Daughter of Lachish

Daughter of Lachish

A Novel

TIM FRANK

RESOURCE *Publications* · Eugene, Oregon

DAUGHTER OF LACHISH
A Novel

Copyright © 2011 Tim Frank. All rights reserved. Except for brief quotations in critical publications or reviews, no part of this book may be reproduced in any manner without prior written permission from the publisher. Write: Permissions, Wipf and Stock Publishers, 199 W. 8th Ave., Suite 3, Eugene, OR 97401.

Resource Publications
An Imprint of Wipf and Stock Publishers
199 W. 8th Ave., Suite 3
Eugene, OR 97401

www.wipfandstock.com

ISBN 13: 978-1-61097-029-7

Manufactured in the U.S.A.

Scripture quotations marked AT are the author's translation.

All other scripture quotations, unless otherwise indicated, are taken from the Holy Bible, New International Version®, NIV®.
Copyright ©1973, 1978, 1984 by Biblica, Inc.™
Used by permission of Zondervan. All rights reserved worldwide.
www.zondervan.com

To Dr Alice Sinnott

who opened my eyes to the stories of loss and joy

in the words of the Prophets

PART ONE

Chapter 1

No! It could not happen to him! Not now! Not so close to victory. He'd thought he would live, would see the fall of the enemy, would experience the triumph over the rebellious city. He had hoped for the spoils of battle, the rewards of war. And now? Now he was dying. He was sure of it. An arrow had pierced his skin and opened a gaping wound in his forearm. It was not only his arm that hurt. The pain surged through his whole body. He lay on the wooden deck of the siege machine, unable to move, close to death. He couldn't even protect the siege machine. Would it make it through the battle? Would it survive if he did not?

"Ishtar! Oh, Ishtar!" Itur-Ea called out to the goddess. "Draw me from the claws of death," he breathed. The pain lessened, the clamor of battle receded. But Itur-Ea felt no peace. Panic seized him as he seemed to rush along a tunnel of darkness, as he fell into the regions below the earth. He tried to call out, tried to remain among the living. Times when he had visited the temple of Ishtar flashed before his eyes. Was he going there? Into her embrace? Itur-Ea let go. Only fear met him in the darkness.

A cold wave hit him. He shivered. Itur-Ea opened his eyes. The archer poured more water over his face.

"Get up!" the archer yelled, then slapped Itur-Ea's face.

Itur-Ea moaned. "I can't."

"It's only your arm," the archer insisted. He cut strips off Itur-Ea's bloodied sash and wound them round the injured arm. Itur-Ea gasped in pain. But the archer seemed to hardly notice. He propped Itur-Ea up and slapped him on the shoulder, the one that was not injured. "We need you. The machine won't last long under this fire if you don't do your job. So do it!" Turning away, the man took his bow, stretched the string and released the arrow that would surely find its mark.

Itur-Ea got up. He didn't think he could lift the ladle. Gritting his teeth he plunged it into the caldron of the siege machine. He poured the water over the side, methodically keeping the siege machine wet, dousing the flames that threatened it. He had seldom seen such tenacious defenders. The men of Lachish threw fire and torches at the attackers without pause. They threw everything else they could as well: boulders, grindstones, wagon wheels and jars. And of course their archers fired arrows and their slingers shot stones at the Assyrian army.

But they could not succeed. Lachish would fall. Itur-Ea was sure of it. Had the city not rebelled against the god Ashur? Had it not broken the treaty of the god? The people of Judah might put faith in their god, the god of Jerusalem, but their god could not help them. For the Assyrian army would crush Judah, the arm of Ashur would utterly destroy the land. Itur-Ea looked back across to the hill where the king of Assyria sat enthroned. King Sennacherib, the lord of the empire, king of all, directed the battle from above.

Itur-Ea could hear the heavy breathing of the soldiers below operating the battering ram. With a thud its iron tip crashed into the city wall. Again and again it was rammed into the same spot so that the wall would slowly begin to crack. Each time it struck, the siege machine shuddered slightly. Whenever they found a crack between stones, the crew would lever the ram with all their strength, trying to dislodge stones in the wall.

"Cover!" one of the archers yelled as he dove to the front of the machine. A heavy rock struck the machine. Itur-Ea could feel the impact as the timber framing shook. No real damage. The siege machines were built to withstand such bombardment. Stepping back, the archer had already released his next arrow. By the glint in his eye Itur-Ea could tell that it had found its target.

Despite his weary arms, Itur-Ea continued to pour water over the hides that covered the siege machine. He looked back over the Assyrian troops fighting their way up the siege ramp. "By Ishtar!" Instead of continuous rows of advancing soldiers, he saw a large gap in the attacking ranks. An intense barrage of arrows and sling stones held back the Assyrian fighters. How could they allow their vanguard to become separated? They could never hope to weaken the city's defenses without the cover provided by the archers and the steady stream of reinforcements.

A glimpse along the city wall through the windows of the siege machine was no more encouraging. The attempt to scale the wall with ladders had been repelled. Attackers lay fallen beside remains of siege ladders.

The siege machine lurched. Instead of the full thud, the ram just scraped the wall. The crew on the lower level was caught by surprise and a few fell over as the ram swung out. "Chains!" The defenders had managed to put a chain around the ram and were hauling it up. The three soldiers sent forward to free the ram were immediately felled by lances and rocks thrown from the wall. "Cut the rope!" the captain of the siege machine shouted from below. Itur-Ea fumbled the dagger out of his belt and began sawing the rope from which the ram was suspended. "Now! Cut the rope!" The voice of the captain sounded desperate. Itur-Ea worked feverishly. Finally the last strand snapped. The ram fell down. In one movement the crew thrust it forward and tilted it back. The chain around the ram became loose and the soldiers were able to haul it back into the machine. Not that the machine was much use now! It provided some cover for the archers, but could no longer damage the wall.

The captain clearly must have seen the difficulty and decided to use the ram unsuspended. What little effect that had!

Theirs was not the only siege machine in trouble. No water was splashed over the side of the closest machine. Had they run out? Or had the pourer been wounded? Frustration and despair surged through Itur-Ea. The attack was not going well.

The king saw the situation. And he acted. The signal for retreat was given. Feelings of relief and disappointment overcame Itur-Ea. But he could not think of their failure now. Retreat was always a dangerous phase of battle. The rear of the Assyrian army pressed forward and sent a cloud of arrows and sling stones onto the defenders on the walls. The brake blocks were removed and the siege machines descended the ramp slowly. The captains shouted orders to keep the machines in line. The maneuver surprised the defenders. They had fought the attackers at close range; their weapons were not aimed to cover the distance. But no soldier could drop his guard, even for one moment. The archer next to Itur-Ea suddenly gasped as an arrow struck him under the arm. Here the body armor was no protection. Wounded, he fell onto the deck.

* * *

"Do you think the Assyrians will enter the city? Will they destroy it?"
"They can't. The LORD will not allow it."

Rivkah looked at her friend Simchah. How could she be so sure?

"My mother prays every day to Amun-Re for the deliverance of Lachish. But she is afraid. I've seen her weep at night."

"We should not bow down to any other gods. The LORD alone can save," Simcha countered. How often had Rivkah heard her say that? Simchah came from a very strict family. Unlike most other people in Lachish, they prayed only to the LORD, the national god of Judah.

"My father said that only Egypt can help us now. If Lachish can hold out long enough until help arrives, there's hope."

"But has the Pharaoh of Egypt been able to stop the Assyrians so far? We should hope only in the LORD."

"Yes, but..." Rivkah knew any argument would be useless. Simchah was her best friend, but when they spoke about the gods she could be so stubborn. She always had to be right, she just wouldn't listen to anything else.

A group of soldiers hurried past on their way to the southern wall. Simchah followed them with her eyes, "Warriors of the LORD!" If anything could distract Simchah, it was strapping young men, especially soldiers. But which boy wasn't a soldier these days? Due to the siege every last body was used to defend the city. Even women and girls worked to strengthen the defenses.

When they had realized that the Assyrians were constructing a siege ramp on the southwestern corner of the hill, the people of Lachish had built a counterramp. They hoped to give the wall extra strength and get more defensive weapons to where they were needed. If the Assyrians did break through, they would be surprised at the opposition they would find. Father had explained it all one night when they were sitting down for their meal. Rivkah had helped to build it, too. Well, a bit anyway. It had been hard work and she certainly didn't complain when her mother had asked her to stay home the next day and put her to work on the loom.

"Do you think they'll take chariots to the southern wall too?" Simchah found chariot drivers even more fascinating than foot soldiers.

"Why would they?"

"To fight the enemy of course."

"I don't know whether chariots would help a lot." Rivkah lived on the main road and saw plenty of chariots going by. They didn't really excite her.

"Of course only if the Assyrians break the wall. And I don't believe that will happen."

"There you have it. They've come close, though." And today, it seemed, the Assyrians had mounted an all-out attack.

"Do you think the Assyrians will leave once we've repulsed this attack?" Simchah mused. "Oh, I so want this siege to end."

Rivkah wished that too. In better days they had sat here in front of the house and had eaten dried figs or nibbled some honey cake. Now everything was rationed.

"It will pass," Rivkah said, sounding rather more assured than she really was.

"I know. We sometimes have to go through hard times to get to a blessed future. Just imagine, I will marry a warrior who has defended our city!" Simchah had a dreamy look in her eyes.

"Oh, Simchah! Really, do you call some of those boys warriors?"

"But what if I marry a soldier from the garrison?"

"Dream on!"

"You'll see."

Rivkah had no doubt that Simchah would get the attention of a soldier if she worked at it. She certainly had the looks and the right manner. She was no longer a girl. Men started to notice her. "But what would your parents say?"

"Oh..." Simchah gave a little wave with her hand as if that would never be any cause for concern.

Rivkah laughed, "Simchah, the commander's wife. I can just imagine it." Simchah joined in. She got up and struck a ladylike pose.

"And who will you marry, Rivkah?"

"I don't know. Mother hopes we'll get rich husbands."

"Maybe a tax official or a rich farmer?"

"Most farmers are poor. You see them coming through the gate leading a skinny donkey. Or at least they used to come . . . before the siege."

"The farmers from the villages. I don't mean those. That would just be horrible! No, the landholders of Lachish, they're well off. And they don't have to work so hard that they get dirty and grimy." Simchah sat down again. "I could come and visit you. And we'd drink wine and have cake and fresh melons."

Rivkah rolled her eyes, "Don't talk of food. I'm starving." She ran the hand over her empty stomach.

"You're impossible," Simchah scolded her. "Always so negative. Why not dream of days to come?"

Just then the noise at the southern wall grew louder. "What's happening?" Rivkah asked.

"Probably fighting back the Assyrians."

"I'd better go home, I think." Rivkah suddenly felt guilty. Why had she stayed away from home for so long? What if the Assyrians entered the city now and she was not would not be with her family?

"Be careful," Simchah warned.

"I don't think their arrows will reach that far into the city. I'll be careful". She gave Simchah a quick kiss, jumped up from the bench and waved as she strode off down the street.

It was quiet in the side streets. Not many people were outside. Most were probably cowering in their houses during the attack. The men fought on the walls—or slept. Few mothers allowed their children to play outside. The shops on the main street stood forlorn. People did not go shopping in such a desperate situation. And yet, she knew, some people had dug out their heirlooms to exchange for food.

There were no customers milling around the workshop of Rivkah's father. Usually, a few passers-by would stand and watch the blacksmith at his work. Especially the farmers, who would wait while their plowshares or ox goads were repaired. The fire and his skill fascinated them.

Rivkah ducked into the house past her father, who was busy stoking the fire. But her mother noticed her when she came into the back room, "Where have you been?" It was clear that her mother was not pleased. "It's dangerous outside. What if you get hit by an arrow? Or if, God forbid, the Assyrians break through the wall? There's a war going on, Rivkah."

She stepped away from the loom she had been working on. "There's still plenty of work to be done around here. Your sister and I have been working most of the afternoon and you were nowhere to be seen." Rivkah's older sister, Shomer, stood at the other loom and turned the back to her. Shomer always did what her parents wanted and her weaving was really exquisite. She looked after her little brothers and sisters and would never be late home.

"I was just at Simchah's," Rivkah tried to defend herself.

"Running around in the streets at this time," her mother shook her head. "Can't you see how dangerous it is?"

Right now Rivkah could see that the best thing to do was to be quiet and somehow appease her mother. She moved over to the loom her mother had been working on. A simple linen cloth hung there half-finished. She could do that.

"Shall I continue weaving this?" Rivkah asked her mother.

"Please. But make sure the rows are tight. And take care to make it nice and even."

"Yes, mother." Why did her mother always say that? After all, Rivkah wasn't a beginner and had woven many garments over the years.

Shomer turned to look at her. Her eyes seemed accusing and yet hurt and afraid. She always took it personally when Rivkah went outside the boundaries set by their parents. But what was wrong with going and talking to her friend? Mother was just overanxious.

Weaving was tedious work. Rivkah wasn't a bad weaver—there were just other things she'd rather do. Suddenly she felt something tickle her back. "Hey!" Rivkah lashed out and hit her youngest brother, Shallum. He had snuck up behind her and had managed to stick some stalks of straw into her dress. Nepheg, the older of the two, peeked around the doorway to see how his sister would react. "Leave it!" Rivkah yelled. Shallum ran away. Rivkah pulled the straw out of her clothes. Annoying little brothers!

But they didn't give up that easily. Soon Shallum was back and tried to stuff some feathers down Rivkah's neck. She knew who was behind that. Just wait, Nepheg! When she saw him again at the door, Rivkah jumped up and ran to grab him. She nearly got him, but Nepheg saw her coming and fled to Mother. "Mother, Rivkah wants to hit me." He clung to her dress.

Mother turned round angrily, "Can't you leave your brothers alone, Rivkah?"

"But they started it," Rivkah said.

"I don't care who started it. I'm trying to cook. And I thought you wanted to weave."

Nepheg smirked triumphantly at Rivkah. But Mother pulled his ear. "And you two stop annoying Rivkah. Go and find something useful to do." With that she sent him away. Addressing Rivkah she continued, "The boys are bored. This war's affecting them quite badly. Just be a bit considerate, please."

Of course they were bored, stuck in the house the whole day. Other boys still went out on the streets at times. Some boys, little older than Nepheg, even helped out along the walls, carrying ammunition and conveying messages. But mother was too worried to allow any of her children out except, maybe, for essential tasks like getting water.

Rivkah returned to the loom. "You're so easy to tease." Now Shomer was giving her sisterly advice! "Just ignore them. Every time you snap and hit them they are even keener to try it again."

"They asked for it."

"Exactly. They want you to get upset."

Rivkah knew Shomer was right, but she wouldn't admit that now. What else should she do? Just stand there and let them annoy her and ruin her dress?

Concentrating on her work again, Rivkah passed the yarn through the warp suspended on the loom. After lifting the rod, the alternate threads of the warp came up, so that she could return the yarn to the right again. With one deft movement she pushed up the rows she had just completed, ensuring they were tight.

* * *

As darkness fell, a multitude of fires illuminated the Assyrian camp. While many shone dimly through tent covers, others glowed brightly under the starry sky. Soldiers gathered in their units to eat the evening meal. In the shadows, the stomping of horses could be heard. Near the palisades a squadron of bullish structures stood silently in formation. These were the siege machines, parked up after battle. In the tents nearby, the maintenance crews prepared for the night. Most of them had participated in the attack. Many nursed wounds, all had lost comrades. They discussed the performance of their machines, the effectiveness of each iron ram and the strength of the enemy walls. But nobody dared to voice their disappointment—they had failed to take the city. For weeks the army had been constructing a siege ramp. They had carried boulders from the valley and the hillsides. Under constant enemy fire they had heaped stones and boulders against the city mound and had constructed an incline. It was exhausting, dangerous work and had resulted in many casualties. Finally the ramp had been covered with lime plaster to ensure stability and give a smooth surface. The limestone had been quarried and processed at a site several leagues up the valley. All previous attempts to attack the gate or to scale the steep sides had been unsuccessful. And now they had mounted the first attack against the city with the siege machines. The siege machines did not always guarantee success. But they had all hoped that this would be the breakthrough, that the walls would be breached and the city of Lachish would be no more. Instead, a long, drawn-out siege seemed to loom. Yes, they had inflicted damage, but they had not dealt the fatal blow.

Itur-Ea angrily kicked a stone. He was angry that their rear guard had not withstood the vigorous enemy bombardment, angry that the defenders fought so determinedly and had hurt the Assyrian forces, angry that those rebels dared to defy the great god Ashur. And it was his siege machine that had been disabled by that chain. The situation had been grim. He was sure it was only the protection of Ishtar, the goddess of war, that had finally saved him from further harm.

The damage would mean more work on the siege machine tomorrow. He wasn't sure whether he could repair it in one day. Nobody really knew when the king would order the next assault. Oh, there would be little skirmishes and the archers would do their best to prevent the strengthening of the defenses. They had to keep up the pressure. But siege machines would only be involved in large-scale offences.

The arm was playing up again. Itur-Ea had washed it and his mate had applied storax balm and a bandage. It would have to do. Those with more serious injuries were treated by the diviners. After a battle there were always scores of wounded soldiers. In his case it was quite obvious what caused the pain. He hoped that no demonic fever would enter his body through the wound. Then it would be necessary to ward off the evil forces and appease the gods.

"Does it still hurt?" Naid-Marduk looked at him.

"What do you think?" Of course it hurt. At times Itur-Ea could get annoyed with his friend.

"It's a pretty nasty wound," replied Naid-Marduk.

"I'll be alright. Certainly not dead yet. You're lucky they didn't get you!"

"That's true," he acknowledged, "It didn't look too good at one point. Of course down below you're protected a bit better. The whole machine really needs to come down before they can get at us." Naid-Marduk had been assigned to power the ram of a siege machine. "On the one hand I prefer to be down there," he continued, "but when you see who they've put on top to splash the water around on my machine . . . he's useless."

"Yeah, doesn't really know much about our machines," Itur-Ea agreed. "He only recently joined the division—originally he was an engineer and sapper."

"Those guys are not much use here at Lachish with that bloody glacis they put around their hill. There's no way of burrowing under the walls."

"The whole place is a nightmare. May Ashur give us victory soon!"

* * *

If anyone had still been asleep, they would be awake now. The donkey protested loudly and strongly at being roused from its rest. Head down, flanks heaving, sucking in the air as it loudly snorted its "ee-ah," panting like a dog on heat. Meshullam had expected as much from the beast. He gave it an irritated slap on the back. Normally, most people would have just turned over on their mats, if they were not up already. The braying of donkeys could be heard in the town any time of the day. But today it might just remind them that they had to get ready. The last possessions had to be packed, the belongings loaded on donkeys and carts. The people of Moresheth-Gath were leaving their town today, heading for Jerusalem, the capital. It was no longer safe here. So far the Assyrians had not attacked the town, but some of the smaller villages not far away had been raided, cattle and sheep had been stolen. It was only a matter of time before Assyrian troops attacked the small town itself. Meshullam's father, Ehud, was sure Moresheth-Gath would not be able to withstand the Assyrian force. They had to leave.

Little groups had already left the town in the previous few weeks. Some had gone to the fortified city of Azekah, others to the government centre of Socoh, still others all the way to Jerusalem. Father had been clear that only at Mount Zion, in the city of the LORD, could they find refuge from the mighty army, the tool of the LORD's wrath.

Most of the people that still remained in Moresheth-Gath had decided to go with Ehud. After all, he was the most influential town elder these days, even though he was among the younger men at the gate. Two days ago Ehud had urged them that they had no time to lose. It was now or never. So Meshullam got the animals ready for departure this morning.

The sun was rising above the eastern hills when the group set out from the town. They went across the narrow saddle at the northern gate to reach the wide ridge that ran nearly all the way to Azekah. The cows bellowed in front of the carts, the donkeys snorted as they were hurried along, the sheep called to their young as flocks were herded together. The goats bleated in protest. The excited shouts of children mixed with the determined commands of men, the crying of babies with the calming words of women and the busy hisses of girls herding the animals.

Meshullam dragged the donkey behind him and made sure he kept his younger brother Shimei in sight. Mother would be furious if anything happened to her baby. Shimei was a good brother, really, but Meshullam thought that Mother spoiled him too much. She always fussed over him.

Now he ran off again!

"Hey! Shimei, come back here!"

Shimei reluctantly came back from behind the bush where he seemed to have discovered something.

"Why?" he asked.

Meshullam didn't give an answer, just looked at Shimei and said, "Come along."

Shimei trotted beside the donkey for a while. Soon he had his hands on the load, fiddling with the ropes. The animal turned its head in protest.

"Leave it!" Meshullam yelled.

"Why?" Shimei grabbed hold of a bag and hung onto it, swinging his legs under the donkey. With a sudden jerk the load shifted, Shimei let go and fell hard on his bottom. The donkey stopped. Luckily the load had not fallen off. But Shimei started crying.

"I told you to stop it," Meshullam snapped.

Shimei only cried louder. Some of the older men that passed them looked at Shimei in disapproval.

"Be quiet!" Meshullam told Shimei.

Shimei did reduce his volume somewhat but continued crying. Meshullam busied himself securing the load again. There were also jars on the donkey's back. What if they had fallen and broken?

Shimei finally calmed down and they were ready to join the drawn-out group again when they saw Mother and the girls coming. Shimei ran towards her, seeking comfort from her. She set down the bundle she carried, took him up in her arms and embraced him.

"What is it Shimei? What has happened?"

Shimei just buried his face in her dress and put his arms around her neck.

"He thought it was funny to hang from the donkey and drag the load down. When it shifted he fell and hit his bottom. That's why he's crying," Meshullam told her.

"But Shimei! Don't you know you shouldn't do that?" she scolded him gently. She hugged him again tightly and set him down. Picking up her bundle she told him to go with Meshullam again.

"We're walking a long way today, Shimei. Just stay with Meshullam."

Somewhat unwillingly Shimei went to Meshullam and walked along behind him. At least for a while he was quiet.

* * *

Rivkah let her eyes rest on the horizon for a moment. Across the hills the city of Mareshah was clearly visible. The mound rose prominently among the dark-green belt of olive groves surrounding the city. In a land dried out by the summer heat, the trees provided a stark contrast to the brown fields and pasture around them. The whitewashed houses of Mareshah stood out in this landscape. Rivkah had taken the street outside the citadel yard today to walk to the well. Under her arm she carried the empty jar. She always enjoyed this view over the hill country. The rolling hills, wide open spaces and then this city on a mound that looked nearly symmetrical. She knew the place wasn't as large as Lachish, not as well-fortified. Most people here didn't speak well of Mareshah at all. It was considered a cultural backwater, a "peasant hole." Still, it looked pretty from the distance.

Rivkah wondered whether they were harvesting their olives this year. Or did the Assyrians combing the countryside prevent it? At least the olive trees were still standing. Around Lachish the Assyrians had chopped down the trees and destroyed all the orchards. Maybe the same disaster would yet strike Mareshah.

As Rivkah walked further down the street, the city wall and nearby houses blocked the view over the landscape. Pushing any musings about Assyrians or neighboring cities out of her mind she quickened her step. Not far to the well now. She noticed a few other women ahead of her on their way to get water. She followed them down the steps to the northeast corner of the city. A tower guarded this section of the city wall. The well was in its basement.

* * *

Rivkah placed the water jar on her head. She had listened long enough to the chatter of the women at the well. Everyone talked about the siege these days. Some thought that they would be able to hold out, that help would arrive from Jerusalem or from Egypt. Others believed that they were all doomed to die, that the Assyrians would conquer the city. One woman even thought that this was the calamity foretold by the prophets. Rivkah shuddered. Was there no hope?

She did not like this war. Nothing was the same anymore. All the life had gone out of the city. The little shops along the main road were all closed. In the past she had stopped and looked at the jewelry. How she had longed to get one of those bangles. She had watched the potter shape the clay on the wheel. Back then, the little shops and street vendors had been eager to sell their food. The farmers had brought their produce to the market. The fresh milk had tasted so good. And the fruit! Now, they just lived on a meager ration of twenty shekels of grain per person per day. A few lentils and a small, bony piece of meat each week provided the only variety. She was starving.

Few people were out on the street. They did not linger, afraid of being exposed to enemy fire. To the right the citadel's walls rose high above the city's humble houses. When Rivkah passed the gates she could see the activity in the citadel. It was the command centre in the defense effort. From the citadel the commander issued orders. From here soldiers were dispatched to the fighting. Here the garrison was stationed. Provisions and weapons were stored here.

The townspeople had to come here for their daily rations. Even though the commander discouraged people from congregating at the citadel, a few milled around the gate. They were anxious to get food to provide for their families. They came to get some comfort in this place. Here they felt some safety. Nobody greeted Rivkah. They seemed too absorbed in their own misery.

As Rivkah walked on down the main street, she suddenly noticed a little boy staring at her. He was standing at the side of the road, pressed against a house wall, looking up with big dark eyes. She wasn't sure what she read in his face. Fear? Surprise? Or was it a guilty conscience? He seemed somewhat disorientated and unsure. Just as Rivkah was about to ask him what he was doing all alone on the street and where did he live, a young woman came running down the road. When she saw the boy she clapped her hands in relief and shouted, "Here you are! I've been looking everywhere for you, Yotam. What are you doing here?"

The boy's eyes left Rivkah and he looked at his mother. He pulled up his shoulders, uncertain how to respond. But then a smile crossed his face. The woman scooped him up and carried him in her arms. He let it happen and then snuggled against her as he wrapped his thin arms around her neck. The woman turned and hurried back down the road. Over her shoulder the boy looked at Rivkah again. In his eyes there was no longer any hint of fear.

Rivkah didn't know whether the woman had even looked at her. She must be one of the refugees from the countryside. Many villagers had sought refuge in the heavily fortified city of Lachish as they heard about the advance of the Assyrian army. The people were poor and did not wear any nice clothing or jewelry. They had had to leave most of their meager possessions behind when they abandoned their houses.

With their arrival, the emergency stores of the city had to last for even more people, but they were a welcome addition to the defense effort. And they did work hard, always willing to help where needed. The houses had become even more crowded accommodating them. Of course, people got annoyed and tempers sometimes flared. But they coped. They had to. After all this was war. Their only hope was in a joint effort to resist the enemy until help arrived, whether from heaven or from earth.

Rivkah's father was busy at work. He did not fight on the walls. He supported the defensive effort through his trade. There was plenty of work for a blacksmith when a war was on. Normally he made agricultural implements. Now he was beating plowshares into swords and pruning hooks into spear tips. The demand for arrowheads just could not be satiated.

As Rivkah walked through the room, her father looked up. "You can leave some of that water here. Just pour it into that small jar over there." He turned his concentration back to the arrowhead he was making. It was delicate work.

Rivkah took the water jar from her head. "Elisaph, can you help her, please." Her father spoke to Rivkah's cousin who just stood there, leaning against the wall, hardly even noticing Rivkah. He helped her father in the workshop treading the bellow to feed the fire with air to increase the temperature, if required. Elisaph gave a grunt but came over and lifted the jar to pour the water.

"Thank you, Rivkah." Her father must have finished the arrowhead. He put his hand on her shoulder. "I hope we'll survive this siege. Keep your head up. I know it's hard on you. But you can be sure we'll fight to save this city. Even if I don't live, I pray you will."

Rivkah was confused. Her father wasn't normally like this. He usually didn't talk that much, especially not with her. But these weren't normal times. The war seemed to have taken its toll on him. Rivkah studied his face. His eyes seemed sad. Was he afraid? Did he have a premonition of what was to come? Rivkah picked up the water jar again and carried it into the inner room.

Chapter 2

Itur-Ea sat in the shade of the tent seeking cover from the fierce midday sun. This morning they had taken off the front panel of the siege machine and he had thoroughly inspected the whole part, made some repairs and replaced a few hides. The machine was in surprisingly good condition after the battle. In the afternoon they would suspend the battering ram again. Getting that just right was always a major operation. He had to admit that it wasn't his strength. He was far more confident in maintaining the shell of the siege machine.

His father was a tanner and Itur-Ea had learned from him. Really, he had wanted to become a tanner himself, but the village had chosen him to join the army when the call came. Now his brothers carried on the trade back in the village. He thought about the village often these days: small houses of sun-baked bricks surrounded by stands of date palms. Irrigation canals watered the barley fields. The land was flat and fertile. Not like here in this wild, barren country of steep hillsides and deep valleys.

They used to catch fish in the canals. But the best and biggest always came from the great river. Of course that was several leagues away. Still, they would sometimes go down to the town on its shore and buy fish at the market. It had always seemed such a journey, like a visit to a different land. He would stand and watch the boats on the river, some of them heavily laden with produce for the big cities. He had dreamed of setting out to discover the world, of seeing majestic cities and temples, of travelling to strange and distant lands.

Itur-Ea laughed. He certainly had done that. Who would have ever thought that he would come to this place, to the end of the world near the Western Sea? But he had hardly journeyed by boat. No, he had had to travel on his own two feet—weeks of marching through inhospitable territory, over hills and mountains, plains and deserts.

And then there were the battles. There were times when he loathed them. The exhaustion, the intensity wore him down. But mostly he savored them. The action, the acute awareness of life and death, the danger thrilled him. The performance of their siege machines gave him an inexplicable sense of satisfaction. Through them, careful design and destructive power combined to overwhelm the enemies of the mighty Assyrian army. Whoever dared to stand in their way had fallen.

Nothing compared to the triumph when the walls crumbled, the last resistance was extinguished, the houses looted and the whole city sacked and burned. Then he knew that he was truly part of the greatest army, that his lot was with the conquerors. Victory was with the king and his god Ashur. It made everything worthwhile.

If the truth be told, he probably couldn't go back and live in the village. Not yet anyway. At the moment life was too exciting to give it all up and lead a sedate life. Wouldn't he get bored in a sleepy village where everything moved to the same rhythm year in, year out, where village politics was the most exciting topic of conversation?

Military training had been hard to begin with. The new environment had intimidated him. And he had never been any good with a bow and arrow. Actually, if he thought about it, you could count on one hand the birds he had shot as a boy in the village. Still, he had shown some promise with the spear, especially in close-quarter combat. He proved to be very skilled with the dagger and the sword. On his first military campaign he fought as a shield-bearer, providing cover for his archer. The experience had taught him some valuable lessons.

It must have been that survey when he returned to Nineveh that had matched him to his current role in the siege machine division. He had immediately taken to this job. With it, his future had been decided. He had become a professional soldier and now knew siege machines like few others.

He had never been back to the village. The army barracks was his home now. The last two years he had been stationed in the big city of Nineveh itself. Its massive walls and grand scale still awed him. But he knew the city well now and had adapted to its life. He was a stranger there no longer.

"Master?" The voice of his assistant interrupted Itur-Ea's thoughts. "We are ready to install the battering ram."

"Thank you. I will inspect it in a moment." As Itur-Ea walked into the sunlight, he felt as if he was leaving behind memories of the village. His military knowledge was needed.

* * *

Rivkah's hands slowly moved through Kaleb's fur, from his ears down his back to his tail which twitched when she touched it. Kaleb moved his head around and licked Rivkah's face. She drew back. "Don't!" she laughed. "Leave your tongue in your mouth." Kaleb stared straight ahead again as she stroked his head. He gave a sigh as he yawned and shifted his paws. "Hey what's the matter, eh?" She pulled his ear. He just looked at her with those deep, trusting eyes only a dog could have. Rivkah wrapped her arms around Kaleb and buried her face in his fur.

He was her best friend. Others just called him dog—keleb—but she called him Kaleb, the mighty warrior from the tribe of Judah. Others thought he was a dirty mongrel but she thought he was beautiful. Others just saw a sly stray roaming the streets; she saw how crafty and fast he was. People might try to kick him just like any other dog, but he was far too clever and alert to ever receive a blow. Some people were even afraid of him. He could put on quite a fierce show. He certainly never let anybody near him—except for Rivkah. He trusted her and she trusted him.

Suddenly Kaleb stood up and growled. But whatever had attracted his attention must have gone. He sat down again, only his ears twitching alertly. He nuzzled Rivkah, sniffing her clothes. "No, I didn't bring any food this time. Hungry?" She held his mouth between her hands. "If Mother knew that I sometimes give you food, she would get awfully mad. She would make sure I got a decent thrashing." Rivkah tickled him under the jaw. "There's not much food round these days, old pal. My stomach's empty, too. I'm sure you'll still be able to catch the odd mouse, eh. But I'll try to sneak something out for you next time."

Kaleb must have been satisfied with that for he slumped down and rolled over onto his back. Rivkah rubbed his tummy. He closed his eyes and pulled his legs up against his thin body. A contented growl came from his chest.

* * *

They had barley soup for their evening meal today. It certainly made the grain go further and filled the stomach. The feeling wouldn't last long but for now the tummy felt so warm and full that the soup seemed like a sumptuous meal. Rivkah could even detect a faint taste of meat. A few bones had been thrown into the pot to give the soup some flavor.

While Nepheg had already finished his bowl and was greedily asking for more, Rivkah slurped her soup slowly, relishing each gulp. There would be no seconds tonight. That's all they got.

"You're not hungry, Rivkah? Can I have some of yours?" Nepheg was trying to get more food.

"No, I'm just enjoying my meal. I don't pour it down my throat like you."

Nepheg clearly wasn't happy with Rivkah's answer.

"I'm hungry! Father, can I have some more? We must have some food in the house."

"You know there's only enough for tomorrow morning. We'll get a new ration in the afternoon. So be quiet. Maybe you really should eat your food a bit slower."

Father was emptying his bowl and cleaned it out with a small piece of stale bread. These days they didn't have fresh bread anymore. Old bread was more filling.

The whole family sat in a circle on the floor, Father on his ibex skin, the others just on the packed-mud floor of the upper storey. They always ate up here. It was much more pleasant than down in the workshop. Rivkah looked around. She was still hoping for an opportunity to quietly put some cooked barley to the side for Kaleb without anybody noticing. Shomer was busy feeding little Susannah. Nepheg was just explaining to Shallum how he could single-handedly defeat the entire Assyrian army. Mother was complaining loudly that she suspected they had not been given the full ration today. Nobody seemed to listen to her. Father certainly didn't appear to. He had closed his eyes and leaned back, reclining on his right hand. With the left he stroked his beard. It was the perfect time! Rivkah took a small shard and scooped some gruel out of her bowl. She quickly hid it under a fold of her dress.

"What are you doing there?" Of course, Shallum must see it!

Rivkah inwardly screamed at her brother, Shut up! She could have strangled him. "Just eating." Rivkah knew she was blushing.

"Leave your sister alone and make sure your own bowl is clean." Mother came to Rivkah's rescue. She had heard enough complaints from the boys for one day. "But . . . " Shallum began.

Mother didn't let him finish, "You won't get any more tonight. So you better eat what you've got. I see your bowl is not that clean."

Shallum just looked at Rivkah in puzzlement but proceeded to lick his bowl as he had been told. Normally Mother would have scolded him for not using a piece of bread to wipe the bowl. But today they didn't have enough bread.

That was close! Rivkah was sure Shallum wouldn't bring it up again during the meal. She just had to disappear immediately afterwards before he could ask any questions. Hopefully he would forget about it later on.

After the meal, Father uttered a short prayer to Baal asking for an abundant supply of food. Everyone rose. It would have been Rivkah's task to wash the dishes. But she had something else in mind. "I've got to go outside." Nobody really seemed to listen, but Rivkah was already halfway down the ladder. Outside the house, she did turn towards the sewer but then walked further up the lane. Here she sat in the shadow of a wall and waited.

It was dark by now. Stars shone in the night sky and a breeze rustled through the streets. The lane was quiet. In the distance she could hear the shouts of men and the subdued hum of a city under siege.

And then he was there! A moist tongue licked her feet. "Kaleb!" Rivkah flung her arms around the dog and drew him close. He eagerly ate what she offered him. "I know it's not much. A handful of barley and a small piece of bread. But it's all I have. I have to eat something too."

Kaleb licked her hands. He seemed to understand, but clearly could have done with more. After a while he realized there was no more and stopped searching, just lying across Rivkah's legs.

"Oh, you're still heavy enough. I thought you might have lost a bit of weight, Kaleb." Rivkah stroked his fur. Kaleb snuggled against her. He was content and could have stayed there till morning.

"Hey, old pal, I can't stay too long. Have to go back to do the dishes. So you better get off." Rivkah pushed him off her legs. Kaleb got to his feet reluctantly and shook himself from head to tail, as if he had just emerged from the side of a warm fire into the frosty air. He whimpered. He was no longer the fierce, wily dog, but more like a small puppy seeking comfort and warmth.

"Kaleb, I'll see you again tomorrow." Rivkah caressed his ears. He trotted beside her, head down, as they walked along the lane. One last pat and Kaleb scampered off into the darkness. Before Rivkah entered the house she turned around and looked down the street and let her gaze wander across the starry sky above.

* * *

The city on the hill loomed dark ahead. Its towers and walls were clearly visible in the pale moonlight. The impressive fort in its centre rose above the jumbled assortment of houses crowding inside the city walls. No light came from the city. But round the base of the hill the odd fire flickered—evidence of the Assyrian army that had encircled Lachish.

This was how it had been for the last two months—two whole months since they had first set up camp on this low hill. But tonight felt different. Itur-Ea paced the open platform of the camp tower. He had asked to have another look at the city before the attack tomorrow. Opposite him, the siege ramp rose steadily against the city mound. It still seemed impossibly steep, but they had brought their siege machines up that slope before.

"Nervous?" The guard on watch grinned at Itur-Ea.

"No, just assessing the likely direction of any possible major resistance. I have to know where the fire might come from."

"Right." The guard didn't look convinced. "You know," he continued, "the king has consulted the gods and tomorrow is a favorable day. Ashur will grant us victory."

"Oh, I do not doubt that tomorrow is the perfect day. It's just . . . you have to be prepared for battle." How could Itur-Ea explain what he felt before a battle? Everything stirred within him. In battles he felt the presence of the great goddess Ishtar so acutely. In the night before a battle he always longed for the mystic union with Ishtar as he had experienced it in the temple of Nineveh.

"Well, I'd better go back to the tent." Itur-Ea nodded towards the guard. He had to be alone. He didn't want anybody watching him right now. Nor did he need any glib comments. Placing his feet carefully on the ladder, he climbed down from the tower to the dark camp below. Finally he felt the ground under his feet. Turning around he walked past tents where soldiers were still making their last preparations for the battle ahead. He did not go to his tent immediately but, rather, felt his way to the siege machines. Placing his hand on the leather shell of his machine, he breathed in the scent he knew so well. It was darker here—no fires were nearby. And so the thoughts came flooding back.

Itur-Ea was a follower of Ishtar, a worshipper of the goddess of war and love. He could still remember the first time he had gone to the temple. Its splendor was inspiring. The surroundings had awed him. The vivid pictures of the brazen and sensual goddess had set his heart racing. The chants and swirling clouds of incense had taken hold of his mind. The union with the temple maid had set his whole body aflame. And he had realized who Ishtar was, had felt her presence. He had taken his fill and was satisfied; he had given his everything and was spent. Life until then had just been a hazy drudge, but now he had burst into a new reality, a clarity of life as if he had finally surfaced from the dark, primeval waters.

Itur-Ea had stumbled like a drunk when he walked back out onto the street. The encounter with Ishtar had overwhelmed him. And he had known that he was a new man—that he was a man. From then on he would return often to the temple. Yes, Ishtar was demanding—the temple fees were significant. Ishtar was fickle—his life was no longer so settled since he had devoted himself to her worship. But she had often blessed him these past years and he would continue to worship her as long as he could, as long as she did not turn against him or tired of him.

His religious life had changed completely since he lived in Nineveh. Back in the village they had mainly worshipped Ea, the god of the deep and of wisdom. Each year at the festival of Nin-aha-kudu, the manifestation of Ea as the god of rivers and irrigated gardens, the image of the god and his daughter had been carried through the village. He himself was even named after the god—Itur-Ea: "Ea has become merciful". While he had become excited as a boy when the festival of Nin-aha-kudu approached, it could not compare with the experience in the temple of Ishtar. How he longed for that experience now!

In the dark night Itur-Ea pressed himself against the cold leather panels. What would tomorrow bring? Would he feel the presence of Ishtar? With a sigh he turned and went to his tent which he shared with a dozen other soldiers.

* * *

Was Nepheg dreaming of a sumptuous meal, fresh fruit and juice? He loudly smacked his lips in his sleep and chewed on non-existent food. Now and then it sounded as if something had got stuck in his throat. But with a sudden rasping noise he always cleared it again, took a deep breath, and then moved his lips once more, smacking and slurping. He's probably drooling, too, Rivkah thought. It was pitch dark, so she couldn't see his face. Nepheg had never been a quiet sleeper, but he must be really hungry tonight.

In the evening, like every evening, they had taken the mats and blankets from the alcove and spread them on the floor in the main room of the upper storey. The children slept together here, except for Susannah, who was with Mother and Father in the little bedroom. In summer they would often sleep on the roof, but Father had thought it unsafe while a war was going on. So they had to endure the night in the heat of the living room. And it did get quite warm up here towards evening, with the day's heat trapped inside the house.

Shallum was sleeping peacefully beside Rivkah. His breathing was quiet and regular. To her left lay Shomer. She had rolled over again and was leaving precious little space for Rivkah. When they went to bed they had had enough room, but Shomer encroached on Rivkah's space during the night. Why did she always have to twist and turn? Could she not remain still when sleeping? Shomer pushed her elbow into Rivkah's side. Rivkah sat up. She gently tried to nudge Shomer to roll back away from her, but had little success. At long last Shomer did move a little.

Rivkah did not lie down again immediately. She stared into the dark and listened. The sounds of her sleeping siblings seemed to recede into the background and she thought she could hear the footsteps of soldiers hurrying across the street below. Even at night they kept watch over the city, defending it against the enemy outside its walls. What did they see as they watched and listened into the dark, trying to detect any movement by the enemy?

And what did the Assyrians see? A city fortified by strong walls, defended by determined men? Did they dream of riches inside the walls? The governor in the citadel had some opulent furniture and the incense stands in the sanctuary were beautiful. But Rivkah had heard of the wealth of Assyria. They had buildings covered in gold, intricate ebony reliefs on temple walls and purple curtains on windows. The city of their great king was so large it took three days to cross it and all its houses were fine and luxurious. No, they wouldn't find any such riches in Lachish, where people had just enough to survive.

Maybe it was the brutality of the Assyrian army that caused them to continue this siege. Rivkah had heard of their viciousness and violence. Were they out to plunder and to kill?

Rivkah shuddered. She put her hand against her chest and clasped the amulet. It was a figure of Isis with the infant Horus. Rivkah felt the outline of the goddess's face framed by the full Egyptian hair. In her lap Isis cradled the child-god Horus.

Would the charm of the goddess help her? Isis was a protector in times of strife, a helper to those in trouble, a source of life. Powerful and skilled in magic, she was the great healer. According to legend, the goddess had prevailed against the cruel god Seth, who had slain her husband. Everything had seemed lost. Through her determination and magic she had conceived a child—Horus, the falcon, who would avenge his father and banish the evil Seth. From death and despair, Isis persevered to the birth of a child who would give victory and life.

Rivkah's fingers glided over the hieroglyphs at the back of the little figurine. Through these marks the power of Isis was with her, the protection of the goddess effective for her. Would Isis guard her at this time of danger? Would the power of Horus keep her safe?

But what if the violent goddess Anath thirsted for blood with a vengeance neither men nor gods could prevent? Anath exulted in human blood and may have set her face against Lachish. Maybe the gods of Assyria would prove victorious. Had they not swept away the gods of all the nations they conquered? And what about the LORD, the God of Judah? Was he powerful to save Lachish? Rivkah knew that people throughout the city called on their gods to save them. Would the gods protect their followers? Rivkah sensed the cosmic struggle that was being waged over Lachish.

As she lay down again she held the amulet tightly. In all the uncertainties it gave her hope. She breathed calmly and closed her eyes. Nepheg, too, now slumbered peacefully beside Shallum. The pangs of hunger must have passed. Rivkah gave Shomer another nudge and was rewarded with a handbreadth of space.

Chapter 3

In the east, above the outline of the hills, the pale sky heralded the breaking of a new day. The light of morning grew ever brighter, reflected in the western sky in a subdued red glow. As the shadows waned and the tide of light reached the valley floors, the ranks of the Assyrian army became plain to see. Myriads upon myriads surrounded the city of Lachish, ready to storm its walls. The standards of the gods were held aloft before each regiment. The rows of helmets stood as if in devotion to the greater powers they followed.

The sun rose in the east and its rays glinted on the weaponry of the defenders on the city wall. The trumpet blew. Assyria attacked. First the archers stepped forward, coming up the hill and sending a hail of arrows upon the men on the walls of Lachish. Behind them the siege machines were pushed up the hill. As the advance of the archers slowed, the siege machines passed through their lines and continued their crawl up the ramp. The ranks of the archers closed immediately behind them and followed these monsters of war up the hill. Arrows struck the machines like enraged bees stinging an intruder. As they got closer to the wall, stones and torches, chariot wheels and furniture were thrown from above—anything that might inflict some damage.

It was time to wet the sides of the machine. Itur-Ea filled the ladle and poured the first scoop over the front. The archers beside Itur-Ea methodically loaded their bows and released the arrows.

They had arrived under the city wall. The machines were rolled into position, the brakes applied, and the battering rams started swinging. Thump! Itur-Ea felt the tremor as the ram struck the wall. To his left and right more machines were pounding the city defenses. The blows were aimed at cracks left by previous attacks. Sooner or later the cracks would widen and the walls would crumble.

"Chain coming down!" Itur-Ea glimpsed it through the window. The siege machine captain at once shouted orders. This time they wouldn't allow the machine to be disarmed again. The crew down below stopped swinging the boom and, on the captain's signal, four soldiers protected by shield-bearers, rushed forward. Even though one was killed by enemy fire, the others were able to get hooks into the chain. Pulling hard, they managed to rip one end of the chain out of the defenders' hands. The chain snapped against the wall, hitting an Assyrian shield-bearer so hard that he went down in agony. But the threat was over for the moment and the battering ram resumed striking the wall.

The defenders did not give up, tried harder still to disable the siege machines. They let down a stone suspended from a rope. A hole was bored in its centre where the rope was attached. The men of Lachish swung it like a pendulum. The rope became ensnared in the battering ram of a machine, halted the constant attack on the wall for a moment. But it proved no hindrance to the determination of the Assyrian soldiers. Itur-Ea saw the stone thud to the ground, the cut rope swinging harmlessly against the wall.

The sun stood clear in the eastern sky by now. Itur-Ea was unsure how much time had passed. Suddenly he heard a loud, shattering sound and the screams of terrified men. Itur-Ea looked to the left. The defenders had managed to roll an enormous boulder onto the next siege machine. The timber framing had not withstood the force of the impact and had crumpled and broken. Loud cheers from the city wall greeted the destruction. Another huge stone was pushed from above and further shattered the machine.

"Ishtar, have mercy!" Itur-Ea's friend Naid-Marduk had been in that machine. There seemed little hope, as the men of Lachish targeted the heap of timber, hides, and men, throwing torches and shooting arrows. The unthinkable happened: the wreckage caught fire. Flames fed on the wood and singed the leather. Smoke rose from the burning heap, drifted against the city wall, was spread upwards, and clouded the sky. The stench was penetrating.

Itur-Ea worked feverishly. He drenched the left side of his siege machine. He had to protect it. It would be a disaster if this machine too was severely damaged or caught fire. He could feel the heat. How much more could it take? At this rate the water in the caldron wouldn't last long. He was able to get the captain's attention. "Captain, we require more water, sir."

"Urgent?"

"Yes sir, priority two."

The captain sent a messenger with the request.

The worry must have distracted him, for Itur-Ea did not see the rock that struck his helmet. In pain, he let go of the ladle and fell onto the deck. Everything seemed to disappear into a haze and stars of light danced before his eyes. Itur-Ea willed himself to crawl to the caldron. He splashed water over his face. Still dazed, he stood up slowly. As he looked over the side he again became aware of the fire smoldering not far away. No time to waste! He grabbed the ladle.

It seemed like an eternity until a mule with jars of water arrived. Making its way through the rows was not easy. The siege machine captain helped to haul the jar onto the upper deck before pouring the water into the caldron. As the mule made its way to the next machine it went down, pierced by arrows.

The siege machine shook. It had been struck by a large stone. Itur-Ea could hear it groan and creak, but the bracing did not give way. They must have launched more boulders, thought Itur-Ea close to panic. But as he peered forward he realized that the rocks now falling down on them were not thrown by men. They had been dislodged out of the wall. It was finally crumbling! An avalanche of stones fell around the siege machines as a whole section of the wall gave way. The wooden galleries on top of the wall dropped down, the defenders scurrying to flee the collapsing structures. The inner side of the wall still stood—strong, yet damaged and vulnerable.

The Assyrian storm troops seized the opportunity and climbed over the rubble, scaling the wall. After the initial shock, the men of Lachish defended the breach violently. Dozens of Assyrians fell by their swords. But wave after wave of attackers pushed forward, climbing over fallen comrades and foes.

Around the city, the Assyrian army stormed the walls. Ladders were carried up and leaned against the walls. And the first attackers began to penetrate Lachish.

* * *

As Simchah moved the grindstone back and forth, Rivkah poured grains of barley onto the quern. They were gathered up in Simchah's next movement, crushed under the stone and ground to flour.

"Put a few more on, Rivkah!"

"Hey, the flour will be far too coarse if I pour on too much barley at a time. And I don't want to be around when your mother looks at the flour then."

"But just look how much we still have to do!" Simchah nodded towards the bowl of barley beside Rivkah.

"Not that much, really." Rivkah drew up her eyebrows. "I wished we had more. At least then we would get bigger chunks of bread."

"I suppose you're right. But why do I have to do it now?" Simchah complained.

"I don't know, but I already had to do it at home this morning. So stop complaining!"

"You're nearly as bad as my mother. And you're supposed to be my friend."

"Ah, come on Simchah. I'm just pointing out the obvious. I am helping you after all."

"Thanks, but it's still not fair." Simchah clearly had other things in mind than preparing tomorrow's bread.

"Your mother would probably have you doing something else if you weren't occupied with the flour. So don't hurry too much," Rivkah whispered.

"But I really want to find out what's been happening at the southern wall. They've been fighting since dawn. Soldiers are hurrying along the street from the citadel. Even my father has gone to fight today," Simchah complained.

Yes, today was different. Everybody sensed it. People were following any news from the clashes with apprehension. Rivkah had helped around the house earlier today, but then slipped off to see Simchah at the first opportunity. Mother was so irritable and unreasonable today. Even Shomer got confused. You were never quite sure just what you were supposed to be doing. First she sent Rivkah to the loom, then realized she didn't have the wool she wanted for the fabric; next she told her to get more water and, after frantically searching for an empty jar, had thought it too dangerous to go to the well; then she had given dozens of contradictory orders and became upset when Rivkah wasn't doing what she had told her. Mother must be totally confused. But then this siege got to quite a few people. Father, of course, was just busy in his workshop, hardly saying a word. He certainly didn't want any girls standing in the way.

"Rivkah, another handful."

"Sorry." Rivkah hadn't paid any attention. She poured a few more grains onto the quern.

"Do you think it's true?"

"Think what is true?" Rivkah asked.

"That some people are selling their jewelry just to get a bit more grain?"

"Oh, I can believe some people are doing it. They are hungry."

"But their jewelry!" Simchah put in vehemently. "It's normally so expensive. And they won't be getting the full price now."

"No, they're not getting a good price," Rivkah agreed.

"I would never give away my shell necklace."

Simchah had a beautiful necklace of white shells and narrow, red faience beads. She wore it only on special occasions, but the two girls had looked at it together many times, admiring its beauty. Once, Simchah had even allowed Rivkah to try it on.

"But your necklace is special, Simchah. Nobody would give that away. Some people just sell what they don't need. Even you said that you'd be glad to get rid of your earrings."

"Only if I would get new ones, I said. Mine don't really suit me. They're just too plain. No decoration, no color at all. I really need to get some nice ones. Do you think anybody would sell me theirs?"

"And how would you pay? Barley?"

"I could put a bit away each day. Nobody would notice and I'll just eat a bit less."

"You would never be able to pull that off. You're already starving now. Even if it's only barley bread, you'll still want something to eat."

"I reckon I could do it." Simchah sounded offended.

"But what if your parents found out? They wouldn't be happy," Rivkah put in another word of caution.

"They won't find out. I'll make sure of that. I know where I'll put the grain."

"Will it be safe from mice there?"

The question seemed to throw Simchah a bit. She frowned, moved her tongue across her lips and answered slowly, "Yes, it'll be alright. I just have to ensure the lid fits well."

"Do you think it's a good idea? It does sound a bit risky."

"It's the best way to get some new earrings soon. I desperately need them." Simchah's mind seemed set. She moved the stone furiously across the quern.

Suddenly she stopped. "Hold on. How much to go?"

Rivkah showed her the bowl. There wasn't much barley left in it.

"Just two more handfuls, Rivkah. I'll put the rest away."

Rivkah giggled, "Suddenly you'll be all keen to grind the flour each day. Just imagine that."

Simchah looked directly into Rivkah's eyes. "You won't tell anyone, will you?"

"No Simchah, I will not tell anyone. I'm your friend."

* * *

Only one siege machine was still battering the walls of Lachish. The others stood, surrounded by the rubble of the crumbling city defenses, as battle platforms. Archers crowded on their decks providing cover for the stormers pouring into the city.

The Assyrians met stiff resistance. The Judahites drove chariots up the counterramp, turning the siege into a field battle. But the close-quarter fighting gave the unwieldy vehicles no advantage. Horses and drivers fell.

It did not take long until Assyrian troops had conquered the first tower. Shouts of triumph came from the soldiers now standing on the open platform. They were echoed by those still outside the walls. Without the threat of attacks from above, ladders were placed against the tower and a lieutenant led his platoon of archers upwards. From the elevated position they commanded a wide area, inflicting further damage on the defenders.

Itur-Ea took a deep gulp from his water flask. His lips were dry and his throat ached. The occasional arrow still struck the siege machine, but there was hardly any danger of torches reaching it now. He no longer had to keep the sides moist.

Looking back over the siege ramp and across to the hill, Itur-Ea could see the Assyrian camp and nearby the seat of the king, the great Sennacherib. There was a hive of activity with messengers arriving at, and departing from, the command center. The king must be assured of victory now.

Soon the order came for the siege machines to withdraw from the southwestern ramp. They could do no more damage to the city walls and stood in the way of the attackers entering Lachish. They had done their part.

It was a staged withdrawal. One machine after the other descended the ramp past lines of soldiers climbing up the hill.

After the heat of battle, Itur-Ea felt strangely weak and tired when he returned to the camp. He ate some bread and grapes—not much, but it felt good. He couldn't rest long anyway; the battle still continued. They would take the city, he was sure, but not without more fighting. It seemed those Judahites were eager to fight to the bitter end. Somehow they were not able to accept the fact of their weakness when faced with the might of Assyria. Their stubbornness may have something to do with their trust in that strange god of theirs. The city itself did not even have its own god, he had heard it said. Rather, they had one god for all of Judah—the god of Jerusalem. This god, they were convinced, could never bow to Ashur. Now they were taught their lesson.

* * *

"They have broken into the city! The Assyrians have breached the wall!"

Simchah's father rushed into the house, the sword strapped to his side. Simchah's mother hurried down the ladder from the upper floor. Her face looked ashen. "What did you say . . . ?" she asked with a wavering voice.

"The Assyrians are in the city. They are fighting back our men. They will come here," Simchah's father shouted in wide-eyed panic. When his wife looked at him, she gasped. Now that he leaned against the wall, the wound on his left shoulder showed clearly. It was a deep, open gash. He was losing blood quickly.

Rivkah looked at him in horror. It took some time for what had happened to sink in. She saw Simchah's father, pale, exhausted, weakened, and yet agitated, ready to fight. As she glimpsed Simchah's mother moving towards her husband to tend to the wound, she suddenly realized what she had to do. Her family! They would be in trouble!

"I have to go back home," she told Simchah.

"Wait!" Simchah pleaded, but Rivkah got up and was already moving to the door. She didn't take any heed of the protests of Simchah's father as he shouted that it wouldn't be safe for her to go into the street.

Rivkah was already out of the door and couldn't catch the warnings of Simchah's mother. She ran down the street. Home! She had to get to them. Mother! Father! Tears were streaming down her face. She knew they were in danger. What if they would die today? She couldn't leave them alone now. She'd rather die with them. Oh, why had she gone away this morning? Why hadn't she stayed at home? Everybody had felt the danger today. And she had left her family, why? Just because she didn't want to work, because her mother had been a bit upset and got a few things wrong. It all seemed so trivial now, so stupid. Rivkah stumbled and fell. Her knees and hands hurt and stung. Sobbing, she got up again and hurried on down the street.

As she rounded the corner, she saw something coming towards her. A grey furry, animal with light brown splotches ran down the street and passed her. She wiped the tears from her eyes with her arm and could see clearly. "Kaleb!" she shouted. The dog didn't stop. "Kaleb, Kaleb!" Rivkah called again. He stopped, turned around and wagged his tail, but didn't move. Rivkah ran towards him. She threw her arms around him. "You can't go there. They're fighting down that way. Come with me!" She grasped the fur on his back and dragged the dog with her. At first he struggled against her, but then relaxed and let himself be led. The two ran towards the main road, Rivkah in a hurry, bending down to clutch the dog, Kaleb trotting along reluctantly.

Rivkah thought she could hear noises coming from the main road. Shouts, the clash of iron, moaning, the hollow thud of shields. Had the battle reached the main road already? Was she too late? She hurried on, dragging Kaleb with her. Suddenly arms encircled her shoulders, gently but firmly, and held her back. "You can't go there, child."

Rivkah let go of Kaleb and whirled around. It was a woman. Rivkah noticed the delicate nose-ring, the precious earrings only partly hidden by the shawl the woman had draped over her head, the eye-shadow which gave her eyes that delicate, yet sad look. She wore fine clothes, better than Rivkah's mother would ever wear. Who was she?

"You can't go there," the woman repeated. "They are fighting on the main road, if the Assyrians haven't killed everybody already."

"But my family! I have to get home! I have to reach them!" Rivkah cried.

"Where do they live?" the woman asked gently.

"On the main road, near the tanners' lane."

The woman shook her head. "I'm sorry. You won't get there. The Assyrians are totally in control of that area. Their soldiers are continually passing up and down the main road. Even if you were a bird of the air, they would shoot you with their arrows if you tried to fly there."

Kaleb looked up at them unsure what to do. He cowered down confused, looking around him. He flinched when Rivkah stamped her foot. "But I have to see them," she insisted. "I can't leave them alone now. I need to talk to my mother, even if I die!" She struggled to free herself, but the woman held her.

"It's no use, child. You will not get there."

The realization struck Rivkah. "Too late!"

She stood still. "Too late," she echoed again. She gave a stifled cry as her legs buckled underneath her. Everything felt black and empty. The woman held her.

"Come on, we have to get away," the woman pleaded.

Rivkah took a deep breath and tried to steady herself, tried to get command over her body. She shook herself as if to wake from a bad dream. Slowly, feeling returned to her legs. "And now . . . what happens now?" she asked, still in a daze.

"We have to hide. Come!" The woman turned her around and led her by the arm down the street. Trembling Rivkah allowed herself to be guided. Suddenly she stopped. "Kaleb!" She turned her head and saw Kaleb still sitting there. "And the dog?"

"What about the dog?" the woman asked.

"It's Kaleb," Rivkah answered as if in explanation. The woman didn't seem to understand. But Rivkah just shouted, "Kaleb, Kaleb!" The dog leapt up and came to her side immediately. He licked her hand and jumped up, nuzzling her. "I can't leave him behind."

The woman sighed. "Bring him along then. But come now!"

The three figures hurried through the empty street. The tall woman walking with determined steps and holding the girl's arm; the girl following and grasping the dog's fur tightly; the dog scuttling along bewildered, yet alert.

"Where are we going? To your home?" Rivkah asked.

"No," the woman shook her head. "The Assyrians will be there, too, by now. It's right in the centre of the city. We have to get somewhere close to the wall, some place the enemy is not really interested in. We have to find a nook where we can hide. If we hold out, there's still a chance we can flee the city before they raze it to the ground."

The woman led them down several streets. It seemed to Rivkah that she wasn't taking the most direct route. At a corner the woman stopped and peered around the house wall. "Hurry!" She crossed the street and dragged Rivkah into a lane near the city wall. There she chose an old shed and gestured to Rivkah to go in. Then she followed herself, before Kaleb scampered after them. The dirt floor was covered with a thin layer of straw in places. Rivkah thought she could even smell the faint odor of goats, but no animals had been here recently. In one corner stood an old storage jar, while the pieces of a cooking pot were scattered over the floor. A few implements leaned against the walls. What was this handle for? A winnowing fork?

The house that the shed formed part of seemed deserted. It was near the counterramp the defenders of Lachish had constructed. It appeared as if the house had suffered somewhat from the battle. Rivkah thought she had seen rubble toward the back of the yard before they ducked into the shed. Weren't there some stray arrows and a sling stone in the lane outside? She could hear the shouts of the Assyrian soldiers only a block away.

"Why did we come here, so close to the fighting?" she asked, perplexed.

"They are not fighting here anymore," the woman assured her. "We'll be safest here. They won't look so close to the breach. The battle has passed on."

Rivkah sat on the dirt floor, leaning back against the wall. Her eyes closed, she lifted her head, regaining her breath. Feeling the woman looking at her, she opened the eyes and gave her a hesitant glance. The woman smiled back, "Here we are."

Rivkah didn't know what to say, but managed a cautious nod.

"I am Bath-Shua," the woman told her. The name didn't mean anything to Rivkah, though she was sure she had seen the woman many times before. She just didn't know where and when. Rivkah just muttered yes and looked away. The woman, however, seemed to expect more and spoke again, "And your name, what's your name, girl?"

"Rivkah."

"The daughter of the blacksmith?"

"Yes."

"I thought so."

The woman nodded and lightly brushed the dirt floor with her hand. Did the gesture trigger a memory? Rivkah suddenly thought she knew where she had seen the woman. She did not know why, but somehow the question burst out, "Do you live . . . do you live in the citadel?"

The woman smiled at her. "The citadel? No, but I am in the citadel quite often. And I do live close to it."

Rivkah waited for a further explanation, but there was none. The woman removed the shawl covering her head and combed her hands through her long, silky hair, brushing it back from her face.

Turning to Rivkah again, she broke the silence. "Well, it seems we'll have to sit here for a while. We cannot get out of the city now. Maybe later. For the moment we are safe here."

Safe? Rivkah could clearly hear the sounds of war. They were not far from danger. How could she feel safe? And yet this woman appeared so confident, so quiet and assured that Rivkah felt less threatened in her presence. The battle noise didn't overwhelm her. Like the distant rushing of a mighty river, it was present but not drowning out other sounds. She could hear herself breathe, could hear a fly buzzing round Kaleb's head. He snapped at the irritating insect. It escaped his jaws again and again before it decided to settle in a distant corner of the shed. Satisfied, Kaleb turned his head and licked his fur. After a while he must have felt clean enough, for he stopped and looked at Rivkah. She took both his ears in her hands and rubbed them. "Oh, Kaleb." The dog edged a bit closer to her and shut his eyes in satisfaction. He opened his mouth and relaxed his lower jaw, revealing a long row of sharp teeth. Rivkah stroked his neck and proceeded to run her hands over his back. Kaleb yawned lazily.

The woman watched them. "Your dog?"

"Yes," Rivkah said, even though Kaleb did not belong to anybody. He roamed the streets a free dog. But he was her friend.

"He looks nice," the woman commented. "Not like a lapdog, more like . . . a warrior dog, strong and skilful, fast and clever. Yet he seems so gentle."

"He can be fierce," Rivkah assured her.

"His name is Kaleb?"

"Yes, like the warrior of Judah," Rivkah explained.

"A good name."

"He is just as courageous," Rivkah said, turning her full attention to the dog again.

"Do you know the story of Kaleb, son of Jephunneh?"

Of course Rivkah had heard stories about the great hero, but she was never tired of listening to them again. "Tell me."

The woman seemed to have waited for the invitation. She settled down comfortably and began:

"The children of Israel had wandered many days through the wilderness. They had walked through that barren land for a long time. They longed for a good land, a land of trees and fields, of vineyards and gardens. So Moses sent twelve men to explore the land of Canaan, one from each tribe. From the tribe of Judah he chose Kaleb. He was a leader of Judah, a courageous man, a warrior among his people. He was tall and handsome, strong and clever.

"And Moses sent the men up and said to them:

'Go up through the Negev and then go to the hill country. Observe the land and the people who live there, whether they are strong or weak, few or many. What is the land they live in, good or bad? And what towns do they live in, unwalled or fortified? What is the soil like, fertile or poor? Are there trees or not? And bring back from the fruit of the land.'

"So the men went up and explored the land. And they saw that the land was good. They saw the vineyards, the orchards, the harvested fields. They saw that the people were wealthy. They lived in big cities, fortified by strong walls. And the people seemed like giants, tall and strong. They saw that the people were skilled warriors, that they had weapons of every kind. And the men exploring the land were afraid. They hid during the day and crept close to the cities in darkness to judge their strength. And they said to each other, 'The people here are strong and powerful. Their cities are fortified and large. We can never defeat them.' But Kaleb was a courageous warrior and he was not afraid. He knew they would conquer the land.

"And the men took with them from the fruit of the land, from the Valley of Eshkol a cluster of grapes. Two of them carried it on a pole between them, along with some pomegranates and figs.

"And they came back to Moses and the children of Israel. They gave their account and said, 'We went to the land to which you sent us and it does flow with milk and honey; here is its fruit. But the people in the land are powerful and the cities are fortified and very large.' The children of Israel were afraid because of their words."

"Were the children of Israel not courageous warriors?" Rivkah interrupted.

"Oh, they may have been. But, you know, men often lose their courage when faced with a mighty foe. And sometimes it is very real fear. After all, a great army can utterly crush a weaker people. But there is always hope," the woman replied. Somehow the story had come dangerously close to their own situation. She continued:

"But Kaleb, he stood up before the people and said, 'We should definitely go and take possession of the land for we can accomplish it.' But his words did not prevail. The people complained bitterly against Moses and against the LORD. So they wandered through the desert for forty more years. All those twenty years of age and older did not enter the land of Canaan, but died in the desert. Only Kaleb, son of Jephunneh, and Joshua, son of Nun, entered the land."

The woman was silent as if the story was over.

"But did he fight?" Rivkah asked.

"Kaleb? Oh yes, he fought. He was an important military leader. But being courageous does not always mean fighting. Kaleb stood before his people and showed them the way to follow, even in the face of strong opposition. To challenge the fear of the people, that is courage too."

"That is courage too," Rivkah repeated.

"Yes, when we overcome our fear and do what we are called to do, that is courage. It is hard to speak against a crowd. But Kaleb had the courage. He believed in the LORD's promises."

"And what happened later? Kaleb lived in the promised land, didn't he?" Rivkah asked.

"Yes, he entered the land with the children of Israel and fought bravely as one of their leaders. Later he led the tribe of Judah and conquered the land around Hebron." Bath-Shua pointed with her hand towards the east, where somewhere beyond this shed, beyond this city, the hills of Judah rose. "The hills of Hebron are not far from here. Sometimes you can see them in the distance from Lachish," she explained.

"Are they near Mareshah?"

"No, farther away. But if you look towards Mareshah you might see the hills of Hebron away in the distance. Joshua apportioned Hebron to

Kaleb and that is where he lived to the end of his days. He had many sons and a beautiful daughter."

"A beautiful daughter?"

"Yes, her name was Achsah. Kaleb gave her in marriage to his nephew Othniel. For when Kaleb and his men marched against Debir he said, 'I will give my daughter Achsah in marriage to the man who attacks and captures this town.' Othniel was a courageous warrior and he desired Achsah because she was beautiful. And so he fought bravely against Debir and took it."

"Did Kaleb have a beautiful wife?"

Bath-Shua lifted her eye-brows. "Kaleb had many wives."

"Why?"

"Because he was a rich man, a leader of his tribe."

"But why did he not love one? Was one not dearer to him than all the others?"

"He may have liked one more. And she was probably very beautiful. But Kaleb was a man. And men are not easily satisfied. They always want more. Still, Kaleb was a great man, a courageous man."

* * *

"The gate has fallen!" The news was greeted with joy by the Assyrian troops assembled in the camp. Ready to be deployed in another phase of the attack, they stood awaiting orders. "No need for us then," one of his comrades whispered to Itur-Ea. No, if the main defenses had fallen, there was no longer any use for the siege machines. It would be street fighting and close-quarter combat until all resistance had been crushed and the inhabitants flushed out of the city.

Something was not quite right though: a small battering ram was ordered to go into the city. Had the defenders barricaded themselves in somewhere? Were they mounting a last stand? They must be. Itur-Ea got the chance to find out. His unit was sent into the city to clean up and find any pockets of resistance. As they were marching up the roadway, prisoners were herded through the gate, out of the city. Itur-Ea had seen it all before: women dressed in dirty, shabby rags, the loss and fear clearly etched into their tear-stained faces; skinny children afraid and confused, clinging to their mothers; old men without hope or dignity, staring at the ground with empty eyes. They were clutching bundles of their most important belongings, of food and drink.

Somehow the suffering repulsed him. But it made the difference so obvious—he was part of the resplendent, victorious Assyrian army, they were the dirty, defeated scum that had been trodden into the dust.

And then Itur-Ea saw him. Head erect, looking proud and controlled, the Judahite warrior was led down the road. Even in defeat he would not submit. He wouldn't be like that for long. The Assyrian army had ways and means to crush a proud spirit. Would he still be silent if his skin was torn off, or would he scream and squirm in agony? It was men like him that had defended the city for so long and those stubborn men would surely feel the anger of the Assyrian soldiers.

The gate was a massive structure. Of course, it was nothing in comparison with the gates of Nineveh. Still, the courtyard between the outer gate and the inner gatehouse formed a large square any city could be proud of. Surrounded by walls and towers, any enemy that had the misfortune to get stuck here would be attacked from all sides. But the inner gatehouse was even more impressive. Itur-Ea guessed it to be nearly fifty cubits long. It had three chambers on each side. Assyrian soldiers now guarded the gate.

As the unit entered Lachish, it became clear that the fight was not over yet. At the end of the road leading straight from the gate, Itur-Ea could see the Assyrian army attacking the citadel. Apparently, the defenders had fled there and were determined to fight to the end.

But Itur-Ea did not join the fight at the citadel. The captain led the unit away from the main road and into the maze of narrow streets. The first few houses they entered were empty. But then they found a family huddled together in the backroom of a house. "Look what we've found here!"

"Get up! Out with you!" The Assyrian soldiers shouted at the frightened group. No matter that they couldn't understand them. The daggers in their hands talked loudly enough. Dragging some meager belongings with them, the captives were dispatched to the gate under the guard of two soldiers.

They found only a few more people hiding in houses. Most surrendered without resistance and joined the other prisoners outside the city. One man tried to defend his family. He must have been involved in the fighting earlier, for a fresh bandage covered his injured shoulder. With a determined look he brandished a sword, shouting at the soldiers. Itur-Ea stepped forward and feigned a thrust with his dagger. The man swung his sword, attempting to strike Itur-Ea. As the man committed, Itur-Ea stepped aside and the sword cut through the air. Catching the man off-balance, Itur-Ea turned around and thrust the dagger into his enemy's chest. Easy! Blood spurted from the wound as Itur-Ea drew back the dagger. The man collapsed to the ground and breathed his last.

There was reason why he had tried to protect his family: his daughter was quite pretty, even in the rags. A couple of soldiers ensured she would not leave Lachish undefiled. That man had been a fool! Had he thought he could save his family by his sacrifice?

* * *

"Do you know the story of the hero, Keret?" Bath-Shua asked.

"I've heard it before, but can't remember it," Rivkah replied. They were still sitting in the shed waiting, though Rivkah did not know what for. Bath-Shua seemed to know. She was so calm, so unafraid. Telling stories, she made Rivkah forget the dreadful destruction around them, made her turn her mind on other things.

"Keret was a great king, a good man. He protected his people from the swift raiders. He passed judgment at the gate. He fed the orphan and heard the cause of the widow. But he did not have a son, no rightful spouse at his side.

He did take a wife, but she departed;
the second passed away before she could bear children;
the third one died in her prime;
the fourth was snatched by the plague;
the fifth Rephesh, the messenger of death, carried off;
the sixth the servants of Yam, the god of the sea, claimed;
the seventh was felled by a spear.
So Keret was crushed, his family had come to an end."

"Did he mourn for his wives? He must have been heartbroken?"

"He may have been sad. But he was a king. It was important for him to have a son, to continue the line. He could not mourn a wife when he needed to continue his quest for an heir. All of his wives failed him, for they did not give him children. That was their role, that was why he married them. He was heartbroken because he had no son. He entered his chamber weeping and the tears streamed down his face.

"Sleep overcame him and on account of his tears the god El visited him in his dreams.

'Why do you shed tears? Do you not have silver and gold, slaves and cattle, chariots and horses?'

"But Keret spoke and said, 'What need do I have of silver and gold, slaves and cattle, chariots and horses? I am weeping because I have no spouse who might give me an heir.'

And the bull-god El answered: 'Cleanse yourself and bring a sacrifice on the walls, a sheep and a ram to offer to the bull-god El, your father. Lift your hands to heaven and call upon his name. Make Baal come down with your sacrifice, the son of Dagon with your offering.

Then gather a multitude and march into the desert. On the seventh day you will come to Udam. And when Pabil, the king of that city, sends you a message, only ask for the maiden Huray.' And Keret awoke and it was a dream.

"So he cleansed himself and went up to the walls. A sheep and a ram he did offer. He sacrificed to the bull El, his father. He made Baal come down with his sacrifices, the son of Dagon with his offering. He gathered a multitude; even the single men came, as did the newly-married and the sick."

"Why did even the newly-married and sick have to come? Should they not stay behind?"

"Keret got everyone he could so that his army looked large. He wanted to intimidate Pabil rather than fight him. So when they came to Udam they besieged the city and Pabil became afraid. On the seventh day he sent a message to Keret, 'Take silver and gold, slaves and cattle, chariots and horses. Take this peace offering, but do not besiege Udam.'

"But Keret sent a message back to Pabil, 'What need have I of silver and gold, slaves and cattle, chariots and horses? Give me what I do not have. Give me the maiden Huray, the most gracious of your family, your firstborn daughter, whose grace is as the grace of Anath, whose beauty as the beauty of Athirat.'

"When the messengers carried these words to Pabil, he wailed. And the people of Udam moaned for Huray. But the maiden went and joined Keret. And he carried her to his palace as a wife to bear him children."

"Did she have children?"

"Yes, seven sons and seven daughters. For Baal had blessed them."

"So everything turned out well?"

"Yes, but one of his sons later rebelled against Keret when he had become old. So Keret cursed him."

"But had Baal not blessed the family? Why would the son then rise against his father?" Rivkah was puzzled.

"Baal's blessing gives fertility, but not peace. For he provides and makes things grow, but also incites strife and trouble."

"And the maiden Huray? What happened to her?"

"She cared for her children and served Keret to the end of his days. She organized the household and ensured the guests were well fed at the dinner parties."

"So Keret loved her?"

"She was the rightful spouse at his side. She fulfilled her duties as his wife admirably. And she gave him what he was hoping for—sons and daughters. Yes, Keret must have valued Huray."

"Is that why a man marries a woman? Only to get children? Is it not because he loves the woman?"

"Oh, some men certainly love their wives. But that is not everything. They always have to think about continuing the family line, especially kings. And men are certainly attracted to women. But they are never satisfied."

"What do you mean?"

"They seek more. Rich men may get a concubine. But they tire even of her. That's why many men come to prostitutes. It makes them feel like the gods."

Rivkah looked at Bath-Shua. She wanted to know more and yet she was agitated by what she heard.

"Like the gods?" she asked. The urge to find out was stronger.

"You know how Baal, the rider of the clouds, lies with women and beasts, mounts them like the sacred ram. You must have heard of Pidray, the daughter of Baal, a maiden so desirable, the daughter of mist. Whether they imitate Baal or seek union with his luscious daughter, men take their desires to the prostitute. With her their heavenly fantasies are enacted. She has to be for them whatever goddess they desire. Many worship the union of the heavenly spouses, whether it be Osiris and Isis, El and Athirat, or the LORD and his Asherah."

"They do? You know?" Rivkah knew that some of the happenings during the religious festivals were hidden from the children, but what Bath-Shua told her was so new it threw her old certainties into confusion.

A frown went across Bath-Shua's face. "I know. I am one."

Rivkah hardly dared to ask, "What?"

"A prostitute." Bath-Shua said nothing more. She lowered her face.

Rivkah opened her mouth but did not speak. A cold shudder went down her spine. Quietly she edged further away from Bath-Shua."

"My father would never do that!" The challenge burst out.

"Your father is a man," Bath-Shua replied quietly.

"But he never came to you," Rivkah insisted.

Bath-Shua looked at her sadly. "Let's not talk about this any more."

"He never comes to you, does he?" Rivkah pleaded. When Bath-Shua did not answer she nearly shouted, "Does he?"

"Shh!" Bath-Shua signaled her to be quiet. "I shouldn't have told you that much. I'm sorry." She came closer towards Rivkah as if she wanted to comfort her. But Rivkah moved farther away. She didn't want that woman to touch her.

Kaleb growled, but not at Bath-Shua. His attention was directed towards the lane outside. And now Rivkah could hear the footsteps. Voices carried into the little shed, though Rivkah couldn't understand them. It didn't sound like Hebrew. They must be Assyrians.

Kaleb became tense. His growl got louder. Rivkah held on to him, frozen in fear. Kaleb stood up and moved forward, even though Rivkah tried to hold him back. It sounded as if the men were quite close now. Suddenly Kaleb growled loudly, barked and rushed forward. He leapt over the low wall in front of the shed. Rivkah tried to stop him. She went after Kaleb and was ready to follow him over the wall. But Bath-Shua jumped onto Rivkah and wrestled her down, pressing her to the floor behind the low wall. Rivkah struggled and kicked, but Bath-Shua held her with an iron grip. She wanted to scream but Bath-Shua clasped her hand over Rivkah's mouth. She bit Bath-Shua's hand. Bath-Shua clearly felt the pain, but did not loosen her grip.

Outside in the lane the fight was fiercer. Rivkah could hear Kaleb barking and growling. She could hear the men shouting and screaming. What was happening out there?

* * *

Itur-Ea whirled around. He thought he'd heard a growl. There were only the three of them in this small lane near the southern wall. Suddenly it was upon him. From behind some stones darted a snarling ball of fur and fangs that sank its teeth into Itur-Ea's arm. Itur-Ea tried to ward it off.

His comrades, Arad-Nergal and Samaku, thrust their daggers into the dog as it hung onto Itur-Ea. He screamed in rage and pain. Finally the animal gave up the struggle and fell limp to the ground. Itur-Ea kicked it. "Mongrel!" Without looking any further the three of them hurried out of the lane.

* * *

The sound of the soldiers' footsteps echoed in the lane as they hastened away and seemed to fade in the distance. Out in the lane it was eerily quiet. Rivkah no longer struggled. She just lay there, afraid and exhausted. Bath-Shua relaxed her grip and took her hand off Rivkah's mouth. Then she let her go and stood up. Slowly Rivkah got to her knees. Bath-Shua helped her stand up. Rivkah shook the dust off her clothes.

Afraid of what she would see, Rivkah looked over the wall into the lane. She caught her breath. There, lying in the middle of the lane was Kaleb. He didn't move. He made no sound. Blood was oozing from his side. She hesitated a moment, then ran round the wall and through the yard entrance into the lane. She threw herself down beside Kaleb, took his head into her hands and cradled him in her lap. There was no response. He had already gone. "Kaleb, oh Kaleb!" Rivkah sobbed his name. She stroked the blood-spattered fur, moving her hands across the limp body. She saw the knife wounds in his side out of which the blood still flowed. She did not try to stop it. Leaning down she kissed the dog's head. Tears welled up and fell on his nose.

"He really is a hero, a warrior." Bath-Shua had come and knelt beside Rivkah. "He fought to protect you. He fought bravely and with courage. But he paid a warrior's price: he gave his life." Bath-Shua touched Kaleb. Rivkah didn't move. The words hardly got through to her. She struggled for breath as her throat closed. Finally the loud sobs broke out of her chest. She cried freely now, broken only by moans of anguish. Bath-Shua let her be.

When Rivkah's breathing became more regular and her weeping ebbed, Bath-Shua got up. "Come, we must bury him now."

Rivkah shook her head. She wasn't ready to bury Kaleb. She wanted him to live. Was he really dead?

Bath-Shua stood by as Rivkah fondled Kaleb's fur. The flow of blood was starting to dry.

Bath-Shua looked around worried. She put her hand on Rivkah's shoulder and said: "Rivkah, we really can't leave him here. There's not much time. A warrior like Kaleb deserves a burial. We have to do it."

Rivkah looked at her blankly. She gathered the will to get up and wiped the tears from her eyes.

Bath-Shua leaned down. "We'll carry him over there to the collapsed wall." She indicated the pile of rubble with her head. When Rivkah didn't move she added, "Help me, Rivkah."

Rivkah lifted Kaleb's head and held him by his front legs. Together they carried him to the wall. Bath-Shua's nice clothes became stained with the dog's blood. She didn't seem to notice.

Carefully they put Kaleb's body down in front of the fallen house wall. Bath-Shua moved away the stones and mud bricks to make a space in the rubble. "We have to lift him in here." They laid Kaleb in the hollow. Rivkah stroked his head one last time. She didn't look as Bath-Shua piled stones and bricks on the dog. "Here rests a great warrior," Bath-Shua said. She mumbled a short prayer and cursed anyone who would disturb the burial place. Then she took Rivkah's hand. "We have been in the street for too long. We have to hide. What if the soldiers return?" Bath-Shua led Rivkah back to the shed. At the entrance she turned and said, "If you stand up you can see Kaleb's grave from here." Rivkah looked. She sighed and then sat down, leaning with her back against the wall.

Chapter 4

After the citadel of Lachish had fallen and its defenders massacred, Sennacherib gave the city over to looting and plunder. With no temple in Lachish, there was no grand ceremony leading the gods out of the city. Normally, the temple also held the greatest riches of a city. The temples of Nineveh would not receive any treasures from Lachish. Of course, there would be some valuables in the fort. Some soldiers counted on finding treasures there; others thought that the residential quarters might yield more. Rummaging through houses to find anything valuable, they destroyed whatever came across their path. Greed and a lust for destruction seized them.

Itur-Ea sat on a stone gazing beyond the miserable mass of captives. The bite wound hurt. He had been sent to escort some prisoners out of the city and had now ended up among the guards watching the vanquished Judahites. Maybe that was his duty as a professional. Meanwhile the auxiliaries, who had been provided for the war effort by Assyria's client kings and governors, plundered the city. Quick to loot and quick to flee! Those amateurs were all the same. You couldn't rely on them in the heat of battle, but when they saw the opportunity to enrich themselves there was no holding them back.

Itur-Ea knew he would receive a handsome share of the spoils of war at the end of the campaign. Earlier in the campaign he had already had the luck of snatching a few precious ornaments from the city of Timnah. Still, it grated him that he had to sit here.

"Sit down," Itur-Ea snapped. The child looked at him with a blank expression. Itur-Ea stood up and drew his dagger. The child's mother dragged it down to her and Itur-Ea sat down again. He needed to rest. It had been a long day. Another sip from the water flask felt good. But still, somehow, he would have preferred to be in action. He felt so far away from Ishtar at the moment. All the excitement had drained from him.

* * *

They hadn't talked much. The death of Kaleb had shattered Rivkah even more than the Assyrian invasion of the city. She sat there numb and weak, her eyes unfocused. Several times she felt like getting up and running—anywhere. But she couldn't gather the strength to get to her feet. Even though she felt like crying, the tears which had flowed so freely before had now dried up.

Bath-Shua sat further inside the shed and watched Rivkah with concern. She seemed to sense that now was not the time for more stories, but did not know how to help. Rivkah was grateful she left her to grieve. Somehow she did not resent Bath-Shua anymore. In these few hours they had been through too much together. And Bath-Shua really seemed to care for her. Who else could she trust in the middle of this war now?

From somewhere Bath-Shua got out some bread. She gave Rivkah a piece. "Eat, you must be hungry." Rivkah shook her head. She didn't feel like eating. But Bath-Shua insisted, "Rivkah, eat something! It'll give you the energy to keep going. You have to stay strong."

Hesitantly, Rivkah took the bread. It seemed she had to eat it. When she took the first bite she suddenly realized how hungry she really was and quickly ate the rest.

"Do you have more bread?" Something like a sudden panic overcame Rivkah.

"Just a little. We'll have to keep that for later," answered Bath-Shua.

What were they going to eat after that? "Just one piece of bread? How are we going to survive?" The dire situation they were in overwhelmed Rivkah.

"We won't stay here forever. Remember, Rivkah, that the LORD is able to make a thousand loaves out of one piece of bread. He is a god that provides. Never forget that, Rivkah! Even in your darkest moments, even in times like these, don't give up."

"Do you really think we can escape?"

Cooped up in this little shed the chance of escaping the Assyrians seemed so remote.

"I hope we can. We have to try. When they burn the city, that will be our best opportunity."

"Burn the city?"

"That's what they are bound to do. The Assyrians don't leave a conquered city standing."

Every question seemed to bring to light more difficulties, but Bath-Shua knew of them already. And yet she appeared calm and hopeful.

"Where will we go?"

"Into the hills. We'll find a place where we're safe. Maybe we can even reach Hebron, the city of . . . ," Bath-Shua didn't finish the sentence. She didn't want to mention the name of Kaleb again. But Rivkah knew. Thinking of him hurt. Still, the name of the city held a promise. It was as if Kaleb pointed to that city, that maybe there she would find safety and peace.

"Do you think we'll be safe from the Assyrians there?"

"I believe so," Bath-Shua answered. "The Assyrians have no reason to move against Hebron. And the LORD will never give the city of his servant to destruction."

"And then, will we ever return here?"

"The Assyrians will not stay in the land forever. One day you may be able to return. It may be a long time until then. Now it is important to find a safe place. If you make it, Rivkah, remember you are a daughter of Lachish, a child of a once-great city. Let no one tell you otherwise. Do not let them destroy your dignity. Even as a refugee you are a woman worthy of respect. You come from a skilled family, from a city that guarded the entrance to the hill country, a city valued by the kings of Judah."

Bath-Shua looked at Rivkah, huddled against the bare, mud-brick wall.

"And Rivkah, you know that you are a beautiful woman, don't you? Do not listen if others mock your appearance. They're lying. Even clothed in rags and overcome by disaster you are graceful. Don't ever feel you are worth less than any man. Otherwise they will exploit your weakness." Bath-Shua lowered her tone. "Don't let men use you in the service of the gods. Listen! There is nothing good in the sexual encounter with the gods. It only gives room to the vain imaginations of men. Maybe they experience the chaotic traits of some gods, such as the lust of Baal or the deviousness of Anath. But you serve what is good of the gods, the faithfulness of the LORD, the perseverance of Isis. Don't let the good be overcome by evil."

Rivkah clasped her amulet as Bath-Shua's words swirled around her.

"You are a capable girl who can find a way through adversity. You know how to conduct a household, how to work with your hands. You can cope in any situation. Do not fear. There is still hope."

* * *

Lachish was to be set to the torch that day. The city would be erased from the face of the earth. Only a smoldering ash-heap would remain after the fire had ravaged the city. Wooden beams and mud bricks do not offer much resistance to fire.

This would not be a random conflagration, but a fire carefully planned to ensure the thorough destruction of the city. Itur-Ea's unit was involved. They were to enter the city through the gate and set the southeastern corner alight before leaving the city through the breach at the top of the siege ramp.

They marched into the city torches in their hands. Rushing through the empty streets they reached a corner opposite a great shaft. Other units had already started fires in the north of the city. Now it was their turn. Entering the houses they set fire to anything they could: furniture, straw mats, clothes, jars of oil. The dry material burst into flame. It was a nightmarish scene: flames shooting through roofs and doors, smoke pouring over the city, soldiers running through empty streets, their footsteps echoing from bleak walls. As they advanced, Itur-Ea could hear houses collapsing as walls gave way and beams were consumed by fire.

* * *

Rivkah could smell the smoke. "They're really burning the city."

"Yes. We'll have to make a break for it shortly." Bath-Shua stood up and walked out of the shed to peer into the lane. "We have to try."

"Will there be other people trying to escape the city?" Rivkah asked.

"I don't think so. Most of them would have been killed or taken captive. We're lucky the Assyrians didn't find us."

"What about my family? Mother, Father? Would they be able to escape?"

"Not many will survive the conquest of Lachish. Many have died. Others the Assyrians will take away as captives. Maybe your family has been able to escape, Rivkah. Let's hope so, but this is war."

"Will the LORD not protect them? You said the LORD will provide." Rivkah raised her voice.

"He does provide," Bath-Shua assured, "but he has given Lachish over to destruction. Many will be destroyed with the city. Some will live, others will die. We do not know why. The LORD knows."

The explanation didn't comfort Rivkah at all. As if fear and sorrow could be explained.

"Rivkah, you have to be strong now. This is our only chance to live. It will be dangerous. But don't be afraid of dying. It is better to die seeking freedom than to cower and entrust yourself to cruel Assyrian caprice."

Bath-Shua took Rivkah's hand and pulled her out of the shed. "Come, we have to go. I'll lead you. Just follow me."

They went into the lane. Bath-Shua let go of Rivkah's hand. Keeping a careful watch they walked along the rubble-strewn street. Rivkah turned around and looked one last time at Kaleb's resting place. Would his body be consumed by the flames? He had to be left behind at the place of his final battle. She didn't have much time to mouth a farewell as she hurried to keep up with Bath-Shua.

At the corner Bath-Shua stopped. Holding Rivkah back with one hand she surveyed the street. "It's all clear. Come quick!" They ran along the street and up the counterramp. Bath-Shua kept to the side of the rise, in the shadow of any remaining walls.

The signs of the battle were evident: an overturned chariot, helmets, spears, shields. Arrows and sling stones were scattered amongst the rubble. Blood seemed to have seeped into the dirt. Apart from four dead horses there were no bodies on the ramp. Even in their haste Bath-Shua seemed to have noticed it. "The Assyrians must have allowed them to gather the fallen. They're probably in a mass grave by now."

Rivkah just concentrated on getting out of this hell. She felt sick in this place of death. Behind them clouds of smoke were billowing from the burning houses.

But instead of rushing through the breach in the wall and out into the open, Bath-Shua slowed down. When Rivkah tried to push past her, Bath-Shua stopped her.

"Careful! The Assyrians might be just out there."

Bath-Shua's worry was real. After they had crept to the edge of the breach, they could see the soldiers on the slope below. The men were standing in small groups, talking among themselves, watching and pointing as flames engulfed more of the city. Rivkah and Bath-Shua pressed themselves against large blocks of stone that had once formed part of the city wall.

"We'll wait a moment. I hope the soldiers will go further down the slope. Then we have to make a dash for it. Luckily it's getting dark now. The night will protect us," Bath-Shua told Rivkah. She studied the horizon, taking in the location of the main enemy forces. "It seems there are no posts up the valley. We will have to go left along the wall, down the hill and across the dry stream bed. From there we might be able to go up the valley or we will have to flee into the hills."

Movement came into the soldiers on the slopes below. Someone shouted commands and the men came together.

"Right, get ready now," Bath-Shua whispered. Just then Rivkah heard footsteps coming up the ramp from the city behind them. She tugged Bath-Shua's dress. Now Bath-Shua heard them too.

"Let's go now! Quick!" There was no time to wait for the soldiers outside to get lower down the slope. Bath-Shua clambered over the rubble and out onto the slopes that dropped away from the city wall. Rivkah followed her. They kept close to the wall as they hurried away from the breach.

Looking back Rivkah could see a group of Assyrian soldiers emerging from the city and stopping for a moment. Rivkah prayed they wouldn't notice the two women hurrying away under the city wall.

Bath-Shua stopped briefly. No-one seemed to have spotted them. "We'll have to get down the hill here. Keep low! We have to be quick, but be careful not to stumble. There are no Assyrians straight down there. We should make it."

Rivkah followed Bath-Shua down the steep slope. They could make it.

* * *

The smoke became thicker and the heat more intense. Itur-Ea's lungs were burning. It was easy to get disorientated in this labyrinth of streets.

The captain signaled his troops to assemble. Once everybody had joined the group, the unit rushed out of the narrow lane and rounded a corner. On the road they met another unit heading for the siege ramp. Following their lead they passed through streets filled with the rubble of destroyed buildings. As they ascended the counterramp, the valley spread before them with the Assyrian camp pitched on the mound across the saddle. This must have been the view the defenders had from these walls. Through the breach, across the loose stones of the wall, they left the city behind and exited into the open.

Itur-Ea turned around and watched the high walls, now crumbling. Flames were raging throughout the city now. The end of Lachish!

As his eyes swept over the city mound, he just glimpsed them out of the corner of his eye. In the dusk he wasn't sure at first. But yes, there below the wall two figures were making their way down the hill. They were trying to get away as quickly as possible. Fugitives! Itur-Ea shouted and ran after them. He did not turn around to see whether anybody else joined the pursuit.

* * *

When they reached the valley below, Rivkah heard a loud explosion as a beam burst in the heat of the fire. She turned to look at the burning city. Glancing across the mound she saw a figure running down the hill, coming directly for them.

"Bath-Shua!" she cried, "they're following us."

Bath-Shua looked back and spotted the soldier. She grabbed Rivkah's arm and shoved her forward. "Run Rivkah! Straight ahead to the stream! Don't stop!"

Rivkah ran ahead with Bath-Shua right behind her. Her lungs felt like bursting. Her dress got in the way. When she looked back over her shoulder she saw that the soldier had gained on them. The momentary distraction had diverted her concentration. She didn't look where she was running. Rivkah stumbled and fell forward. She was able to catch herself and got up again by the time Bath-Shua was at her side. It was only a tiny delay.

Running right behind Bath-Shua now, Rivkah followed her into the dry, rocky stream bed. They got out on the opposite bank. There Bath-Shua stopped and turned towards Rivkah.

"You have to go on alone now, Rivkah. Don't wait for me! Run up into the hills and hide."

At first Rivkah didn't understand. She should leave Bath-Shua?! She hesitated.

Bath-Shua's voice was full of emotion as she put her hand on Rivkah's head.

"The LORD bless you and provide for you. The LORD grant you life and peace."

Then she slapped Rivkah's arm to send her on her way.

"Run Rivkah. Run, my daughter! Run and live!"

Bath-Shua turned to face their pursuer. Rivkah's legs started moving again. Bewildered she ran across the valley to the hills. Behind her she could hear the struggle. As she fled into the night, the screams followed her. Whatever the men of Lachish had done to Bath-Shua in the past, however they had hurt her, nothing could have come close to this.

* * *

Itur-Ea ran down the city mound, pursuing the fugitives. He was catching up. He could see now that he was chasing two women or, rather, a woman and a girl. They would not escape! The girl stumbled on the uneven terrain, but picked herself up again and carried on. The distance was narrowing. Now they clambered over the rocks of the dry stream and reached the opposite bank. Suddenly they stopped. The woman spoke to the girl and placed one hand on her head, then turned to face Itur-Ea as the girl started running again.

Itur-Ea stared at the appearance. She looked beautiful, like a goddess of the night, wild and yet sensuous. And then he realized. He rushed forward and overpowered the struggling woman. With his dagger he ripped open her clothes. Ishtar had bestowed her favor upon him and given him this woman. And Itur-Ea met Ishtar, the goddess of war and love.

PART TWO

Chapter 5

Thorns tore bloody scratches across her legs. Her hands were bleeding. She had fallen countless times, hurting her hands and legs. Bushes caught her dress and ripped it. She stumbled on the loose rock. And still she ran. Even though it was now completely dark she did not stop. Her heart was beating wildly. She was gasping for air. Sobs broke the frenzied rhythm of her hard breathing. Tears streamed down her face. She wiped them away with her arm.

Since that horrible moment at the brook of Lachish, Rivkah had been running. She had not looked back after Bath-Shua had sent her on ahead. The screams told the story. And she knew: she was alone now. Fear and horror had driven her on. First across the valley and then into the hills. She had to get away from that place. Rivkah couldn't hear anybody following. Twice she stopped and listened. Still, the fear persisted.

Rivkah slowed to a walk. She just couldn't continue any more. She was totally drained and exhausted. Her whole body trembled. A few hundred cubits more and she collapsed on the ground. The sobs became a loud wailing cry which Rivkah tried to stifle with her hands.

"Bath-Shua, what have they done to you? How cruel can men be? You never deserved this." Grief for the woman who had protected her in those last dramatic hours broke her heart and now she let everything pour out. The grief that had been held back could no longer be contained.

"Kaleb, you mighty warrior! You are no more. You fell in battle, fighting for your people, for me. Kaleb, you were more than a dog, you were my best friend. No soul was as noble as yours. Kaleb! Oh . . . " Words failed her at the thought of the faithful animal. In agony she tore her fingers through her hair until it hurt. The picture of his lifeless form lying there in the street, killed by the Assyrian soldiers, still haunted her.

Then the realization hit.

"Mother, Father, little Susannah, Shomer, Shallum, Nepheg! Are you dead too? Gone? Or do those vicious Assyrians still torment you?"

She could see their faces now. She longed to touch them, to be with them. How dear they were to her. Rivkah regretted every harsh word she had ever said to them, every time she had disregarded her family. Other things had seemed more important, other people more interesting. Now she realized that her family was the most precious thing she had ever had. That's where she belonged.

She had lost so much. It came before her eyes in a flash: the house she grew up in, the streets she played in, the city she knew.

"Lachish, oh my city! You have fallen! Nothing but ashes, nothing but ashes! Oh Simchah! The LORD did not save us! Why? Had the gods abandoned the city? Did Amun-Re or Baal or the LORD not hear the prayers of the people?"

She had no answers to the questions. How the people had hoped for deliverance! Now they were dead or condemned. The names of friends and neighbors crowded her mind. In an incomprehensible babble a torrent of names burst from her lips. The names of her family were mixed up in the flow. Slowly the stream of names grew calmer, the torrent ebbed. She only mentioned a few names now, until at last she breathed only one name into the silence: "Mother . . . Mother . . . Mother."

* * *

Meshullam thought he had heard somebody call his name. He forced himself awake and opened his eyes, staring into the blackness of the night. He listened carefully, but could hear only the breathing of his cousins and his little brother Shimei beside him. But yes, now he heard a voice calling somewhere far away. It was faint and no, it was not his name it was calling. Maybe it was a soldier on the walls, keeping watch during the night. It must have just been a dream.

But now he was awake and couldn't get back to sleep again. Meshullam turned around and bumped into his cousin Michael on his right. Michael only grunted in his sleep and hardly moved. Meshullam turned back again. He drew his knees up to his body and turned to his other side. Why couldn't he sleep? Carefully he got up and went to the door of the tiny room. Here in Jerusalem they were living in the small house of a family that had moved down from Samaria several years ago. There wasn't much space. The house was as crowded as the rest of the city. The family of his uncle Nahshon lived in this house too and, of course, Grandfather.

Meshullam had not gotten used to the big city. Everything was so cramped, so close together, so crowded. It was worse than usual now. Thousands had fled to Jerusalem from the countryside. And now the Assyrians were outside the city, besieging the gates. Nobody could go in or out. Their life was bounded by the walls of the city, their movements enclosed by its gates. Meshullam longed to walk through fields again, to wander through orchards and hurry through scrub and forest. But he knew they could not have remained at home. It was too dangerous.

He wondered what was happening there now. Had the Assyrians already taken Moresheth-Gath? Had they destroyed the houses, torn down the walls, felled the fruit trees and olive groves? Had the Assyrians swept across the country and taken the towns and cities? Tonight he could not help but think of the cities that were under siege in the west, the people that hid behind walls that were not as well fortified as those of Jerusalem. Would they be able to hold out? If not, what would happen to them in the hands of the Assyrians? Reports of their cruelty had travelled ahead of the army. Could the people expect any mercy?

In the dark Meshullam uttered a short prayer: "LORD God, do not forsake your people, spare your wrath, be merciful."

He stood still, then quietly returned to his place between his cousin and his brother. Sleep did not come quickly. This night, he had no peace.

* * *

House walls collapsed behind her as she ran through empty streets. Somewhere Rivkah could hear Kaleb bark. She tried to get to him, but was not sure which way to go. Where was he? Suddenly Bath-Shua was beside her, pressing her hand. "You must leave this city now. Run, my daughter, run!"

Rivkah wanted to ask her something but Bath-Shua was gone. Instead her hand held onto a burning post. She drew it back and started to run. Then she heard them behind her: the Assyrians! They were following her. She tried to run faster. But her feet seemed like stones. She could hardly move them. In agony and fear she cried out. They were closing in on her. Rivkah turned to confront her pursuers. The faceless form of a soldier thrust a metal blade into her stomach. She gasped with pain.

In shock Rivkah woke from her dream. Her whole body was hurting and her head ached. She got up slowly. Shivering with cold she drew her moist clothes tighter around her. She must have cried herself to sleep last night.

Now it was light. In the east the first rays of the sun crept over the hills. She fingered her Isis amulet. It gave her strength. She got up slowly. Hesitantly, Rivkah took a few steps: away from the conquered city and towards the sun. Her steps became firmer. She became aware of her dry throat. Her stomach felt empty. In search of food and water she walked on.

When Rivkah came to the top of another low hill she could see the rocks of a small stream in the shallow below. In the hope that she would find water she scampered down. To her disappointment the stream bed was dry. But Rivkah did not give up that easily. Clambering upstream she searched between the rocks and did indeed find a pool of stale water. She knelt down on the rocks beside the pool. Cupping her hands she brought the water to her mouth, drinking hastily.

Her thirst quenched, she continued up the stream. She walked slowly, not really having an aim. Yes, she was hungry, but where on earth could she get something to eat?

The sun stood high in the sky by now and was beating down on her. Rivkah sat down. She felt sick. Her stomach was churning. Lying down in the dry grass she just wanted to close her eyes and sleep. But scenes from the previous day's disaster crowded her mind. The memory overwhelmed her. That wouldn't do! She got up again, willing herself to do something—anything.

She walked on, further uphill. It was some time later when Rivkah—out of the corner of her eye—suddenly noticed a strange movement. She thought she had seen somebody. But no, she must have imagined it. Surveying the surroundings she couldn't make out any trace of another being. Still nervous, she continued on.

"Hey, little girl, what are you doing here?"

The voice startled Rivkah. Frightened she wheeled around, her heart pounding. A man stepped from behind a bush. Rivkah stared at him.

He studied her. Then he nodded. "So, where are you going?"

"I . . . don't know." Rivkah couldn't think of an answer.

"You don't know. See, see. And where are you from?"

Rivkah was silent. She just looked at him. An unkempt beard surrounded his face. The head covering was wound over his ears and hair. He wore coarse, woolen work-clothes just reaching over his knees. A simple rope served as a belt. The sandals he wore seemed to consist more of patches than any original leather. The man came closer.

"Come on girl, speak to me. I just heard you talk plain Hebrew. Can't be too difficult. Where do you come from?"

Rivkah looked at his eyes. They seemed kind. There was no anger, no cunning or malice in them. In fact, he looked anything but dangerous. Rivkah decided to trust him.

"From Lachish," she managed to say.

"From Lachish? Isn't the city surrounded by the Assyrians?"

Rivkah nodded.

"How did you get out then?"

"Through the breach in the city wall."

"The breach in the city wall? What do you mean?"

"The one the Assyrians made," she answered.

"They've entered the city then?"

"I fled from the burning city."

"So the great city of Lachish has fallen?"

"Yes," Rivkah confirmed quietly.

"Oh Lachish, your walls were thought to be impenetrable,
your gates were meant to repel any attack,
your steep slopes were told to hold back any enemy,
your towers were counted as a sure defense.
Now you are no more;
you have been erased from the face of the earth,
your warriors have lost the battle,
your chariots will drive out to war no more.
Oh Lachish!"

The man proclaimed his lament over the fallen city. His eyelids were pressed together and with pain etched across his features he lifted his face heavenward. Then he opened his eyes again and looked at Rivkah. "So you fled the city? All alone?"

She nodded.

"Poor girl. When did it happen? It's the first I heard of it."

"Just yesterday," Rivkah said.

"Have you had had anything to eat or drink?"

Rivkah shook her head.

"Oh my, you must be starving then. Come on, I'll show you where we're staying. I suppose we can always share our meager provisions with another fugitive."

* * *

Sennacherib, king of all, king of Assyria, sat on his royal throne while the spoil of Lachish passed before him. In his left hand he held the royal bow, in his right he clasped two golden arrows. Truly, here was the leader of the mighty army that through its weapons, its skill and fighting prowess had carried out the will of the great god Ashur. The king's feet rested on an ornate footstool, his left arm inclined on the armrest of the magnificent throne. Eunuchs stood behind the throne waving richly-adorned fans, moving the air that was still heavy with the smoke of the smoldering city. Robed in precious garments, the figure of the king on his high throne commanded the attention of all. His head erect, crowned with the ornate, peaked cap of Assyrian kings, Sennacherib surveyed the procession before him. The Tartan, the commander-in-chief, led the train followed by commanders of divisions, the strategists and the Musarkisu officers. Among them was Ashur-bel-amati, the commander of the archers. It was said he could split a hair from a distance of two hundred paces, so accurate was his mark with the arrow.

The Tartan then remained at the king's side while the other officers moved on past him. Next, the leaders of the vanquished city appeared before the king. They had their hands held in supplication to the king, silently beseeching him for mercy. As they came closer, they shuffled forward on their knees, repeatedly bending down low, kissing the dust. There was no dignity left in them. They looked like dogs that slink through the city streets. Their clothes were tattered and torn, their feet bare; they wore no jewelry and carried no weapons.

As he watched the pitiful display, Itur-Ea could not imagine that these were the leaders of the men that had determinedly held the mighty Assyrian army at bay for months. His rage and anger against them turned into disgust. Now these wretched fools would pay for their obstinacy. Their weakness and stupidity was now plain to see.

While the leaders of Lachish were still groveling in the dust before the throne, a crowd of prisoners was herded past the back ranks amongst which Itur-Ea was standing. Women, children, and old men were now brought before the king, who gave them scant attention as they filed past. The great king showed renewed interest as Assyrian soldiers came forward carrying past the most valuable booty taken from the city. There were intricately carved incense stands and ornate furniture with ivory inlay, jewelry and musical instruments. The city must have had a sanctuary after all, even if there was no grand temple. Soldiers carried past shields and spears, swords and bows, which had been taken from the defenders. Now they would be added to the weaponry of the Assyrian army. But the war chariots received the most attention as they were wheeled past. Their workmanship was admirable. They looked sturdy and yet maneuverable—a most welcome addition to the military inventory.

The Tartan also appeared pleased at the less notable, but more practical, loot of jugs of oil and jars of barley carried from the city. Clearly, Lachish could have held out longer. Now the food would be used to sustain Assyrian soldiers and to give the prisoners provisions on their long journey into exile.

The parade concluded with an offering to the gods. Two rams and a bull were killed in honor of the great god Ashur, the chief army priest conducting the rites. The king watched in solemn silence as priests burned the entrails of the animals. He raised his voice and dedicated the victory to Ashur. Ishtar of Nineveh also received a bull. Itur-Ea's heart beat faster as the animal expired with an angry bellow. He joined fervently in the prayers to Ishtar. She had protected him in this campaign. She had given victory. And he had encountered her on the battlefield on the night that Lachish fell.

Sennacherib, king of all, king of Assyria, stood. The celebration was over. Soldiers cheered as the great king came down from his throne and went into the royal tent.

* * *

The pace was just crazy. Rivkah could hardly keep up with the man's strides. She followed several cubits behind him, but always seemed to be dropping back, so that she frequently had to break into a quick run to keep up with him. They hadn't been walking that long, but to Rivkah it seemed like hours. The man hadn't spoken since he'd made that offer of food and drink.

Rivkah had to stop and catch her breath again. She fell even further behind. The man suddenly seemed to notice and turned around. "Sorry, I totally forgot that you must be tired. I'll slow down. Are you all right?"

Rivkah tried to replicate his smile. "Just a bit tired and hungry."

"It's not far now," he promised.

Whatever did "not far" mean? She couldn't see any houses anywhere. Not a sign of a village. It must still be miles away.

The man kept his promise and slowed his pace. Rivkah was closer behind him now, following his steps. He made his way through the low bushes and thorns covering the landscape. She watched him place his feet carefully on the dry ground as they walked uphill. Suddenly he seemed to remember something and stopped. He turned to Rivkah, "What's your name, girl?"

"Rivkah."

"And your family?"

"Amzi, the smith, is my father."

"Oho, he was a good tradesman, your father. One of our neighbors once went to Lachish to get his plow repaired."

Rivkah nodded.

The man continued, "I am Amnon from Shechar. Our village was in the valley across there. See, just over that ridge? I was a farmer there, working the land of my fathers. We fled before the might of the Assyrian army. But come on. I'll show you where we are living now."

Now that he mentioned it, Rivkah could faintly smell human waste. It wasn't quite as strong as in the back alleys of Lachish, but it was unmistakable. And then she noticed the fireplace: a simple circle of stones on the ground. Somebody must have used it today. A few pots and bowls lay beside it. Next she saw the cave towards which Amnon walked. He stopped in front of the entrance. "Welcome to our home." He didn't get any further. From inside the cave came a voice, "Son, who have you brought here?" An old woman crawled out of the entrance. Her weathered face was framed by long, flowing hair that once must have been shining black, but was now streaked with grey. When she was out in the open, she stood erect, her hair nearly touching her waist.

"I found her in the hills south of here. She's fleeing from the Assyrians, mother. They have captured Lachish! The city has fallen! May the LORD have mercy on us! Will the Assyrians really rule this land? We all know their cruelty.

The mighty one has broken the gates of the city,
he has plundered the villages round about,
he has felled the people by the sword
and destroyed their children with fire,
so that they will be remembered no more
and their inheritance has been laid to waste."

Amnon was silent again, deeply troubled.

"So you have brought her here," the woman brought him back to the present.

"Yes, she is hungry and needs rest. She was wandering aimlessly through the hills. And mother, she looks as if she could do her share of work."

The old woman inspected Rivkah. "And who is she?"

Amnon leaned over to Rivkah and whispered, "It's Rivkah isn't it?"

"Yes," she answered.

"Mother, this is Rivkah, daughter of the blacksmith of Lachish."

"Shalom Rivkah, daughter of Lachish. Come in." The old woman turned to the cave again.

"This is my mother, Ayalah," Amnon explained as Rivkah followed.

Rivkah climbed down the steps into the cave. At first she could hardly see in the dim light. But then her eyes adjusted to the dark. She was in a rectangular room with a low ceiling. It was about four by six cubits wide. Opposite the entrance there was a door to another chamber. To the left, too, another room went off the main chamber she was now standing in. Rivkah knew immediately: this was a grave! What were they doing among the dead?

* * *

The wind had turned. The westerly breeze now blew the smoke of the smoldering ruins of Lachish away from the camp. The stench had hung over the valley throughout the night and day. Itur-Ea hardly noticed the change of wind. He stood among the other soldiers watching the leaders of Lachish being tortured. Their pleas for mercy to the king had gone unanswered and he had handed them over to the wrath of his officers. The anger of the officers knew no bounds. One of the Judahites had been hurled to the ground. An officer hauled him up by his hair and at the same time thrust a dagger into his side. The man tried to wriggle out of the way, but a soldier kicked him in the belly, causing the man to double over. Silent tears welled in his eyes. The officer drew him up again and began to hack the skin from the flesh. The man's screams of agony were met by the laughter of the soldiers. He did not last long. The screams died away as the man sank into a lifeless form, the blood draining red into the dust.

The Assyrian fury was not spent yet. Several archers grabbed two Judahites and stripped them naked. The two stood motionless, giving no resistance as derisive shouts pelted them like stones. The sport had only begun. Four archers stepped forward and each took a leg of the men, pulling them off their feet. Like a cat swung by its tail, so the men were used as living slings and swung through the air. Their heads smashed together before being bashed onto the ground. As one soldier became tired, another took his place and grabbed a leg. The spectators howled in delight. They participated in the sport by dealing an occasional blow to the victims lying on the ground or as they swung through the air. Where was the courage of the Judahites now, where their defense?

Itur-Ea laughed out loud. Just watching them suffer released his anger. He shoved his way to the front of the group. One of the Judahites lay in a crumpled heap on the ground, a shattered body fighting for breath. There was still a spark of life in him. In rage Itur-Ea kicked the man's head. Other soldiers joined in and stomped on the limp body. Its life was snuffed out and when the horde moved on, it left only a dismembered mess of blood and cracked bones in the dust.

Itur-Ea watched at least a dozen men being tortured and killed that afternoon. It was part of the sweet victory over such determined a foe. As the cool of evening approached, the Assyrian soldiers went to their tents where they celebrated the fall of Lachish with streams of beer. The beer had been distributed for the occasion, to celebrate the victory of Ashur.

* * *

Outside, the raindrops were pounding on the parched ground. The fall rains had arrived. From the safety of the cave Rivkah was staring at the showers outside. How cold it had become! Rivkah shivered. Drawing her knees up to her body she hugged them tightly. Her clothes just weren't warm enough. Not on a day like this.

Amnon sat opposite the entrance and greeted the arrival of the first rain:

"Blessed are you LORD
for you have remembered your people.
You send the rain in its season,
both the early and the late rains.
The ground is thirsty and dry,
the fields are withered and parched
and you bless them with showers of gentle rain,
you moisten them with downpours of water.
O LORD, you ride on the clouds,
like a warrior you pass through the heavens.
Listen, listen to the thunder of his voice
and the rumbling that comes from his mouth.
He thunders with his majestic voice
and he does not restrain the lightnings when his voice is heard.
From heaven's chamber comes the whirlwind,
and cold from the scattering winds.
God loads the thick cloud with moisture,
the clouds scatter his lightning.
God thunders wondrously with his voice,
he does great things that we cannot comprehend."

The hymn had built up to a climax as Amnon's voice grew louder. Now he suddenly broke off and continued in a gentler voice.

"O LORD, pour your strength into the earth,
make the ground fruitful, oh God,
that the dust may bring forth fruit
and the fields stand heavy with grain.
May the ears of wheat stand like rows of soldiers,
sons of the mighty one.
Blessed are you LORD
for you have remembered your people.
You send the rain in its season,
both the early and the late rains."

Amnon gazed out into the rain. His old mother Ayalah sat beside the smoldering embers of the cooking fire. Head down, eyes closed, she had listened intently to the old hymn. Beside her sat Naarah, Amnon's wife. With a rapturous expression she looked at her husband. Nestled in her arms lay Tilon, her son. He had fallen asleep, snuggling against his mother.

The others sat across the room on either side of the door to the southern chamber. There was old Joab. Rivkah understood he was a farmer, too. She had met him only when he came back in the afternoon. Together with Achan, the young boy, he had foraged for food. Not that they had found much. A few grains of wild barley and a quail was all they brought back. Still, Naarah had managed to cook a filling meal.

Joab was carving a wooden spoon while he listened to Amnon's voice. He worked slowly, his mind wandering to times long past. How often had he greeted the coming of the fall rains? Each new year, he had waited for the rain in its season. And today it had come in its due time. But today was different. Today there was no home, there were no fields.

Engrossed in thought Joab's hands stopped working. Then he lifted his head, looked at the group assembled in the dim light of the cave and said, "In my village the children always greeted the new rain with a short song. It's not solemn at all, but . . . "

Joab smiled and started to sing:
"O bull of my father
don't stuff yourself on green.
Fresh grass do not gobble
for death is in its leaves.

O bull of my father
be sturdy and be strong.
The yoke you shall carry
and wheat shall crown our fields."

It can't have been one of the better renditions of the song. The tune was hardly discernable and the mood of the ditty entirely lost to the listeners. Nevertheless, Naarah seemed to have liked it.

"That's good! Tell the old bull what to do." She sighed. "Our bulls were beautiful animals, were they not, Amnon?"

Her husband just made an unidentifiable sound, apparently in assent. He didn't seem too enthused about the whimsical song. Or maybe he did not want to be reminded about what they had lost. Not getting the expected response, Naarah mumbled something quietly and concentrated on her son sleeping in her arms. Tilon had not been disturbed by the singing and slumbered peacefully.

Outside it was completely dark now. The occupants of the tomb could hardly make each other out. Ayalah got up and felt her way to the western chamber.

"Time to lie down. Tomorrow is another day." She encouraged the others to follow her lead. Amnon helped his wife to carry Tilon into the adjacent room.

Rivkah had been allotted a place in the southern room with Joab and Achan. She curled up on a bench there and wrapped the woolen blanket tightly round herself. Her first night in the grave! Fear crept up inside her. She shuddered. Hardly daring to breath she stared into the dark. The walls seemed to threaten to fall in on her and bury her alive in this grave. Or was this just a dream and she was already with the dead?

She closed her eyes. But now she saw images of the burning city, the flames licking the buildings, the horror of destruction. The oppressive dark seemed welcome when she opened her eyes again. Careful not to make a sound, she turned over. Reaching out she touched the cold walls of the tomb. Somehow she was sure she shared this fate with her family, her city: they had descended to the shades of the earth, a place of darkness and emptiness, where there was no light or food and the dreaded Lord Mot controlled the weary captives. Rivkah shook. She felt goose bumps on her skin. But with the horror came sadness. Death had taken them and Rivkah would see them no more. The separation hurt. She could feel her throat tighten and her chest ache as she thought about the loved ones she had lost, the family that would never be together again. Tears stole into her eyes. She let them flow freely in the dark. Trying to keep quiet she suppressed her crying. Only once did a sob escape her lips.

She didn't know how long she had lain there, lost in her misery, but she slowly became aware of another sound. It was the snoring and rattled breathing of her companions; or, rather, of one of them—Joab, the old man, made plenty of noise in his sleep. It brought her back to the present. It was both annoying and comforting.

She still had not fully fathomed what had happened this day. She had been so thankful after the simple meal of bread and herbs that Naarah had prepared for her. The woman had told her their own story of woe, of leaving behind all that they cherished. And she described their present situation in desperate terms. The long walk to get water from a stream bed, the arduous task of collecting firewood. The constant search for food in a land swarming with the enemy, where any day could mean discovery, any step might lead to captivity.

Naarah complained about the few implements with which she was expected to manage the household. She showed obvious disdain for their current accommodation. Naarah had confided to Rivkah that she had buried a dove in the ground outside, just opposite the entrance. Hopefully it would ward off demons and keep the inhabitants safe. In places like these you just had to be careful.

Rivkah had looked with apprehension towards the cave entrance. The place had seemed so unwelcoming, so strange. Naarah's chatter certainly didn't ease her mind. It was Ayalah, Amnon's mother, who made Rivkah welcome. She had shown her round their living quarters, made sure Rivkah was comfortable with her bed and given her the blanket. And then they had talked. Ayalah had explained how the little group of refugees had organized themselves, how they survived and how they made the best of their situation. Ayalah was thankful for this refuge. It may be just a cave, but it was a place to stay. She had told Rivkah how glad she was that she had joined them. Rivkah would fit in so well. She could contribute to the group by helping with little things. She had not suggested any arduous tasks; no, Rivkah had felt welcome just for who she was and hoped she could prove herself useful in some way.

Later on the men had returned—if you could call little Achan a man. Dinner had been a quiet affair, though the first drops of rain had been greeted loudly. When Amnon sang the solemn hymn she even felt thankful, gained hope, even if it was only for a fleeting moment. That had been her first day in the grave.

* * *

The heavy goat-hair tent-canvas muffled the sound of the raindrops that pelted against it. But outside drops fell into the puddles that had formed throughout the camp and drummed an arbitrary rhythm through the night. Water dripped inside the tent. The dew, which some nights had drenched ground and canvas, had never really tested the tent. But the heavy rain and wind drove the water through slits and small holes. Itur-Ea had moved his bed to a dry place. Now the narrow bedstead was wedged between two of his fellow soldiers.

The beer had done its part and Itur-Ea had slept soundly after the festivities. But now something had woken him and he just couldn't get back to sleep. The closeness of the others irritated him. He hardly dared to move, even though he couldn't find a comfortable position. He had gotten used to cramped quarters, but not this close.

Pictures of today's killings came to him: the lifeless forms of the Judahites mutilated by the frenzied mob of Assyrian soldiers; the triumph on the faces of the officers as they dealt blows to the enemies; the delight in the eyes of his comrades pouring out their hatred. Those prisoners had been dealt a lesson, but . . . somehow the question rose within him whether killing these pitiful, vanquished people brought any glory. It needed no courage to attack the defenseless. He suppressed the thought. After all, that was what victorious armies did. They did not show any mercy, they exacted the wrath of the victorious god on his foes. The leaders of the losers always suffered the wrath. Most of the prisoners were kept alive. They were needed for the empire.

Itur-Ea thought of the burning city. Its flames had lit the night sky. Now the rain would quench the embers. The night of the battle, Ishtar had kept him safe and given him her spoils. In the end he had killed the woman. Her body had carried him to excitement and ecstasy, had made his blood boil within him. But when it was over, he had not felt fulfillment, only emptiness. Ishtar had bestowed her gifts and yet they were hollow. He had walked back to the camp feeling weak and strangely sad. He tried to rekindle the excitement by recalling the shape of her body. He thought back to his experiences in the temple of Nineveh. But it did not work: there was no excitement, only a desperate restlessness.

Itur-Ea turned onto his other side, touching the soldier to his left. The festivities of the day had overshadowed his desperation, but now in the night it returned. A great loneliness overcame him. How had it come to this? Had Ishtar played him a cruel trick? She had given him his wish and it had turned out to be false comfort.

*　*　*

A green shimmer covered the land after the rain. The dust had been washed off the plants and the moisture allowed fresh shoots to appear. Among the dry, brown grass, new blades pushed out of the ground and slender leaves sprouted on the bushes. The parched earth had her fill and, ever so gently, bore fruit again. It wasn't the strong exuberant growth of spring, but the hesitant signs of life after the long dry of summer.

"That rain was heaven-sent," Ayalah remarked to Rivkah as they slowly walked down the hill. "We may not be able to plow fields and sow seeds, but at least the plants grow again. We should find some fresh herbs today."

Ayalah had asked Rivkah to accompany her. The old woman was not comfortable venturing far from the cave on her own. Rivkah didn't mind. She always enjoyed the time with Ayalah.

"You really don't know anything about gathering greens?"

"No, sorry. We didn't eat a lot of green plants from the field. Only now and then did we buy some on the market. And I didn't always like them."

"Ah, another of those spoiled townspeople," Ayalah laughed, "but greens are good for you, they really are good for you. Besides, if you want to eat you have to find something. We don't exactly have barns full of wheat."

"No, not really. We are lucky we still have bread. Where did you get the grain from, mother Ayalah?"

"We were able to get the barley harvest in before the Assyrians entered the country. I insisted we take some jars when we fled from the village across to the cave here. Amnon wasn't so sure. There was so much else he wanted to take. 'First we have to eat,' I said, 'and then you can worry about your clothes and tools!'"

Ayalah stopped and leaned closer to Rivkah whispering, "You know, I got him to bury his plow. What would he do with that on our flight? It's still there. He has checked on it after the Assyrians came and destroyed the village."

She started walking again and continued in a louder voice, "And I believe we will return to our village and build houses again. These armies flood the lands, but they will pass on. Thousands will be swept away by this war. The land remains. Bare and forlorn it may be, fallow and devastated, but it will bear fruit again. It needs people to till the soil, sow the crop, plant the trees and gather the harvest. I pray that my family will return to their heritage, to work the land once more. The LORD may have deserted his people for a while, but he will not root them out completely. Rulers may change and kingdoms may falter, but his faithfulness endures."

"And my family?" Rivkah asked.

"They suffered with their people. I cannot comprehend it. I do not know why some share the fate of their nation and others remain. But were you not plucked like a brand from a burning fire? Rivkah, I believe there's hope for you. Maybe your family, your city will continue through you."

The two walked on in silence. Suddenly Ayalah stopped and bent over, looking at the ground.

"Do you see these shoots of wild cress, Rivkah? Just what we are looking for. Nice and tender. They should make an excellent salad. Come, dear can you pick them for me?"

"Which ones?" Rivkah wasn't quite sure what she meant.

"These ones here." Ayalah pointed to some crinkly leaves barely sprouting out of the hard ground. "It's hard for an old woman to bend down and pick them. I'm no longer that fit. That's where you come in. Prick them off just below the leaves. That's it . . . Now put them in the cloth bag we brought along."

Rivkah plucked the shoots, gathering them in a bundle.

"Give me one of those leaves, Rivkah."

When she chewed it Ayalah smiled satisfied. "Very nice. I didn't know it grew so well around here."

They found more plants at other spots as they moved over the hill. Wild, prickly lettuce and shoots of shrubs and pines were added to the bundle.

After they had walked through a small grove of trees they came out into the open again.

"Take a few leaves of that," Ayalah pointed at some sorrel that had sprouted a few green leaves again.

"Can you eat that?" Rivkah had often seen it outside the city walls and along some of the roads.

"Yes, you can eat it. It may be a bit bitter, especially as the leaves grow bigger, but we can't be picky, can we? You know, in these times you eat food you would otherwise just walk by or leave to the animals."

Rivkah took the leaves.

"I think we should have enough now. These greens don't keep long. So you'll have to get more in a day or two. But come, we'll go back home now and prepare lunch."

As they walked up the hill Rivkah remembered the earlier conversation on their way down from their home.

"So you have only barley now. No wheat? Is that why the bread tastes a bit . . . umh . . . funny, mother Ayalah?"

Ayalah tapped the ground with her stick.

"Oh, we do have some wheat. When we found this place and the others joined us, we realized that the barley wouldn't last us through the winter. Amnon was able to get some wheat from the fields near Mareshah. It was not easy with the Assyrians snooping around. He couldn't exactly harvest the fields, just picked a few ears and brought them back. It wasn't easy threshing the wheat as we don't dare to be out in the open much. So we often grind it husks and all. Of course the bread is sometimes a bit hard to get down, but if it fills you, it's good. In late summer we gathered wild emmer and darnel, whatever wild grain we could find. That's even harder to thresh and you don't get much out of it. It's not easy baking bread with that sort of flour. I tell you, Naarah normally bakes delicious bread, but she has her work cut out for her. As you know, we don't have a good millstone either. That makes it even harder to grind fine flour. It's the only one we were able to pull out from the rubble of the destroyed village. But you know, we should be grateful for what we have, even if the bread is sometimes a bit crumbly and hard to chew on."

By now they had come to the saddle on the ridge above the cave. It was not far from here and only downhill. They reached the cave and crawled through the entrance. Inside Naarah had finished cleaning the bowls and jars. A jar of thickened milk stood beside her. She must have just carried it in, out of the morning sun. Rivkah was still not used to the sour taste of the thickened milk the fugitives seemed to like for lunch.

"We've brought you enough greens for a nice salad and a hearty meal at night," Ayalah told her daughter-in-law.

"Good. I hope you're not too thirsty after carrying all that. There's not much water left. Somebody will have to get some more."

"Rivkah will get some water after lunch, Naarah," Ayalah assured her.

While little Tilon crawled around the cave, the three women prepared the salad washing the leaves, then tearing them into little pieces. They added roasted fennel seeds and thickened milk.

Soon the men drifted in. Joab had been lucky and had found some clay to make pottery. He told them that this clay was better than the one he had discovered previously.

"It's also a bit easier to dig out: the soil's softer." And while he discussed with Naarah and Ayalah what dishes would be needed, Amnon and Achan turned up.

They had been out hunting, but did not have much to show for it. A thrush had been caught in the bird trap that Amnon had made from sticks. All the nets were empty. But they had collected quite a few worms and reset the traps.

"I think we'll get some decent catches in the next few days."

Amnon turned to Rivkah, "If you see any worms, pick them up. We really need them. You should find a few now after the rain. Outside, just beside the entrance, there's a jar with soil and some food scraps. That's where we keep them."

"One thrush is not much for dinner," Naarah remarked.

"We'll see whether we can get some more," Amnon remarked. "Swallows are best caught in the late afternoon."

Joab and Amnon complimented the women on the fresh salad.

"I suppose that's what we'll have to live on now." Achan didn't seem pleased hearing that. He only nibbled hesitantly on the leaves.

Chapter 6

The column of soldiers seemed endless, disappearing over the crest of the rise. The troops marched to the beat of the drum, the land reverberating under their steps. Even during the climb their steps were firm, their advance persistent. Behind him Itur-Ea could hear the shouting of the drivers goading on their oxen, mules or camels. The animals' backs and the carts were laden with tents, cooking pots, jars of food, weapons, ammunition, and siege machines. The whole army camp was on the move. When he turned around, Itur-Ea could even see the rear guard protecting the end of the train.

Hauled by mules, the carts carrying the siege machines were at the head of the freight section. Itur-Ea walked beside the cart on which his machine had been packed. He liked to keep an eye on it. He even carried his tools in a bag on his back.

As he arrived at the crest of the hill, he could see the full might of the Assyrian army marching down the gentle slope into the wide valley ahead. The banners shone in the early afternoon sun. The soldiers' mail shirts glistened in the heat. The spears of the infantry stretched across the land like a forest. It was the splendor of Assyria on display. And up ahead where the outer reaches of the plain merged into the hill country was the city on a hill, Libnah—their destination. This city, too, had not yielded to Assyrian power and now the full weight of the Assyrian forces would fall upon it and smash it.

As the army came close to the hill of Libnah it stopped. The war chariots and cavalry swept round the city in a wide circle, cutting off any escape route. The main corps of the army crossed the little stream and stood to face the city. Behind them the vassal forces and sappers began to erect the camp. Trenches were dug. The first palisade walls were rammed into the ground. As it was only a short march from Lachish, they had taken much of the camp's fortifications with them. Still, some troops swarmed into the countryside to cut down trees for building material.

Itur-Ea was involved in erecting the officers' tents. They were far larger than those of the ordinary soldiers and canvas overlaps were carefully sewn together. By nightfall, walls surrounded the whole camp. The war chariots and horses had been brought within its walls. Not all of the soldiers yet had a roof over their heads. There would be more work in the days to come. Meanwhile, they had to be alert in this first night of the siege. Often, defenders rated their chances to inflict losses on any army weary from its march.

* * *

Rivkah inhaled the fresh, morning air deeply. The sun had already risen high on the horizon and the morning clouds were scattering. Soon the sun's rays would strike the land unhindered by the mist. It would be a warm day. The birds were still chirping and swarming through the still air. Rivkah took her eyes off the ground and watched their incessant activity. They were darting from branch to branch, flying high into the sky and then hopping across the leafy ground. A smile crossed Rivkah's lips as she contemplated the exuberance of their fluttering and singing.

She had come out here with Amnon and Joab to gather more herbs and greens. Well, the men were not here to look for food. They had come out to these straggling trees to look for wood. Amnon wanted to see whether he couldn't find some reasonably straight branches to construct a turntable for building pots. They had made a few pots in their time here, molding the clay with their hands as best as they could, but the ware was not particularly even or durable. Joab and Amnon had resolved that this time they would try to do better. And Naarah agreed that it would be much easier if they could turn the pots and work on them evenly, adding coil after coil to build a vessel.

When Rivkah had heard about their plans at breakfast, she suggested she could go with them and search for greens. Under Ayalah's guidance she had become quite good at picking edible plants. She certainly preferred it to working round the cave and looking after the goats.

Amnon and his family had brought two goats with them. They kept them in a cave nearby—just a few paces away. Every morning and evening they milked them. One morning Naarah had taken Rivkah with her to do the milking. Naarah had squatted down beside one of the goats and started to squeeze the milk into a bowl. She had looked at Rivkah and told her that she should not just stand there but get on with milking the other goat. Rivkah had never ever milked a goat before nor, in fact, a sheep or a cow. She had stood there, not knowing what to do. After watching Naarah and trying to see how she did it, Rivkah got down beside the other goat and hesitantly placed the bowl under the udder. The goat had stood placidly. Rivkah took the teats into her hands and tried to squeeze some milk out of them. But nothing came, not one drop. She had tried again. Nothing. The teats felt so awkward in her hands.

Maybe I have to slide my fingers down the teat, she had thought. Trying this technique she got a thin squirt of milk from the udder, which even landed in the bowl. Try as she might, though, she had not been able to coax any more milk from those teats. Meanwhile the goat had become irritated and kicked Rivkah. She no longer stood still. Rivkah trembled. She wanted to get this right! Finally Naarah had come over, looked at the few drops of milk in the bowl and the nervous goat and told Rivkah to get up.

Well, Naarah had told her in no uncertain terms how useless she was—not even able to milk a goat. Naarah had finished the milking and had made Rivkah carry the bowl with milk back to the cave. Since then Rivkah avoided the goats at milking time. She did not want to show her ineptitude again. She always found something else to do. Today it was foraging for food.

While the two men searched through the open forest, Rivkah wandered through the clearings. She found a good patch of sorrel. Using a small flint knife she cut the leaves off. That was easier than plucking them. And with sorrel it was totally impossible to pull the whole plant out.

Rivkah hummed a tune as she worked. She could remember only some of the words and did not even attempt to sing them. They spoke of love and longing, that much she knew, but the music expressed those feelings far more deeply than words ever could. She dreamed of a prince who would drive out the Assyrians and rebuild Lachish, a hero who would ask her, Rivkah, to be at his side to bring the city to life again. How Naarah would look then! And her parents would be so proud of her. But they were no more. As the melody became more melancholy so her thoughts turned to the people and places she had lost. With pained expression she repeated the sorrowful chorus of the tune.

Silent now, Rivkah suddenly noticed that she had cut more than enough sorrel. It didn't taste that good on its own. People would also want something else. She had to see what more she could find. She stuffed the leaves into the bundle and walked on.

It was then that she noticed the figure at the edge of the clearing. A man stepped out of the shadow of a tree. It wasn't Amnon or Joab, Rivkah could see that immediately. She froze, uncertain what to do. Panic crept up in her. It seemed as if the man had watched her for some time. He came towards her. He was a Judahite. His clothes showed that. They must have been very nice clothes once, those of a rich man. But now they were torn and dirty.

"Shalom."

Rivkah didn't know how to respond to his greeting. Her instincts told her to keep quiet. But then she thought of Joab and Amnon. How could she alert them that there was someone else in the woods?

"Shalom, traveler," Rivkah said loudly.

"How do you know I am a traveler?" the stranger asked.

"The towns and villages here have been destroyed by the Assyrian army, my lord." Rivkah kept up the loud voice.

"That is true," acknowledged the man. "But what are you doing out here?"

"I am gathering herbs and leaves."

"So far from a village?"

Rivkah did not want to reveal or talk about the cave they lived in. In these times you couldn't really trust anyone. It would be best he didn't know.

"The herbs are best here." It sounded like a good enough reason. Of course, Rivkah had never really looked for herbs before she started living in the cave. But it was true: this forest did yield the best green plants in the areas she had covered with Ayalah so far.

The man did not look convinced.

"So where are you from, girl?"

"What do you mean, my lord?" Rivkah tried to deflect the question.

"What is your town or village?" the man asked.

Rivkah didn't answer at once. Somehow she did not want to mention Lachish. But what else should she say? She didn't even know the names of any of the other villages in this area. In that moment her conversation with Ayalah came to mind. And so it was, that the name of the village Amnon and his family came from quietly passed her lips, "Shechar."

"Shechar? But didn't the Assyrians destroy that village, too?"

Rivkah did not know what to say.

The silence that followed felt uncomfortable. The man clearly expected an answer and wanted to press further. How could she explain? Just then a twig snapped loudly somewhere to the right of Rivkah. Both she and the man turned towards the sound.

It was Amnon, striding into the clearing. Rivkah couldn't see Joab.

Amnon greeted the stranger, "Shalom my friend."

The man responded, "Shalom."

He was clearly surprised by Amnon's confidence.

Amnon walked right to the centre of the clearing, beckoned the man to come closer and sat down. Reluctantly the man walked towards Amnon and seated himself on the ground opposite him.

"Let us talk plainly," Amnon began.

"So be it," the man affirmed, casting a fleeting glance at Rivkah as she came nearer to listen to what was said.

"I can see you are a Judahite." Amnon looked at the man's clothes.

"I am," the man confirmed.

"So are we," Amnon continued. "We all know about the calamity that has befallen our land. These are troubled times. We have to be cautious and yet we have to help each other. As for us, we are simple peasants, living in the hills. But tell me about you, my friend! What brings you here? You do not look like a peasant."

"No, I am the secretary to the governor of Libnah." As he spoke he seemed to have decided to trust this peasant who was welcoming him as confidently as if he sat in the city gate and not on the ground in a remote forest.

"I am Beriah, son of Jesher. For two years I have been the governor's secretary in Libnah. The Assyrians have attacked Libnah. The city is still resisting, but unless it gets help, it will fall. When we saw the advance units scouting the land, we knew that the Assyrians were about to come against the city. I was sent to Jerusalem to warn the king and ask again for reinforcements. I took two men with me. We escaped just in time. Soon the country was swarming with Assyrian soldiers. We constantly had to be on our guard. We did not travel along the main roads, so our journey to Jerusalem was slow. But when we arrived there we soon realized that Jerusalem was completely encircled by the Assyrians. There was no way we could get through the siege lines to bring a message to the king. Nor would the king be able to send his soldiers out of the city—not without a battle at least. Our mission had been to no avail. I finally decided to send one of the men to try and make it through the lines to Jerusalem. He did not succeed. We saw his body the next morning, thrust on a spear."

"Horrible!" Amnon showed his disgust at Assyrian cruelty.

"The Assyrians are merciless. I knew we had to flee. Who knows, maybe the man had told the Assyrians of our presence? So we made our way back to Libnah again. When I saw the city from afar my heart stood still. The whole countryside around it was covered with Assyrian soldiers. Like ants around a dead jackal, they swarmed around the city. Libnah is not dead yet. It is still fighting. But it cannot withstand the might of the Assyrian army forever. For this is the main unit of the Assyrians. The force surrounding Jerusalem is a small band by comparison. And Libnah is not Jerusalem. I would trust Jerusalem to hold out against the mightiest army. Its walls are strong, its towers high and thick. It has supplies for thousands. But not little Libnah. We watched the city from a distance for two days. But then we were discovered when we were getting water. I escaped, my comrade did not."

Beriah said no more. He swallowed hard. Grief and concern clearly showed on his face.

"Now you have come here?"

"Yes, I fled into the hills. I cannot reach Libnah, cannot get to Jerusalem."

"You are alone now?"

Beriah lifted his hands and shoulders: "Totally alone."

"And your family?"

"My father's house is in Jerusalem." He lowered his eyes and stared at the ground before adding quietly, "My wife and son are in Libnah."

Amnon didn't ask any more questions. Gathering a twig in his right hand he scratched a meaningless pattern into the dirt. Rivkah, standing behind Amnon, chased away a fly in the uncomfortable silence that followed. Beriah sat there on the ground, occasionally nodding his head as if to remind him of some important thought that came fleetingly back to him. Finally Amnon snapped the twig in two and threw the pieces away. He stood up and said to Beriah,

"I am Amnon of Shechar. My family and I have sought refuge in the hills. There is a group of fugitives here. We would be glad to offer you rest for a while. Ours is a very humble abode, but you are welcome, secretary to the governor."

"Thank you, Amnon. The LORD bless you. I gladly accept your hospitality."

Beriah got off the ground, brushing the dirt off his clothes. Amnon turned and saw Rivkah standing just behind him, watching the men. He spoke to Beriah, "This is Rivkah of Lachish, one of the other refugees living here."

"Lachish?" Beriah looked confused. He gave Rivkah a questioning glance.

She did not reply but gave a slight nod.

At that moment Amnon called out, "Joab! Come, we will bring the stranger back to the cave."

Joab appeared from amongst the trees, smiling nervously. Amnon introduced him to Beriah, "This is Joab, another farmer who fled to these hills."

Turning to Joab he added, "This is the secretary to the governor of Libnah. He has been pursued by the Assyrians. I have offered to receive him in our home."

With Amnon leading, the little group left the clearing and entered the forest.

They stopped briefly to allow Joab to get a few pieces of wood they had found. The group continued in silence when he joined them again.

Amnon led the group most of the way. But when they were partway up the final hill he fell back and walked beside Rivkah.

"Are you sure your bundle is not too heavy? I can help you if it's too much for you."

Rivkah assured him that it was alright. In fact, it was not even as full as it normally was.

Strange, Amnon had never before worried how heavy her bundle was. Did he just want to show his concern in front of a stranger?

He leaned a bit closer and asked quietly, "Rivkah, did you hear what his name is? Hm, I can't remember it."

So that's what he was really worried about!

"It's Beriah," Rivkah told him.

"Ah, thanks," Amnon mumbled and then hurried back to the front of the group.

Rivkah smiled. That was Amnon! So confident, but sometimes he forgot to listen.

* * *

Leah stood in line with the other women collecting their ration of bread from the bakery. The bread was baked in large ovens in Jerusalem, each supplying a whole quarter of the city. No one baked bread at home, not now during the siege. Here at the bakery the women and girls exchanged the latest gossip, talked about the situation of the city and the land, voiced their fears and their hopes.

"Have you heard? The field commander of the Assyrians delivered an ultimatum to the king."

"When?"

"Just yesterday."

"My husband heard it, too. He had gone up to the wall and stood near the gate when the Rabshakeh read out his message."

"Was the king there, too?"

"No, but Shebna, the state secretary, was there."

"And Joah, the chief of the records office."

"Eliakim, the palace administrator, was there as well."

"They will have delivered the message to the king."

"What did the Rabshakeh say?"

"He asked King Hezekiah to surrender. He made it clear that Jerusalem could not withstand the might of the Assyrian army. He said that they had conquered all the other cities in their path, so, why would Jerusalem be any different? The gods of the other cities were not able to save them."

"What did the officials say?"

"I don't think they gave a response."

"No, I heard they didn't."

"But they brought the words of the Rabshakeh to the king."

"And the king?"

"He is considering the demand to surrender."

"Do you think he will?"

"Will what?"

"Surrender."

"No, I do not think so."

"Does he think this city can repel the Assyrians?"

"The king will not allow the Assyrians to enter."

"But if the Assyrians conquer the city?"

"Their cruelty will know no end."

"They will rip open the pregnant women and smash the babies against the walls."

A hushed silence fell on the women. The cruelty of the Assyrians was well known. Fear gripped them, they all felt it. Would surrender not be better than facing an enemy out for revenge?

"The LORD will not allow the Assyrians to destroy Jerusalem," Leah spoke into the silence. The women looked at her. What did a girl like her know? Her confidence was not reflected in any of the faces around her but nobody dared to contradict her. After all, the LORD was the god of Judah, the god of this city. But fear, not hope, held the women.

"Miriam, how is your son today?"

"Much better. He was really poor yesterday, but today he ate and drank again. He would have eaten more if we had more to give."

The women turned to other topics: their families, their daily cares, their tasks in the home.

Nobody seemed to notice Leah when it was her turn to collect bread for the family. The women seemed to totally disregard her. The clerk counted out the flat loaves of bread and marked the amount down in the register. Leah wrapped the bread in a bundle.

"Next please!"

Another woman came up to collect bread for her household.

Leah took the bundle and walked back to the house, not talking to anybody.

* * *

The rain had started early in the morning. It was only a drizzle at first but now the showers had set in and a strong wind drove the heavy drops across the land. Nobody wanted to be out in that weather and the whole group of refugees was huddled inside the cave today. Most of them took it slowly. But Naarah seemed to be busy and somewhat annoyed with the lazy demeanor of the others.

"I don't have time to just sit there and stare into the rain," she told nobody in particular. "There's still so much work. I have to prepare those six tiny birds you brought in yesterday. Then I have to get the fire going and put the stew on. Washing and preparing those roots will take some time and the stew has to be stirred continually. In this weather I'll have to look after the cheese, too. And then little Tilon needs looking after. There are also the goats. Who is going to look after them?"

Ayalah stemmed Naarah's flow of words.

"I know it's best if we don't get in your way when you are cooking. Rivkah and I can look after the goats."

"Are you sure?" Naarah expressed her doubts. "Rivkah is not very good with the goats."

"We'll manage."

"Just don't make the goats too nervous."

"It'll be alright," Ayalah assured her again.

Rivkah looked at Ayalah. Why did she have to volunteer her for that? Now Ayalah would also see that Rivkah couldn't even milk a goat. At first she thought about asking to help with the cooking instead, but then decided to rather go along with Ayalah's suggestion. Naarah would only find something else to complain about if she stayed here. And what if Ayalah really needed her help? In any case, there would be less trouble with the goats if she went with Ayalah now, rather than being told to go with Naarah later.

Ayalah and Rivkah fought their way through the rain to the other cave. They carried a bowl and a jar to collect the milk.

The two goats seemed pleased to see them. One of them greeted the women with a soft "baa" before turning the head to nuzzle its side. The other shuffled her feet, straining at her rope to get to them. But to Rivkah this was not a welcoming scene. She felt nervous. What would she do if Ayalah asked her to milk one of the goats? She decided to tell her straight away.

"Mother Ayalah, I really can't milk."

"You can't milk? Have you ever tried it?"

"Only once with Naarah. Not before. We didn't have any animals," she explained.

"And Naarah didn't teach you how to do it."

Rivkah shook her head.

"Now is the time to learn then," Ayalah said. She walked to one of the goats and stroked her hair. "This is Kala. She is the quieter of the two. Come and give her a pat. She loves the attention."

The goat turned her head when Rivkah rubbed her side.

"That's good. Take that stone over there and put it beside Kala. It's easier to sit down rather than to crouch, especially when you're not used to milking."

Rivkah took the stone and placed it next to the goat. She looked at Ayalah.

"Yes, sit down. Maybe move a bit closer. That's better. Here's the bowl. Just place it under the udder."

Rivkah didn't feel comfortable at all with her head pressed against the goat's side. She placed the bowl on the ground. Now came the difficult part.

"Just rub the udder gently. Not too much. A few strokes will do. Put your hands around the teats. Now squeeze the teat with your thumb and index finger and push the milk down with your other fingers. Close one finger around the teat and then the next one. That's it."

The first stream of milk squirted into the bowl.

"Now the other hand."

It didn't go quite as well with the left hand but on the second try the stream of milk was stronger. The first few squirts came slowly. But then the flow stopped.

"Remember to release your thumb after each squirt."

"I did." Rivkah got a bit annoyed. Why didn't it work?

"No need to worry. Just place your hands again and do it slowly."

Rivkah knew she didn't go half as fast as Naarah had done. Kala, the goat, did get a bit restless, but she didn't kick. Soon the bowl was nearly full.

The milk came a bit slower now.

"I don't think there's much more milk there," she told Ayalah.

"You're right. You're just about finished. Now strip the last bit out by running your thumb down the teats."

When Rivkah carefully took the bowl of milk and got up, she was exhausted. She emptied the bowl into the jar.

"Well done, Rivkah. You've milked your first goat. Now the other one. That's Tera."

Rivkah looked less than enthusiastic.

Ayalah smiled at her and gently laid her hand on Rivkah's arm.

"You know what, Rivkah? I'll start Tera off and you will finish the milking. Just move the stone here."

Rivkah took the stone and placed it beside the other goat.

"Oh, and help me to sit down," Ayalah laughed quietly.

"Are you sure, mother Ayalah?"

"I may be old, but a bit of milking won't kill this woman. It's alright."

As she milked the goat, Ayalah showed Rivkah again what to do, commenting on her own every move.

"Squeeze and push the milk down. Loosen your grip and squeeze again. Come on Tera, old girl. You're not going to make trouble for this woman."

Ayalah's words seemed to comfort the goat. It all looked so easy when she did it. Soon it was Rivkah's turn. The milk flowed and Tera didn't get nervous. Maybe milking was not that scary after all.

* * *

Libnah did not hold. The splendor of the Lord Ashur overwhelmed it and the might of the Assyrian army broke down its walls. Soldiers poured across the breaches and the defenders could no longer avert the destruction of their city. The siege machines had yet again shown their effectiveness. They had pounded the walls and loosened the stones. Despite the missiles hurled at them, the torches raining on them, the arrows shot at their sides, the siege machines had worked without ceasing to open up the city. Now they were drawn back from the walls, making way for the forces that would finish the job.

Their crews still had to remain cautious. They were still in battle. Itur-Ea kept a wary eye on the walls. Some towers were still held by defenders. Their arrows could still reach him. As the machine lurched down the ramp, Itur-Ea became more relaxed. At least there was not much danger to the siege machine now. He felt for his water flask and drained the last drops. The days were no longer as hot, but the heat of battle still exhausted him.

Itur-Ea inspected the siege machine after it was parked near the camp. There was no serious damage. He would have to make a few small repairs later on. But it would have to wait, for now the battle continued. He was eager to join in the fighting again. Not that there would be much resistance anymore. They would just have to get the people out of the city, plunder it and set it to the torch. Victory was already theirs!

On the way to the assembly ground, Itur-Ea snatched a bit of food from the mess tent. Chewing on roasted barley, he joined the others. Standing to attention they faced the city. A runner reached them from the central command tent and delivered his message to the captain. The standard was lifted high, the signal given and they marched into battle again. Itur-Ea wondered why they did not head towards the gate. Did the defenders still hold it? Instead they climbed the ramp again. This time they did not have to worry about any arrows shot from the walls. It seemed the defenders on this side of the city had been taken out. Itur-Ea stepped across the fallen body of an Assyrian soldier. They had not yet cleared the dead away. Only the wounded had been taken back to camp.

They entered the city across the rubble of the wall. The unit immediately turned left and marched along a street that ran parallel to the wall. At the next intersection the captain led them towards the wall again. Here the defenders were still controlling a tower. Itur-Ea's unit joined other Assyrian troops engaged in the fight for the tower. Below the tower lay fallen soldiers, pierced by arrows. Using their shields as cover the Assyrians managed to reach the tower and break the door at the base. The defenders fought bitterly in the confined space. But the discipline of the Assyrians and their force of numbers prevailed. The attackers were able to fight their way to the next level in the tower. Itur-Ea stormed into the building and made his way upwards. Suddenly a sword crashed against his shield. A Judahite fighter attacked from a side room. The first stroke had been poor but now the defender pressed Itur-Ea hard. Itur-Ea blocked the blows, anticipating his opponent's frenzied moves. After he was able to neutralize another blow, Itur-Ea lunged forward. His opponent had left himself exposed for just a moment. It was enough. Blood and guts poured from the Judahite's open stomach. He lifted the sword again, but the blow was weak. Itur-Ea rammed the shield into the man's face. He fell over backwards. Another thrust across the throat made sure the defender had breathed his last.

Itur-Ea stepped back but slipped on the blood-drenched floor. That saved him. For as he fell, the spear aimed for him passed just a handwidth over him. Itur-Ea had not seen the other Judahite who now fell on him in despairing rage. Sitting on the floor, Itur-Ea felt fear rise in him. He struggled to get up. But he needn't have worried. Two Assyrian soldiers came to his aid and fell upon the Judahite, who had no hope against the combat training of the Assyrian military. He fell beside his dead comrade.

The Assyrians took the tower. Itur-Ea promised to offer a prayer of thanksgiving to Ishtar. Today Ishtar had protected him.

Chapter 7

It must have been the light that reached even the inner chamber of the cave. Rivkah could not sleep tonight. She tossed and turned. Outside, the full moon bathed the countryside in an even glow. Not that Rivkah could see outside from the sleeping bench. But she saw the light that seemed to come from the main chamber of the grave. Rivkah sat up on the bench, drawing the knees to her body. She looked around to see whether the others were sleeping. The light was not sufficient to see them clearly, but she could make out Achan's small form on the near bench. Joab was a little easier to distinguish as the moon's rays seemed to filter to the bench on the opposite side of the chamber. They were both lying still. Rivkah could make out Beriah's irregular breathing. He was sleeping in the main chamber.

There had been some debate about the sleeping arrangements the day that Beriah arrived. Amnon had suggested that Rivkah should move into the western chamber, joining his family, to make room for Beriah. Naarah had flatly refused. Beriah rescued the situation by proclaiming that he really preferred to stay in the front room. At first, Amnon had insisted that this was not a place fit for a guest. But Beriah had maintained that really it was the most pleasant place for him to stay. Gladly Amnon had accepted the solution.

Rivkah rubbed her face with her open hands and took a deep breath. She was tired but the bright moonlight made her restless. Unfurling her legs she stretched out again and leaned on her elbow. With tired eyes she stared through the passage into the moon-lit front chamber. Suddenly she saw a shadow flit across the room. Was Beriah also having difficulty sleeping tonight? The moonlight must fall directly onto his bed. But why would he go outside and scrape in the dirt? For now Rivkah could hear the shallow soil outside the cave entrance being scraped away.

"Woman, what are you doing there?" It was Beriah's voice. Rivkah could hear a woman's gasp outside the cave. Who was it? She sat up. Should she go outside and have a look?

"But Lord, I am protecting this home from the demon Resheph."

It was Naarah! Her voice sounded frightened, not with her usual confident tone.

"Protecting it from the demon Resheph? Woman, you will only bring evil upon us with your detestable deeds. What do you have there?" Beriah's angry voice reverberated around the cave. Rivkah could see the others stir on their benches.

Naarah's response had a measure of surety again, "A piece of bread wrapped in bitter herbs. Burying it at the door will ward off the demon at the time of the full moon."

Beriah was clearly upset. He sounded even more agitated: "Cast away these vile practices! Trust in the LORD alone! You have shown that you betray him in your heart. You seek protection from other gods, even bring an offering to pestilence itself. Woman, throw away your offering! Into the night with it!"

"But . . . the full moon . . . night . . . death . . . " Naarah broke into an incomprehensible babble, sobbing.

By now Rivkah stood in the middle of their room wanting to go outside to see what was happening. She hesitated another moment and then moved forward slowly. But she was held back.

"Stay!" Joab said firmly, grasping her arm and pulling her back.

"But . . . " Rivkah had to see. She shook her arm free and looked at Joab.

"No. Stay!" he repeated quietly. Why couldn't she go outside?

"Let them deal with it," Joab said, pointing with his chin towards the opening. Rivkah also spotted the shadow now hurrying across the front chamber to the cave entrance. It must have been Amnon. As she quietly sat back on the bench and listened to the voices outside, she could hear him.

"Woman, what have you done?" Amnon's voice was calm but sad.

Beriah cut in angrily, "She is offering to demons and creatures of the night, offending the LORD, our God. She is doing evil in our midst. See, she still holds onto that bread of betrayal."

"Show me!" Amnon ordered. What did he want to see?

"Perfectly good bread," he proclaimed. "Woman, why do you waste bread when we are in need?"

Naarah offered no reply. But suddenly Rivkah heard her gasp.

"You can't do that. It's unclean bread offered to demons," Beriah shouted, horrified.

Rivkah could just hear Amnon's mumbled response, "Not offered to demons. Just a woman frightened by the night." His mouth was clearly still full as he swallowed the last bits of bread. He cleared his throat and spoke clearly, "My wife, come! Go back to your bed. May the LORD forgive you, for you have acted foolishly."

Rivkah could see the figures make their way slowly across the front chamber. Only now did she become aware of Tilon's crying and Ayalah's soothing voice as she tried to comfort the child.

The cries of the child mingled with the sobs of the mother as they sought solace in each other. Soon the noise in the family's chamber faded away.

Outside the cave, Rivkah could hear Beriah:

"Have mercy on me, oh God, have mercy on me,
for in you my soul takes refuge;
I will take refuge in the shadow of your wings,
until the disaster has passed.
I cry out to God Most High,
to God who fulfils his purpose for me.
He sends from heaven and saves me,
rebuking those who hotly pursue me;
God sends his love and his faithfulness."

* * *

It sounded like a whole cavalry battalion galloping across the hill. The air reverberated with the explosions of wooden beams and the thunderous collapse of mud-brick houses. The billowing smoke rose from the burning city and darkened the sky, enveloping the valley in a murky haze. It was the end of Libnah. The city had succumbed to the same fate as the other cities across Judah.

Most of the prisoners sat dejected, keeping their eyes on the ground. Only a few looked up, tears welling up into their eyes. One woman started to chant a wailing song. Two or three lonely voices joined her in feverish pitch. But soon the lament ebbed away into intermittent sobs and cries.

Itur-Ea watched them in disgust. How utterly pathetic! It was their own rebellion against the great god Ashur that had brought them to this misery. And he would never understand why they bewailed the loss of their squalid little hovels. He had been in the city and was disgusted.

There was no grandeur—no great temples, no avenues, no gardens. Soon the prisoners would be settled in a city just as bleak as the city that was now burning before their eyes. They would serve the empire in one of its far-flung provinces.

Itur-Ea only hoped it would not be him escorting them across the hills and plains of Syria to the Euphrates and beyond. Things had not gone well for him today. Instead of being left to repair and ready his siege machine he had been ordered to guard prisoners. Did the king not expect any more sieges on this campaign? Was the task of departing prisoners now a higher priority? The success of the siege machines during yesterday's battle had clearly demonstrated their value and the professionalism of their crews. Why then was he sitting here?

Itur-Ea got up, a resentful eye on the prisoners. Two women started to wail again, tearing their hair. How they got on his nerves!

"Quiet!" he shouted in Aramaic. "Your city is gone! Your gods have left you! Your land is lost!" Even if they didn't understand him, the tone of his voice would have conveyed the meaning clearly.

But one person had understood him. It must have been nearly half a watch later when the young man approached him and interrupted Itur-Ea's morose thoughts.

"Our God has not left us," he said in broken Aramaic, "our land is not lost."

Itur-Ea laughed derisively. "You tell me! You are a prisoner and you say to me 'our land is not lost' and 'our god has not left us'! Can you not see plainly?"

Itur-Ea's Aramaic was a little better, even though it was not his mother tongue.

"I can see," the young man replied, "but I know our God is with us. Defeat and death, yes, but our God does not leave us. In exile, even in Assyria, he will be with his people. And he will bring his people back to their land."

"Hah, take your god with you to Assyria! But there, the Lord Ashur and the great goddess Ishtar have dominion. They have even shown their power here."

"We do not take our God with us. Our God will go with us. Our God has power, yes, our God has mercy. He does not leave his people. And you will see the power of our God."

"The power of your god? He bows before Ashur."

"Ashur has won today, yes, but our God is with us. He is not with a big army." The man moved his arm and indicated towards the Assyrian camp. "Our God will have mercy on his people."

"How? Will he send a big army? You need to turn to Ashur for a god of power, to the goddess Ishtar to win a battle."

"Our God has mercy and life."

Itur-Ea had enough of this deranged prattle. He pushed the young man hard.

"Quiet!" he commanded.

Then he turned and walked to join the other Assyrian soldiers. Soon his watch would be over.

* * *

Rivkah could hear the men from a fair distance.

"The Assyrians may have destroyed the cities of Judah, carried off their treasures as plunder and slaughtered their inhabitants, but the Assyrians shall not stand forever. They shall fall." That was Beriah.

"But their armies cover the whole land. You have just seen the ruins of Mareshah, the charred remains of the olive trees that once surrounded the city. I just cannot imagine how life will be possible there again." Amnon sounded less hopeful today, nearly defeated.

The entrance of the cave darkened as the two men came inside. Rivkah smiled at them, "Lunch is nearly ready."

They didn't even seem to hear her.

Rivkah tossed the sorrel leaves she had washed into a bowl and poured a dressing of herbs and thickened milk over the salad.

"And yet, life will return to Judah. Here, in this desolate cave, I despair at times. The Assyrians have taken everything." Beriah angrily kicked the ground with his foot. "But their pride will be their downfall. They will not fill this land forever. For they have insulted the LORD and his people. And so their strength will fail them."

"The strength of the Assyrian army? But their might is great," countered Amnon.

"Oh, I well know the size of their camps teeming with soldiers, the deadly accuracy of their weapons, the strength of their shields, the practiced skill of their archers. By land and by sea they have come here. On ships of Sidon did the Assyrians travel along the coast to attack the cities of the plain and invade the land of Judah. Cursed be they! All their ships and camps shall not bring them triumph in the end."

Beriah turned and faced the northern wall.

"And from this cave we will curse them. There shall be a lasting memory of our hope and their downfall."

Beriah took out a knife and began to scratch in the soft limestone wall. Rivkah craned her neck to see what he was doing. It looked as if he was drawing a tent into the stone.

"They have pitched their tents in this land, sought to claim it for their own," Beriah mumbled. He wrote a few letters above the drawing.

"What does it say?" The question popped out of Rivkah's mouth before she realized.

Beriah turned and faced her, "It says 'cursed'. May all their military might and splendor be cursed."

Rivkah drew her breath. From the depth of this cave Beriah dared to curse the might of the Assyrian army and he was etching it in stone. It was an act of defiance, an act of power in weakness. For the written word would not remain without effect. The curse would seek out the army depicted on the wall, unless . . . unless the one who uttered and committed the curse to stone was struck first.

Beriah was still drawing on the wall. Rivkah could see the outline of a camp.

"Cursed be the camps of the mighty army!" Beriah breathed.

He did not turn around when Naarah entered the cave. Tilon was strapped to her back. Naarah looked somewhat puzzled at Beriah. Amnon motioned her to keep quiet and sit beside him.

Beriah drew more forms: ships, and soldiers—both infantry and archers.

Then he wrote more words on the wall.

"Cursed be the one who insults you!"

"Does it say that?" asked Naarah.

"Yes, for they are insulting the living God."

Beriah turned his face towards the entrance, "LORD, how long will the enemy insult you? Will the foe rage against you forever? With your right arm, oh LORD, shatter the enemy; in the greatness of your majesty throw down those that oppose you. Unleash your burning anger to consume them like stubble."

Beriah let his hands fall back to his side. He took a deep breath and turned to the others sitting in the cave. Slowly he opened his eyes.

"I know, here in this cave, driven from your home you may doubt whether the LORD has dominion over this land. The cities around you are destroyed, the enemy has taken over the whole land."

Looking straight at Amnon he continued, "You despair when you see Mareshah in ruins, when great Lachish is no more. You ask in your heart whether the LORD has forsaken his people, whether the gods of the enemy have triumphed. Has not the king of Assyria grasped the cities of Judah with his hand?"

In the silence Rivkah avoided Beriah's eyes and looked at the ground. In a loud voice he cut across their despair: "But know this: the LORD is the God of the whole land. He will not forsake his people. He is the God of Jerusalem and the whole of Judah."

Beriah walked across the room. Nobody spoke as he incised more words into the rock: many words, letter upon letter, one line and then another. Amnon, Naarah and Rivkah sat quietly, not wanting to disturb him. Even little Tilon was still. Ayalah came in, ready for lunch. After her eyes had adjusted to the dim light in the cave, she scanned everyone in the room. Somehow Ayalah seemed to understand the situation immediately. She sat down near Beriah. When he had finished the second line, Beriah stepped back from the wall. Ayalah looked at him. He answered her question even before she asked.

"These letters proclaim:
'The LORD is god of the whole land,
the mountains of Judah belong to the God of Jerusalem.'"

Ayalah nodded her head in approval. It seemed Amnon had found new strength. He sat erect and confident.

"Yes, the mountains of Judah are the LORD's. So it is written."

Hope had entered the cave.

* * *

It had been a decent midday meal. Today they had had plenty of fat beef. Itur-Ea belched, satisfied, as he wandered through the camp. Samaku was with him.

"At least these Judahites know how to feed their cattle," Samaku commented.

"I really don't know how they were able to fatten their calves that nicely with an army just around the corner."

"They probably didn't intend them to end up on an Assyrian grill, hee-hee..., but thank you."

"It really made a nice meal," Itur-Ea agreed.

"Now we only would have needed a nice woman afterwards, eh?" Samaku nudged Itur-Ea. He smiled but couldn't shake off the image of the appearance of Ishtar at the battle of Lachish. It had ended with blood and without any real satisfaction.

"Come on! I hope we won't have to wait until we're back in Nineveh to get access to shapely ladies." Samaku egged him on.

"We can dream," Itur-Ea mocked him. Samaku smirked.

By now they had come to the eastern end of the camp, where the priests and slaves took care of the wounded and sick.

Their comrade Arad-Nergal was here. He hadn't even been wounded. He had suddenly become sick a few days ago and complained loudly about his headache. Later on large lumps formed on his thighs and little, finger-width boils appeared on his legs. The last time they saw him the lumps had opened up so that pus flowed from them onto the bedding. Initially, he had had complained about the excruciating pain, but then later, he only lay there listlessly, moaning occasionally. Samaku and Itur-Ea kept their visits short. They never stayed long in the tent of the sick.

They were just about to enter the tent, when Arad-Nergal suddenly appeared in the doorway, greeting them exuberantly and rushing out into the open. What had happened? Yesterday he couldn't even get up from his bed.

"It's hot in there," Arad-Nergal told them. "I need to breathe the wind." Arad-Nergal stood in the lane, arms outstretched, taking a few deep breaths. Suddenly he stumbled to one side and fell to the ground. He sat there shaking.

"Get a slave to take him back to his bed," Samaku told Itur-Ea. Itur-Ea rushed off into the tent, but could only see rows of sick soldiers listlessly staring into nothingness. He went to the priests' quarters but was told by the priest at the door that nobody was available. Samaku was not impressed when Itur-Ea turned up alone.

"Nobody there!" Itur-Ea told him.

"Stay here, I'll look," Samaku said.

Itur-Ea watched Arad-Nergal in horror. He lay in the dust shaking and whining. Samaku returned soon—alone.

"We will have to get him back to his bed," he concluded. They looked at each other.

"Now!" Samaku urged.

At first Arad-Nergal struggled against them, flailing his arms wildly. But the effort must have exhausted him. Whimpering, he sank to the ground. Samaku and Itur-Ea were able to haul him up and half-carried, half-dragged him into the tent. Some of the other patients looked at them silently, but most seemed not to notice. Samaku and Itur-Ea let him fall onto his bed.

A slave suddenly appeared from the back of the tent. "Ah, he's crazy! Many of them go crazy and then . . . die."

"Look after him," was all Itur-Ea managed to say before he fled this place of misery, Samaku on his heels.

They went their separate ways. Itur-Ea still had to get some provisions for his company. He walked the streets of the camp dejected. Maybe that's why he noticed the rat. Of course they saw rats every day, but normally the animals would run away. Not this one. It just sat there, blinking in the sunlight and made no effort to move as Itur-Ea came closer. He avoided the miserable creature. He was sure its appearance had some significance. Was it an omen?

* * *

Rivkah angrily gritted her teeth. She had pulled and twisted the branch and still it didn't come off. It looked so dry and about to break. It should have been easy to just rip off. She angrily kicked the brushwood. It didn't help of course, only hurt her toes. Rivkah had already collected wood yesterday and this morning, but Amnon had insisted they needed more.

They had sent Achan out with her. But Achan wasn't much help. At first he had pulled enthusiastically at some branches. But when they didn't snap off immediately he lost interest and didn't even try to find good wood. Rivkah couldn't get him to carry much either.

She twisted the branch one more time. There was a distinct breaking noise, but still the branch didn't come off. "If it doesn't break now, I'll just leave it," Rivkah mumbled to herself. She gripped the branch and strained against it, yanking it back a couple of times. Suddenly it broke and Rivkah fell backward, right into a thorn bush. That hurt! She let out a little scream and then proceeded to extricate herself from the bush. Those thorns were stuck all through her clothes. Wiping tears off her face she walked a few steps from the bush, not even looking at the branch which had finally broken off.

"Achan!" she yelled, "come here!"

No response.

"Achan, you get here now!" Her voice was shrill. Still no Achan. Just wait! She would get that boy!

"Achan, you better come at once! What are you doing?"

Finally, Achan slowly wandered round a group of bushes.

"Hurry up!" screamed Rivkah. She was livid.

Achan listlessly ran a few paces. He pulled a face.

"Amnon told us not to shout or make loud noises," he said.

"I don't care about Amnon!" Rivkah shot back.

"But what if the Assyrians hear us?"

"If you useless boy would have helped and didn't wander off all the time, I wouldn't have to shout."

"I don't wander off all the time."

"Yes, you do! Now take that branch there and carry it back to the woodpile."

"But it's far too big for my bundle," Achan complained.

"Where's your bundle then?" Rivkah asked him.

"I dropped it when you called me. It's just behind those bushes." He looked at the branch, "This is too big."

Rivkah sighed. That boy! Calmer now, she saw that he wouldn't get far with a huge bundle of wood.

"You carry that branch. I'll take half of your bundle, alright?" she suggested.

Achan still wasn't happy, but he pulled the branch behind him to the bundle. Rivkah picked up the wood she had already collected, then added half his bundle. On the way back she realized she had come off worse in the deal. Trying to hold together all those small sticks and twigs was hard work.

The men wanted to fire the pots they had made. That's why everyone had been out collecting firewood. Down in the valley, in a clearing enclosed by trees and bushes, they had built up a sizeable woodpile. Beside it they had dug a pit and lined its top with some stones. That's where they would fire the pottery tonight. They didn't dare to make a big fire during the daytime. The smoke would be seen for leagues around. It was still risky enough during the night, but they should be able to avoid a fire with open flames. The trees would prevent the glow being seen from a distance.

"Oh, good. Just add it to the pile." Beriah welcomed the wood Rivkah and Achan were carrying. He had been helping Amnon and Joab to stack the few pots. In his previous life he might have used shards to write messages and notes, but he had never handled dry, unfired pots before. Still he was always willing to help and Rivkah thought she had never seen anybody placing pots so carefully.

"That looks good. Nicely stacked. Maybe there should be a larger gap between these pots here." Naarah joined the group around the pit. Clearly enjoying showing off her expertise in pottery firing, she commented on the position of every pot,

"Do you think this is stable enough on this side? No, I think you can leave it. You would not get it much better... And that pot over there, yes that one, it might just have to come out a bit... Careful!... I think that's enough."

She walked approvingly round the pit. "It should be ready to be covered with wood now," she told her husband Amnon. He nodded.

"I should really stay, but the goats still need milking and the food..." Suddenly Naarah noticed Rivkah there, "Rivkah, you're just standing there. You can see I'm busy. Please, go and milk the goats."

Rivkah hesitated for a moment. After hauling wood for two days, she wanted to see the fire. Not that she minded milking that much anymore. Even the goats had become used to her and she was able to tease milk out of their udders without getting them upset. But why now? She wanted to say something, to plead to stay just a moment longer. And yet ... "please". Naarah had actually said "please" to her. It must have been the first time Naarah had used the word when speaking to her. Rivkah managed a smile and turned to get the milking bowl.

It was dark by the time Rivkah had milked the goats and joined the women in the cave for dinner. The men were still busy with the fire. Amnon and Joab soon crawled into the cave for their evening meal. Rivkah asked them whether she could go down to the fire.

"Just head on down. Beriah is looking after it."

The night was cold outside; clouds covered the sky; no stars shone above; the darkness seemed impenetrable. Rivkah stopped at the entrance. Should she turn back? But then she slowly stepped forward. She knew every bush and every stone here. Her eyes adjusted and she was able to distinguish shapes. Still, her bare feet were bruised by thistles as she made her way down to the valley. Soon she could see the dim glow of the fire through the bushes.

Beriah sat not far from the pit and seemed deep in thought. He was startled when Rivkah appeared out of the dark. "Oh, it's you!"

He got up, went to the woodpile and put some branches onto the fire. After he made sure it was burning evenly, he sat down again. The warmth of the fire felt good. Rivkah stretched out her hands towards the heat. She touched her cheeks with her warm hands. Going to the other side of the fire opposite from Beriah, she hunched down, staring into the pile of flames and smoldering wood.

"Are you cold?" Beriah asked from across the fire.

"A bit."

"It's a cold night."

"Yes." Rivkah couldn't see him.

"I hope it doesn't start raining."

"Yes."

"Why don't you come over here, Rivkah? It's difficult to talk across a pit. There's a blanket here too."

Rivkah was unsure for a moment. Then she got up and sat beside Beriah, wrapping the blanket around her feet.

"You know, all these years I have eaten out of earthenware bowls and scratched notes on potsherds, but I've never really thought about how pottery is made, never really watched it being fired. And now I'm sitting here watching over a pottery fire." Beriah grabbed a stick beside him and poked the burning wood. "Amnon told me to just feed the fire carefully, to ensure it burns slowly and at an even temperature. I hope they'll come back before I make a mistake. I'd hate to see these pots broken. It took quite some time to make them. And then it took a long time to dry them. Once the winter rains have really set in, it'll be even more difficult to dry them."

"The weather will become so much colder," Rivkah added quietly.

"Yes, and the dew in the air will moisten the pots. So we have to get it right tonight. As winter comes, making pots will only get harder.

Amnon said so and I believe him. And . . . " there was suddenly a humorous tone in Beriah's voice, "you probably wouldn't want to collect that much wood again."

"No." Rivkah had to laugh. "But it would be so much easier if Achan did his share of the work. He didn't get much wood at all," she said bitterly.

"I know it's hard, Rivkah." Beriah looked directly into her eyes. "But do not let anger take hold in you. For the LORD watches from heaven and sees if you scheme evil against your brother. Rather, put your mind to what is good, to build up his people. If you do your daily tasks conscientiously and work for the good of his people, the LORD will watch from heaven and will see it.

"At times it may seem as if the LORD does not care, does not act. Great suffering has fallen on his people; misery has overtaken me, his servant. And yet I have acted justly and his people have not conspired against the LORD. If some people have strayed and I have sinned in my youth, may the LORD be merciful and forgive. And so I continually turn to the LORD, beseeching him to take care of his people, to acquit them and free them from the oppression of their enemies. For if the LORD attends to his people again and declares them free from guilt, he will deliver them and they shall be truly free."

Rivkah looked at the wafts of smoke rising from the fire before they were swallowed by the darkness of the night. A small explosion could be heard from the pit as it released a few sparks.

"I hope these pots are alright," whispered Beriah. He stood up to tend the fire, but must have decided otherwise for he sat down again. Somewhere nearby an owl screeched in the dark.

"And us, what will happen to us here?" Rivkah's question broke the silence.

Beriah lifted his chin. "The LORD will deliver us, even here in this wild part of Judah, seemingly so godforsaken."

Deliver? What did that mean? What hope was there for her? Rivkah could not see any future. A restoration of Lachish? But it would never be the same again. The city had gone, its people dead. She was only able to live day by day, to do her work and eat the little food she got. Rivkah moved her hand down her neck and pressed the little pendant of Isis hidden under her clothes. It was her link to the past. Would it also lead and protect her in the future?

Beriah must have also been deep in thought. He stood up.

"Even here we can pray."

Lifting his arms, he tilted his face towards a heaven covered by dark clouds.

"Be merciful to me, O LORD, for I am in distress;
my eyes grow weak with sorrow,
my soul and body with grief.
But I trust in you, O LORD;
I say, 'You are my God.'
My times are in your hands;
deliver me from my enemies
and from those who pursue me.
Let me not be put to shame, O LORD,
for I have cried out to you;
but let the wicked be put to shame
and lie silent in the grave.
Let their lying lips be silenced,
for with pride and contempt
they speak arrogantly against the righteous.

"How great is your goodness,
which you have stored up for those who fear you,
which you bestow in the sight of men
on those who take refuge in you.

"Be strong and take heart,
all you who hope in the LORD."

As Rivkah looked up, she saw the clouds breaking and for a moment stars shone through. A feeling of deep comfort and sadness overcame her. Even though she felt like weeping, no tears came. Somehow she felt safe here beside the fire in the dark, and yet also lost and confused. She snuggled into the blanket and closed her eyes. And then she must have fallen asleep.

Beriah shook her gently.

"Come Rivkah. We're going back to the cave."

It took Rivkah a moment to realize where she was. Ah yes, out here by the pottery fire. Joab was here to look after it.

Beriah took a branch and held it into the pit until its tip burned. He held the torch and took Rivkah's hand.

"Quick, we'll take this to lighten our path."

The burning branch dimly lit the way to the cave as shadows flitted across bush and stone.

* * *

Naarah was already up. Rivkah could hear her fussing around with pots and bowls in the front chamber. She must have surely woken Beriah by now with all that noise. If Naarah was up, Rivkah should also get out of bed and help her. But she was so tired. She slowly turned around on the bench. Just one more moment. She snuggled into the blanket. The noise seemed to recede into the background as if it came from far away.

It seemed only a little later when Rivkah heard somebody call her name, "Rivkah!"

Ayalah stood over her, shaking her gently. Startled, Rivkah sat bolt upright, blinking as she searched with one hand for the blanket that Ayalah must have pulled away.

"What . . . ?" Rivkah tried to focus as she rubbed the sleep from her eyes.

"Get up Rivkah. It's not the time to laze in bed. It's well into the day. You've been sleeping too long," Ayalah scolded her gently.

Rivkah swung her legs onto the floor.

"But I wanted to get up, I really did. I don't know why I fell asleep again."

"Come on now. There's plenty to do. Soon we'll open the pit and take out the pots. Don't you want to see?"

Ah, that's right! The previous evening came back to Rivkah. They had been firing pottery. She tried to remember Beriah's words beside the fire before he had walked her back to the cave. She had not been able to go to sleep immediately. Somehow she had felt restless and peaceful at the same time. Now in broad daylight the emotions had evaporated.

"Are you coming?" Ayalah asked.

"Yes. It'll be interesting to see how the pottery turned out. I'll be right along."

Rivkah stood up and straightened her dress. She followed Ayalah out of the cave and down to the valley. On the way, Ayalah told her that

Naarah hadn't been too pleased when she had realized that the goats hadn't yet been milked this morning.

Down in the valley they saw the men taking the pottery out of the pit and stacking it in convenient bundles. The pots had already cooled down.

"The men put out the fire at dawn," Ayalah said. "We didn't want the Assyrians to see the smoke."

"Over there, take those pots over there," Amnon told Rivkah. He had more words for Ayalah, "The pots seem to be well fired. Only two of them cracked. The bowls look alright, too. Not professional, of course. A few of them are quite black in places."

Ayalah examined a few pieces.

"You can be satisfied, son. Considering the circumstances, you've got some nice pieces here. These vessels will serve us well."

Rivkah went to the bundle Amnon had indicated. She carefully put the pots on her back and tied the cloth around her shoulder.

Amnon and Joab were still discussing the outcome of the firing with Ayalah. Beriah stood with them but seemed to be deep in thought. When she passed him, Beriah looked at Rivkah. She smiled hesitantly at him. He smiled back, but then a distant look came across his face.

Rivkah didn't wait for the others and carried the bundle immediately back to the cave. Naarah was there. And she did complain about having to milk the goats this morning and then continued to comment on Rivkah's laziness and tendency to sleep in. It would have been no use to point out that it was the first time it had happened, no use either to let her know that she could have simply woken her up. Rivkah just had to endure the barbs and resolved that it wouldn't happen again.

It wasn't long before the men and Ayalah arrived at the cave. Naarah was fully occupied with looking at the pottery. It gave Rivkah the opportunity to eat some bread and stop that grumbling in her stomach.

Naarah arranged the pots and bowls, looking them over with a critical eye, "This one would just be right for a milking bowl—if we could get our sleeper up in the morning and she remembers that somebody actually has to milk the goats." Joab didn't seem to hear the last remark, but totally agreed on the bowl's purpose, "That's what I intended it for when I made it. It turned out well, didn't it?"

However, Rivkah was more interested in the quiet discussion between Amnon and Beriah.

"Do you think we've got enough bowls and storage vessels now?" Beriah asked.

"Enough for this place. We don't really have any wine or oil to store and we haven't saved any wheat or barley," Amnon pointed out.

"You're right. Food is much more of a concern."

"I don't know how much longer we can hold out in this cave. We cannot stay here forever. And all the while the Assyrians are threatening," Amnon said.

"Yes, our situation looks desperate. We are hiding from the enemy. We are pressed hard and cornered. We cannot fight the enemy ourselves, weak as we are. Life in this cave is hard to endure. So in our need we cry to the LORD to save us. For he has power to set us free, to give us life and hope once again." Beriah closed his eyes. Lifting his hands he just said two simple words, "Save, Lord!"

Amnon repeated them, "Save, Lord!"

Beriah stood up and spoke in a loud voice so that even Naarah stopped commenting on the pottery and looked at him. "From this cave we have called upon the LORD to curse the enemy. And so we will also call upon him to save us, to bring hope to us again."

Taking his knife, Beriah carved letters into the stone beside the entrance to the southern chamber. He turned to the group watching him, "'Save, LORD,' I have written. For we pray for the LORD to save us, to come to our aid in this place."

He smiled at Rivkah as he continued, "In this past night I prayed before the LORD, our God, beseeching him to hear us and incline his ear to our pleas. For if the LORD takes care of us in his mercy, he will restore us and give us life anew."

Beriah took a few steps across the room and ran his hand across one of the inscriptions he had incised earlier.

"We have proclaimed that this land is the LORD's, the God of Jerusalem. And so we turn to him now:
'He is the LORD, LORD,
the compassionate and gracious God,
slow to anger, abounding in love and faithfulness,
maintaining love to thousands
and forgiving iniquity, transgression and sin.
Yet, not acquitting the guilty,

he visits the iniquity of the fathers upon the sons and the sons' sons
to the third and fourth generation.

'And so LORD, LORD, gracious God,
visit us in our distress
and acquit us according to your promise.' "

Rivkah had heard the solemn confession before, had listened to it in awe and fear, but only now did she understand the hope of which it spoke. For the LORD would acquit the innocent and take care of the wronged.

Only the scratching of Beriah's knife could be heard as the others watched him write the words beneath the earlier declaration. Finally he stood back from the wall and read:

"Take care, LORD, gracious God.
Acquit, LORD, LORD."

Ayalah closed her eyes and quietly recited a prayer. Naarah held up her hands in supplication. The new pots were forgotten. Rivkah was the first to slip out of the cave. She had to gather herbs. Nobody was going to accuse her again of being lazy.

* * *

The sun was already high in the sky as they set out. With Libnah behind them, they were heading towards the Philistine plain. The splendor of the mighty Assyrian army was on full display as column after column marched down the valley. Weapons gleamed in the sun and the wheels of the heavily laden wagons shook the ground. And yet, Itur-Ea did not feel any pride, could not look at the spectacle without a sense of loss and despair. For not far from the ruined city his friend Arad-Nergal had been buried in a shallow grave. His body had been disfigured by the disease, his limbs wasted by the plague that had ravaged him. He was not the only one to be left behind in foreign soil. Disease had taken away so many of the soldiers.

Still, the force that left Libnah was larger than the one that had arrived here weeks earlier. The strike forces that had harassed and sacked towns and villages across Judah had been called back to join the main force. Not all had reached the camp at Libnah by the time the army set out for the plains. The division that had encircled Jerusalem had only arrived the previous night after a hasty retreat from the Judahite capital.

There must be something to the rumors after all. Had the Egyptian forces really regrouped? Were they about to stage another attack with additional troops? Everything pointed to it: the sudden departure by the Assyrian army, the halt to further raids. Just a few days ago they had still thought they would actually be going to Jerusalem and finally flush out that rebel Hezekiah, the king of Judah. Jerusalem had been shut in for months now. It could not hold out for ever. At least that's what had been concluded by the Assyrian soldiers round their camp fires at night. Some had feared that troops would have to stay behind to continue the siege through winter. So it was good news that the plan had been changed. But another encounter with the Egyptians, was that really any better?

They had routed them in their first battle. When Egyptian chariots had launched their raid, the Assyrian army had successfully fought them off. But would this new Egyptian threat be so easy to fight off? Or would they be a larger force, equipped to meet the Assyrians? Itur-Ea was sure the topic would be discussed once they had erected the camp.

Chapter 8

The wind shook the bushes and rushed through the trees; branches bent under the sudden gusts. The rain had petered out to intermittent drops. Traces of the heavy downpour were still visible in the scoured soil, the streams foaming wild and brown. Puddles covered level sections of ground and the soil was soaked and heavy with water.

In such weather the goats were content to stay in the dry cave. Not even the thought of some choice leaves could entice them into the open. Rivkah had just finished the milking. There was noticeably less milk today, but she had not been able to coax another drop out of the teats. Naarah would be none too pleased. Rivkah patted Kala, the goat next to her, "Maybe better tomorrow, eh?"

Then she took the bowl and walked out into the drizzle. Leaning over the bowl to shield the milk from the rain drops, Rivkah hurried to the main cave where the others waited for the rain to abate.

Naarah did question her about the milk, "You really weren't able to get any more out of them?"

"No, that's all they had."

"Tonight I'll come and see myself." Naarah didn't fully trust her. She glanced at Amnon who returned her worried look, wrinkles creasing his brow.

"As long as we get plenty of greens we'll have enough food," Ayalah said.

Joab groaned audibly. By now everyone was well aware of his dislike of "those bitter leaves". For a few days Joab had painted mouth-watering pictures of fatted calves and strong wine, of fine bread and sweet honey cakes. And when he talked, the herbs they ate seemed even more bitter, the bread they chewed even more coarse. Beriah or Amnon must have said something to him for he no longer spoke about feasts, even though he left no doubt that the current diet was not to his liking.

Ayalah dismissed Joab's grumbles. She thought the wild plants were good for them. Now she stood at the cave entrance and looked outside. She turned around and talked to Rivkah, "Speaking of greens, come,

Rivkah, we'll go out and gather some more. The rain has stopped. The sun is shining."

"But Mother, so soon after the rain. It is still wet and slippery. You don't have to go," Amnon cautioned.

"Son, your old mother does not fear the wet and cold. I want to go outside and gather herbs. As the year passes we will find new plants springing from the earth."

Rivkah got herself ready. Together they stepped into the open space outside the cave. The sun was indeed breaking through the clouds.

They hadn't gone far when Rivkah asked, "Is there something wrong with the goats? It seems Amnon was worried."

"You know, Rivkah, goats don't give milk just to feed humans. They give to feed their young. It's been nearly a year now since Kala and Tera had their kids. They really should be in kid again, and about to give birth. We took only the two mother goats when we fled. There's no billy goat. If there are no young, the milk will stop. The two will give milk for some time yet, but it will become less and will be not as creamy. That's why Amnon is worried. He won't get much of the cheese he's so keen on!"

Ayalah laughed, but behind the humor Rivkah could also see her concern.

"Will we have enough to eat?"

"The LORD will provide."

That should've been enough. But it didn't settle Rivkah's concerns. What did it mean? And because she knew she could ask Ayalah, Rivkah voiced the question, "How will he provide?"

"Has he not given us all these herbs of the field to feed us? The LORD will give what we need."

"But even now we struggle to find good leaves and plants. How much farther do we have to go in search of food? And no one can live on leaves alone."

"It will be hard, Rivkah. But we have been given knowledge of herbs and leaves, so we have to use our minds and hands to find nourishment. We have to do our part."

"Shouldn't we do something more to give us food, to bring about good luck? Why don't we invoke the powerful gods of Egypt, utter words of magic or make the earth fruitful through sacred rituals?"

"No Rivkah! We do not know what we will bring upon us. Those gods and demons not only give, they also take. And they are capricious, full of greed and fancy, fickle and demanding. If you rely on other gods, you have to continually please them. They may help you briefly, but then they turn against you and cast you into utter ruin and torment. Here in Judah we pray to the LORD, for he is the God of this land and this people. We cannot escape him. He is our hope. That's why Beriah continually pleads with the LORD, the God of Israel, even though Beriah has experienced great calamity. He has no one else to turn to."

* * *

The clash of swords, the thud of shields, the shouts of men and the neighing of horses sounded across the plain. The two great armies were locked in battle. Already the archers had released volley after volley of arrows. The infantry had advanced and man fought man, swords killed and wounded, spears found their deadly mark.

Amidst the ranks of his company, Itur-Ea stood on a gentle rise, craning his neck to get a glimpse of the battle. His company, the siege machine experts of the Assyrian army, was prepared for battle. Equipped with the weapons of the infantry they would only join the fight if the king deemed a tactical change was necessary. These were men that had developed the skill of attacking walled cities and the success of the army depended on them. But they were not skilled in open field battles. Here their siege machines were no use. Other troops trained in field warfare led the charge. Alongside them the large mass of vassal soldiers was thrown into battle.

Even though sickness had spread through the Assyrian camp and claimed many soldiers, they were still a formidable force. Still, sometimes when Itur-Ea saw the many rats dying in the gutters of the camp and heard the cries of his comrades, he wondered whether the gods had forsaken them. With the plague, unrest had spread through the camp.

But the might of the Assyrian army displayed in battle pushed all these doubts aside. Itur-Ea could not see the Assyrian cavalry charging to harass the Egyptian flanks. The only indication of their attack was the dust cloud moving across the plain, raised by hundreds of horses. He could hear the hooves pounding the ground, the chariot wheels thundering across the dirt. Both riders and chariots advanced in formation.

At first he did not notice the other dust cloud speeding across the plain from the south. Only when it suddenly came up behind the Assyrian cavalry did he realize that the Egyptian chariots had mounted an unexpected counter attack. Nor had the threat been noticed on the field. The arrows that now hailed down upon horses and riders, on drivers and archers, created havoc among the Assyrians. Those shield bearers that survived the first attack adjusted quickly and were able to protect their vehicles from the rear. But others had fallen. Driverless chariots swerved erratically, injured horses dragged their vehicles to the ground, and riders halted their advance and wheeled around. The formation was broken. After the first confusion, the commander of the Assyrian cavalry gained control of the situation. But to Itur-Ea their reaction seemed painfully slow. He stood on the rise clutching his sword tightly with one hand, rubbing his thigh nervously with the other. Blood shot to his face as his heart beat violently. He willed their fighters to confront the enemy, to repel the stealthy attack.

Rather than turning in one flowing movement, the chariots and riders stopped and laboriously changed direction, leaving them exposed to more arrows shot by the departing Egyptians. By the time the Assyrians were ready to fight, the Egyptian chariots were leagues beyond the reach of their arrows. The Assyrians chased the attackers only briefly. Following them would be futile. The commander slowed the pursuit and changed direction again, resuming their advance toward the flank of the Egyptian infantry.

Now the cavalry would be able to do some damage, and weaken the Egyptian fighters. But before the chariots and horses could discharge their arrows and join the battle, the swift Egyptian chariots were on them again. Itur-Ea saw how they had turned round and swooped on the Assyrian cavalry at speed. Would the Assyrians stand up to them this time? Clearly the cavalry commander had also noticed. And they were prepared this time; they turned in one swift movement to face the threat rushing towards them. Now they would loosen their arrows and halt the Egyptian charge. But the volley of arrows never ascended into the air. Did the commander not give the order? Did the archers crumble under the pressure? Impossible! Bow and archer were a finely-tuned combination, war machines that were deadly and scarcely assailable.

Itur-Ea and his whole company gasped in horror as the Egyptian chariots advanced unchecked, the occasional wavering arrow proving no hindrance. The Assyrian cavalry stood in confusion, overawed by the swiftness of the attack and their own inability to fight back. The Egyptians burst upon the apparently paralyzed troops. Itur-Ea could see that it wasn't only the Egyptian chariots that were now involved: part of the Egyptian infantry broke away from the main battle and set upon the Assyrian cavalry, slaughtering the horses, butchering the men. The very target of their advance had now turned upon the Assyrian cavalry. The men on the rise behind the battlefield watched in horror as the elite force of their glorious army was being decimated.

The panic spread to the Assyrian troops in the centre of the battle. Instead of taking the opportunity to attack the distracted Egyptians, they fell back and slowly retreated.

"Attention!" The order startled Itur-Ea. Mesmerized by the drama unfolding before him, he had totally forgotten his own part in the battle. Gripping his shield tightly, he stood erect and firm. Assyrian military discipline was what counted now. The banner of their company was lifted high and the company of siege machine fighters marched to join the field battle. They would bolster the flagging infantry. They would stand against the enemy, strengthen the battle lines, so that the Assyrian army could regroup and take the upper hand once more. And so Itur-Ea headed into battle one more time.

* * *

"Isis! An amulet of the goddess Isis! Oh Rivkah, what have you done? Why do you carry this abominable image?" Beriah screamed at Rivkah, clenching the small statuette in his tightened fist. The string cut sharply into Rivkah's neck as he forcefully pulled the amulet. Rivkah's head snapped backwards when he violently yanked the figurine trying to rip it off.

She started to sob, "It's only a charm. I always wear it."

"Cast it away! Away with this scandalous idol!"

Rivkah remained motionless, her arms hanging limply at her side.

Beriah tried to pull the string over her head, but in his haste he only managed to tangle it up in her hair.

"Where did you get it from?"

"My mother gave it to me."

"So your mother and father ensnared you, gave you over to sin and idolatry! Away with it!"

Beriah drew his knife and cut the cord. He hurled the amulet into the bushes. Rivkah saw the amulet drop and then she ran, away from Beriah.

"Rivkah!" Beriah shouted. But she did not stop. Halfway up the slope she looked back. Beriah did not follow her. He just stood there staring at the ground. She continued on.

Fighting for breath, Rivkah finally flung herself to the ground, sure that nobody would find her here.

The power and protection of Isis were gone, taken from her! The one thing that bound her to her family, to her city, her past, had been snatched away. Her security, her confidence had been flung aside.

"Mother," she breathed. She held her hair tightly in clenched fingers.

What now? It had all started so well today. Beriah had offered to accompany her to the cistern to get water. She had felt happy and had walked lightly down to the valley. He had told her funny stories about the letters of the alphabet, promising to teach her to read. And then she had bent over to haul water out of the cistern. The amulet must have slipped out from under her dress and hung openly from her neck. She hadn't even noticed, but he had. His anger Rivkah still could not fathom.

The sun had gone far beyond its zenith when she returned to the cistern. The water jar was no longer there. Had Beriah taken it? What had he done after she ran off? Standing at the place where it happened, she could picture the figurine of Isis slamming into the bushes. She could not just leave it. She ran over to the spot where she thought it fell. On hands and knees Rivkah searched among straggling branches and prickly thistles. Finally, she found the amulet loosely wedged between some branches. She took it reverently, tracing her fingers over the hieroglyphs on its back. She knew she could wear it no longer. Beriah would not allow it.

And so Rivkah buried the amulet of Isis there at the edge of the clearing behind the cistern. As she patted down the soil she was finally able to weep.

"Mother, I must leave Isis here in the cold. But I will not forget. No, I will get back to her," she whispered.

Wiping away the tears she walked back to the cave. Dusk was already falling. The others would be eating now. She waited a long time before she entered the cave.

"Rivkah," Beriah said softly. But she did not listen and went straight to the sleeping chamber where she curled up on the bench. Joab and Achan came in later but did not talk to her. Rivkah felt so drained, so tired, and yet she could not sleep, not this night.

* * *

Itur-Ea knelt in the dirt beside the road. Behind him the unending column of the Assyrian army marched by. The dust stirred up by thousands of feet and hooves covered his hands and stung his eyes. He rubbed an arm across his face. It only made it worse. His whole body shuddered again. He felt cold, his cheeks were hot and flushed. He struggled to get up, but felt too weak to rise from his knees. Then it came again. His stomach contracted and he spewed out the rest of his breakfast, adding to the vomit on the ground. "Oh!" the weak cry scarcely passed his lips as he crawled onwards.

The bullock wagon with the siege machine and his belongings was leagues ahead by now. He had to reach it again. Nobody seemed to care when they saw him kneeling by the roadside. They all looked away. It was a sight far too common these days. Another sick soldier lying by the roadside. There was no point in stopping for them. Most died within days. They only held up the troops on their march home. Itur-Ea tried to get up again. He had to make it!

The pain! Oh, the pain! It surged through him as he struggled to his feet. He stumbled several paces before he fell again. He touched his legs, felt the swellings chafing against his balls. Yes, here they were: the inflamed lumps in his groin. He winced. What tricks were the gods playing on him now? The Assyrian army was on its homeward journey. He had been looking forward to returning to Nineveh again or, at least, to being quartered in a nice provincial city over winter. Would he make it now?

In the end, the decision to return to Assyria and withdraw the troops from the hills of Judah and the plains of Philistia had come quite suddenly. After the Assyrian troops had fallen back during that battle with Egypt, the great king had ordered every last unit into action. But Itur-Ea's company never fought. The Egyptians had been content with their surprise triumph over the elite cavalry wing. They thought better than to attack the formidable force massed above them on the rising terrain. Nor did the Assyrians advance again. The two armies faced each other as morning turned to the mid of day. Finally, emissaries from both sides met near a grove of trees to the west. Hours passed while the soldiers stood in the sun. Thank Ashur, it was not the height of summer anymore! The wait was exhausting, the stench and sweat grew nearly unbearable. Their uniforms weighed heavy on the soldiers. And then came the order to stand down. At first they did not know what it might mean. When they got word that they were to return to Nineveh within days, joy mingled with disappointment. They were leaving behind the dangers and exhaustion of battle, the hardship of camp life, but they were also leaving an enemy unvanquished, a land not yet fully brought into submission. The events of the battle still grated many, hurt the pride of professional soldiers. Some thought the gods had turned against them. There even was a rumor that the archers had not been able to use their bows because rats and mice had eaten the strings. But then, many rumors swirled around the rodents that lay dying throughout the camp. Were they punishment from the gods?

Despite it all, they were going home. Itur-Ea had hung onto that. And now! Here he was, struck by the gods with this disease.

The last wagons were passing him. Someone had pity on Itur-Ea and handed him a water flask. Itur-Ea drank in hurried gulps. The cool water refreshed him. He tried again and was able to stand. Making his way to the road he steadied himself against one of the wagons. It was slow enough. Despite the pain Itur-Ea could bring himself to take one step after another, to continue on the road home. He had to make it! Behind him the rear guard watched the withdrawal of the great Assyrian army.

* * *

Achan was sick. Nothing had seemed wrong with him the night before. But in the morning he wouldn't leave his sleeping bench and complained about headaches. He looked weak and drawn. His cheeks glistened red. Rivkah felt his hot skin, laid her hand on his glowing, sweating brow.

At first they didn't know what to do, shrugged their shoulders and left Achan alone. But the fear was growing. Was it a demon that tormented Achan or had the LORD struck him down? Joab, who had spent so much time with the boy, was worried the sickness would pass to him too. He suggested sending Achan away before the sickness would befall them all. Naarah feared for the life of Tilon, her young son. Even

Amnon agreed that keeping Achan with them might expose them all to disease. He remembered occasions when person after person had been struck down, and recalled reports of whole villages being wiped out by disease. And so it seemed to them that Achan could not stay, that to save themselves he must be abandoned.

But Beriah would have none of it, "Do not forsake our brother in his time of need. Should we abandon the fatherless? The LORD defends his cause and will surely reckon it to us if we take care of him. Even if this sickness is judgment upon the boy, it is our duty to care for him, to restore him to peace and health again. And if we do not succeed, we are to abide with him lest he depart alone."

Beriah looked at Joab, saw Amnon's worried eyes on his son Tilon.

"If we seek to save our lives and the lives of our children by giving our brother over to death, we have grasped a life of iniquity. The sin will be upon us and our children. Better to lose our lives than to turn against God and our brother."

The men still did not seem fully convinced. Rivkah, too, could not shake her fear.

Beriah sighed.

"I will look after him. You don't have to touch the boy. But don't throw him out."

That's why it was Beriah who brought Achan food, helped him eat and carried him outside when he needed it. It was Beriah who wiped away the sweat from Achan's brow, helped him clear his blocked nose and made him inhale the fragrance of healing herbs Ayalah had gathered.

Naarah was even scared to touch Achan's bowl, did not provide meals for him. That left Rivkah to cook, to help with anything that Beriah requested. Often Ayalah went out alone to look for greens, as Rivkah spent more time around the cave. She was able to observe the diligent care Achan was receiving. He seemed to respond to the attention and his health improved each day.

* * *

"Water!" Itur-Ea cried out. He couldn't be far from the spring. He knew they had camped near one. It must be just down there past these rocks. The animals that had been watered there had torn up the ground; the soldiers that had carried water from there had trampled the dirt. He crawled along on hands and knees, too weak to stand. Again he collapsed onto the ground.

"By Ishtar!" he breathed, "am I going to just die out here like a dog?" He tried to get up again, but only managed to drag himself a few paces.

"No!" he screamed bitterly. "No," he moaned, tears now streaming from his eyes. The choking sobs shook his body. The pain seemed unbearable. He let out a piercing cry that soon faded away, the effort too much for him. Itur-Ea just lay there, the late morning sun caressing the lonely figure left behind on the abandoned camp site.

He couldn't even remember them breaking camp. The activity around him, as the troops got ready to move again, had hardly penetrated his feverish stupor. One or two soldiers had prodded him. He thought he had recognized Samaku's face. It came back to him only now.

As morning passed he had suddenly noticed the stillness. Nothing moved. Nobody was there. That's when he had become aware of his dry throat. But they had left no water for him. The tents were all gone. Just the trampled ground, the discarded food scraps and the smells were unmistakable signs of the army camp. In his thirst he had finally decided to search for the spring. Now he couldn't even reach it.

The sun that at first seemed welcome now felt uncomfortably hot. It seemed to burn his legs, his arms; it felt like fire against the back of his head. He crossed his arms behind his head, trying to ward off the searing rays. He nearly choked as his head pressed into the dirt.

He placed his arms on the ground again, pushed himself up on his elbows and lifted his head. Not far to go to the spring!

He hauled himself forward two or three cubits. His legs were hardly able to push him. In exhaustion he fell onto the trampled ground again. His head buried in his arms, he lay motionless, though his throat stung with thirst and his head drummed in pain. He could not even will himself to try one more time to get up.

So that was it! Left out here in a foreign country to die. That was where Ishtar had brought him! That was the price of Assyrian might! Not on the battlefield, not when storming a city he would die, but abandoned by his people on their homeward march, ravaged by a consuming disease. There was no glory in this, no honor. Itur-Ea couldn't even see any point in the conquest of so many cities, the battles they had won, the power of Ashur they had shown to the world. He may have been a tool of the gods, but now they had cruelly discarded that tool, had cast him aside. Before their fickle moods he felt helpless. But he was afraid no more. They had already broken him, had had their sport with him. Now all the horror of their deceit and cruel disregard for mortal man was exposed.

Ishtar had promised so much, but her charms were empty. Even the encounters in the temple of Nineveh, a memory he had treasured, now filled him with disgust. They were a sham. Ishtar had shown her true face in the companions that had been killed by enemy fire, in the sleepless nights when he called for answers and received none, and in the disease that killed without dignity. Ishtar had received her bloody offering: the lives of thousands of men.

And yet, despite their power, their might, their playful disregard for human lives, the Assyrian gods had not fully prevailed. Did the great army of their god Ashur not retreat in haste? Did not the tiny state of Judah, though deeply wounded, still mock them? Did that god of the Judahites still protect his people? Would he really restore the land to his people? Itur-Ea could still dimly remember the words of that prisoner: our god has mercy and love, he had said. What was a god of mercy and love like? Was he weak like the people that worshipped him? But maybe such a god would endure, would take care of the sick, the stricken.

Itur-Ea coughed. By Ishtar! He could hardly breathe. Oh, that the god Ea would have prolonged his life and led him back to the village of his birth. He could see them now, processing through the fields of his childhood home, past the canals he had played in as a boy. They sang for joy as they carried the god through the fertile fields. How he longed to be there! He reached out and pain surged through him. Blackness, hopeless blackness, engulfed him and all he could see was the mocking smile of Ishtar as he slipped from this world.

Chapter 9

Achan was better soon. The fever left him. His nose cleared and he was able to breathe freely. Though still weak, he could walk slowly. No one had anything against him joining them at meal times. Joab and Rivkah moved back into the southern chamber. Beriah spent the nights in the front room again. He no longer dedicated all his efforts to Achan, but often went out with Amnon and Joab, roaming through the area to hunt and get wood. He seemed to have grown restless.

One night, as they were sitting in the cave with a small fire giving welcome, but meager, warmth Beriah declared his intention to venture out into the world again, "I'm going to Jerusalem."

"To Jerusalem?" Amnon asked surprised.

"Yes, we haven't heard anything from anyone for weeks. We do not even know whether the armies of Assyria are still in this land. Has the king of Assyria conquered Jerusalem or is the city still holding out? Or has the LORD utterly destroyed the king of Assyria? And what about the towns of Judah? I am going to find out."

"Will you come back?" asked Rivkah.

"I do not know. If I am needed elsewhere I will set to work. And if I am taken by the Assyrian army I cannot come back. But if my path leads me to these lands again, be sure that I will return to you and give you a report."

Amnon turned to Beriah, "If at all possible do come back and let us know what you find out."

"If I can, I will let you know. I will not forget you, for you have shown me hospitality in my time of need, Amnon."

What would life here be like without Beriah? Rivkah thought of his kind words, his willingness to help out. She remembered his trust in the LORD and the anger against any other gods. He had no regard for those that he thought offended the LORD. His faith was unflinching and uncompromising. Isis! How he had reacted when he saw the little figurine, ripping it from her. She felt so unsure without it. Rivkah placed her hand on her chest where, normally, the amulet would have touched her skin. But Beriah had also given them hope. She squinted to see his inscriptions in the flickering light. Time and again he reminded them that not even the Assyrian army was invincible, that there was a tomorrow beyond the present trouble. When he called on the LORD, he comforted the people around him. Rivkah knew she would miss him. Beriah come back soon!

He left early the next morning. Naarah gave him bread baked with the best flour she could grind from the poor grains they still had. Ayalah gave him advice on herbs he might or might not find. Amnon embraced him warmly and ensured he also took some cheese with him. Achan tried not to cry as he said his goodbyes. Joab clasped his shoulder, proclaiming that Beriah would find the Assyrians vanquished.

"God be with you, Rivkah," Beriah said to her as she stood at the edge of the small group. He fleetingly touched her hair.

"May the LORD direct your ways."

Then he turned, swung the bundles across his shoulder and walked up the hill to reach the valley beyond. They watched him as he made his way through the damp grass and bushes. When he disappeared behind the crest of the hill, they went inside the cave to eat the morning meal.

* * *

They all said they had never seen the stream appear this early in winter. The water bubbled from the ground, filled the channel at the centre of the Kidron valley, brought the dry wadi to life, rushed past stony banks, and trees rooted firmly in the alluvial soil. Leah sat and watched the spectacle. It was good to see water flowing from the spring in abundance, pouring over rocks and stones, gathering in pools and pushing against banks, not with destructive violence, but in joyful abandon. It was good to feel the sun after days of rain, to be warmed by its rays after days of cold. It was good to be outside the city, to leave behind the gates and look up at the imposing walls from amidst the trees of the valley below.

The siege of Jerusalem had been lifted weeks ago, but Leah was still amazed what a difference it had made. After the fear and depression of the siege, the sudden departure of the enemy had created confusion and uncertainty, to be replaced by joy and triumph at the news that the Assyrians had indeed withdrawn and were returning to their own country. They had celebrated and thrown open the city gates, had prepared lavish feasts and danced to the sound of flutes and lyres. The king had proclaimed a festival of thanksgiving at the temple. But people only slowly ventured outside the walls again, still uncertain what to expect. When they heard about the destruction of so many cities, towns and villages of Judah, and the thousands of prisoners that had been taken by the Assyrians, their joy was dampened. Slowly, the cost of the Assyrian occupation became known. The tribute demanded by the Assyrians and the pledges paid to Egypt had exhausted the royal coffers, and would be a burden for the ravaged country for years to come.

But still, the relief was great, confidence in the future restored. The thankfulness of the people was profound: God had saved his holy city and had shown himself loyal to his servant, the king from the house of David. Leah savored the freedom, drank in the promise of a hopeful future. She leaned back, let the sun caress her face and shook her long hair.

"Hey, Leah, are you coming?" One of the girls shouted to her. "We're going back up to the city."

"Coming!" Leah replied. She got up and followed the other girls. They went up the valley past the spring. Several cubits farther on they came to the well at the junction of the Kidron and Hinnom valleys. "The shepherds water their flocks here in summer," another girl explained. That was Basmath. Her family was of old Jerusalem stock. Most of the other girls had only arrived in Jerusalem as refugees in the previous months. Others had been in Judah's capital for longer or had even been born here, but their families were mostly recent arrivals, whether from other parts of Judah or from Samaria to the north. They all lived in the new, southwestern part of the city, where houses crowded on the slopes of Jerusalem's hills. After the days of rain, they had decided that there was no better place to enjoy a sunny, winter's day than out here in the valley.

Chattering among themselves, they walked up the Hinnom Valley to the Valley Gate in the south. By the time they reached the city, many of the streets were already in shadow as the sun started to slip low in the western sky.

* * *

Rivkah struggled through the reeds. The stalks were thick and strong, with fresh leaves cutting into her bare feet and ripping her dress. It was hard going. She had thought it might be quicker through here. Not so!

Why had she not taken her usual route across the stream? Crash! She broke through the reeds and landed right in a shallow pool of water. Her dress was wet and even the bundle of herbs she was carrying fell into the water. By Astarte! What else could go wrong? Not that it did the herbs any great harm, but still. She had been trying to keep them dry. Rivkah fought on. No use going back, she was nearly across the stream and the worst of the reeds was already behind her.

When she had finally fought her way across the short distance to the open, Rivkah collapsed onto the grass. She felt totally exhausted. She was a lot weaker these days. It had been ages since she last had a decent meal. For days now they had practically eaten only the herbs and leaves she collected. All the grain had been used up. The men hardly ever got any birds in their traps. Naarah wasn't pleased at all with the precious grain that had been wasted trying—mostly unsuccessfully—to attract birds.

The goats didn't give much milk at all now. That's why Joab and Amnon were talking about killing one of them for meat. Rivkah dreaded it. She had grown fond of the two goats. They were both such individuals, had their own distinctive character. Tera was like a haughty, old lady who immediately got upset if things didn't go her way. Kala was a lot sweeter, but also a lot more clever. You never knew where you stood with her. And now—to kill them! Impossible! But when her stomach complained at night Rivkah would have done anything to get some food, even if it meant . . . meant that one of the goats would no longer be there.

Rivkah got up and tied the bundle over her shoulders again. She trudged along the valley. The final hill up to the cave seemed so steep today. She could walk only slowly. Often she'd walked up here with a heavy water jar, but it had never felt as hard as today with just a bundle of herbs.

She saw Ayalah farther up the hill, probably walking to the grove in the sheltered depression just below the hilltop. Maybe she wanted to pick herbs among the oaks there. Not that there was a lot left so close to the cave.

Rivkah crawled into the cave and threw the bundle onto the floor. Only Naarah and Tilon were there.

"Where have you been so long?" Naarah hissed.

"I had to go further down the valley," Rivkah responded as she sat down.

"You were dawdling. Let me see what you've got there."

Naarah was rummaging through the bundle. "Yuck, it's all wet. What did you do with it?"

"I fell into the stream."

"You fell into the stream. Can't you even cross a little watercourse?"

Rivkah said nothing.

"Just look at how little you've brought! These leaves don't look nice at all." Naarah dug her hands deeper into the bundle and pulled out a bunch of wild cress. She held it up.

"Can you eat these?"

"Yes."

"I don't think so. We'll just end up with stomach cramps again. I wouldn't be surprised if you put them in here on purpose."

Naarah glanced sideward at Rivkah. Then she deliberately threw the cress outside.

"What are you doing?" Rivkah couldn't believe what she was seeing.

"Shut up."

"But that is perfectly good cress."

Ayalah had shown it to her on one of the first days they had gone out together and they had eaten it often since then. What was Naarah on about?

"Girl, don't speak to me like that. And don't think I'll take your excuses. We've also run out of water again because you couldn't carry enough up here."

"But I got some first thing this morning. There should be enough. Why...?"

"There's not enough," Naarah cut in. "You are just plain lazy and not prepared to do any hard work."

Rivkah became incensed. They were all outrageous and false accusations. It was so unjust!

"I milk the goats every morning and evening. I get water twice a day. I help with the cooking. I go out and get most of the food."

"You eat most of the food, you mean. Just another mouth to feed. You've lived on our provisions and drink more than your share of the goats' milk. Don't think I don't know what you're doing when you are milking."

"I am not taking any of the milk!" Rivkah screamed. She had always resisted the temptation. It was a baseless accusation.

"Of course you are! I don't know why Amnon let you stay with us, you, a city bird who has never learned to work. You just live off our family and take what's not yours. Well, we've had enough of you!"

"But . . ." Rivkah stammered. A lump formed in her throat.

"Don't think you can just sweet-talk Amnon again, you devious little scab!"

Rivkah ran out of the cave. It was all so unfair! She thought of going and finding Ayalah to tell her everything. But then she ran down the hill, down to the clearing behind the cistern. There she fell to her knees and dug in the soft soil. She knew the exact spot. Slowly she took the figurine of Isis and brushed off the dirt with her fingers. She wiped it clean on her dress. She kissed the head of Isis and felt again the familiar hieroglyphs on the amulet's back.

* * *

"The Assyrians have left our land, have returned beyond the Euphrates, even to the Tigris River. The LORD has rescued Jerusalem, he has redeemed the Daughter of Zion. The LORD has not given the city over to her enemies, he has protected his holy mountain.

"But the fields of Judah lie fallow and bare; the cities of Judah are in utter ruins.

Jackals fill their houses and owls dwell amongst their broken walls.

Thorns and briars cover the fields, wild goats leap across the lonely pastures.

And now, you will not return to your inheritance?

You will not go back to the fields of your fathers?

You will not rebuild the houses, nor till the fields of Judah?

Return to your cities and fields! Take care of your inheritance!"

"But, Father," Meshullam's uncle Nahshon argued, "we cannot just go back again. The Assyrians have given the land over to the cities of the Philistines, to Ashdod and Ekron. They will not let us dwell in peace in the land. The walled cities are destroyed, the towns are no more. We will not be safe; there will be no protection, no refuge."

"And what shall we eat?" Meshullam's father asked. "No plow tilled the ground after the early rain, no seed sprouted in the late rain. The enemy has cut down the olive groves, torn out the vineyards and destroyed the orchards. Our flocks have been decimated, our oxen sold or butchered. There is nothing to return to."

In the silence Meshullam looked at the men: there his grandfather, Micah, convinced that Judah had to be resettled; his own father, Ehud, and Uncle Nahshon, both scared about returning to an unprotected border zone; then one of the other elders of Moresheth-Gath, who now saw his future in Jerusalem; and their host Gamaliel, who had given hospitality to the family of Micah during the siege. Meshullam sat among them after supper, as Grandfather once again urged them to go to the land destroyed by the Assyrians. Was he finally tired of arguing? Could he see his sons' concerns? Even if he did, Micah was not one to give up. Had he not spoken to this stubborn people for many years? Had he not warned them again and again where their actions were leading them? He had even dared to speak out against the leaders of Judah, to point out the injustice that flourished in the country. Meshullam sensed that he would not capitulate to some frightened men from a country town, especially not his sons.

"No, my sons. Fear has clouded your sight, trembling has seized your mind. Have you not heard what the LORD has said to the king through the prophet Isaiah?

'This year you will eat what grows by itself and the second year what springs from that.

But in the third year, sow and reap, plant vineyards and eat their fruit.

Once more a remnant of the house of Judah will take root below and bear fruit above.

For out of Jerusalem will come a remnant, and out of Mount Zion a band of survivors.'

Do you not know that you are the remnant of Jacob? The LORD has preserved you to settle this good land again, to work the fields, plant vineyards, build houses and teach your children."

"But, Father, our future is here in Jerusalem. We will make this city great, build houses here," Uncle Nahshon interrupted.

"The Daughter of Zion is forlorn without her children, the cities of Judah. Jerusalem will not be able to stand alone in the land. And are not the fields of Jerusalem also destroyed, the vineyards of the city also rooted out? Just as you build up Jerusalem, so you must build up the towns of Judah, yes even the small villages and farmsteads. So, go and live in the land!"

The other elder from Moresheth-Gath shifted uneasily. "But our families! They have endured enough in the past months. We should not force them to live among wild beasts and empty hills, to face hunger and the threat of the Philistines, without protection from the weather or marauders. Our children will starve, our women will be too weak to give birth, our young men will not be able to hold the plow."

Micah looked at him, his eyes burning. It was the prophet speaking:

"Writhe in agony, O Daughter of Zion,

like a woman in labor,

for now you must leave the city to camp in the open field.

There you will be rescued.

There the LORD will redeem you out of the hand of your enemies."

* * *

The string was a bit shorter now. But once again the figure of Isis hung against her skin, hidden under her dress. Somehow the amulet felt different. Somehow she was more aware of the power of Isis.

Rivkah slowly stirred the stew inside the pot. They had had plenty of meat in the last few days. Amnon and Joab had finally butchered Tera, the goat. At first Rivkah had only swallowed the meat with difficulty, but now she was glad for the food. Still, whenever she went over to the other cave to look after Kala, the place felt empty without the second goat. It was obvious that Kala missed her companion, too.

Rivkah tossed a few herbs into the stew. It would be ready soon. She looked up to the ridge. Amnon and Joab should be back soon. Inside the cave Naarah and Ayalah were repairing blankets. Ayalah had suggested cooking outside on such a fine winter's day. Rivkah was glad for it.

When she glanced across the ridge again she saw Amnon running down the hill. What had happened? Then she saw Joab on the ridge as he came over from the valley beyond. He was running too, with Achan bounding along behind him.

"They're coming back," Rivkah called to the women inside the cave.

"Good," came the reply.

But this was not a normal homecoming. Amnon was out of breath when he arrived.

"The Assyrians have gone!"

Rivkah looked at him blankly.

Ayalah and Naarah rushed from the cave.

"The Assyrians have gone!" Amnon repeated.

"They've really gone?" asked Ayalah.

"Yes!"

Joab and Achan arrived.

"The LORD struck the army of the Assyrian king and decimated their strength. Humbled, the Assyrians have left for their own country."

"Glory be to the LORD," Ayalah shouted.

"Hallelujah!" Naarah exclaimed.

The smile on Rivkah's face grew until she burst into joyous laughter. The others were shouting. She hugged Ayalah and danced with Achan.

Naarah was the first to stop and remind them that the stew would burn if nobody looked after it. But tonight nothing could dampen the mood. They sat down to eat the evening meal inside the cave and no one complained about that slightly nutty, burnt flavor. The meat had never tasted that good.

"We met a fellow Judahite who was returning from the hill country in the east. He was going to the valleys," Amnon explained. "He told us how the Assyrians had threatened Jerusalem, but could not take it. And so after he had suffered heavy losses, the king of Assyria returned home."

"The man was going back to see what had happened to our lands," Joab added.

"The Assyrians took many prisoners with them. Their king destroyed the cities of Judah and gave the land to the kings of the Philistines. But nobody knows whether the Philistines have come to work the land or if the fields lie fallow and bare," Amnon continued.

"Some are going back, he said," Joab carried on.

"We should return to our village, too," Amnon proclaimed.

"But it is all destroyed. How can we . . . ?" Naarah began.

"It is our land, our inheritance. And if we go now, we have the best chance of claiming it back before others settle there." Amnon looked around the cave. "We will go there tomorrow and start building the houses again."

"Now? In winter? Will you build a house now?"

"Once spring arrives there will be work aplenty, if we want to cultivate the land again. We have to start now, even if it is only a small house. No, we have to start building now."

"But what about Beriah? Shouldn't we wait until he returns?" asked Naarah.

"We cannot wait for him. We will move as soon as we can. I don't think he will come back any time soon. He will be busy in Jerusalem."

"Do you think he got to Jerusalem?" enquired Rivkah.

"He shouldn't have had a problem. There were no Assyrians left there," responded Joab. "He'll stay there."

Ayalah looked at her son, "So you want to go back to Shechar and build there?"

"Back to Shechar," he confirmed.

Turning to Joab he continued, "Joab, come back with us. It's better to stay together at times such as these. Help us to build a new house and a new life."

Joab stroked his beard.

"My village is destroyed and I do not have any descendants to pass my inheritance on to. I will go with your family."

Amnon nodded, then looked at Rivkah. "You are welcome too, Rivkah . . . and you, Achan. Come with us."

Welcome? Rivkah couldn't believe it. Did Amnon know the things his wife had said to her? Rivkah could not imagine continuing to live with Naarah. But where else could she go? Maybe Beriah?

"Thank you, Amnon. But I really want to go to Jerusalem."

"To Jerusalem? All alone?"

"That's just madness! How will you get there?" Joab couldn't understand it.

Even Naarah seemed surprised. "So you really want to leave us. Don't you think there is space in our house for you?"

Only Ayalah seemed to understand Rivkah. She knew of Rivkah's sorrows. "Let her go. She will make it to Jerusalem. And she can seek a future there just as well."

"But, Mother! A girl alone on the road."

"I think Rivkah can manage. It's not that far. Only three days or so."

Amnon turned to Rivkah. "Do you even know the way?"

Rivkah shook her head. "But I will find it."

"You will find out how hard it is. We've warned you. Think again, girl."

Doubt began to rise in Rivkah's mind, but she wouldn't give in now.

"I will go to Jerusalem."

* * *

It wasn't a large group that left Jerusalem. Leah looked back over the little caravan of people and the few cattle, sheep and donkeys that were setting out from the gate. Eight families, that was all. Uncle Nahshon and his family weren't coming. They had decided to stay in Jerusalem, to make their home in this city. Others from Moresheth-Gath had done the same. But some families were heeding the call of Micah, and not only those from Moresheth-Gath. Families that had fled to Jerusalem from other Judahite towns had decided to join the group.

Leah's father Ehud led them. Her grandfather Micah had insisted on coming too, even though the journey would be hard for him and he could no longer do any heavy work. He was determined to return, to see the people settle again in the land. He walked back there with Meshullam, alongside their donkey. The two of them looked back at the city they were leaving. Grandfather was talking loudly to Meshullam, moving his arms dramatically as he was bringing home his points. Leah couldn't understand him from the distance, but she did know that Grandfather always had plenty to say about Jerusalem—Daughter of Zion as he often called it—and its relationship with the land of Judah. She had heard so much of it before.

"Leah, when will be back home again?" her little sister Tirzah asked her, "I so want to see our house again."

"You know, Tirzah, I don't think our house will be there anymore. Mother told you already, didn't she? The enemy has gone through all the land and destroyed the houses," Leah warned her. Tirzah would be upset when she saw the devastation. For Leah was sure they would find only ruins by the accounts she had heard. A few people had seen the destruction. Apparently the Assyrians had not left one stone upon another.

"But our house was so big," Tirzah said.

"I know it was nice and big. But the soldiers have destroyed all the houses, the small ones and the big ones too."

"Where are we going to live then?"

"We will build a house, Tirzah. Father said we would. It will be totally new. It will be nice."

"Will it be big?"

"Yes, it will be big. Bigger than the house in Jerusalem. And there will not be so many people."

"But there will be animals?"

"Yes, we will have more animals. We will need cows to pull the plow, and we'll have sheep and goats."

Tirzah was quiet for a while. Then she looked at Leah again. "When will we be there?"

"I don't know exactly, but it will take us two or three days. It's a long way."

"Not that long, really," a voice said suddenly behind Leah. She turned around. It was the boy she had noticed before, when they were setting out. She didn't know him. He smiled at her. Dark curls framed his handsome face with that strong chin. His robe wasn't anything special, but the way he draped his elegant belt around the waist spoke of refinement. Leah smiled back at him.

"It's not that far, really. Yes, we might not get there that fast with all these people and will have to spend a night or two on the way somewhere. But I could probably walk it in little more than a day," he continued.

He stopped and leaned his head to one side, looking at her. "We haven't met. I am Nadab from Shaphir. My mother and father, my brother and sister, we have come with you to settle the land. May the LORD bless you."

"My name is Leah, daughter of Ehud from Moresheth-Gath," Leah responded.

"Shalom, Leah, daughter of Ehud. I am so happy to be here with you, to travel back to reclaim the land and restore dominion to Judah. This journey has been blessed by the LORD."

He closed his eyes briefly as if in silent prayer, then looked directly at Leah. She felt herself blush. He raised his eyebrows briefly, then winked at her. "We will get to know each other well. I do not doubt it."

Tirzah must have felt left out. "And I am Tirzah," she interrupted.

Nadab looked at her.

"This is my little sister Tirzah," Leah said.

"The LORD bless you, Tirzah." Nadab turned his full attention to her. "How could I not notice such a pretty girl? I am sure you will become a beautiful young woman." He leaned forward and tousled Tirzah's hair. "Eh?"

Tirzah laughed.

Leah looked at them, not sure what to say, not sure whether she liked the way he touched her sister. But when Nadab turned to Leah again she basked in his attention. He walked beside her for several hours that day.

* * *

Rivkah stayed while they built the house. Every morning Joab and Amnon would go down the valley to the site of Shechar. Using stones from the destroyed houses they built a new house for the family. It wasn't big: only three rooms and no upper floor. "We can add that in summer," was Amnon's comment. They worked each day, even when heavy winds drove rain across the land, and the cold penetrated to the bones. On those days they arrived wet and exhausted at the cave in the evening, eagerly stretching their arms towards the fire, leaning towards it and enjoying the heat warming their frozen faces. They ate the little food that the women could offer them and fell on their sleeping benches dead tired. But they would sleep only fitfully. At least, Rivkah noticed that Joab did not lie quietly at night. Sometimes he would not go to the sleeping chamber in the evening and instead curled up beside the fire, dozing there until it burnt down before retiring to the bench. And yet, every morning they went out again, trudging to Shechar to continue with the house.

Rivkah came with them only twice. The first time was on a fine winter's day. The site of the village was on a hillside facing the rising sun. Two streams joined in the valley that stretched to hills in the east. Joined by other streams, the waters turned towards the west where they flowed past the city of Lachish, or rather the ruins of what was once Rivkah's home. Amnon told her that. She gazed at the bubbling waters and thought of the stream that wound its way past Lachish. How often had she looked down into the valley and hardly noticed it circling past the city. The last time she had seen it, it was dry. The last time she had been there, darkness was already falling. The last time she had crossed it, she had feared for her life. She had lived, but only through the sacrifice of another. She remembered Bath-Shua's scream that night. She shuddered. It seemed so unreal in broad daylight, but the memory still came to her.

The outline of the house was already clearly discernible, though the walls were still low. Amnon and Joab had used the larger stones to build up the outer courses of the wall and now filled the centre with smaller stones. Once it was level they would build more courses to get the walls to the required height. The destroyed buildings gave them plenty of stones to build with. And since the sun was still too weak to dry any mud bricks they had decided to use stones for the greater part of the house.

The second time Rivkah went with them the sky was grey. Drops of rain fell intermittently and a cold wind blew from the west. The walls of the house were already complete. From the distance it really looked like a home, not just like the uninhabited shell that it was. Only when she got closer could Rivkah see that it was not yet complete. The roof beams were already in place, but the house was still open to the sky. It was their task today to find branches for the ceiling. Together with Joab she dragged whatever she could find in the surrounding area to the house. Each time she deposited another load she stood behind the house wall for a moment, sheltering from the biting wind. Yes, she could imagine the house giving protection from the cold. And though she could hardly picture it, she was sure it would provide welcome relief from the searing sun during the heat of summer.

They gathered sufficient branches that day, but Amnon decided not to start work on the roof when the rain became heavier. The mud layer covering the branches would only have been dissolved by the water. They walked back to the cave in the pelting rain. Rivkah got totally drenched, her clothes heavy with water. That night she eagerly crouched beside the fire, but even it could not really warm her. She shivered when it had finally died down, just a few embers glowing at its centre. Still the exhaustion helped her to fall asleep. She woke later in the night, feeling numb with cold.

Luckily Amnon and Joab decided not to go back to the house the following day. Amnon did not trust the weather. However, it was another few weeks before the house was finally finished. They spent part of the time carving tools to again start farming the land. Amnon retrieved his plow and repaired it lovingly. Not that it would see much use this year. The season for sowing was already past and they had hardly any seed to sow, anyway. This year they would have to rely on the wheat the land itself provided. There should be enough, with little pockets of wheat and barley growing here and there in the fields devastated by the enemy. Harvest would be difficult. Naarah was not sure they would find enough food until then.

"Amnon, and what will we live on until we can harvest some barley?" she asked him again, after he had tried to calm her, assuring her that everything would be alright. He had said it so often these weeks and Rivkah was sure he believed it. But even she shared some of Naarah's doubts. Would the land really provide?

* * *

A few charred beams rose from the flattened rubble. Amongst burnt and shattered mud bricks a few stones stood out. All traces of walls were obliterated. The winter rains had carved small channels amongst the ash and clay debris. In some places puddles had formed, spreading a muddy sludge over the surface which now started to dry. The place looked barren, razed to the ground. It was nearly unimaginable that once houses had stood here, that once this had been a lively town, their town. Meshullam walked amid the scene of destruction. It must have happened months ago, but the ferocity of the fire was still evident, the vengeance with which the enemy leveled the place plain to see. Meshullam could hardly orientate himself. Where had their house been? Somewhere over there near the western edge. It had been near the town wall. There was no wall now, only a tumble of stones scattered over the slopes of the hill.

Meshullam walked over to the place where their house had been. He sank down when he reached it. He sat there, right in the dirt and ash. His knees just wouldn't hold him. They felt too weak. He combed his hand through his hair. His breathing was heavy as if in pain. Only a single tear stole into his eye. The memories that came flooding back only increased his sorrow. How often he had felt secure and comforted in this home and now it was flattened, unrecognizable. Nothing indicated that this had been their home, that once it had been full of life, of laughter and longing, of daily grind and celebration, of meals shared and work planned. It had once been at the centre of his life.

Suddenly Meshullam noticed his father beside him. He looked up. Father's face clearly showed the emotion at the sight. "I don't think we'll bring the others here," he said. Meshullam nodded and looked at the ground again.

"Come, we'll go back," Father said. They walked across the hill slowly, calling the other men who had come up here with them. They had all expected the destruction, but seeing the reality still shocked them. Their faces reflected the pain they felt.

That night they got together and decided not to build their houses on the remains of the old town. They would not go back. No, they would build on the ridge to the north, where the small band would not be surrounded by the remains of the destruction. Here, the fields and water were close-by, too. The hillsides were not as steep, the location not as defensible, but had those things stopped the enemy before?

Their former home would not be far away, though trees and shrubs would largely shield it from view. Here, near their chosen location, the Assyrians had left an olive grove intact, giving the settlers the oil they needed.

Micah, the prophet was led to the destroyed town the next day. Meshullam did not go with them, but Leah later told him that she had heard that Grandfather had wept when he saw the place where once their town had stood. But he accepted the judgment. Meshullam heard him say so later on. Judah had sinned greatly and it had felt the consequences. Praise to God that he had preserved a remnant.

* * *

They had already brought many of the tools, the pots and jars down to the house in Shechar. Today they would leave the cave and move to the house. Their few provisions were easily packed. They did not have much food left and would be forced to gather what they could find. But winter was nearly over and spring would bring new growth, the promise of life. When the flowers started to bloom, birds would again move across the land in greater numbers, migrating from their winter homes to the north. Grain would grow until it matured in early summer. Life would be hard, but there would be an end to the hunger. For the winter had brought abundant rain and the soil was moist, waiting to bring forth plants when the sun warmed its surface.

They stood in the front chamber. This had been their home for the last few months. Here they had eaten and worked, talked and sang. Rivkah's eyes wandered over the drawings and words that Beriah had incised into the walls. Amnon must have been looking at the drawings too.

Daughter of Lachish 137

"Beriah was right. The LORD answered his petition and has come to our aid. Now even the Assyrians know that the LORD is indeed the God of Judah. The Assyrians were indeed cursed in their pride. They insulted the LORD and his people. And now the curse has come upon their heads."

Amnon walked along the walls.

"No one should disturb these words for they are consecrated to the LORD. Joab, give me your knife. I will write on this wall to protect these words."

Joab gave him the knife. Slowly and laboriously Amnon set to work.

"'Cursed be the one who erases!' These are the words I have seen protecting the messages on tombs. But though we are in a grave here, the words will protect messages of hope, prayers and curses fulfilled."

Amnon thought long before he started to slowly etch each letter into the limestone.

"You can go outside. I'll be finished soon."

Did he not want them to watch his slow progress?

Outside, Ayalah called Rivkah to her side. They walked several paces away from the others.

"So you are going to Jerusalem, Rivkah?"

Rivkah nodded.

Ayalah continued, "You are right. I don't think you could live with us in Shechar. Life would have been too difficult. Naarah has still not accepted you and I don't think she ever will. But I will miss you, Rivkah. You have been a good companion, quick to learn and always willing to work. You have been a great help. May the LORD bless you. May you find a home. Don't forget to look in unexpected places. You never know what the LORD has planned for you."

"Mother Ayalah, I will always remember you. You were always kind to me. I am thankful for the way you taught me to recognize leaves and herbs, the way you taught me to milk."

Both of them smiled at the memory.

"It is done!" Amnon shouted as he came out of the cave. He and Joab placed a stone in front of the entrance. Amnon went to get Kala the goat. She came willingly out of the cave. He handed the rope to Achan and then went back to put a few stones in front of the entrance. "These caves should not be a place for owls and jackals," he commented.

The group slung the bundles over their shoulders, ready to go. Rivkah stood a little away from them.

"We are ready to leave."

Amnon turned towards Rivkah. "You are welcome to come with us, even if you want to go to Jerusalem. The journey is dangerous and you do not know the way. Stay with us for a while. You can travel on later. Someone may pass on his way to Jerusalem, but do not go alone."

Rivkah shook her head. "I am going now."

"But think, girl."

"It may be a long time before someone passes Shechar. I can't wait until then. I'm going to Jerusalem."

"Shechar is not far from the road into the hill country," Amnon tried to argue.

Rivkah just shook her head. "No, I'm going now. Amnon, thank you for your concern, but I have decided to go to Jerusalem."

"Let her go then," Naarah told Amnon. "She always does whatever she fancies without thought of the consequences. And she hasn't learnt to be thankful for the help we offer."

Naarah's words only confirmed what Rivkah already knew: she couldn't stay. "I am deeply thankful for all you have done," she told them, "but my face is set towards Jerusalem."

Amnon sighed. "You have decided to go to Jerusalem. I am sad you do not want to join us. But go in the name of God and may his face shine on you. May he keep you safe." He placed his hand on her head as if in a blessing and then lightly ruffled her hair.

Joab wished her "God be with you" and Naarah mumbled something similar. Rivkah gave Achan a kiss on the cheek and patted the goat. She embraced Ayalah as she fought back the tears stealing into her eyes.

Amnon set off first. He led the little band down the valley. Rivkah stood to watch them go, then turned and set her face towards the north wind walking with her back to the midday sun. When she reached the top of the ridge she stopped and looked back. She could still see the others walking along the valley, past the reeds. She had said goodbye to all she had known in the past few months. Where would the future lead her? With a sigh she continued, descending into the next valley.

PART THREE

Chapter 10

Trembling, the sheep lay on the bare ground, its sides heaving with effort. Its breath came fast, its mouth was half open. A weak "baa" escaped its throat as it labored in pain.

"Come on, girl," Meshullam urged quietly, "come on, push!" He rubbed its woolly belly. The sheep hardly responded. It was too exhausted to push, too weak to try again. Shimei held the sheep's head, stroked its ears and neck. Sometimes the ewe looked at him fleetingly before closing her eyes again. Would she make it? They had been kneeling beside the ewe since morning. She was straining and pressing but, so far the lamb had not been born.

No one had realized the ewe was pregnant when they had purchased her cheaply at the market outside Jerusalem's walls. She wasn't much of a sheep, not well proportioned and far too thin. Meshullam had seen that immediately. But then, many animals were not in the best condition this year. And she had come as part of a deal. And so Father had bought her. Who would have thought that she would still give birth so late in winter? Most ewes had already had their young weeks ago. It had come as a surprise when Meshullam had seen her prancing around the meadow nervously, lying down frequently before getting up again and walking a few steps. There really had not been any signs. Meshullam had put her growing girth down to the better food she was getting now. But her udder had not swollen to alert him that she was about to have a lamb.

When he had seen her pushing and straining, the vulva opening, he had suddenly realized what was happening. The whole family had been excited at the news. They would have a lamb this year. And so they had waited. But nothing had happened. The ewe became increasingly distressed, lying down for longer but still getting up frequently. Then the water bag had broken, but she hadn't given birth. Father had felt the lamb inside her, had tried to assist, but it did not come.

"We have to get the lamb out," Father said, "otherwise both the sheep and the lamb will die." He put his hand inside the uterus and took hold of the front feet. He was able to pull them out.

"Merab, can you hold the sheep?"

Mother knelt beside the ewe putting her arms around the woolly body.

"And Meshullam, you pull the lamb out. I'll guide it."

Meshullam grabbed the soft feet and started to pull. They were so wet and slippery he could hardly get a good handhold.

"Again," Father urged him. The sheep groaned. "It's alright," Shimei told the sheep, continuing to rub its neck and holding its head.

As Meshullam pulled, the lamb's head appeared. "More." Meshullam leaned back. The head, then the shoulders slipped into the open. Meshullam paused.

Father looked at him. "Gently now."

Slowly, Meshullam pulled out the lamb's thin body. It flopped onto the ground. He wiped away the membrane covering the lamb and cleaned its nose and mouth. Was it alive? Father took the lamb and blew into its nostrils. It spluttered and began to move slowly, starting to breathe. It was so small, so thin, as it lay there on the dirt. Father moved it to the ewe's head to let her lick it, but she was so exhausted she did not really take any notice of the lamb.

Shimei guided her head to the lamb, made her smell her own young.

"What is it?" he asked, "a boy or a girl?"

Meshullam looked.

"It's a boy."

"I'll call him Uzi." Shimei rubbed his hand across the wet body of the lamb.

"Uzi, little lamb, welcome to this world."

Later, Meshullam lifted up the sheep while Mother and Shimei held Uzi to the teat. Uzi felt it and began to suckle.

*　*　*

Leah tossed another handful of dry grass into the mud sludge. Meshullam mixed it with a strong, wooden stick, lifting parts of the mixture and folding it back again, turning and pressing it. Beside him was Nadab and a few of the older boys stirring and trampling the mud. It had a thick consistency by now with the long stalks of grass making it hard to move and shape. Leah could see it was hard work for the boys, even though they tried to look strong and easily able to handle the task.

"That's good now," Meshullam gasped, motioning her not to put any more grass into the mixture. Of course, he had to tell her! After all she was just his little sister.

Nadab smiled at her. "Thanks Leah, I think that should do." His voice did not betray any effort. He seemed so much more at ease with this work. He was a strong man!

"You can put it into the frames now." Once more, Meshullam thought he had to tell her what to do. Leah did not bother to reply. While the boys leaned on their sticks and forks, Leah and the women carried the mud mixture to the drying area on the level ground above the pit. They patted and packed the mud mixture tightly into the frames, then removed the frames and set them down in line with the molded mud squares.

The frames were filled again and again until long lines of wet mud bricks stretched across the area. Now they would have to wait for the sun to do its part. Today there were no clouds in the sky, the sun shining bright and clear. But only two days ago they had had a downpour which moistened the earth and had brought out the spring flowers, now that the sun warmed the ground. If only the weather would hold! The mud bricks would need a few days to dry. And they urgently needed the bricks. During the last rain, the settlers had crammed into a few caves and under a tent or two. It was less than satisfactory, really. Leah could see that her mother hadn't been pleased. She wasn't the only one. The women wanted a home, the men a house to call their own. And that's why house construction was the most important task, even if it meant they couldn't start building animal pens or caring for the land. The men had already decided where to build the few houses for the eight families and had started to lay the stone foundations. They would not be big houses. There was no time for that now. But they could always add to them later on.

A cloud cast a shadow across the bricks. Leah looked up anxiously. But it was nothing to worry about. It was only a small band of cloud wafting in from the west. It carried no rain and soon disappeared.

* * *

The fields shone red in the early afternoon sun. Like a carpet of crimson wool, the anemones covered the valley sides among the freshly green hills. On slender stalks the flowers swayed in the gentle breeze, ripples of red wafting across the earth. Rivkah stopped and looked at the spectacle spread out before her as she topped another ridge. She had come across a few flowers on the way, had even stopped occasionally to admire them but, the concentration of red, the sheer number of flowers in this little valley overwhelmed her. There, at the edges of the red meadow as it blended into green bushes and the newly green forest, spots of yellow stood in contrast with the dominant red. Wild flax had found a hold in the stony soil.

Rivkah stood and watched. All the anxiety, all the fear of wandering alone through this empty land drained from her and was replaced by a deep joy. With a happy cry she bounded down into the valley. Jumping across stones she descended the gently sloping sides. Halfway down she let go of her bundle. It fell among yellow flax and small violets. And then she was among the anemones, plunged into the sea of red. Laughing, she parted the stands of flowers as she ran. Somewhere in the middle of the field she spread her arms and danced. Twirling her body round and round until she felt dizzy, she fell into the flowers. The petals caressed her face as she knelt among the anemones.

"Uh," she whispered and with a laugh flopped backwards onto the ground. Lying there, her breathing became quiet. It was so still here on the ground among the green stems of the anemones. Closing her eyes, she inhaled deeply. It was the scent of flowers, of fresh growth, of moist soil. She peered up the slender green stems to the red blossoms waving lightly above her. And beyond the red was the brilliant blue of the sky with just a few streaky clouds adding touches of white.

Rivkah did not know how long she lay there, enjoying the peace that flowed through her. Nothing disturbed the stillness, until Rivkah noticed the beetle that wandered down one of the stalks. She watched it coming down gingerly, before losing it from sight. Was it the same one or another that little later climbed back up one of the stalks nearby? When it reached the flower, it crawled along the petals and squeezed its way inside. It must have been there for a while, but then Rivkah saw it unfold its wings and buzz off across the field. Gone!

Suddenly her thoughts came back to her journey, to her aim of reaching Jerusalem. She wasn't sure whether she was going the right way, had not met anyone yet. She had come across a few destroyed villages, had found cisterns and abandoned orchards. But she had not come across any good road, only small tracks and paths. And so she had walked northward across hills and through small valleys, sometimes retracing her steps, uncertain where to go. Each time she came to another ridge she had looked down, hopeful to find a sign. Worry had overcome her. But that was gone now. She would make it! She had to go on.

Slowly Rivkah got up and walked up the valley again to retrieve her bundle. It took a while to find it, but she never had any concern she had lost it.

She walked slowly down the valley, making her way through the flowers, her hands gliding across the red beauty, the soft petals touching her fingers. She still would have to find water somewhere and a place to spend the night. And maybe she would even find the way.

It was late in the afternoon when she noticed the hill rising steeply ahead. Behind it, a ridge seemed to stretch into the distance with the valley narrowing to its east and ending in a line of rolling hills. She walked past the steep hill as the sun sank lower in the west, the hill casting its shadow across the valley. Rivkah drew her dress closer around her, feeling the sudden cold. Up on the hill there must have once been a sizeable town but, now, only the boulders strewn across its slopes, the debris of mud bricks and charred beams indicated that this place once had a wall and houses. It did not look inviting. But there must have been a road to Jerusalem from here. Rivkah was sure of it.

Rather than trudging up the steep sides she decided to approach the town from the ridge to its north. Rivkah made her way past the caves set in stark, white limestone formations opposite the former town. She chose a gentle route up to the ridge trying to avoid the densest of growth. As she walked she suddenly noticed she was on a path, a path that must still be used today. She could make out the imprint of a sandal at one point. She was less than halfway up the hill when she heard singing. It was a woman's voice, clear and gentle. Rivkah froze and stopped. Should she continue? What if . . . ? But maybe the woman knew the way to Jerusalem, maybe she could even show her a good place to stay for the night, something better than the cold caves she had passed in the valley below. Rivkah took another few steps. To her right she could see a water jar bobbing above some bushes. The woman must be fetching water. Yes, she would go and meet her.

* * *

Leah lowered the empty water jar from her shoulder. She dipped the pitcher into the pool below the spring and slowly filled the jar. The spring would only flow in winter and spring, but a channel led to a series of cisterns. Plastering the cisterns had been one of the first tasks when the settlers had arrived and chosen the location of the settlement. They were not being filled yet, but soon the water would have to be diverted into the cisterns. In the past, when they still lived on the knoll, they had carried water from the well below the town. This spring was used to water the animals and some of the orchards nearby.

When the jar was full, Leah placed the pitcher beside the spring again. She was a bit late tonight and so had come here on her own. The other girls from the settlement had already fetched water tonight. But she had been busy today. They had moved into their new house. The family of Micah had a home again. It was the second house to be finished. A few things still had to be completed, of course, and it was not yet fully furnished—but that would come. It had been exciting to get their belongings under the roof, to put them where they belonged. Mother had immediately designated a use for each room and each corner. There was a place for everything. And everybody knew where they would eat, work and sleep. Mother made sure there was not even the chance of a discussion. Ah, it would be good to sleep under their own roof again.

Leah took the water jar and placed it on her head. She sang a song as she walked back. The jar might be heavy, but her heart was light.

"Like an apple tree among the trees of the forest glade
is my lover among the many young men.
I delight to sit in his cooling shade
and his fruit is so sweet,
oh, so sweet to my taste."

Suddenly she stopped. The song died on her lips. Hadn't she just seen somebody? Yes, up ahead a strange girl stood on the path. Who was she? What was she doing here? Slowly, Leah edged forward. The girl smiled hesitantly.

"Shalom," she said.

"Shalom," Leah responded.

The two looked at each other. Leah guessed the girl was about the same age as her. She seemed to come from a very poor family. Her dress was torn and patched. She had no real shoes; nothing but a few scraps of leather and cloth covered her feet. A dirty scarf covered her head; the hair underneath it seemed unkempt.

"What are you doing here?" Leah asked.

"I am on my way to Jerusalem," the girl answered.

"You are travelling then?"

"Yes, I am travelling. Do you live here?"

"Yes, we do. We have just moved back here from Jerusalem."

"So you know the way to Jerusalem from here?"

"Yes, but you better speak to my father. He will be able to tell you more."

"Thank you."

"Come with me. I'll take you to him."

The two girls walked up to the ridge, Leah ahead.

"Where do you come from?" she asked.

"From Shechar."

"From where?"

"Shechar. A village near Lachish."

"And you are going to Jerusalem?"

"Yes."

"Do you know anybody there?"

"Yes, I do. His name is Beriah."

The name didn't mean anything to Leah. She had heard of a few people with that name, but didn't really know any of them. They walked on in silence.

"My name is Leah."

"I am Rivkah."

They reached the settlement. Leah walked towards the new house. A dim glimmer of light shone into the darkening evening outside. She turned around at the threshold.

"Come in."

* * *

Rivkah entered the small house. In the light of one oil lamp she saw the family gathered for supper. The mother was ladling the stew into bowls held by the eager arms of the children. Two men sat to one side of the circle holding their filled bowls. It was the older man who first noticed that Leah had not returned alone. After studying Rivkah for a few moments he directed a questioning look in Leah's direction.

"This is Rivkah, a traveler on the way to Jerusalem."

The heads of the others shot around, curiously looking at the girl standing there just inside the door.

"She needs more information about the way to Jerusalem, Father. So I invited her to the house."

The younger of the two men nodded.

"Welcome to this house, Rivkah."

Rivkah came closer to the circle. By now Leah had set down the water jar and came to join the meal.

"Come, sit down, girl, and have something to eat. Join us in the meal," the old man said.

Rivkah sat down beside Leah. The woman got up quickly, returned with another bowl and after filling it, gave it to Rivkah. Leah passed her some bread. Now that she was part of the circle, the light fell on her and the family studied her more closely again.

"Where did you say you came from?" Leah's father asked.

"From Shechar near Lachish."

"Oh yes, I have heard of it. Small place. Does it still stand?"

Rivkah shook her head.

"I thought so. The Assyrians destroyed just about all of that area."

"And you escaped the Assyrians?" the old man asked.

Rivkah gulped down a mouthful of hot stew before she answered.

"I hid with others in a cave. They went back to the village. I am going to Jerusalem."

"Do you know somebody there?"

"Yes, Beriah, son of Jesher."

They did not recognize the name.

"The secretary of the governor of Libnah," she added.

"I had not heard of him, even in the days when Libnah was still standing. He is in Jerusalem now?"

"Yes, he was going there."

"Is he your relative?" the woman asked.

"No, but he was with us in the cave. We gave him hospitality."

They didn't ask any more questions, instead talking excitedly about houses.

After a while, Leah's father looked at her.

"You are welcome to spend some time here in this house, Rivkah."

"And you can't go to Jerusalem in that dress, girl. I will give you one of Leah's old ones," Leah's mother added.

"Which one?" Leah queried.

"The one you wore the other day. You complained it was a bit small for you. It should be just fine for Rivkah here." The woman looked at Rivkah, measuring her size in her mind.

"Thank you." Only now did Rivkah become aware of her clothes, realized that she must look dirty and unkempt. Her dress was just hideous. And she didn't know when she had last combed her hair. She wanted to cover it up again with the scarf, but it would not be good manners to do that inside when eating a meal. And her headscarf was in fact little more than a dirty rag. Rivkah felt ashamed.

The boys across from her were poking each other, giggling and saying something she couldn't understand. Were they laughing at her? Rivkah felt the color rise to her face. She concentrated on her food and, after draining the bowl, cleaned it with bread. She set it down in front of her. The others had finished their meal, too.

"Come Rivkah, we'll look for the dress now . . . Leah, come with us." The woman lit another lamp. The two girls left the circle with her and climbed to the upper storey. Rivkah realized that the house must be very new, the wood just hewn, the mud bricks recently formed and laid. They did not have a clothes chest yet. Leah's mother hauled a bundle of clothes from a corner. Leah held the oil lamp. Finally her mother seemed to have found what she was looking for. She held up a simple dress.

"That's it, isn't it?"

"Yes," Leah agreed. Her mother held it against Rivkah's body. "That should fit."

Rivkah changed while the two waited. When she put on her new dress her fingers touched the figurine of Isis that still hung from her neck. She stroked it, traced the hieroglyphs again. Isis was with her. Now the figurine lay against her skin under a new dress. Her old dress lay discarded on the floor.

"Take it down with you and leave it by the door."

From downstairs strains of music drifted upwards. The others had obviously gotten their instruments out and started to sing. Rivkah climbed down the ladder with the others, dropped the old dress by the door and joined the family circle again. The old man was busy plucking the lyre, the older of the boys played the flute. Now the women joined in the chorus:

"In God, whose word I praise, in God, I trust.
I will not be afraid.
What can mortal man do to me?"

In a croaky voice the old man sang verse after verse, sorrowful when lamenting his anguish, joyful when giving thanks to God.

"Today we are celebrating because we have a house again," Leah told Rivkah.

Song after song gave praise to the LORD, song after song spoke of his power and love. From the young boy to the old man the whole family joined in the singing, clapping the rhythm with their hands when the melody became more animated. Rivkah knew only one of the psalms, and then, not well. She joined in quietly. Somehow she felt so out of place here, and yet also accepted.

"Just one more psalm now and you should all be off to bed," Leah's father said.

"Let's sing 'Praise awaits you, oh God,'" the small boy said.

Leah groaned quietly, but the old man's hand was already plucking the strings. The whole family joined him and sang:

"Praise awaits you, oh God, in Zion;
to you our vows will be fulfilled.
O you, who hear prayer,
to you all men will come.

"You care for the land and water it;
you enrich it abundantly.
The streams of God are filled with water
to provide grain,
for so you have ordained it.
You drench its furrows,
level its ridges,
soften it with showers,
bless its crops.

"The grasslands of the desert overflow,

and the hills are clothed with gladness.
The meadows are covered with flocks
and the valleys are mantled with wheat.
They shout for joy and sing."

Chapter 11

"Meshullam, come! Uzi is hungry," Shimei called him.

"Just wait. I'll come soon," Meshullam shouted back. He was carrying mud bricks to the new house they were constructing. This would be the third. The village was growing steadily. At the house he put the mud bricks down on the pile. The men took them from there to construct the walls. Father was working with them, too.

"Father, I have to be off to feed the lamb again."

"That's fine. We have quite a few bricks here. The other boys should be able to keep up until lunch."

Meshullam ran over to their house. Outside, they had built a pen for the sheep. Right now only Uzi, the newborn lamb, and its mother were in there. Meshullam jumped into the pen.

"Couldn't you have come earlier?" Shimei greeted him.

"Sorry, I still had to carry the bricks to the pile."

Shimei held the little lamb. It was hungrily pressing its mouth against the body of its mother, searching for the teats. The sheep just lay there, legs folded under its belly, head resting on the ground. It was not interested in its young. It had never recovered from the difficult birth and had hardly been able to stand up, let alone walk around. For over a week now, Meshullam had cut grass for the sheep and given it water. For over a week now, he had lifted the sheep up every time Uzi needed a drink. Shimei always held the lamb, guiding it to the teats.

Once again Meshullam lifted the ewe's weak body. She was so light now. Her flanks had sunk in, her eyes were unfocused. Her breathing was shallow. Shimei guided Uzi to the teats. He drank hungrily. But there was not much milk and the udder was empty all too soon.

Meshullam lay the sheep down again. There was not much life left in her. She did not respond to any of his efforts. She did not take the grass he offered her, did not seem to notice the water he gave her. Even when he poured some over her nose she did not flinch. Meshullam was worried. The ewe's life was ebbing away. But she still had a lamb to feed. In his panic Meshullam tried to make her drink some water at least.

Turning her mouth to one side, he dripped some into her throat. But she didn't swallow and the water just flowed out of the side of her mouth. It was no use. The ewe had no strength left to live.

"What's happening?" Shimei looked at him.

"She's dying, Shimei."

"Can't we do something? Should I get Father?"

Meshullam shook his head.

"I think she is beyond help. But yes, go and get Father. He had better see for himself."

Shimei ran off.

Meshullam held the sheep's head in his hands. Her breath was so faint he could hardly feel it. He did not know exactly when she slipped away, but as he finally let go of her head, he knew she was dead. He stood up and looked at the sheep, the little lamb rolled up peacefully by her side.

Shimei came back hauling Father to the pen.

"She's gone," Meshullam informed them.

"Are you sure?" Father asked.

"Yes."

"I never gave her much of a chance. Pity for the lamb. Let's hope it survives. Meshullam, can you get the wool off the sheep, please, and take it away."

Meshullam knew Father did not want to touch the dead animal, did not want to become unclean just to bury a sheep.

"I'll do it."

"Good."

When Shimei realized that even Father couldn't help, tears came into his eyes. He climbed into the pen and took the lamb into his arms.

"Uzi, I will look after you now. Don't be afraid. I will get milk for you. I will feed you. I will protect you." He planted a kiss, wet with tears, on Uzi's head.

* * *

Leah waited while Rachel and her aunt, Tinshemet, filled their water jars. Rachel was not much younger than Leah. They had played together when they were children, had grown up together. They both had known Moresheth-Gath before its destruction, had run through its streets and walked through its fields and orchards. Rachel had not been Leah's best friend back then. No, that had always been her cousin Helah. But now Helah was in Jerusalem. And so Rachel and Leah went to the well together, talked and laughed on their way.

Leah liked Tinshemet. She was new here, but very nice. She had married Rachel's uncle in Jerusalem and had come to settle here with them.

Tinshemet put the pitcher back beside the pool after she had filled her jar. Leah picked up her water jar and put it on her head.

"It is still bigger than the house in Jerusalem," Rachel commented about their new house.

"Once we have furnished it, it should be quite nice," Tinshemet agreed.

"I actually quite like it. I only hope that Father will not try to keep too many animals in it again. They just make it so dirty."

"At the moment our house is still clean too," Leah said.

"I like how the house smells, so new. Fresh mud bricks and freshly cut wooden beams. It's nice."

The three of them walked back to the village. They passed the place where Leah had met Rivkah just a few days ago. She still looked around in all directions whenever she passed the spot.

From here the path led gently up to the village. Going up it was not hard and left them plenty of breath to talk. And so they discussed the plans for the village, the houses in which the families would live, who would be whose neighbor, who would be happy with their house, who would not. They wondered where the gardens would be, whether they would plant more orchards, where the animals would be kept. They asked where the men would gather in the summer evenings. After all, there would be no gate, no city wall either, at least not yet. They thought that someday more families would move to this place again, that it would grow and become a town once more. Maybe they could then celebrate the festivals as they had done before, with dances and music, with choice meat and sweet cakes.

"Shalom, Leah." It was Nadab. Leah had not noticed him there. He greeted them at the edge of the village. "Are you well?"

Leah searched for words, but could only respond with a quiet yes.

"Can I walk to your home with you?"

"I'm alright. Rachel and Tinshemet . . ."

"We will go on, Leah. We have to turn right up there anyway. Why not walk home with Nadab?" Tinshemet smiled.

"Yes, Nadab," Leah said, nearly whispering.

The other two walked on.

"Should I carry your water jar?"

What! A boy carrying a water jar? Leah looked at him somewhat confused.

"But can you . . . ?"

"I'll carry it in my hands."

Yes, those strong hands and powerful arms would have no problem lifting a water jar. Leah took the jar from her head. When she gave it to Nadab she splashed some water on him.

"Sorry."

"No worries," he laughed, "better showered by a beautiful girl than bathed by an old man."

Leah blushed.

"What do you think of the village, Leah? Are you feeling at home again?"

"It's different."

"Not like the old town?"

"No, the old town was a lot bigger. So many more people."

"Did you like the old town better?"

Leah hesitated.

"I think so. But the village we're building will be nice, too. Different, but nice."

"I'm starting to feel at home already. Maybe I will live here forever. And more people will come, I'm sure."

"Yes. Maybe we will have a big town again."

"That would be nice."

They were silent briefly. Nadab looked at Leah. "You know our house will be built not far from yours."

"I know."

"We will see each other quite often."

"Yes."

"Does that bother you?"

"No, not at all. No, it would be quite nice."

"I'm looking forward to it, Leah."

"Really?"

"Seeing a beautiful girl like you is always a pleasure."

"Don't say that!"

"But it's true."

"Nadab!" Leah gave him a light push.

"Now you've made me spill even more water," he protested smiling. "The jar will soon be empty if you continue like that."

"Don't talk like that then."

"Are you forbidding me to tell you that you are beautiful, Leah? Are you punishing me for telling you what I see?"

"Don't," Leah said, but gently touched his arm.

They were close to Leah's home now. They grew quiet. At the door Nadab gave Leah the water jar. She took it from him. Their hands touched briefly.

"Thank you," she said quietly.

"Totally my pleasure."

She nodded.

"Shalom, Leah. Until tomorrow."

Leah turned and disappeared into the house. She heard him walk away. Flushed, she put the water jar in the kitchen. Nobody had noticed.

* * *

"Drink, Uzi, drink," Shimei urged the tiny lamb. He held its skinny body while Meshullam tried to pour a trickle of milk into its mouth. The lamb lay in Shimei's lap, limp and unresponsive. Shimei was propping up its head; Meshullam held open its mouth. Meshullam was able to pour some milk onto the lamb's tongue, but it trickled out the side of its mouth, drenching the lamb's wool and running down its neck. The lamb did not swallow.

"Uzi, drink," Shimei pleaded once more. The lamb opened one eye, seeming to take in some of its surroundings. It lasted just a moment. Then the lamb seemed to turn back into itself, not taking note of anything happening around it. They tried one more time.

"Why don't you drink?" Meshullam felt frustrated. It seemed there was nothing they could do. Uzi had not accepted any of the milk they had tried to feed him. He had not accepted anything since his mother died. They had thought he would come round to drinking from a bowl once he was hungry enough. But Uzi had only become weaker, had only become more obstinate. He just refused the milk of a strange ewe. Now they were at the point of losing the lamb. Meshullam knew it would not last the night if it didn't have something in its belly. That's why he had tried all evening. And Shimei cared too much for this tiny lamb to even think about going to sleep while its life was in danger.

Meshullam feared that Shimei might see his lamb die tonight. He would be inconsolable. But Meshullam did not have the heart to send him away.

And so the two brothers brought Uzi to the stables and stayed with him late into the night. They tried again and again, without success. Uzi would not accept any milk. As the hours dragged on, Meshullam became resigned to Uzi's imminent death. He let the lamb be, though he continued to touch the limp body regularly. There was still life in it. At some point Shimei must have fallen asleep. He lay there curled up next to the lamb. Despite the sadness, Meshullam had to smile at the thought of Shimei's determination to get the lamb through, to keep Uzi alive. Only, it seemed, he had not been able to make a difference.

And then Meshullam must have fallen asleep as well. Meshullam did not know how long he had been sleeping. He was woken by the excited Shimei.

"He's licking it! He's licking my finger!"

It took Meshullam more than a moment to remember why they were here in the stables at this time of the night. Oh yes, Uzi the lamb. The lamp was still flickering, casting dancing shadows across the walls. He can't have been asleep for that long.

"He's licking milk from my finger," Shimei said again.

Meshullam couldn't believe his eyes: there was Uzi eagerly sucking on Shimei's index finger. Apparently not content with the small amount of milk he got each time, he latched onto the finger again. He would never get much milk that way, but it was a start. And the change in temperament was truly a miracle. Uzi had turned from a listless, pitiable creature into a hungry, alert lamb. Shimei still propped up his head and held him tightly, but Uzi seemed to have some energy again.

"He really wants milk now. Finally! What happened?"

"I just tried it and Uzi wanted more."

"Thanks be to God."

Meshullam took the bowl with milk.

"Let's see whether we can give him some more. Keep your finger in his mouth and I'll pour some down your finger."

"Oh, that tickles!"

"Doesn't matter. Keep your finger in there."

"See! Uzi likes it."

"Good. He's drinking."

Meshullam watched with satisfaction as Uzi swallowed the milk and his thin body filled with food. Yes, he would live.

* * *

Rivkah stayed longer than a day or two. She was thankful for the hospitality she received, for the way she was welcomed by the family of Micah. They gave her new clothes, a place to sleep and rest, and better food than she had eaten for months. But she knew she could not stay here, could not again become a burden. She did help, of course. She ground the flour in the morning, helped with the cooking, milked the goats. Milking sheep was a new challenge. It was difficult to really place the hands on their udders; and they were often quite restless too. However, she managed. Luckily they only milked three sheep. Uzi, Shimei's lamb, drank quite a bit of their milk.

In a sense, the rhythm of work, the daily meals spent together, felt familiar to her. And yet this family was different. Was it the quiet peace and wisdom of old Micah? Was it the determination to settle this land again? Was it their faith in the LORD, the God of Israel, whom they praised in their songs and psalms? They were full of hope, were working towards a new future in this ravaged land. Despite the hardship, the uncertainty and obstacles, joy infused their lives. Rivkah rested in the peace, savored the hope, longed for the joy, sought their determination, but she knew she had to go on eventually. Jerusalem was her goal. She wasn't sure what would await her there, but trusted Beriah could help. There must be opportunities for a girl like her in the city. She would build a new future for herself, would start life again, would enjoy all the city had to offer.

She still hadn't asked any of the men for the way to Jerusalem. Somehow she felt uncomfortable talking to Ehud, Leah's father. But surely Micah would know. And he had always been nice to her. So when Rivkah came back from milking and saw Micah sitting in the afternoon sun outside the house, she quickly set down the jug in the kitchen and went out to talk to him.

"Father Micah, can I ask you something?"

"Ah, Rivkah, come sit down."

Rivkah settled down beside him. She was quiet for a moment.

"What is it Rivkah?"

"Can you tell me the way to Jerusalem?"

"To Jerusalem? That's right, that is where you wanted to go. I can tell you the way to Jerusalem."

He paused for a moment. "You know, the roads are not what they used to be before the Assyrians came to the land. Not many people travel on them now. But they are still there.

"Travel north along the ridge from here." With his right he pointed northward, beyond the new houses and along the ridge. "It will drop away gently, a small valley separating it from the next ridge along. Go into this valley and follow it to the east—not far. For then you will come to another small valley which you can follow toward the north, keeping to the edge of the ridge. It will open into a wide valley, where once wheat and barley grew in abundance. This is the valley of Elah. You will see the city of Azekah rising above it, once a strong fortress, now a ruin. When you see the city, turn to the east and follow the stream up the valley of Elah into the mountains. The road there is still good. You should find it. It will lead you past another town that was once great, Socoh. It is no more. As you travel along the road you will come across the remains of many towns and villages, now only inhabited by owls and jackals. As the valley winds into the hills, the road ascends a ridge. Later on it descends into a valley again, the valley of Rephaim. As you get closer to Jerusalem you will notice inhabited villages once more. And then, you will see the city on the hill above you, standing tall on the ridges and mountains. You should be able to make it to Jerusalem in a day or two."

"Thank you, Father Micah." Rivkah got ready to get up.

"Rivkah, do you really want to go to Jerusalem?"

"Yes, I do."

"And once you are there, what will you do there?"

"I will see. I know someone in Jerusalem."

"Yes, now I remember. You told us that first night. You think he will help you?"

Rivkah nodded.

"Rivkah, why are you leaving your family and going to Jerusalem?"

"I am not leaving my family."

"But you said you lived in a cave together. You escaped the Assyrians, didn't you?"

"I did. But I did not live in the cave with my family."

"But you were with others?"

"Yes."

"Were they from your village?"

Rivkah was quiet. Why did Micah ask those questions? She looked at him. His eyes showed only kindness.

"I am not from Shechar."

"Yes."

"I am from Lachish."

"Lachish was destroyed, conquered by the enemy."

"Yes."

"You escaped?"

Rivkah gulped. "I did."

"And those people you lived with in the cave?"

"They were from Shechar, at least most of them. They took me in when I was wandering alone. I had nowhere else to go. But I could not stay with them forever, that was clear. Now that the Assyrians have left, they have moved back to the site of their village, to Shechar. And I am going on to Jerusalem. I can start again in the city."

"And your family?"

"Dead, captured . . . I don't know. They did not escape Lachish when it fell."

"But you did?"

"Yes."

"And sometimes you wish the Assyrians had taken you, not them?"

"Yes."

"I know, Rivkah."

He looked straight ahead.

"I had a daughter, a beautiful daughter, Abigail, my youngest. She was the daughter of my joy and sorrow, for my wife died when she gave birth to her. Abigail was nursed by other women, but I cared for her as best I could, tried to be mother and father to her. She was the light of my eye. How proud I was when she married an upstanding man from Azekah, a man of faith and action. They had children, three lovely children and more to come, I'm sure. I was in Jerusalem when the enemy came, but she stayed in Azekah. The Assyrians conquered the city and leveled it. I do not know what happened to her or her children. We have never heard from her husband. Did the Assyrians murder them or did they carry them into exile? I want to know. And sometimes I wish it would have been me instead of them. She still had life before her, would see her children grow up. I am old. I have completed my task. I have proclaimed the message I was sent to deliver. Maybe God still wants more from me, but how I wish she had lived."

Rivkah sensed the deep loss. And she was sure he did understand her, knew how she felt. For his questions had often been her questions. She looked at the ground.

"Why did I survive and no one else from my family? Sometimes I remember each harsh word, each time I hurt them, and I know I can never say sorry."

"Rivkah, it is hard. But trust the LORD to forgive. And the LORD will make something out of our broken lives. I cannot understand why, but here I am. I have to continue living. And so do you. You are still young, you have life before you. And so you want to go to Jerusalem, to start anew. Maybe you have nowhere else to go. I will not hold you back, but I want to tell you that you can stay here; you are needed here."

* * *

Leah liked Rivkah, but there were a few odd things about her. Take, for example, when they were gathering herbs together. Rivkah discovered even the tiniest leaf of sorrel, but walked right past a big thistle with a juicy root that could be added to any soup. She left the leek, but was sure to discover eryngo. She seemed to disregard some of spring's nicest herbs and instead continued to gather the bitter herbs of winter.

The two girls were out in the fields east of the village, where valleys and ridges started to rise towards the highlands of Hebron. The exuberant growth of spring offered tender shoots and fresh plants, plenty to add to the dining table. Leah knew that they did not go out to gather wild plants only to add variety to their meals. No, this year there would be no bountiful harvest to fill the grain pits and storage jars. Therefore, their provisions would have to last as long as possible.

Leah had always enjoyed harvest time. It was hard work, but always joyful. That was another odd thing about Rivkah: she was good at grinding flour and baking bread, but it seemed she had never participated in a harvest. When they talked about harvest time, Rivkah knew about the festivals, but when Leah asked her about the gathering of sheaves or the threshing floor in her village, the answers became evasive. Indeed she didn't like to talk about life in her village at all. And now that she thought about it, Leah noticed that Rivkah avoided any question about her past. She did like to hear about Jerusalem, though. Not that Rivkah talked any more about going there, Leah had noticed. No, she seemed content to stay here with Leah's family. It seemed as if Rivkah was only concerned about the here and now, not the past or the future

"I don't know whether I can eat these herbs and wild plants for much longer. I really want a bit more bread and meat. What did you have in Jerusalem, Leah?"

"Bread and more bread, with a few lentils maybe. The bread was baked in bakeries. We didn't make it at home."

"In bakeries?"

"Yes, each quarter had one."

"That sounds great. No need to grind the flour and prepare the dough. Did the bread taste alright?"

"Oh yes, it wasn't bad."

"Life in Jerusalem must have been fairly good for you then?"

"We only got a small ration of bread. It wasn't exactly a feast. Then there were the thousands upon thousands of people crammed into the city. They were all afraid, uncertain whether the city would survive. No, it was not a good time. I felt so relieved when we left the gates of the city behind."

"Do you think life's better here then?"

"There's more work here, of course, but we have a home. We are not just another family of refugees. For us it wasn't as bad as for many others. Grandfather is well-known in Jerusalem and has supporters there, you know. We were taken in by good people. I liked Jerusalem, but it's not my home."

"My home is destroyed."

"So is ours. But we are building a new home here and, somehow, I like it."

"Despite the work?"

"Despite the work. In Jerusalem you also have to work hard to earn your bread. Many of the newcomers work as servants for government officials. Life in Jerusalem is not all easy.

"Jerusalem is the centre of Judah, the city of the temple. But Grandfather always says that Jerusalem is nothing without the towns of Judah."

Rivkah was quiet.

"Do you still want to go there?" Leah asked.

"I don't know... What do you think? Maybe I should stay here for a while...? I don't mean to be a burden."

"You are not a burden, Rivkah. You know you are welcome here. And I know that Grandfather is very keen on you staying. I think he likes you. And he believes we need more people here."

"Are you sure?"

"Definitely. And I would be really happy, too. You know—another girl my age. Rachel and Zeruiah are the only others, and they're not like you. Stay with us!"

"For a while at least. You have been so good to me. You know, somehow I already feel part of the village."

* * *

It was Shabbat, Rivkah's second Shabbat here in the new settlement of Moresheth-Gath. Today they wouldn't do any work, today was a day of rest. Here they respected the ancient law, ceasing from their labor and not just slowing the pace of their daily work. The goats still had to be milked, the water still had to be collected from the well, but no bricks were made, no cloth woven, no fields plowed. The children could play together, the adults could sit and talk. Rivkah didn't know whether all the families would do it, but the family of Micah would join together in singing hymns and psalms as the Shabbat drew to a close. That's what they did last week at least.

Rivkah had risen early today. Most of the people and animals still slept, enjoying the rest. Only a few goats grew restless, waiting to be milked and let out to graze. Dew covered the ground, bands of mist drifting across the land in the calm, gentle morning wind. In the east the sun rose above the clouds, sending rays that danced in the mist. Rivkah stopped on the path leading to the spring and watched the sunbeams. She didn't carry a water jar. She had come out here to get away from the sleepers, to be alone and think. Not that she didn't like them or wanted to spend less time in the house; just sometimes it was good to be alone, to be out here in the freshness of morning.

Rivkah fumbled the figurine of Isis, took it from under her dress and held the goddess towards the light. She had seen it so often and still the smooth, worn image of Isis holding her son Horus infused her with comfort, a vision of serenity and power. She traced the familiar hieroglyphs. Had Isis brought her here? Had she been given this place of new beginnings where she had not sought it? Was this where her life would continue? Somehow she felt welcome here, nearly at home. And she couldn't have just stumbled upon this place, these people. It must have been ordained by divine direction. She could not make any sense of it otherwise. Rivkah was slowly beginning to realize that this village was not just a stage on her way to Jerusalem.

Only hesitantly did she relinquish her dreams about Jerusalem; only reluctantly did she come to think of this place as her home. Could it really offer the future she had dreamt of, the excitement she longed for? Was she really meant to be here?

Rivkah was glad that the family of Micah had accepted her into this community. Maybe they thought that the LORD, the God of Judah had guided her steps to their village. Had the LORD really added her to the number of those settling the devastated land? Rivkah did believe that the LORD was still with Judah, was still protecting the nation and would restore some of its former towns and cities. She rejoiced for Judah. But somehow the national God did not seem attentive to her own need, was unconcerned with her plight. She could not feel his power, could not hold his image in her hand. Was she just an instrument in the hands of the gods? Or did their designs, their plans and schemes combine fortuitously for her? Here in the family of Micah she had heard psalms of trust in the LORD. But hadn't he abandoned Lachish; hadn't he been powerless to prevent the death of so many? How can you trust, when the gods dealt so arbitrarily with mortals? Rivkah was not yet ready to trust, not yet ready to be comforted, but she was determined to take hold of the opportunities the gods provided, to accept the gifts of answered prayers. Rivkah kissed the figurine of Isis and uttered a silent prayer of thanks.

The mists receded as the sun rose higher in the morning sky. Soon the family would gather for the morning meal. Rivkah wanted to make sure they would also have goats' milk on the table.

* * *

Rivkah had seen him before. It didn't take long in this small village to meet everyone. Leah had even pointed him out. Nadab was his name. But it was only now that Rivkah really noticed him. There was, of course, his shirt. It was of pure, white wool, embroidered with fine, intricate patterns. It was clearly only to be worn on Shabbat or other holidays. But even more noticeable was his face, framed by those dark curls. His strong chin gave him that determined look, his fine nose and smooth cheeks spoke of tenderness and passion.

Rivkah studied him, but when he turned to look at her, she looked away and showed more interest in the young children playing knucklebones and chasing each other.

The older ones had no interest in the games. They had grown past them. They sat in the shade chatting and watching their younger siblings and neighbors. The other girls were there: Leah, Rachel and Zeruiah. And then the boys: Nadab of course, then Meshullam, Ahiel and the two brothers, Boaz and Jeroham. They leaned against the terebinth or lay on the ground, propped on their elbows.

The new houses in the village were discussed. Only Nadab's family did not yet have a completed house, but they were all sure it would be finished in the coming week.

"Our house in Shaphir was a lot bigger," Nadab told them. "The broad room at the back of the house was nearly as large as some of the houses here. And we had stairs to the upper storey."

"Stairs?"

"Not just a ladder."

The others nodded. Clearly they had never lived in houses as grand as that.

"Maybe we can build big houses here one day," Boaz suggested.

"Houses with stairs," Jehoram added.

"Not anytime soon," Nadab put in.

"No," Meshullam agreed, "that would take too much time and effort. No one in the village has time for that at the moment."

"Did you live in a big house, Rivkah? What was yours like?"

Rivkah's heart jumped. Why did Nadab ask her directly?

"No, ours was . . . small, not big at all. We just . . . we had no stairs," she mumbled.

"But it had plenty of room for all the animals?"

What should she say now? Should she tell them that they never had any? They would think that she came from a poor, unrespectable family. But she knew how she could impress them.

"My father was a blacksmith."

"A blacksmith?" Ahiel asked.

"Yes."

The others did seem impressed.

"Where did you live?" Nadab wanted to know.

Now she had done it. She had told most people in the last few days that she was from the small village of Shechar. But nobody would believe that there could be a blacksmith in such a small village. And the way Nadab looked at her he was clearly expecting her to name an important city. Well, she would.

"Lachish," she said clearly. Now she had told them.

"Lachish, the big city and chariot-division base?"

"Yes, Lachish. I lived in the city, not far from the citadel where the chariots and troops were based."

The others looked at her with respect. Only Leah threw her confused and questioning glances. Rivkah would have to explain later.

"Did you see the soldiers often?" Ahiel asked.

"Yes, we lived right on the main road to the gate. They would pass quite frequently." Rivkah looked past Ahiel at Nadab. She was getting more confident.

"But wasn't Lachish destroyed?" Nadab asked.

"Yes, it was razed to the ground and burnt."

The mention of Lachish reminded her of the loss, but now she would have to continue, would have to sound as controlled as she could. And she was sure they would accept her, would think of her as an interesting girl.

"And you . . . ?"

"I escaped."

"How?"

"I hid, and when the Assyrians were burning down the city I escaped through the breach in the wall and fled into the hills."

Rivkah pushed the harrowing details of the day out of her mind: the death of her dog Kaleb, the tense wait and flight with enemy soldiers on all sides, the desperate race down the city mound, the rape and death of Bath-Shua. The memory of them was still painful, but they did not matter now. All that mattered was the admiration she could see in Nadab's eyes.

"You fled alone?"

"Yes, I escaped alone."

"Rivkah, the girl that took on the Assyrian army."

He smiled at her and shook his locks.

"Did you expect any less?" She was surprised at how confident she sounded.

"No, I should have known the first time I saw you what sort of girl you were," he quipped.

"That's alright. Now you know." She didn't know when he had first seen her. She was glad it hadn't been that first night when she arrived in that horrible dress and with the filthy hair.

"And now, when I look at you, it sure makes sense."

"Oh, does it?" she responded.

"And then, where did you go then?" Meshullam asked. The others were only now finding words again.

Rivkah turned to glance at Meshullam before looking at Nadab again. "I met some people from the village of Shechar. I stayed with them."

Rivkah noticed the flicker of recognition flit across Leah's face. She looked hurt and betrayed. Rivkah was sorry. She hadn't intended it that way. She had just wanted to be careful. And she hadn't been able to talk with anyone about Lachish, only with Ayalah, then old Micah. It always was painful. But it seemed the others found it fascinating, especially Nadab. It certainly was a good story. And if her flight from Lachish earned her their respect, she would have to learn to leave the pain behind.

"You hid from the Assyrians?" Rachel asked.

"Yes." Rivkah just nodded, not even averting her gaze from Nadab. The others went on to talk about the Assyrian encirclement of Jerusalem, their own journey from the city back into the country and how they had bought animals. Rivkah was silent again, didn't listen. But she was sure that she had found her place among the young people of Moresheth-

Gath, that they held her in new regard. But when Nadab smiled at her, she looked at the ground.

* * *

Why had she lied to her? Why? She had thought Rivkah was her friend! And then Leah had discovered that all the time Rivkah had been lying to her. She had never told her the truth about where she really came from, had always let Leah think she was from some small village. And then she had finally changed her story, right in front of Nadab! And Nadab had been impressed. That, Leah could tell by the way he had responded, by the way he joked with Rivkah. Not only had Rivkah broken their trust and friendship, she had successfully gotten Nadab's attention. It hurt. Leah hated her for it! But Leah hated herself even more—nobody seemed to trust her, nobody valued her.

Leah pushed the grinding stone across the quern, crushing the grain, grinding it to flour. Her body moved rhythmically backwards and forwards as she applied even pressure to the stone. But occasionally she pushed harder, moved faster as the frustration took hold of her. Sometimes she stopped grinding altogether, the pain of betrayal overcoming her, paralyzing her for a moment. Then she continued in her task again. Rivkah hadn't even offered to help her. The two had hardly spoken since Shabbat. Rivkah had tried to explain, had said something about being afraid when she first arrived, of the pain of talking about what had happened at Lachish. Leah hadn't listened and let Rivkah know that she wouldn't accept any excuses. A lie was a lie. How could you be friends with a liar? So that was how she repaid all the kindness, was it? Rivkah had said no more after that.

It was the start of a bitter silence between the two. Their friendship was over, that was clear. They still sat beside each other at meal times, but whenever possible they avoided working together. And at night they no longer lay at each other's side. Leah despised Rivkah. Still, she mourned the loss, the loss of a friend.

Leah sat back. She had ground enough for today. Taking a bowl she gathered the flour. Right now she didn't feel like doing anything else. Every task required a strength she just didn't have.

The quiet rest didn't last long. Her younger brother Shimei came into the house, closely followed by Uzi, the little lamb. Ever since that night in which Uzi had finally accepted milk from humans, the two were inseparable. Uzi followed Shimei everywhere; and Shimei took Uzi everywhere, often carrying him in his arms. Through Shimei's constant care, Uzi had grown stronger, was no longer the weak little lamb on the brink of vanishing. Right now the two irritated Leah. Could they not leave her alone for just a moment? And why did they constantly have to tear through house and yard?

"Where's the milk for Uzi?" Shimei asked.

Leah pointed to a bowl on the bench. "He doesn't need another feed yet."

"Oh, it's already late. And Uzi says he's hungry." Shimei turned to the lamb. "You're hungry, aren't you?" In confirmation Uzi nudged Shimei's leg and started to suck on Shimei's finger when he bent down.

"Just don't feed him too much," Leah cautioned.

Shimei didn't even seem to hear her. He went straight to the bowl and dipped his finger in it. "It's cold."

"Of course it's cold," Leah snapped, "and don't put your finger in the milk."

Shimei licked the milk off his finger. He poured some into a smaller bowl.

"I'll warm it in the bread oven."

"Be careful not to disturb the embers."

They usually kept the embers of the fire in the oven from day to day. That way they didn't have to make a new fire again each morning. But you had to be careful not to snuff it out.

Shimei placed the bowl in the oven. Uzi followed his every movement with interest. With the milk warming, Shimei took Uzi in his arms and gently stroked his short wool. Uzi lay totally still in his arms, enjoying the caressing. He leaned back his head, his little feet loosely draped across Shimei's arms. They must have sat there like that for several minutes before the lamb struggled. Shimei set him down and Uzi jumped around the room in leaps and bounds, hopping into the air with all four feet at once.

Shimei took the bowl of milk and tested its warmth. It must have been right for now he called, "Uzi, come here, the milk's ready."

The lamb immediately ran to Shimei, eagerly stretching his head towards the bowl. Shimei held Uzi and put the bowl to his little mouth. He slowly poured the milk. Uzi eagerly swallowed it.

Leah was quiet and watched the two. They no longer irritated her. No, somehow she enjoyed watching them, inwardly laughing at their antics. They did not seem to have a care in the world, and yet they cared for each other. Her brother could be a pain, but the commitment he showed towards the lamb touched her. Were they real friends, a boy and a lamb?

Uzi wiggled his fat little tail with excitement. Food clearly was one of the highlights of his day. When the bowl was empty, Shimei put it aside. Leah said nothing, did not ask him to clean it or put it back. She could do that herself later. She did not want to disturb them now. Shimei held Uzi and gave him a gentle rub. Uzi was still licking his lips, though he looked decidedly content with his full tummy. The peaceful scene did not last long. Soon the two were on their way again, running around the room and leaping out the door. Leah could hear Shimei's excited shouts as he called Uzi. His voice receded, but Leah still smiled.

* * *

Meshullam led the donkey down to the valley. It had the plow strapped to its back, the long shaft trailing behind it. Father led the two cows. Only one cow belonged to the family. They had to borrow the other. They were the only cows in the village. That's why the pair was used by everybody to do the plowing. Not that they did much plowing this late in the year. It was far too late for barley and wheat. They would have to make do with trying to harvest the few stalks that struggled to grow in fields planted in previous years. But they could at least try and sow some of the summer crops, like sesame and chick-peas. Meshullam had heard some of the men say that it was too late even for that. Clearly Father thought they still had a good chance. It would have been better earlier, but there had been so many things to do when they first arrived.

For the sesame, Father had chosen a field that had belonged to them before, when they had lived in the old Moresheth-Gath. It had yielded good fruit then. Of course, the settlers had divided the land again, had allocated it by lot when they arrived. With towns and fields destroyed, so many people displaced and killed, new families moving in, they had decided not to cling to the old, inherited plots, but to start anew. If more people returned to Moresheth-Gath to reclaim their inheritance, they could be accommodated. Grandfather had been sure of that. And so, not all the land in the vicinity had been distributed.

When they came to the field, Meshullam first took the sack of sesame seed from the donkey and put it on the ground, then the plow and shaft. He helped Father attach the shaft to the plow, linking them with two iron rings. He hammered them tight and made sure they fit. Together they put the yoke on the cows and then attached the shaft.

"That'll do," Father said. He picked up the plow and moved the cows to the edge of the field.

"Cut the edge, cut the edge!" Father called out to the pair to start the first furrow. With a flick of the goad the cows moved forward and Father guided the plow into the ground, pressing down upon it. The iron plowshare loosened the top soil, its triangular form with the sharp tip lifting the hardened ground. The furrow was only a thin line in the ground, but the band of loosened soil clearly showed the width of the plow. It was into the furrow that Meshullam now let the seed fall. By working together Father could concentrate on the plow. And for sesame, furrow planting would provide a better yield than scattering the seed, as they did for wheat and barley.

At the end of the field Father shouted, "Come up, come up!" The two cows slowed down as Father lifted the plow out of the ground and gave the pair a minute's rest, before turning them and plowing the second furrow. Urging them on again with shouts and the goad, Father guided the plow back to the other side, Meshullam following behind. After a few lengths Father and Meshullam rested to drink some water from a flask.

Now it was Meshullam's turn. With a call of "cut the ground, cut the ground" he urged the two cows on and pressed the plow into the soil.

"Good," Father commented behind him, following with the sack of sesame seeds.

Meshullam must have let the plow veer from its line. About midway through the field Father called, "Keep straight!"

Meshullam slowed down and checked his direction. Yes, in the last few yards he had come off the line. Trying to concentrate, he continued on. By the time he shouted, "come up, come up", he could already feel the strain in his hands and arms. He lifted the plow out of the ground, glad for the brief rest. Turning the animals, he started on the next furrow. There would still be many lengths to do today.

* * *

"Shouldn't you be back in the village helping your father finish the house and not out here carrying that bundle of herbs for me?" Rivkah asked Nadab.

"Oh, my father can do quite well without me. There's not much left to do on the house. We've been in there for two days now already. I think you need my help more. And it's certainly a much more pleasant task."

"Carrying herbs? You're kidding? I am used to carrying my bundle of herbs and have done it for a long time now. But thanks for doing it for me."

"I might just learn a few handy things on the way."

"Like what the best plants look like?"

"Exactly."

"Let's start the lesson now, then."

"Go ahead, oh teacher," Nadab teased.

"That's sorrel here. Nice and tender, see?"

Rivkah bent down to pick the young green plants. Gathering a few leaves in her right hand she suddenly shoved them right in Nadab's face as he was watching her movements intently. "Just in case you need a closer look."

Nadab drew his head back quickly, a surprised look on his face. Had she gone too far? But no, he laughed.

"Good one, Rivkah."

She moved the leaves to his face again. This time he did not draw back, but smiled as the leaves tickled his nose and cheeks. Suddenly he brought up his hand and caught Rivkah's wrist, moving her hand to the side. Nadab stared passionately into Rivkah's eyes, his look making her uneasy, excited and confused at the same time. It lasted only a moment, a penetrating, precious moment, and then it was gone. Nadab's face grew into a smile, he winked and laughed letting go of her wrist. Flushed, Rivkah composed herself again.

"What else can you show me?"

"There's more, but first put this in the bundle. That's your job after all."

After Nadab put the first lot of sorrel into the bundle, Rivkah picked some more nearby, adding to their collection.

"That should do. We have enough of that now," she said.

"What, are we finished?"

"I don't think so. But we might want more variety. Come on, let's see what else we can find."

The two walked on, slowly making their way round a hill.

"Ah, here we are. That's marjoram. We'll pick some."

Nadab took the leaves Rivkah was plucking and added them to the bundle.

"Smells nice," he commented.

"Yes, it does add a bit of tang to any meal."

They also found a few good thistles. Nadab helped Rivkah to dig out the roots, discarding the prickly leaves. Just as he was about to throw some thistle leaves away, Nadab suddenly turned towards Rivkah and tickled her with the thistle.

"Ouch," she howled. It didn't really hurt much. Nadab thrust the thistle at her again, this time harder.

"Stop it!"

He laughed and stabbed the prickly leaves at her back.

"Nadab!"

His laugh sounded menacing, out of control.

"Stop it, Nadab!"

"Alright, alright. Don't get upset." Nadab threw the thistle away.

"But it hurt!"

"Sorry, Rivkah. I didn't mean to hurt you." He smiled at her, sheepishly.

He was sorry. That would do for Rivkah.

After adding a few tender shoots from some bushes to the bundle, Rivkah decided they had enough.

"Time to go back."

"What, already?"

"I still have other things to do."

"You're right, the bundle is already quite full," Nadab conceded.

"I think that's plenty."

"If you ever need help again, I would be delighted to come."

"I'm sure I will."

"And I have learned something today; I've learned that the leaves you pick smell really nice."

Rivkah laughed. Together they walked to the village.

* * *

Leah saw Nadab and Rivkah coming back to the village, slowly walking up the hill. Their conversation seemed animated; they were obviously happy in each other's company. The sight hit Leah hard, agitated her. Only yesterday she had thought Nadab had only eyes for her. Of course she had noticed his interest in Rivkah. That's why she had made a point of meeting him as often as possible. And yesterday they had some wonderful moments together. They had talked about love, not just in veiled allusion, but about how God blessed human love, and brought a man and a woman together. It had been a conversation of depth, of surfacing emotion. Nadab had even praised Leah's beauty, had touched her as they said good-bye. And now this!

Leah swallowed hard, fighting back the tears. She wondered whether she should go and meet Nadab and Rivkah or at least walk past them, just to remind them that she was still there. It would make Nadab remember the previous day and Rivkah would see that Leah was still in the picture. But Leah knew she couldn't confront them now, couldn't ask Nadab to his face what he was doing. She would be too emotional for that. In the end, she couldn't bring herself to move and watched the two from a distance as they entered the village.

Leah wasn't sure who she was most angry with. Was it Nadab, who talked of love one day, then so openly flirted with another girl the next? Was it Rivkah, who she had once considered a friend, but who lied to her and was now competing with her for the affection of the same man? Or was it herself? Was she not interesting, not attractive enough to hold the attention of a man like Nadab? What had she done wrong? And why did she not have the courage to step in, or even to push Nadab further when they met?

She could not understand it. Whatever did Nadab see in Rivkah? She was not as tall, not as pretty as Leah. She may have come from an important city, but she had nothing to her name. At first, she had even hidden the fact that she came from Lachish. What did that say? Leah, on the other hand, was the granddaughter of a famous prophet and came from the most important family of this village.

Nadab would regret his little outings with Rivkah. Just wait until he came begging back to Leah. She would not yield easily. No, this time he would have to prove his love, would have to show his sincerity. But, oh, his actions hurt. Leah had been betrayed by those she had thought to be her closest friends.

* * *

Slowly Rivkah squirted the milk from the udder into the bowl. She leaned her head against the goat's side. She was so tired. She had hardly slept last night. Nadab had been constantly before her eyes. She could not get him out of her mind: his smile, his flowing voice, his slim yet strong body. Each different aspect entered her thoughts and fused together into the picture of a handsome man. She had replayed each word he had said, remembered each little gesture.

What did he think of her? Why did he seek her company? Rivkah knew that men sometimes mistreated women, sought to use them for their own selfish needs. But not Nadab. He was so understanding, so sincere. Rivkah felt accepted when she was with him. He saw something in her she hardly ever dared anyone would see. He thought her courageous and yet lovely, fascinating and yet fun. She mattered to him.

She wondered whether Nadab would be the true lover the songs told about. Would he stand by her, no matter what? Would she be the only one for him? Did he long for her in ardent desire? How would she know he was the one? How would she know he was not just playing games? Could she trust him?

If she believed the songs, her heart would tell her, and she would recognize the man who would be true to her. And her heart told her that Nadab was that man. Nadab was all a girl could wish for: strong, handsome, charming. How the others would look if he chose her. Leah, Rachel and Zeruiah would be white with envy. Even the boys seemed to look up to Nadab. Rivkah could stand proudly at the side of such a man. All who doubted her would be silenced. She would never be afraid of someone like Naarah again.

The stomping of the goat tore Rivkah out of her thoughts. "Don't get stupid!" she chided the animal. But then she noticed that the goat's udder was indeed empty. Time to move on to the next one.

Chapter 12

Dark green leaves rustled in the wind, shadows flitting across the tumble of poppies, thistles, nettles, weeds, and flowers that spread out under the rows of olive trees. The fresh, bright colors on the ground contrasted with the more dignified, darker colors in the branches above. The chirping of birds, the constant patter of leaves, swelling to a crescendo in the occasional gust, the buzzing of bees searching for nectar among the spring flowers, all combined to create the gentle symphony of the olive grove, only interrupted by the distant "baa" of a sheep or the braying of a donkey. It was peaceful here. This grove was some way from the village, but the trees were strong and tall. They always yielded a good harvest. That's why they had cared for the trees in the past, and that's why they were even more important now after the Assyrians had devastated so much of the country. Meshullam and Father sat under an olive tree in the shade, eating their lunch. They did not have much: a piece of bread for each of them, some cheese, a roasted thistle root. In other years they would have had more bread. But they had little grain this year, even though they had bought considerable amounts of it in Jerusalem. It had to last until the harvest. That was a few months away and would not be plentiful, they knew. And so they had to make the grain last, only had a little bread with their meals. Meat wasn't on the menu much either. Their flocks were too small to spare any animals. They did have the occasional pigeon, but after the day's work was done who would want to go to the effort to catch one of the birds when they provided so little meat? It was good that the girls managed to gather herbs and greens for salads and thistle roots for stews and roasting. The other boys all talked with disgust about eating the green things, but Meshullam actually liked them, at least for now. He had to admit that Rivkah was quite good at gathering a plentiful supply each day. She had proved herself useful ever since she had arrived here and was certainly a great help to the family right now.

The meager lunch must have given Father food for thought, too.

"Some of the families are not as careful with the wheat as they should be. Tobijah has already complained that he hasn't got enough."

Meshullam nodded. Tobijah was Nadab's father. "But he does not have a large family—only two sons and a daughter."

"I know, but they haven't even started sowing any summer crops, no sesame or chick-peas. Yes, their house was the last one to be finished, but all the men helped. Now is the time to work in the fields, not to enlarge the home. I am worried. I didn't really know them when we set out. They aren't from Moresheth-Gath, as you know, but from Shaphir. I know life isn't easy here. It's not like the other years. This year we have to work hard and for a meager return. This rebuilding will be tough, but we can make it."

Father took another drink from the water bottle and wiped his beard.

"There are other families, too, Meshullam. The house of Joel is also getting low on wheat. They are many people, so their need will be great. But at least the two sons are diligently working the fields.

"I know Grandfather believes we can settle this land successfully. He is sure that the LORD will provide. And the LORD has provided." Father waved his hands towards the trees above them. "He has given us olives for oil, green plants for food, grass in plenty for our sheep, but he is not pouring the blessings of the land into our lap while we sit and do nothing. We have to work to reap the fruit of the land and this year the work will be hard."

"Grandfather says we are the remnant that will make the land bloom and grow again," Meshullam said.

"We are. But then we also have to act like it. That means leading a righteous and diligent life, as a family and as a community. We are just humans, not perfect beings and that will always cause us strife, will make us stumble. Therefore we cannot become complacent, like the people of Judah who became complacent and were disciplined by the LORD. The ways of the LORD are sometimes hard. We, as a community, must make sure we all play our part."

Meshullam nodded. A sudden gust of wind shook the leaves above, causing ripples of sunlight to sweep across his face. With a chirp, a thrush flew across the space between the olive trees and landed on a branch above them. It launched into a song of incessantly repeating notes until Father stood up. Suddenly it was silent, before flitting away to the next tree and then to the next. Father swept the twigs and dirt from his tunic.

"It's time to work." He gave Meshullam a hoe and took the other one himself.

Meshullam went to the row of trees he had been working on before. They were hoeing the soil near the trunks of the trees, loosening the ground and taking out the weeds. That would give the trees more water ensuring a better harvest. They still had to prune the trees as well. Yes, the LORD had preserved this olive grove, but there was plenty of work to do so that it would yield abundantly. Meshullam moved to the next tree, hacking out weeds and turning the soil.

He was sure some of the plants he hoed would be edible. Of course, he didn't really have time to sort through them if he wanted to finish the row in good time. Not that he knew much about the plants anyway. He had always left that to the women. It was their task to gather herbs and greens. His mind went back to Rivkah again. She seemed to know all about plants. Rivkah had certainly done her part. She contributed to the family, willingly did her work each day. Did she feel that this was her village now? Did she believe she was part of the remnant? From the little he had heard of her story, she was certainly like a brand plucked out of the fire; she had survived against all odds. Had God saved her for this, to be a part of the rebuilding of Judah? Meshullam hadn't given much attention to Rivkah. She was a quiet girl—not really remarkable—apart from the few words now and then that gave an inkling of her turbulent past. What had she lived through? Somewhere behind the hard work, the quiet demeanor at the family table, she hid deep pain and hurt. Meshullam thought he could sense it in some of her comments, in the sad expression that spread across her face at times. Had she found in them a new family? He hoped so. Meshullam straightened his back, rested for a while, then stretched his neck, arms, and hands before moving on to the next tree.

* * *

The setting sun bathed the tops of hills in a golden light, so that they stood in stark contrast to the shadows of the valleys. Rolling toward the distant plains, hill seemed to rise from hill, the spaces between them strangely compressed by breaking rays of light. The flaming disc of the sun stood above blue-grey bands on the horizon amongst a spreading layer of golden yellow. Touches of red flared towards the corners of the sky.

Rivkah sat and watched. Was it that beautiful every day? Or had she just not taken the time to observe the western sky as day faded? She turned from the spectacle to look at Nadab. He must have been watching her. Her eyes found his immediately. He did not return her uncertain smile, but enveloped her in a steady gaze, dreamy and yet intense. Sunlight illuminated his right cheek, accentuating his handsome features. His black curls framed his face perfectly, contrasted more intensely in the evening light. He moved his lips slowly, deliberately.

"Re has run his course
is now descending into the deep
to guide his ship through the waters
to hide the world in darkness
before rising again to a new day
to shed light on the world."

Was the splendor of the Egyptian god any more manifest than at this hour, when day was waning, when he descended into the depths of the ocean? They both turned towards the sun that was now sinking beneath the horizon. First, a thin sliver was sliced off the golden disc. Then it lost more and more of its round form, flaming brightly towards the end. Its total disappearance seemed sudden after the gradual farewell.

Nadab moved closer to Rivkah. When she leaned back she felt his strong arm behind her. Rivkah did not draw back at the touch, held still for a moment, then nestled her body against Nadab's shoulder, trusting his arm to hold her.

"It's beautiful, the end of day. I'm glad I could share it with you, for . . ." his voice faded, then continued hoarsely, "for you are beautiful too, Rivkah."

She became tense, did not respond, then relaxed, smiled towards the colorful sky and laid her head on his shoulder, breathing out a quiet sigh. She had never felt like this before, had never felt so wanted, so special. Excited and comforted at the same time, her heart hammered inside her. Did he hear it?

"We have to come here more often," Nadab continued after a long silence.

With the sun gone, a band of glowing yellow stretched across the horizon above shades of red, the pale blue sky darkening in the heights. The magic of the sight worked its spell on Rivkah and Nadab, binding them by its wonder. The gentle breeze from the west stiffened, suddenly feeling colder. Rivkah snuggled closer to Nadab.

"Look!" She more felt than saw him indicating towards the west. "The evening star." Bright as a diamond reflecting the light, it stood above the thinning bands of color.

"It's so bright," Rivkah declared, "will it rise in the sky?"

She felt his curls in her face as he gently shook his head. "No, it will follow the sun and disappear into the deep below. It is only the herald of the night, just as the morning star proclaims the coming of the day."

Rivkah watched as the evening star slowly sank towards the horizon, the dark of night now enveloping the land. Already other stars appeared dimly in the night sky.

Suddenly, howls erupted from the valley below, repeated from side to side, culminating in a high-pitched chorus.

"Jackals," Nadab said. They seemed to move closer, some of their howls coming from nearby. Some voices, only a few, seemed to assemble right below Rivkah and Nadab.

"Let's go back. The family will be wondering where I am," Rivkah said. She sat up straight, moving away from Nadab, no longer leaning on his arm. Nadab stood up, then gave Rivkah his hand to pull her up.

"Yes, it's time to get back."

They walked close together, frequently touching hands.

"What do you have to do tomorrow?" Nadab asked.

"I'll have to milk the goats again in the morning. Merab said something about planting vegetables. I think I have to help there. What about you?"

"We will finish the clothes chest in our house and work on the stalls for the animals. Will you be gathering herbs again?"

"In the afternoon, I think."

"I will help you."

"I would be glad if you came."

They didn't talk when they entered the village, walked silently among the few houses.

"See you tomorrow then," Rivkah said quietly when they reached the house of Micah.

"Rivkah," Nadab whispered. His hands held her face. Rivkah drew in a sharp breath. Then she felt his lips on hers, just lightly.

"Nadab," she said, but he was already gone, swallowed by the night.

Rivkah stood outside the house, leaning against its wall. She had to gather her thoughts, control her feelings before she went inside.

* * *

"Go away!" Tirzah pushed Uzi from her. The lamb was climbing all over her, trying to find out whether the bowl she held contained any milk. The bowl actually did for a change, Meshullam knew. But Uzi generally believed that any bowl held by human hands was a potential food source. This time Uzi didn't give up so easily, didn't let himself be shoved around. He tried again.

"Uzi, don't!" Tirzah shouted.

"Quiet!" Father told her.

"But, Uzi . . . "

"Shimei, go and hold the lamb," Mother cut in.

Shimei stood up and walked over to Tirzah. "Uzi, come here, I'll give you some milk." He put his arms around Uzi and lifted up the struggling lamb. "Uzi!" he scolded him. Uzi stopped kicking and let himself be carried. Even though, together, the two often tested the patience of the people around them, nobody could handle Uzi as well as Shimei.

Shimei sat down at his place beside Meshullam again and clasped Uzi under his arm. With anybody else Uzi would have struggled, but with Shimei he sat peacefully, only prodding the boy's leg or side occasionally to remind him he was still there, still expecting his food. He would not be fed until the family had finished their evening meal. Father had put that rule in place when Shimei had too frequently left the table to look after the lamb.

Tonight they had thistle stew, and a small piece of barley bread each. Rivkah would have collected the thistles, but she wasn't in the circle now, Meshullam noticed. Where had she gone at this time of the day? The goats would all have been milked. She better come quickly or there wouldn't be much dinner left for her.

Just then the door opened and Rivkah slipped in. The others hardly looked at her, but Meshullam studied her for a moment. Her face was flushed. She seemed excited and somewhat shaken, but her eyes shone with joy. What had happened? Was she happy or upset?

"Sorry, it took me a bit longer."

What had taken her a bit longer? Meshullam didn't ask. Rivkah sat down beside Leah. The two didn't say a word to each other, avoided looking at each other. Rivkah ladled stew into her bowl. She took very little, clearly was not very hungry. After a few bites she appeared to stare dreamily into nothingness. Strange!

Shimei was the first to finish his bowl. He looked around him to see how the others were doing, then quietly stroked Uzi when he realized that some of their bowls were still half full. But when Father put his empty bowl down and leaned back, he perked up again and asked, "Are we finished now?"

"I am still eating and so is Rivkah. No, we are not finished yet. But you can go and feed the lamb, if you really can't wait," Mother replied. Shimei jumped up, Uzi following him equally as excited.

"You don't need to bring the house down to feed Uzi. He won't die just because he has to wait a heartbeat or two longer for his milk," Grandfather commented.

Shimei turned to look briefly at Grandfather. No, Grandfather was not angry, just amused. Shimei went to the fireplace where the milk for Uzi stood. Uzi executed a few four-legged jumps in excitement. He drank eagerly from the bowl that Shimei now offered him.

"It's a waste of good milk feeding it to that lamb," Father remarked, "he's a runt and will never grow fat and strong."

"But Uzi needs it," Shimei protested.

"Look at him! We don't want to use him for breeding, he will be rejected as a sacrificial lamb and we won't get much meat off him, even at the best of times. So why should we waste good milk on him?"

Shimei looked distraught.

"Let him be for a while," Mother put in. "He's not drinking that much and soon he'll be eating grass. There's plenty of fresh growth around at the moment. He'll grow bigger. Keep him at least until the heat of summer. Then it might be more difficult to find grass."

Father didn't seem fully convinced, but he muttered, "Just don't give him too much milk."

Shimei nodded, relieved. Meshullam smiled at him. He could see Father's point, but he liked Uzi. After all, it was a little miracle that he lived.

* * *

She had to find out! She just couldn't live with the suspicion, the feeling that something had happened between the two, that Rivkah had captured Nadab's heart. The thought hurt, but Leah couldn't ignore the signs: the time the two spent together quite openly; the instances when Rivkah just seemed to be gone, reappearing later with glowing cheeks and shining eyes; and, most importantly, Nadab's apparently waning interest in herself. Leah had to get certainty.

The opportunity came when Mother left Rivkah and Leah to hoe the garden, to ready it for planting the cucumbers and melons.

Leah went straight to the issue, "Rivkah, you and Nadab . . ."

Rivkah stopped, leaned on the hoe, but her blushed face betrayed the emotion she felt at the mention of his name.

"What?"

"Has he told you . . . that he likes you?"

Rivkah didn't respond, went back to hoeing the soil.

"Rivkah, you can tell me. I won't say anything. I've just seen him help you, seen him be nice to you. Nadab is a really great guy."

Leah smiled at Rivkah, reassuring her.

When Rivkah looked up, her eyes sparkled.

"Yes, he likes me."

"And?"

"And what?"

"Is that all? Have you spent some time with . . . you know . . . alone?" Leah whispered.

Rivkah hesitated. "He . . . he has kissed me."

Leah put her hand to her cheeks, eyes wide open in mock surprise. "He has kissed you?!"

"Yes."

"Really? When?"

"Yesterday, and the day before."

"What else?"

"We watched the sunset together."

"That's so exciting, Rivkah! He really loves you. So sweet of him."

"I know. He's . . . he's just so . . . so sensitive. And such fun," Rivkah mused.

"I'm so happy for you," Leah managed to say.

"He just seems to know what I think even before I say it."

"Great." Leah couldn't keep up the charade any longer. She felt sick, as if somebody had kicked her in the stomach. She leaned on the hoe pretending to work.

"I've never met such a strong and considerate man before, a man who can really understand me."

"Yes." Leah worked the ground feverishly, not daring to let Rivkah see her face.

Had Rivkah sensed the change in mood? For now she was silent too, seemingly concentrating on loosening the soil. It was too much for Leah.

"I better get some water," she said.

"Do we need it now?" Rivkah asked.

"Yes, we better moisten the soil before putting the seeds in."

Leah had never heard that from Mother, but Rivkah wouldn't know any better.

"Alright."

Leah was already running back to the house to get the jar, to be alone.

Leah shouted to Rivkah when she passed her on the way to the spring, "I'll be back soon!"

Rivkah stopped briefly and straightened. She waved.

Once Leah was on the path to the spring, she felt she would be alone now, was sure she would meet no one else. Her breathing became fast, as if in pain, interrupted by sharp sobs. She had suspected it, but now that Rivkah had confirmed what Nadab was up to, it hurt. Had he rejected her? "Nadab, what have you done? You broke your promises, only to cavort with a shameless refugee and a liar."

All her frustration, her anger was directed at him and at that enchantress, Rivkah. Leah didn't know how she did it. Rivkah was nothing special, but maybe city girls had their tricks.

Leah raged on in a babbling monologue, "Go and get your whore then, Nadab. That's all she is, a girl from a whoring city. It is all you deserve anyway. You can't even tell an honest girl when you see one."

But then her anger turned against herself. The shame of being upstaged by that girl, of finding out that she, Leah, had adored a man who had no loyalty, no principles. How could she have given her heart to a man like that?

Daughter of Lachish 185

"I hate myself. How could I have been so foolish, so taken by him?"

When she came to the spring, Leah quietened down. She filled the jar and drank some water. That was nice! She leaned over the basin and splashed the cool water over her hot face. With it her anger dissolved and a new determination set in. It wasn't over yet. She had heard only Rivkah's story so far. Did Nadab see things differently? Leah decided to confront him when she met him alone, to ask him directly about his relationship with Rivkah.

Leah met Nadab sooner than she had thought possible. Walking back from the spring, she saw him near the path, coming from the fields toward the village and the vegetable gardens. He was alone. Leah walked faster.

"Nadab!" she called. He heard her and stopped. In a few steps she caught up with him.

"Shalom, Nadab."

"Leah," he smiled.

He wanted to walk on, toward the village, but Leah didn't move.

"How are you?"

"Fine," he answered and turned around to look at her. His gaze still excited her, still made her heart beat faster. But she wouldn't let her emotions cloud her thoughts.

"Nadab, I want to talk to you."

"You know you can always talk to me," he said earnestly.

"Nadab, do you still care for me?" She had to be direct.

"Leah, I do. Don't ever doubt that. I love you."

Leah closed her eyes, could hardly contain the wave of emotions welling up in her. He really loved her, he did! It was the first time he had explicitly declared his love for her. Here he was, looking deeply into her eyes! In her joy, her heart seemed to skip a beat. It was wonderful. But she had to get certainty.

"Why have you never kissed me then, Nadab?"

For a moment he looked perplexed, as if found out. Doubt came washing back over Leah. But then he leaned his face to one side and smiled at Leah. Slowly his hands reached for her face, touched her hair, her cheeks. "Leah," he breathed and leaned towards her.

Leah responded to his kiss, drew him closer towards her. She savored the moment, wanted it to last forever. Nadab released her, stepped back and gazed into her eyes. Leah didn't want to break the moment, but she had to ask the question, "Nadab, did you kiss Rivkah? Do you love her?"

Nadab let her go and laughed loud.

"Rivkah? That scrawny thing? No, I don't love her. Why would you think that?"

"But you spend so much time with her."

"Oh, I helped the poor girl a bit. That must have gone straight to her head and now she thinks I'm madly in love with her."

"She says you kissed her."

"Yuck! My attention must have totally confused Rivkah. Who would want to kiss a girl like her? Skinny little thing with that weary, drawn-out face. She looks dreadful. Not only that, she has no passion at all, no sense of beauty, no time for fun. No, don't you worry about her, Leah."

Nadab laughed and shook his curls.

It was not what Leah had expected to hear, but then it seemed to make sense. How could she have believed a liar? Rivkah had probably just been dreaming, had been out spying on Nadab and gotten carried away in her fantasies.

Leah pressed her body against Nadab's, leaned her head against his chest. He lifted up her chin and kissed her again.

Hand in hand they walked towards the village. What a face Rivkah would make when she saw them! All her lies would be exposed.

But when they came to the garden, Leah could not see Rivkah anywhere. The vegetable patch was finely hoed, ready for the seeds. Where was Rivkah?

Mother came from the house, walking towards the garden. As soon as they saw her, Nadab and Leah separated.

* * *

Where was Leah? Rivkah had hoed the whole vegetable patch. She went over some of the rough pieces again. Leah should have returned with the water by now, especially at the speed with which she had disappeared down the path. Maybe she had broken the jar. Or was the water too heavy in the late morning sun? Rivkah decided to go and help her.

It seemed the rift between them had finally started to heal. Leah had talked to her again, had confided in her again. Could they renew their friendship? Rivkah hadn't intended to hurt Leah. It was just . . .

not until she had met Nadab, had she left behind all caution and talked openly about Lachish. He had liked the exciting story. But it had meant a break with Leah. Somehow she was upset that Rivkah hadn't trusted her with it.

Still, it all seemed to be working out. Her relationship with Nadab had caused Leah to talk to her again. Nadab was the subject of their first proper conversation after the misunderstanding. Everything was falling into place. She had found friends, and love. Rivkah hummed a happy tune, her heart flowed over with thankfulness.

Suddenly her song stopped. Wasn't that Nadab up there on the path? He had his back turned towards her. Who was he talking to? Leah? Yes, it was Leah. Nadab leaned forward and caressed Leah's face and then he kissed her. Rivkah stood still, the shock paralyzing her limbs. Leah responded to the kiss, put her arms around Nadab. Heat and cold tingled through Rivkah's body. Her knees felt weak, seemed to buckle. It couldn't be! Nadab wouldn't do that to her! Her joy suddenly turned into shock and anger. She wanted to scream but no sound came. She wanted to run, to get away from the dashed pieces of her dreams. But something held her. Was it that tiny flame of hope, that small persistent voice that told her it couldn't really be true? She decided to get closer, to hear what they were saying. Ducking behind some bushes, she silently scurried the short distance until she was only a few cubits away from them.

Nadab laughed aloud, then mentioned her name. Rivkah couldn't understand what else he said, but they were clearly talking about her. She pressed farther into the bush, trying to get a little bit closer. Leah said something she couldn't understand, but she could hear Nadab clearly:

"Yuck! My attention must have totally confused Rivkah. Who would want to kiss a girl like her? Skinny little thing with that weary, drawn-out face. She looks dreadful. Not only that, she has no passion at all, no sense of beauty, no time for fun. No, don't you worry about her, Leah."

Nadab laughed again. His mocking voice cut right through Rivkah, not only destroying any remaining hope, but also any confidence she had ever had. So that was what he really thought of her, how others really saw her: ugly, insipid, without passion, and with no time for fun. What else did he have to say about her?

Rivkah could see Nadab and Leah kissing.

Her own lips felt as if they had been seared, as if touched by poison. What had Nadab meant when he kissed her? Was she just an ugly girl he had used to make Leah jealous? Or was she just another girl he played with, to be discarded when he saw fit, a girl stupid enough to take a kiss and a strong arm for real love?

Nadab and Leah walked towards the village. Rivkah glimpsed them passing hand in hand. Did Nadab really love Leah? Leah was certainly a lot prettier than her. Everyone could see that. And she came from a good family. How could Rivkah ever have imagined Nadab would choose her, when there were so many more beautiful girls in the village? Girls from better families too. What had she been thinking?

Now the truth had finally come out. But it hurt, oh it hurt! Tears came streaming down Rivkah's face. She was just a skinny little thing with a weary, drawn-out face. Would any man ever look at her? She had felt so special when she was with Nadab, had been sure he had seen something beautiful in her. Now she knew it had all been a lie. How could Nadab do something like that to her, betray her like that? All along he had just been fooling her, using her. He never really loved her. She hated him!

Behind the bush Rivkah cowered on the ground. She had never felt so alone, so rejected. She fumbled the figurine of Isis that hung from her neck, but it did not bring any comfort. From somewhere words came into her memory: "Do not listen if they mock your appearance. You are beautiful." Who had said that? She couldn't remember. She wanted to believe it, to hang onto it, but couldn't. Hadn't Nadab just plainly said otherwise? And she believed Nadab.

* * *

The sun stood in the western sky, had long passed its zenith, when Rivkah crawled out of the bushes and hesitantly made her way back to the house. It seemed someone had finished planting the vegetable patch without her—Leah? The sun had already dried the newly watered soil.

No one seemed to be in the house. She might just be able to slip in unseen. Later she would milk the goats and life would continue as it had before. But would it? Everything had changed. It would never be as it had been before. How could she live here now? What held her to this place any longer? Only the fear of starting again.

As Rivkah was about to enter the door, she noticed old Micah sitting in front of the house, leaning against the wall. He had been watching her, Rivkah sensed. She shot him a glance full of pain.

"Rivkah, come here." Rivkah hesitated.

"Come, sit." He pointed to the ground beside him.

Rivkah had to obey. There was no way out of it now. She didn't look at him when she sat down.

"We've been looking for you, wondered where you were. You didn't come back to the house for lunch. Merab couldn't understand why you did not help them finish planting cucumbers. Even Leah had no idea where you were."

Rivkah didn't try to defend herself, didn't think of any excuse.

"Rivkah, you have been deeply wounded. Your face tells the story. I don't need to know what happened. But I want to tell you, you are not alone. Whatever you have done, whatever others have done to you, you are not alone. You are part of the people of the LORD. That will not protect you from every harm, but it means that you are not forsaken. Take your sorrows, your pain and anger to the LORD and he will hear you. Bring your shame before him and he will forgive and heal. The LORD will restore you again. He takes up the cause of the humble and the weak. You will stand among the people and gladness will come again to your heart."

As comforting as Micah's words sounded, Rivkah could not fully believe them, could not even imagine joy and gladness. And how do you take sorrows and pain to the LORD? What would she have to do, what rituals would she need to perform? She doubted that rituals and prayers could fill the emptiness she felt.

Then there was the other question, a question she decided to ask, "What will the others think?"

"You don't need to worry about that," Micah assured her, lightly placing his hand on her shoulder, "but I see it troubles you." He swallowed, gathered his thoughts before he continued, "This family, this house has no cause to think ill of you. You always carry out your duties conscientiously, treat others with kindness and have shown that you are an upright woman. If you have sinned against any of us, unintentionally or deliberately, I forgive you and may they forgive you. If we have hurt you, Rivkah, I hope you can forgive. But it is no sin to feel pain and sorrow when you have been hurt." Micah paused. "They will want to know what happened, of course, where you have been. Let me handle that. I am sure you were praying in your sorrow. And if the LORD calls us to prayer, neither work, nor lunch can keep us back."

Rivkah looked at Micah. He smiled at her. Understanding showed in his eyes. Rivkah was sure she would cope. She knew he would help her. It was one comfort, at least.

Chapter 13

Nadab grinned at Meshullam and lifted the wine cup in a silent cheer. Meshullam only sipped at his wine. This was pure luxury! Who could afford wine in times like these? But the table Nadab's father, Tobijah, had spread before Ehud, Meshullam's father, was more than sumptuous for these times of want. There was a tender leg of lamb, wheat bread dripping with oil, fine cheese, and a spiced lentil dish. Mint, marjoram, and herbs were delicately arranged on a platter to add any desired flavour or cleanse the palate. And over in the corner Meshullam could see the dessert: sweet honey and raisin barley cakes, dried dates, and figs. It was a feast the likes of which Meshullam had not seen for years.

They were the only guests. Father had brought his oldest son, Meshullam, with him, when he was invited to dinner by Tobijah. Father did not know the reason for the invitation but, as the chief elder in the village, he was always willing to listen to the concerns of any of the families. The rich table did make him uncomfortable, though. Meshullam could sense that.

"Ehud, do you want another piece of this leg?"

"Thank you. It is very nice, perfectly cooked, so tender. But first, let me take some herbs."

"And you, young man. Can I offer you some lamb?"

Meshullam was already nearly full and cast a longing eye in the direction of the barley cakes in the corner. He would have to save room for those. But how could he refuse the offer of more lamb?

"Thank you, sir. It is indeed delicious. But first, let me enjoy what I have already eaten," he replied. He hoped it sounded respectful and not too stilted.

Meshullam and Father sat back, resting from the fat food. Father drank a little more wine. He swirled it round his mouth appreciatively, then set down the cup again.

"How is your father Micah?" Tobijah asked.

"He is very well and full of hope for this village. The promises of God's restoration are bearing fruit, here and in Jerusalem."

"Is he in regular contact with his followers in Jerusalem, with the king and his officials?"

"No. He does not send letters to the people who keep his message alive in Jerusalem. They are not many and are not organized. I knew of a few scribes who committed his words to paper, a few temple musicians and priests who admired the power of his words, a few tradesmen and former farmers from the country who saw the truth of his message. But it is not a large group. And while he was respected at the court, he never had direct access to the officials of the king. My father never had the influence the prophet Isaiah had."

"He is too humble. He is well-known across Jerusalem."

"His name is remembered, but his main concern is for the nation, not his standing at the court."

It was clear that Tobijah was not pleased with these answers, but he continued to enquire into the well-being of the family.

"Your wife, Ehud, how is your wife these days?"

Meshullam was sure Mother talked often with Nadab's mother. She could have told her husband many a detail about the families of the village.

"She is busy in the house and in the field. As you know, spring is a season of work."

"It is indeed, Ehud. And can your wife provide good meals for the family each day now that our supplies of food are diminishing?"

"Merab cooks good meals each day, not plentiful . . . " Father cast his eyes over the delicacies spread before him, "but adequate to feed the family. The girls help her with that task, of course."

"Oh yes, you have two older girls in the household who help your wife. Is it two?"

Father signaled agreement.

"My daughter is still young and cannot give my wife a helping hand," Tobijah continued.

Meshullam wondered where he was going with the conversation.

"And your fields? Are they producing?"

"The land here is good. I have known it from my youth. We have had plentiful rains this year. I think what we have sown will grow. Of course, that is not much. But I have seen the green wheat and barley shoots spring up in many of the fields. The seed from the last harvest has sprouted, even though it was not sown by human hands. I believe we can get enough wheat this season. The harvest will be difficult, the threshing laborious, but it will feed us."

"That's true for your fields."

Did Meshullam detect a bitter tone in Tobijah's voice?

"I have also seen the seed sprout in the fields allotted to you, Tobijah. You will have a harvest."

"Some more wine, Ehud?"

"Thank you." Father held his cup as Tobijah poured.

"Woman, offer our guests the cakes and sweets."

Nadab's mother came hurrying from the back of the room and took the dessert platter to Father. This was what Meshullam had been waiting for. After the main guest had taken a cake and some figs, Tobijah's wife offered the food to her husband. Only then could Meshullam get a cake. He savored the sweetness.

"That was what I wanted to talk to you about, Ehud—the fields," Tobijah picked up the conversation again. Ah, now they were getting to the heart of the matter. At last! What did he want?

"The harvest, if there will be a harvest, is still months away. How can we live until then? How am I supposed to feed my children?"

"But you have plenty." Father swept his hand across the half-empty bowls still standing on the table, the leftovers of the lamb, the cakes and dates.

"That is all we have left," Tobijah said. "We need more food."

"But Merab would have fed the family for a whole week with what you have set before us today." Meshullam could detect the simmering anger in Father's voice.

"It was a choice meal, I agree, but it was the last of our food. We need your help, Ehud. We need the village to give us food and money."

"Did you not bring sufficient from Jerusalem?" Father asked.

"We brought the food you advised us to bring, but now we have no more. If the village cannot help, can Micah's friends send us provisions?"

"I don't think my father can call too freely on the goodwill of others. People are struggling in Jerusalem, too. But I will talk to the others in the village. Maybe we can help you until the harvest arrives. We do not have much, though."

"I tried to raise more money from Jerusalem, but no one would accept our fields as security nor would they buy them," Tobijah complained.

"Take your fields as security?" Father exploded. "Are you trying to bring this village into debt, to sell what we have given you? We came here in the name of the LORD to settle the land, to claim it for Judah once more, and you grab land to make money from it. You sell out our inheritance so that the rich govern the land once more and suck the people dry!"

While Father was speaking, Tobijah's face grew red, anger written all over it.

"How dare you speak to me like that, Ehud? Who made you judge over me? Fine, I tried to raise some finance using the fields as collateral, but you can't even leverage your connections in Jerusalem to secure some financial backing for us. A stinking hamlet of hunger and sweat, that's all you're offering. Well, I tell you, that's not what I came here for! I believed the great prophet Micah could offer something better.

"Well, keep your fields of weeds, with the odd barley plant thrown in. Keep your tiny houses of crumbling, mud brick. I'm leaving!"

"Go then, just go!" Father shouted.

"We'll pack up tomorrow. We'll cut our losses and leave this abominable hole. Life's better in Jerusalem. But I warn you, Ehud, do not gloat over me. Do not count yourself lucky that you have got rid of me. You will rue the day you threw my hospitality back in my face. And you will pay for all the lies you've told, all the great promises you made in Jerusalem."

Father jumped up. "Watch your tongue, Tobijah. I am no liar, nor is my father. The LORD will keep us in this land, but we cannot sit back and do nothing. No, we have to move our hands and work. Apparently you are not cut out for that."

Meshullam also stood up awkwardly.

"Leave this house now, Ehud! It is still mine tonight. Just remember you have not won."

Father moved towards the door. Meshullam followed.

Nadab sidled up to Meshullam. "So then, I'm going back to Jerusalem and you'll be staying in this hole," he spat. "Serves you right. You always thought you were better than us."

Meshullam was already at the door.

"And one more thing, Meshullam—tell that whore of your sister that there are plenty of prettier girls in Jerusalem. She is just a slut, an ugly slut! Tell her that!"

* * *

Leah watched them go, did not let her eyes wander from the little group making its way along the ridge. Only when they disappeared from view, descending to the valley beyond, did she cease straining her eyes. She still could not believe they had gone. They wouldn't even stay one more night, although they certainly would not get far today. They would have to camp out somewhere tonight. Why the haste?

Nadab had told Leah that it was her father's fault, that he had made them leave. But Nadab had also added that he was glad to get out of this place, that he was looking forward to returning to Jerusalem. Leah hadn't been able to get much more out of him. He had simply refused to talk to her, had ignored her, claiming he was busy. All her desperate pleas he had just brushed off. As the family left the village, grim-faced—farewelled by few, but surreptitiously watched by many—Nadab had finally told her that Meshullam had a message for her. What could that be? She would have to talk to Meshullam later.

Her eyes returned again to the spot where she had last seen Nadab's figure before he had disappeared over the brow of the hill. Now he was gone! He had walked out of her life so suddenly and left behind a wounded heart and broken dreams. Leah sat down on the crumbling wall encircling the orchard behind the village. So that was it? She would never see Nadab again? This was not how she had seen their future.

It was just a few days ago that he had declared his love, had first kissed her. Leah's lips still burned at the thought of his kisses. She longed for his touch, his sweet words. Only yesterday he had held her close, had murmured promises into her ear as his hands had explored her body. And today he had been angry and aloof, acting as if he hardly knew her. What had brought about the change? She would have to find out, she would have to ask Father! Had Father found out about their love and disapproved? Had he forbidden Nadab to speak to her? Had he sent the whole family away because of her?

She jumped up from the wall and hurried towards the house. Mother was there.

"Where's Father?"

"He can't be far. He came back from the orchard early today. I think he went to talk to some of the other men."

"I need to see him."

"Why, what is it?"

"I need to talk to him."

Mother sighed audibly. Leah was sure she was meant to hear it. It didn't matter. She needed answers now.

She didn't have to wait long for Father. As soon as he came into the house, Leah questioned him, "What have you done? Why did Nadab have to leave, why?"

"Leah!" Mother called.

"Nadab? Ah, the son of Tobijah. Yes, the whole family left . . . , went back to Jerusalem," Father said quietly.

"Why? What happened?" Leah shouted, agitated.

"Leah!" Mother repeated.

"They tried to sell the land that was allotted to them. Tobijah wanted to use this village to get rich. He didn't intend to work the land, didn't regard it as our inheritance, did not strive for the good of Judah. He wanted to live off the back of this community while he alienated the land from us. Luckily, he did not succeed. It is better that he and his family have left—for this village and for him. His family wasn't able to endure the hardship and would never have been able to farm the land with dedication."

"So, that's it? It is all about land?" The disappointment in Leah's voice now overshadowed the anger.

"Leah, I am sad, too, that one family could not pull through. It is a difficult time for the whole village. We came here with such great hopes. And I still have hope. It is just so . . . so disappointing."

"Did you tell them to leave?"

"I did not. But when I discovered Tobijah's plans I did not shrink from pointing out the error of his ways. Such acts cannot be allowed in our midst. And so he left."

"And you are pleased with that?" Leah's anger was rekindled.

"Pleased? No. But I have been concerned for some time. They didn't work the fields, didn't plow or sow. Even though they had enough, they squandered their provisions. We have to live prudently. Everyone in Moresheth-Gath has to know that!"

Father was clearly agitated. The events had shaken his confidence, but also hardened his resolve. His mood did not improve when Shimei came tearing into the house, inevitably followed by Uzi. Father looked hard at the lamb. "That also means that we can't squander our milk and grass on a weak lamb like that. It will never grow fat and it would be better to butcher it now."

Shimei heard the remark.

"No! You can't hurt Uzi!"

"Son, be quiet! What has to be done, has to be done. That lamb will have to be killed soon. You'd better get used to the idea."

Shimei threw his arms around Uzi, holding him protectively.

Leah sensed that she would not be able to get more out of Father at the moment. He was in a sour mood. She had heard all she needed to hear.

So it was just a dispute about the use of the land. She knew there would be no going back on that. When it came to land, Father had strict views. He would never compromise. Tobijah would not be able to return. But what about Nadab? Could he return? Would his love for her bring him back? Or could she join him in Jerusalem? She had to find out what message he had given to Meshullam. Maybe that would tell her what to do.

Leah sneaked out of the house. Meshullam would be getting their goats and sheep from the village flock that one of the other boys had led today. She hurried through the village, past the terebinth where they liked to sit on the Shabbat. The first boy she met was Boaz, his family's animals following behind him. She passed him quickly. He looked at her somewhat puzzled, but she took no notice. Meshullam would still be nattering with the others. Typical! But Leah did recognize the next sheep coming towards her. Meshullam was following right behind it, calling it back while leading the rest of the flock. Looking around to see whether any of the other boys were close, she pounced on him. "What's the message?"

He didn't seem to understand. "What message?"

"The message from Nadab."

"He didn't leave any message."

"He told me he had given you a message for me."

Meshullam didn't respond immediately, apparently trying to remember Nadab's message. How could he ever forget that? A flicker passed across his face. He did remember!

"What did he say?" Leah demanded.

Meshullam hesitated.

"He said . . . " Why didn't he continue?

"Yes, he said . . . " she prompted him.

" . . . that you shouldn't worry about him." Meshullam paused and looked up. "That there are many pretty girls in Jerusalem."

"He didn't say that!"

"He did," Meshullam assured quietly.

"You liar!" Leah exploded. "Nadab would never say that! Tell me! Tell me what the message was!"

Meshullam shook his head sadly. "I've told you, Leah."

"It can't be true!"

Meshullam called the sheep again. They had started to slowly wander away. He set out towards home at the head of the flock, leaving Leah standing alone. She saw Rachel approaching with her family's flock. She certainly didn't want to face her now. And so Leah followed their sheep, walked back home. What else could she do?

* * *

So Nadab had left. It would lessen the pain. Over these last few days Rivkah had been trying to avoid him anyway. And yet, she still wanted to see him, still hoped that the bond they had once shared would come alive again. It would never be the same again, of course, after his betrayal. She knew that. But now it seemed definitely over. She told herself it was better that way. At least she could continue with her life here without being constantly reminded of him. Without being reminded? Who did she want to fool? Every stone, every bush, every path spoke of him. Here in the fields, he had accompanied her when she was gathering herbs and green plants. Up in the village between the houses and trees, they had first seen each other, first exchanged words and glances. And on that hillside, they had watched the sunset together. Memories of Nadab were all around her. Only he was gone.

Rivkah sat down, looked around her. She put the bundle of herbs beside her. Here she was, doing the same tasks day after day—the same tasks she had done to help Amnon and his family. Was this her dream?

What this really home? When she had met Nadab she had been sure this was the place for her. But now . . . was it still true?

She had marveled at the mysterious ways of the gods who had brought her to this village, to this family and this man. She had given thanks to Isis, her personal protector, and to the LORD. But now the ways of the gods seemed confusing and even cruel. Why did they bring her here? To give, only to take away again? To offer hope, only to dash it in pieces? Or was her stay here just a diversion from her proper way? Maybe she was really always meant to go to Jerusalem? Maybe it had been wrong to stay here, to accept the apparent hospitality of Micah's family. They had been good to her, but she had worked hard in the household. She was not just another mouth to feed; she had made a contribution. Rivkah was sure she could earn her keep in Jerusalem, too. She could make herself useful there. Nadab was there, of course. The thought filled her with anxiety. She wasn't sure whether she wanted to meet him. She certainly didn't want to appear to be running after him. Maybe she would not leave for Jerusalem just yet. But she would go there. She would wait for the right time.

Rivkah felt calmer, more certain. This place was not her home, she knew that now. Someday soon she would go on to Jerusalem.

* * *

Shimei! Wherever could he be? It had seemed strange when he hadn't turned up for lunch. Shimei was not known for missing a meal. Meshullam had shouted loud enough for the entire village to know that lunch was being served in the house of Micah. In the end they had eaten without him. Maybe he was out playing in the fields and had simply lost track of time.

After lunch, Meshullam had gone round the whole village and asked whether any anybody had seen Shimei. Nobody had. He got really worried when Shimei still had not turned up at sunset. Mother shared his worry. And so, Meshullam found himself hurrying down the hill into the darkening valley as the last rays of the sun lit up the hills of Hebron. He stopped now and then shouting, "Shimei! Shimei, where are you?" He listened, but heard no response, no voice calling in answer. Rushing on again, he thought about all the places where Shimei might be. The orchards or the fields? Or maybe even the caves? He'd better check them first. Meshullam did not stop until he came to the first cave. But by now, it was too dark to see even a few steps past the entrance. He called into the cave, but only a dim echo of "Shimei, Shimei" returned. His voice sounded frantic. He felt his way into the cave, touching the walls. But even at this slow pace he stepped into a hole in the floor, fell, and hit his knee. It hurt! This was absolutely no use. He would never find Shimei this way. Carefully, he made his way back toward the cave entrance, the fading light guiding him to the outside. He tried another cave, loudly shouting Shimei's name. He didn't really expect a reply, just hoped for the improbable. Meshullam realized that he could not achieve much with darkness falling. Soon he would not even be able see where he was going. He had to return to the village and just hope that Shimei had returned home. Stumbling over stones, roots, and scrub he found the path leading up to the village. By the time he got to the houses it was pitch dark. Light filtering through the cracks of doors and windows guided him on his way home.

Shimei was not there! Meshullam met Mother's expectant look with a quiet shake of his head. "I have not found him." Wherever could he be? What had happened to him? "We have asked everyone. No one has seen him."

"The shepherd boy has not seen him either," Leah confirmed.

"None of the other children know where he is," Rivkah added.

"What about Uzi? Is Uzi with him?" Tirzah asked.

The others looked at each other. Uzi would be wherever Shimei was. The two were inseparable.

"No, I don't think anyone has seen Uzi either. Otherwise they would probably have told us," Mother surmised. Seemingly studying the floor, she repeated the lamb's name several times, "Uzi, Uzi . . . Uzi."

Suddenly she lifted her head and looked straight at Father. "Uzi! That may be why. Do you think Shimei has run away?"

"Run away? Why would he do that?" Father didn't understand.

"To hide Uzi. He may be afraid that Uzi would be killed."

"Uzi . . . killed? Why would he think that?" Meshullam asked.

"Father said he would have to kill Uzi soon. He told Shimei we could not waste milk on a weak lamb like that," Leah cut in.

"That boy, that boy . . ." Father shook his head.

Meshullam's heart sank. If that was true, if Shimei feared for Uzi's life, he would do anything. Shimei would not even think of the consequences, he would just want to protect his lamb.

"Did you . . . did you really tell him that?" Meshullam managed to ask Father.

"We cannot disregard our situation. In times like these a pet lamb is something we cannot afford. That lamb just guzzles milk and feeds on our pasture, but is no use to us. I tried to explain it to Shimei. The boy just won't listen."

Father's reasonable words sounded absurd tonight. Did he not see how much Shimei loved Uzi? How could he talk about butchering the lamb? Of course, Father was right about not wasting milk or feed, but cold reason was not always the only consideration and certainly not how Shimei saw the world.

"I think Mother is right. Shimei would run away if he feared for Uzi's life," Meshullam said quietly.

"We will have to find that boy," Father stated.

"That will be difficult. He will run from us. He won't answer when we call his name," Mother cautioned. Then she leaned over and put her hand on Father's shoulder. "Will you promise not to hurt the lamb if he comes back? Will you do that?"

All eyes were on Father. He sat still, not wanting to give an answer.

"For your son," Mother added.

"My son has to learn. But this time I will not hurt the lamb. It will live—for this year at least. We cannot have anything detract us from our task. The death of this lamb will only create sorrow and dissent. It will detract us from the work at hand."

"Well spoken, my son." Grandfather expressed his agreement. "Tomorrow we will look for Shimei. We will tell him he can come home unafraid. We cannot search for him tonight. But we can pray and ask that the LORD will protect him from all the evils and dangers of the night."

Grandfather raised his voice, the others lifting their faces upwards.

"Protect, oh LORD, our son from the troubles of the night
and guard him against the powers of darkness.
Keep him safe from the fangs of the wild beasts
and may your angel keep watch over him,
so that he may greet the dawn of another day
and we may yet praise you as morning passes to noon.
You are our help and our deliverer,
oh LORD, the God in whom we trust!"

"Amen," Meshullam affirmed the prayer that reflected his own worries and wishes. If only Shimei was safe. Oh, let him not be hurt tonight! Let him not get lost in the wide lands! There were wild beasts and snakes out there. He could fall into old cisterns or wells. Or he could wander into the land of the Philistines. So many dangers! Meshullam hoped that Shimei had not gone far. He could picture him out in the dark alone, shivering, with Uzi pressed against him. He would be listening into the night, every noise, every shadow frightening him. He would be hungry and tired, but unable to sleep. Did he have any milk for the lamb with him? Yes, that would have been the first thing he thought of. Shimei cared more about the needs of Uzi than his own.

"But now we must eat. We have to be ready to look for Shimei tomorrow. It's no use letting our worries carry us away." Grandfather signaled Meshullam to sit down and join the circle. Leah carried the pot from the hearth and set it down in the middle of the family gathering. Mother passed out the stew. One bowl remained empty—Shimei's.

* * *

Tirzah ran ahead through the plowed olive grove, looking behind every tree, repeatedly calling, "Shimei! Shimei!" Leah combed through the olive trees to her right, and Mother was walking through the trees farther up the hill. Leah wasn't convinced that all their shouting and searching would achieve anything. Shimei would come back sometime, she was sure. He would get hungry and cold. He'd realize that he had to come home. Of course, something could have happened to him. But would they ever find him in that case? He could be anywhere.

Leah looked behind a shrub at the edge of the grove and pulled apart its springy branches. Nothing. Not that she had really counted on finding any sign of Shimei there, but each potential hiding place and shelter raised a weak glimmer of hope only to be repeatedly disappointed. She did care about Shimei. She couldn't deny that. Even though he was plainly annoying at times as most little boys were, she was quite fond of him. She could still remember him as a little child. He had been so tiny and helpless. She had been keen to help Mother with everything, had responded to his every cry. There had been nothing more important than her little brother. Times had changed, of course. He wasn't so cute anymore and thought much more of Meshullam than Leah. It seemed

Meshullam was his great example. Anyway, these days Leah generally had other things to do than follow her little brother around.

Tirzah was already sitting on the ground, leaning against the stone wall, when Leah got to the end of the grove.

"We still haven't found him," Tirzah said. The disappointment was plainly visible on her face. She didn't have any energy left. The fruitless search had exhausted her. Leah also felt like a rest. She sat down beside her sister. "I don't know where he could be. The others are searching for him, too. Maybe they have found him."

Mother came over, clearly not willing to give up the search for her son yet.

"Come on girls. We have to find Shimei. We have to go on. He could be among those rocks over there."

"I can't anymore," Tirzah groaned. Leah wasn't any keener to go on.

"We have to find Shimei. Just sit here for a while, but then you go and look over there beneath those rocks. I'll go uphill and look there."

Mother wouldn't rest until she found Shimei. She hurried up the hill, searching behind bushes and rocks, in shallows, and under limestone overhangs.

"We'd better get up," Leah told Tirzah after they had sat silently for a while. Tirzah was clearly still tired.

Leah stood up. "Come on!"

"But . . ."

"Tirzah, we don't need to go far."

Tirzah finally got up and shuffled after Leah. It didn't look very hopeful over there beneath those rocks. It wasn't really the place anybody would hide or seek shelter in. It would just be another futile search.

All this was really Father's fault. If he hadn't lost his calm and suddenly become obsessed with not wasting that tiny amount of milk on the lamb, Shimei would have never run away. Father was just so unreasonable at times and hurt a lot of people. Did he now see what he had achieved? He had scared his son so much that he had run away from the village. And Shimei was not the only one. Through his uncompromising views Father had already driven others away.

The two sisters looked among the rocks. A pair of quails fled from them and they disturbed a hare, but there was no sign of Shimei or the lamb.

* * *

High in the sky, a hawk soared, circling above the summit of a low hill. Rivkah watched it swooping down at ever increasing speed and racing across the rolling landscape. She lost sight of it when it disappeared behind a gentle rise. Had it discovered something? A pigeon? There were plenty around. The afternoon wind carried their cooing across the land. As the wind snatched away the sound of one, another pigeon called, their cooing creating a chorus of sound, ebbing and rising, distinct voices at times hovering above the general chorus.

Rivkah searched alone. She preferred it that way. Micah had thought she knew the area well enough from the many times she went to gather herbs. He had told her to search the rolling countryside to the west. She actually didn't come here that often, but she knew it well enough. In her search she had gone farther than she had ever gone before. The rise, over which she saw the hawk disappear, was unknown territory to her. And so she decided to look there, to see where the hawk, the messenger of Horus, led her.

The hollow beyond seemed ordinary enough. A stand of trees reached from its lowest point up to the higher sides, denser at the centre than at its edges. Looking at it, Rivkah realized that some of the trees were felled and charred. And there, across from her, she could make out the remains of a house. The place looked abandoned, without a trace of human life. Maybe wild beasts lived there now. Had the Assyrians come here, too? Even in the warm afternoon sun Rivkah felt cold. Maybe she should turn back. But since she was already here, shouldn't she look? She was sure she would find edible plants among the trees. She could come back for them later.

Rivkah walked down slowly. She didn't want to shout. Not here. She just quietly said Shimei's name a few times. There were a few fruit trees in the hollow, their fresh green leaves cheering up the desolate place.

She strode up to the ruins. It must have been a small hamlet once. There were two farm houses. Some of the walls still stood, or at least parts of them, but the roofs had collapsed and mud bricks and stones lay scattered around the place. She had seen enough. There was nothing here. It was already late in the afternoon and she'd better get back to the village.

Rivkah had only walked a few steps when she noticed a movement among the ruins. She froze. What was that? Slowly, she turned her head to take another look. Yes, there out of the abandoned house came a lamb. Had it escaped the Assyrian attack? No, it was far too young. It could only be a few weeks old. Rivkah looked again. Could it be . . . could it be Uzi? She walked towards it, crouched down, and stretched out her hand. The lamb jumped towards her, and nuzzled her. As she held it, she was certain, "Uzi!" She stroked his wool. "Here you are, Uzi! Now, where's Shimei? He can't be far, eh?"

Rivkah found him asleep in the corner of the house, leaning against a wall, his head lying on a jumble of mud bricks. Beside him was a small jar. She picked it up. It was empty, but the smell of sour milk told her what he had carried in it. She shook Shimei gently. He groaned quietly and moved his head slowly. Suddenly he opened his eyes with a start. He seemed to recollect where he was, what was happening.

"Where's Uzi?"

Rivkah pointed to the lamb. "He's here. He is alright."

Shimei jumped up and ran over to him and sweeping him up in his arms held him protectively. "Don't kill Uzi!"

"We are not going to kill him."

"You won't tell Father where we are, will you Rivkah?"

"Shimei, your father has said he will not hurt Uzi. Don't be afraid. You can come back home now."

"But, Father said he will kill Uzi."

"He has promised he will not hurt him. He wants you to come back . . . and Uzi as well," Rivkah said.

"Has he really said that?"

"Yes, and your grandfather, too."

Shimei was still unsure. He wanted to believe her. "Will Uzi get milk?"

"Yes, Uzi can drink milk. We have enough."

"Uzi is hungry, you know. He has nibbled some grass, but a young lamb needs milk."

"There is plenty of milk at home. Your father said Uzi can have some. He only wants you to come home."

Shimei suddenly seemed eager to go. He put Uzi down and stepped out of the house. Uzi followed him. Rivkah picked up the small jar and left the ruin. She took Shimei's hand. "Come Shimei, I'll show you the way. Let's go home."

* * *

Uzi drank eagerly. Meshullam helped Shimei feed him. Seeing the little tongue licking the bowl, the keen eyes focused on him, the ears standing alertly, he realized that he had missed Uzi. He marveled at the pink nostrils of the lamb, the head of curly wool, the thin legs that had grown so much stronger these past weeks.

Meshullam hoped his obvious care for Uzi did not rile Father. While Father was glad to have his son back safely, he hadn't been that welcoming towards Uzi, acknowledging him only grudgingly. He had told Shimei that the lamb would live, for now at least, and that he had better feed it some milk.

Mother could hardly take her eyes off the son that had seemed lost to her. She had embraced and kissed him when Rivkah had led him back into the village. Now she was busy preparing a hearty meal for him. Leah and Rivkah helped her. Grandfather sat silently observing the others, seeming to enjoy the eagerness of Uzi.

When the bowl was empty Uzi licked the wool around his mouth to get every last drop.

"That's enough now, Uzi," Meshullam laughed, "you are hungry, eh? But don't fill your belly too quickly."

Shimei planted a kiss on Uzi's head. "You're fine now Uzi, aren't you? That milk did you good, didn't it?"

"That's enough milk for the lamb today," Father commented. His words cut coldly into the happy mood. Meshullam let go of Uzi, but Shimei tightened his hold on him.

"Time for dinner," Mother announced lightly, breaking the awkwardness. The family sat in the circle, everyone coming together for the meal. Mother filled the bowls which Leah then passed around, serving Grandfather and Father first.

During the meal Rivkah had to retell how she had found Shimei. It really was amazing that she had stumbled across him. Who would have thought that Shimei had gone there? That was in the direction of the Philistines and who knew what they would do to a small boy from Judah. Meshullam was just glad that his brother had been found. He hoped that Shimei realized the danger he had placed himself in and would never run away again.

After dinner they sang psalms of thanksgiving, even Father joining in with gladness.

Chapter 14

"What is Jerusalem like?" Rivkah asked Micah.

"Jerusalem?" Micah said quietly beside her. "That's right, you've never been there, have you?"

"No." But Rivkah had to know. She still wanted to go and live there one day. The others spoke about Jerusalem now and then, made the occasional remark, but generally talked more about their new village. Still, Jerusalem was never far away from their thoughts and Leah sometimes told stories, giving snippets of information about life in the capital city. Knitting it all together, Rivkah had had assembled a picture of what Jerusalem was like. But they had only been there for a short while, and as refugees at that. Old Micah had spent more time in the city, Leah had told her. Apparently, he was quite well known in Jerusalem.

Rivkah hoped Micah would tell her more. And so she had joined the old man as he sat in the afternoon sun in front of the house. Rivkah always enjoyed sitting with him. He made her see life in a new way, showed her other perspectives. And he really did seem to like her.

"Jerusalem," Micah came back to her question after he had gazed into the distance, gathering his thoughts, "Jerusalem is a city of many faces. You have to learn to see them, to get to know the different sides of the city."

Rivkah looked at him as he rubbed his forehead.

"Jerusalem is a mighty city. Its towers are high, guarding its gates. Yes, it has nine gates. And its walls are so wide that two chariots can pass each other on the wall. The temple stands high on Mount Zion. It is the glory of the city. Right next to it is the palace of the king. What great buildings they are! But spread over the hills and the valley are the small houses of the people, hovels crowded together along narrow streets and packed with men, women, children, and animals. Their lives are hard. Not many own land and so they work for the leaders of Judah, selling their time and skills to the rich to earn enough to feed themselves and their families. Jerusalem is a city of contrasts."

"And you know all the sides of the city?"

"I know it well. I have lived in the houses of the poor and spent days in the palace of the king. I have spoken to the common people and to the high officials of the court as well as the priests."

A sparrow fluttered across from its perch on the neighboring house, landing on the ground in front of them. They watched it as it cleaned its feathers in the dust, shaking its little body. With a chirp it flew away.

"Yes, injustice is plain to see in Jerusalem. The leaders live in luxury while the poor have barely enough to feed themselves. And not just in the city. The leaders pressed the last ephah of barley, the last jar of oil out of the towns and villages of Judah. The holy city had become the haunt of predators. There was no justice. The leaders of Judah did not hear those that were wronged. They did not recognize their own wrongdoing, did not want to see the harm they inflicted on the nation. How often did I warn them! I can still hear the words I spoke to them:

'Hear this, you leaders of the house of Judah,
you rulers of the house of Israel,
who despise justice
and distort all that is right;
who build Zion with bloodshed,
and Jerusalem with wickedness.
Her leaders judge for a bribe,
her priests teach for a price,
and her prophets tell fortunes for money.
Yet they lean upon the LORD and say,
"Is not the LORD among us?
No disaster will come upon us."
Therefore because of you Zion will be plowed like a field,
Jerusalem will become a heap of rubble,
the temple hill a mound overgrown with thickets.'"

Micah's voice grew to a crescendo, then stopped abruptly. He turned towards Rivkah.

"Was it really that bad?" she asked.

"It was that bad. I saw a farmer dragged before the law courts. His landlord accused him of not paying the rent. The farmer called the evidence of his neighbors. They witnessed that the landlord's steward had collected the jars of barley and wheat. But apparently, they had never arrived at the landlord's premises. And the farmer didn't get the promised receipt. Now the landlord was seeking redress. The farmer pleaded, even promised to pay again the rent misappropriated by the steward. He would have had to have given his stock as security to borrow enough to pay—but the court would have none of it. His pleadings were declared to be an admission of guilt. So he and his family were sold into debt slavery to cover the rent and the penalty. Nobody dared to speak against the judgment, but we all knew that the judge had received gifts from the landlord and was frequently entertained at his house.

It did not end there. The king himself was guilty of injustice, condoning the murder of those that stood in the way of his building program. The money for his great projects was sucked from the poor. The grandeur of Jerusalem is built on blood. And therefore, the city stands condemned. For a city built on injustice will not last."

"Did they listen?"

"No, they did not listen. They claimed that the LORD was with them. But they do not know the LORD. For the LORD hears the cries of the downtrodden and the suffering. And the LORD loves justice and condemns those that pervert it, especially if they do it in his name."

Rivkah saw the grim face. Micah's eyes that were normally so gentle now burned with fire.

"I told them often. I said:
'Listen, you leaders of Jacob,
you rulers of the house of Israel.
Should you not know justice,
you who hate good and love evil;
who tear the skin from my people
and the flesh from their bones?

'This is what the Lord says:
"As for the prophets
who lead my people astray,
if one feeds them, they proclaim 'peace',
if he does not, they prepare to wage war against him.
Therefore night will come over you, without visions
and darkness, without divination.
The sun will set for the prophets,
and the day will go dark for them.
They will cover their faces
because there is no answer from God."'"

Micah stared at the ground. "They did not believe me. They thought I was just a radical from among the people, maybe even paid by their enemies. But I did not talk for gain. No, I saw the misery, I saw the injustice and I could not remain silent. The Spirit of the LORD drove me to point out the wrongs. And so I spoke.

I told them:

'But as for me, I am filled with power,
with the Spirit of the LORD
and with justice and might,
to declare to Jacob his transgression,
to Israel his sin.'

But what was the Spirit of the LORD to them? They continued as before. Generation after generation of leaders learned from their fathers and continued their iniquity. They did not change their ways."

"But Jerusalem was not destroyed, was it?"

"No, even when the towns and cities of Judah were destroyed, Jerusalem was spared. As I told you before, it is a city of contrasts. It is, after all, the LORD's holy city, the mountain of his temple where the LORD's presence dwells. Jerusalem is the centre of his people. While its rulers act unjustly it remains under the threat of destruction. But Jerusalem will stand no matter what, even if it has to rise again out of the ashes. Even in the darkest time, when destruction seemed at hand, I was able to speak words of hope to the city. The LORD will redeem it, of that I am sure.

'In that day', declares the LORD,
'I will gather the lame;
I will assemble the exiles
and those I have brought to grief.
I will gather the lame
and the outcast I will assemble.
The LORD will rule over them in Mount Zion
from that day and forever.
As for you, oh watchtower of the flock
oh stronghold of the Daughter of Zion,
the former dominion will be restored to you;
kingship will come to the Daughter of Jerusalem.

'But now many nations are gathered against you.
They say, "Let her be defiled
let our eyes gloat over Zion!"
But they do not know the thoughts of the LORD;
they do not understand his plan,
he who gathers them like sheaves to the threshing floor.

'Rise and thresh, oh Daughter of Zion,
for I will give you horns of iron;
I will give you hoofs of bronze
and you will break to pieces many nations."'

Micah's eyes shone, a smile playing around his lips. His anger had been replaced by hope.

Rivkah could hardly fathom the change. "So Jerusalem will not fall?"

"Jerusalem will stand in the end and the LORD will rule from Zion. That is what we can always look forward to. At times it may seem as if it will never come true. And in those times people lose hope. They do not even see what they still have. When Jerusalem was surrounded and under siege, the people lost all courage, did not even trust the king who called them to endure. They saw only the forces arrayed against them, heard only of the destruction wrought across the country. They could not see beyond the present danger. Many people never can."

"But now the enemy has left."

"The enemy has left and did not destroy Jerusalem. Still, Judah is not a great nation. But trust in the LORD. The days will come when the land will bloom again and everyone will dwell in safety. And other nations will not plunder Judah. No, Judah will rule over them, will tread them into the dust, if they raise their weapons against the LORD and his people. For any nation that seeks to gain riches by the sword will fall by the sword."

* * *

Uzi was still a runt, Meshullam couldn't deny that. He looked thin, even though his wool had grown thicker. He wasn't tall by any measure. But he had certainly grown. He no longer looked weak, as if a gust of wind would carry him away. And he was now munching grass happily. He had

had his last bowl of milk weeks ago, but still came rushing up whenever he saw Shimei. Then he was like a little lamb again, jumping excitedly around the boy.

Ah, it was good to sit in the shade and lazily watch the sheep graze. Meshullam leaned back in the grass and peered up into the dark green leaves of the olive tree. He broke off a stalk of grass and put it in his mouth, wiggling it with his tongue. Tomorrow, the hard work would begin. That's when the harvest would start—if you could call it a harvest. They had not sown in winter, but the barley still grew in some of the fields. The seeds from previous years had sprouted, and Father thought there were pockets where it would be worth their while to cut the grain and sort the weeds from the barley. Until then he would enjoy the Shabbat. All he had to do was watch the family's sheep near the village. No one was going out to find pasture on Shabbat. There was still enough grass close-by.

Meshullam took the stalk out of his mouth and flung it aside. He plucked a flower instead and chewed on its stem. But he spat it out immediately. Yuck, it was bitter! He sat up and tried to get rid of the taste, spitting again. That was better.

Meshullam noticed that Uzi had stopped grazing and was looking around. What was happening? Then Uzi suddenly began to run toward the village. Meshullam now saw Shimei as well. That explained it.

Uzi ran straight at Shimei, lightly ramming his legs. He proceeded to jump around the boy. Shimei took hold of Uzi's wool and dragged him down so that both of them were tumbling on the ground. Uzi got up in a flash, hopped away from Shimei and waited for him to follow.

At times it was difficult to tell who was chasing whom as they ran across the pasture. The other sheep reluctantly moved out of the way when the two came close, some voicing their protest.

Meshullam lay down again, this time on his side, watching Shimei and Uzi.

"Meshullam!" Shimei yelled when he saw him. "Meshullam!" he called again.

Meshullam didn't answer, pretending to be asleep. He watched Shimei through half-closed eyelids.

"Meshullam, come and play with us!"

Meshullam just let out a loud snore.

The expression on Shimei's face changed, suddenly became focused. He whispered something to Uzi. Then he crept towards Meshullam, Uzi following less silently behind him. Meshullam lay still, watching the two coming towards him. Shimei found a dry thistle which he wanted to pick but, after hurting his hands a few times, he abandoned the idea. Uzi meanwhile wandered closer to Meshullam and now proceeded to sniff at his legs. That tickled!

Suddenly Meshullam jumped up, let out a loud cry and grabbed Uzi. The lamb wriggled and kicked. Shimei ran away. That had given him a fright.

"Let him go!"

"If you come and get him," laughed Meshullam.

"Not fair! You weren't really asleep," complained Shimei.

"With all your shouting and running, did you really think anybody could sleep?"

Meshullam suddenly let Uzi go. Immediately, the lamb bolted away, running back to the other sheep, who looked at the excited Uzi, slightly bemused, before turning back to find the next tender blade of tasty grass. Shimei ran after Uzi. This time Meshullam came too.

"I'll get you!" he warned his giggling brother.

"Don't, don't!" Shimei gasped when Meshullam caught up with him and tickled his tummy. He rolled in the grass laughing and shouting at the same time, hardly able to breathe. Uzi joined the two brothers, butting Meshullam in the back so that he fell over.

"Silly sheep!" Meshullam shouted, but Shimei had already launched a tickle attack on him. Meshullam inadvertently kicked Uzi as he tried to roll away to escape Shimei before going on the attack again.

"Stop it!" Shimei shouted.

"Alright," Meshullam agreed.

Shimei sat up, but was still laughing. Uzi jumped around them. It seemed as if he was laughing, too.

* * *

This wasn't like the barley harvest last year. Whole sections of the field were hardly worth harvesting. There, the few barley plants were so smothered by weeds that only a thorough search would have turned up a few grains. However, Father and Meshullam still worked the whole field row by row, making sure that they cut all the barley they could.

Mother and the girls followed them, picking up the stalks and bundling them together. He had to admit that he was still nowhere near as fast as Father. After all, it was only his second harvest as a cutter. And last year they had not harvested any wheat, but had fled when they heard of the Assyrian invasion.

It was hard going, but he hoped he would get into the rhythm soon. Rivkah worked together with Meshullam. She had never harvested before, had never gathered grain. That's why she worked with him. They were the slowest. Mother worked with her at first and showed her what to do. Initially, Rivkah wasn't very fast and fell behind, even though Meshullam did not work particularly fast and Mother helped her, but then she must have gotten it. She kept up with Meshullam. Working as fast as she could, she hardly even stood up to stretch her back.

Meshullam remembered the years past, when he had worked with Mother to gather the stalks, just as many other boys worked with their mothers in the field. The back certainly did hurt when you had to bend down continually so low to the ground. Cutting the grain was a bit easier, at least as far as the bending went. Of course he still had to lean down, but nowhere near as far.

Taking the ears of barley in his left hand, Meshullam brought the sickle down and cut the stalks in one swift movement. Gathering the cut stalks in his left arm he grabbed another handful to cut. He tried to gather the stalks from several cuts in bunches before putting them down on the ground. It would make it easier for Rivkah. That way she wouldn't have to untangle each individual stalk from the many weeds. She could just collect the bunches and tie them together into sheaves.

They had started early this morning, but the sun already stood high in the sky, beating down on the harvesters. Meshullam wiped away the sweat running down his face and lifted the cloth covering his head. It was pretty much drenched, too. And there was still plenty to do. When they reached the end of the field, not far from the tree where they had left the water skins this morning, Meshullam stretched and told Rivkah, "Time for a drink. We'll have a short break."

"Right. I'll just gather these last few bunches into a sheaf."

Meshullam walked over to the tree and put the sickle down. He took the water skin and poured the liquid down his throat. It felt nice and cool in this heat. When Rivkah came along, he gave her the water skin. The way she drank she must have been thirsty, too. And the way she walked showed that her back did hurt.

"Hard work, eh?" Meshullam commented.

"It's alright."

"Doesn't your back hurt?"

"It does a bit. But I'll manage."

"Just make sure you drink enough. Otherwise you'll get tired real quick."

Rivkah nodded and lifted the water skin to her mouth again. She took another drink, but more slowly this time.

"Can you give it to me?"

Rivkah handed the water skin back to Meshullam, who took a quick sip and then moistened the whetstone. Holding the sickle in his left hand and pushing it against the ground, he moved the whetstone rapidly back and forth across both sides of the blade. That was the way Father had showed him to sharpen a sickle. And even if Meshullam wasn't as practiced as Father, it should make cutting that much easier after the break.

"We'd better get back to work."

Rivkah followed Meshullam back to the field. This time she had no problems keeping up with him.

"You haven't done this before?" Meshullam asked her.

Rivkah looked up at him. "No."

"You know you're quite good at this?'

"Really?"

"For years I used to gather the grain, but I don't think I was ever as fast as you are after just one morning."

Rivkah didn't reply.

"Maybe I didn't work as hard. After all, it's not the nicest work," Meshullam suggested.

He cut a few more stalks and put the bunch down on the ground.

"I certainly prefer cutting the barley more than gathering it, especially with all those weeds."

"It must be different harvesting a field that has been plowed and then sown with barley."

"Quite different. You still have thistles and weeds among the barley, but it's better than having the barley among the thistles and weeds."

"But we are getting some grain, aren't we?"

"Oh yes. And we can be thankful for that. I think we will harvest enough wheat and barley. But harvesting will be hard work."

As if to prove it, Meshullam grabbed a thistle when he took the next handful to cut. He let go of the stalks in his left arm.

"Ouch, sorry for that," he told Rivkah as the stalks fell onto the ground, scattering among the weeds. He shook his hand, looked at it and pulled the thistle tip out of it. He didn't want that to happen too often. He would have to concentrate on the field again.

* * *

Those flies! As if the heat and the constant bending weren't bad enough! Leah brushed the little insects from her arms and legs. They seemed to swarm and bite particularly round the scratches from thorns and thistles. They were irritating at the least and sometimes just painful. With each day of the harvest her arms and legs became more swollen and scratched. She bathed them every night in water to cool them. Mother always told her off for it. She thought it best to keep the sweat and grime on the skin as a protective layer. Apparently they shielded the skin from the strong sun and insects alike. Later, after the harvest, you could wash and be clean again, she said. That's what she had been taught by her mother.

But Leah didn't quite believe it. She always looked forward to the evening when she soaked the day's injuries in the cooling water. And the way Mother started to smell—did she not notice? She didn't even seem to care and walked beside the other women on the way home from the fields. True, some of them did just the same as Mother, but were they not ashamed to be noticed by the other women, to be avoided by their daughters and husbands?

And Leah had to work all day with Mother! She usually hung back a few paces, preferring not to be seen working directly beside her. It was not fair! Why did she have to stay with Mother and Rivkah didn't? Only now and then did Mother allow her to work with Meshullam and Rivkah. Then Leah would hurry off as quickly as she could.

Leah trudged along behind Mother, gathering sheaves. She looked at the other two with envy. They were working hard, too, she had to admit that, but they were also having fun. Just now Rivkah laughed at something Meshullam said. Then it was Rivkah's turn to tell a story. Leah wondered what they were talking about. Meshullam continued cutting, but instead of walking forward slowly, he jumped off the ground with both feet at every second step. Strange! What were they doing? It went on for quite a while.

"Leah, concentrate!" Mother snapped when Leah was so distracted she dropped half a sheaf. Leah picked up the stalks again. Why was Mother so upset? These things did happen after all. She hung back but was careful she got all the bunches Mother had left on the ground for her.

Rivkah and Meshullam laughed as they worked. Now Meshullam started singing a song:

"Ears of grain standing tall,
ears of grain do not fall
before the sickle slides
before the thistle bites."

Rivkah joined him in the chorus:
"Rejoice for what you reap;
it gives you pleasant sleep, lalala
the table full of bread;
the house and guests are fed, lelele"

Meshullam must have taught her that one. Rivkah wouldn't know any harvest songs. He sang the next verse:

"Come, join me in the song,
come, know it is not long,
so, go another row;
it's done before you know."

Rivkah came in again, her voice high and clear:
"Rejoice for what you reap;
it gives you pleasant sleep, lalala
the table full of bread;
the house and guests are fed, lelele"

They repeated the song again, drawing out the "lelele" at the end of the chorus. Meshullam added a few warbles. Now he was just plainly showing off. Rivkah tried some variations as well, less successfully, Leah thought. The effort must have exhausted them, for soon Leah could not hear any more singing or talking from the two, just the quiet swish of Meshullam's blade.

"Why don't we sing a song, Leah?"

No Mother! Not now! Whatever gave her that idea? It wasn't the same. It was one thing for Meshullam and Rivkah to sing, another for an adult like Mother to burst into song. Maybe Mother took Leah's silence as encouragement, for she started:

"Oh, come now all together,
come, join us in the field;
and we will harvest thither
whatever it will yield.
When winter comes with vengeance,
when all is dark and grey
we'll have bread in abundance
in houses snug and dry."

Leah didn't join in. She looked around. Good, only the family was close-by. No one else was there. That would have been just too embarrassing. Rivkah, no doubt, would laugh at Leah having to endure Mother's singing. But Leah would make sure nobody thought she was part of it. She hung back even further. When the song was over, Mother did not start another one. They continued working in silence.

* * *

Where in spring mud bricks had dried in the sun, piles of wheat and barley now covered the level ground. Around one of these piles Meshullam drove two cows in a large circle, their hooves treading the stalks of wheat, breaking them into smaller pieces. The grains separated from the stalks and husks by the forceful threshing. Father threw the loosened sheaves of wheat onto the threshing circle, spreading and turning them evenly. And Meshullam led the cows across them, constantly going round in a circle.

When he was satisfied with the result, Father threw the threshed wheat to the side, forming a boundary around the threshing circle. He immediately replaced it with more sheaves from the central pile.

This afternoon they would do the second threshing, throwing the wheat back onto the circle and heaping it in the centre. In a few days it would be winnowed and sieved, not an easy task with so many weeds amongst the grain. But at least they did have some barley and wheat, probably enough to last through the winter. For this they were thankful.

Meshullam looked around the threshing floor. Every family in the village had their piles. All the men were out here to thresh. Over there, Ahiel urged a donkey around a pile of barley. They even had a threshing sledge. His little sister was squatting on the sledge, watching the hooves of the donkey plodding ahead. Most families had not had time to make a threshing sledge and so relied on the hooves of the animals to crush the stalks. The heavy cows were much better at that than the light donkeys.

Shouts of conversation drifted from pile to pile as men discussed the harvest, guessed how much grain the piles would yield. Boys sang songs to urge on their animals and to annoy their friends across the threshing floor. Well, until their fathers cut in and stopped the silly songs.

Meshullam was so intent on listening to Ahiel's song about stupid donkeys that he nearly didn't notice one of the cows in his team stopping and lifting her tail. Just in time he placed the catcher under the beast's rear end to catch the excrement. Once they had resumed their circular route, he threw the stuff beyond the outer pile, outside the threshing floor. He had to pay attention. It just made things so much more difficult later if animal poo was mixed in with the straw and grain.

Watching the two yoked animals more closely, Meshullam guided them around the circle. Their hooves now fell in a steady rhythm, crushing the sheaves, tearing them apart. Meshullam's eyes focused on the treading, He watched as stalks were torn and fractured. And the hooves fell on them relentlessly. What was it that the prophets had been saying, that Grandfather had once proclaimed? Just as the plants were broken to pieces, so the LORD's enemies would be shattered.

When would the prophecies come true? When would the enemies be crushed like wheat under the hooves of oxen?

Father turned some sheaves and Meshullam led the cows across them. Once more their hooves broke the stalks apart.

And who were the enemies of the LORD? Were they the invaders, or did they also live among the LORD's people? What about the power-grabbing leaders, the common thieves and bandits? Meshullam shuddered. On whom would God's judgment fall? Would he not also judge the whole people? For were they not all so often complicit in the rebellion against the LORD and his law? Who would survive then?

What? The cows stopped again. Meshullam quickly thrust forward the catcher. The wheat must not be polluted.

* * *

For several days Rivkah brought lunch out to Ehud and Meshullam. She watched the animals go round in circles, men and boys goading them on. She saw how the wheat and barley was broken and crushed. The plants she had carried from the fields were now just a jumble of torn stalks, shriveled leaves, opened husks, and grain—the seeds of the plants. It was a destructive process to get to the goodness of the grain. Later on, it would have to be ground into flour to make bread. She knew about that part only too well.

Rivkah mentioned all this to Micah when she was sitting beside him outside the house one morning.

"Yes, it requires hard work and good land to provide us with food. And we can be grateful that the land provided its bounty to us this year, even though we did not sow. But the harvest was small and the labor to collect the grain was hard. You still harvest what you reap, Rivkah. Many people can recognize this when they see the fields. If we sow weeds, we will get weeds, if we sow wheat, wheat will surely sprout in the field. But it also holds true in our lives and in the lives of nations: in the end injustice will give birth to injustice, wrong will bring wrong. And though we may see good around us, evil seems to triumph, injustice to remain unchecked."

"Have you seen much of it?"

A sad smile played around Micah's lips when he looked at Rivkah.

"Rivkah, I am an old man. I have seen much injustice and it always seemed to pay its way. The perpetrators seemed so successful, so secure in their position. Nothing could hinder them. I have seen many families stripped of their land. For generations they had worked hard. They plowed the land, sowed, harvested, threshed, and winnowed the grain. And then they lost the land. It requires both land and hard work to survive. And if the land is taken away from them, how can they feed themselves? They have to beg, or sell their labor to others. The number of the landless increased. I could not keep silent. I had to speak out."

"What did you say?"

"I can still remember the words. They still echo in my mind. Rivkah, listen:

'Woe to those who plan iniquity,
to those who plot evil on their beds!
At morning's light they carry it out
because it is in their power to do it.
They covet fields and seize them,
and houses, and take them.
They defraud a man of his home,
a fellowman of his inheritance.
Therefore the Lord says:
"I am planning disaster against this people,
from which you cannot save yourselves.
You will no longer walk proudly,
for it will be a time of calamity.
Therefore you will have no-one in the assembly of the LORD
to divide the land by lot."'

"And did they change?"

"No, they continued as before and they continue still. But I have seen many of the land-grabbers lose their land. They thought they had acquired it with the color of right, sealed the land transfer in the gate and the palace. But now, what they had regarded as theirs has been taken by the enemy, has been wrested from them. Of course, the same fate also struck many of the common farmers but, finally, some of the large landowners had done to them as they had done to others."

"Do you think they will lose the land altogether?"

"They are so secure in their royal bureaucracy. They believe it will stand forever. But has not the northern kingdom, Israel, been destroyed? Have not the officials, merchant bankers, and the landowners of Israel been carried into exile? They have been driven from the land. So also, the kingdom of Judah cannot protect these land acquisitions forever. They forget that the foundations of Israel and Judah go back further in time. For this land was not settled by kings and officials but by the tribes of Israel. Just as Joshua divided the land by lot in the assembly of the LORD, so it will again be divided by lot. And those who have accumulated land, robbing others of their inheritance, they will not be represented at the assembly. No land will be allotted to them. For finally, it is the LORD who allots the land, who judges our actions, who provides justice. It is so easy to forget that when we are faced with the might of the current system. I reminded them often and yet few believed."

"What did they say when you told them?"

"They did not want to listen. They paid the "professional" prophets to preach against me. And people preferred to listen to these "professionals", though they are just deceivers."

"What did they say?"

"Well, I had to defend myself against their accusations, of course; I had to point out the fallacy of their arguments.

'Do not prophesy,' their prophets said,
'Do not prophesy about these things;
disgrace will not overtake us.
Should it be said, oh house of Jacob:
"Is the Spirit of the LORD angry?
Does he do such things?"'"

"That's what they said?"

"Yes, that's how they preached against me."

"And how did you respond?"

"I told them:
'Do not my words do good to him whose ways are upright?
Lately my people have risen up like an enemy.
You strip off the rich robe
from those who pass by without a care,
like men returning from battle.
You drive the women of my people from their pleasant homes.
You take away my blessing from their children forever.
Get up, go away!
For this is not your resting place, because it is defiled,
it is ruined beyond all remedy.'

"Yes, they tried to forbid me to preach. They said it was blasphemy. They told the people that the LORD would never get angry with them. And the leaders and the rich believed them, for that was what they wanted to hear. They wanted to continue in their ways. If, they reasoned, the LORD was pleased with them, they could continue stripping the farmers of their land in the courts, they could continue their little war games along the border and take the land of their brothers. Yet their very actions were offences against the LORD's covenant, against everything

Israel stands for. And the prophets encouraged them. Blood is also on the heads of the prophets, for they condoned driving the people from the land and thereby bringing suffering and tears to women and children. They will carry their sins."

"What happened to them?"

"Some are still there, more arrogant than ever. Some people have seen through their deception, others are still blinded by it. Their message is much more attractive than the one I was given to proclaim. I told them:

'If a liar and deceiver comes and says:
"I will prophesy for you plenty of wine and beer,"
he would be just the prophet for this people!'"

"Did they do that?"

"Close enough."

"It must have been hard for you."

"It was. At times anger carried me away. At times sorrow for my people broke my heart."

"And now?"

"Now I look back and wonder if my words achieved anything. I warned them, but they did not listen. I spoke the words the LORD gave me to speak. I told them what the spirit urged me to proclaim. Maybe that is all that counts."

Rivkah put her hand on Micah's arm.

"Rivkah, despite the disappointment, I still marvel at the LORD's faithfulness, I still give thanks for every person that does hear and turns to the LORD. For these words will not die and the promises of the LORD will come to pass."

They sat in silence. Rivkah rose. It was time to prepare lunch for the men threshing outside the village.

Chapter 15

Leah was glad there was no animosity between her and Rivkah anymore. Over the time of the harvest, as they worked together, the rifts had healed. Rivkah had welcomed any conversation. And so they talked together at meals, maybe too much for Father's liking at times. They shared stories from the past, talked about the present and discussed the future. Leah got to know Rivkah better, enjoyed being with her. She had no problem admitting that she liked her. Actually, Rivkah was probably her best friend.

Leah wasn't quite sure when she realized it but, now it seemed so obvious—Meshullam and Rivkah were the perfect pair. The problem was that the two hadn't realized it themselves or at least they didn't acknowledge it. So Leah took it upon herself to try and get them together. It was somehow exciting playing the matchmaker. She watched them closely at first. They certainly got along well, liked to be in each other's company, but there was no indication of anything more, not really anyway. Leah did sense something that Shabbat evening when Rivkah sat beside Meshullam. He looked up when she sat down, moved aside a little and then slowly edged towards her while they sang. Or did Leah only imagine that? They looked good making music together side by side. By now, Rivkah joined in most of the psalms they sang. The ones she didn't know, she tried to pick up, singing along softly until she knew the words and melody.

Then there was the day when Meshullam showed Rivkah how to sieve the barley. They joked and laughed together as they had done through much of the harvest. And they sat close, Meshullam sometimes leaning over to show her something, and to guide her hands. But their conversation never developed into anything serious. Meshullam's instructions became dry and methodical, explaining the right technique over and over, correcting Rivkah as she tried to get it right.

And so Leah looked for further signs, and for opportunities to get them talking about matters of love and the future. They were alone together occasionally, like the time they brought the first load of grain in from the threshing floor. But talking across the back of a donkey would hardly have been romantic. Maybe Leah had to push them along.

When the three of them walked back home one evening after gathering the first of the early figs from a tree halfway down the ridge, it seemed the right time to bring the conversation to the point. First she tried to talk with Meshullam about the future.

"We we will be able to use the threshing floor for making mud bricks again," she said casually, as they discussed the progress of their work on the grain.

"What would we want to build?" Meshullam looked puzzled.

"Maybe you would want to add your own house," Leah suggested. "It must be getting time. You'll be the first to build a new home."

"I won't build one until I'm getting married."

"So you've been thinking about getting married?"

"Sometime in the future, yes, of course."

Rivkah looked somewhat bemused at the interchange, but did not say anything.

"Have you thought about who you might marry? There are not many girls in the village," Leah continued.

Meshullam seemed to hesitate slightly before he answered.

"I don't know. I'm not in a hurry. No doubt more families will settle in the land again."

That was not the direction Leah wanted the conversation to go in.

"But if you had to choose from those that are here now."

Meshullam would not be drawn.

"Father will settle that." He seemed intent on evading the question. Instead, he talked about how the land would need to be divided if more people came, especially the olive groves. After all, it took so long for the trees to get established.

Leah pursued the topic.

"Rivkah, have you ever stayed out in the orchards in early fall?"

"Stayed out in the orchard? No, we didn't have one."

"We girls go out and live among the vines and trees to protect the fruit until it is time to harvest them."

"And the girls seem to really enjoy it," Meshullam put in.

"We do. We sing songs—songs of love—and we dance. It is a time of rejoicing, of music late into the night."

"Nice," Rivkah commented.

"You know some love songs, Rivkah, don't you?"

"Yes, but they're not really good."

"Why don't you sing one?"

"Now?"

"Yes."

"No," Rivkah shook her head, "not now. I don't think I can remember them. And... you know... I don't really want to sing them tonight. Maybe we'll sing some psalms later on, but not those songs." Rivkah laughed nervously.

Meshullam hung back a few steps. Was he embarrassed by the thought of Rivkah singing love songs or by Leah's own insistence? Maybe, Leah had to admit, this wasn't the right approach. "In the orchards then. It's not that long to go now. You'll see, it really is a good time."

They came close to the village and could hear a dog bark.

"Why don't you two walk on and I'll go and see Rachel on the way home?" Leah suggested. But even this attempt was unsuccessful.

"I'll come with you," Rivkah said.

"But Meshullam, is that alright with you?"

"Oh yes, you two can go and see Rachel; I'll be on my way."

"But..."

"See you later!"

Meshullam walked on ahead alone. The two girls could only do as Leah had said. Together they walked towards Rachel's house.

* * *

The lamps flickered, casting dancing shadows against the walls. The guests had already put their three young children to bed, and now husband and wife were sitting with their hosts, telling their story. Mother passed around some cake made from the harvest's grain. The guests accepted it with gratitude. The man was quietly spoken and Meshullam had to concentrate to hear him clearly. The sounds of the cow and donkey in the adjacent room, the rustling of the sheep, the occasional bark outside, all stood out clearly as he tried to listen.

"We could not stay. They took everything we had. We were glad to escape with our lives."

"The Philistines?" Father asked.

"Yes, men from Ashdod. They claimed that the land had been given to king Mitinti. They had come to demand tribute and taxes, they said.

They took the meager harvest we'd won from the land. The animals—sheep, goats, and donkeys—they herded away. They even claimed our jars, pots, and bowls. The nicer pieces they took away, the others they smashed outside our house. They left nothing. They warned us that they would be back... after the olive harvest; they wanted olives to feed their presses. They made that clear. The consequences would be dire if we could not deliver. But how can we?"

"Are there still any olive trees left standing?"

"There are, but many have been cut down by the Assyrians. We would have to move from lonely tree to lonely tree, from grove to grove to gather what the rulers of Ashdod demanded. How could we do that without tools, animals and food? Life has become unbearable. We had to leave."

"How many houses were there in your village?"

"Only the two families, my uncle and I. We had returned to our ancestral village to claim our inheritance again. But we can live there no more."

"You could not fight them?" Meshullam asked.

The man looked at him, bemused and offended at the same time. Meshullam was glad for the dim light. It hid the color now rising to his face. How stupid could he get?

"No, we could never fight them. Ten of them came with swords and spears. I only had my knife tucked in my belt. I'm glad they didn't strip that off me. We have no protection there and so we bow to their threats."

"Judah will not protect you, will it?"

"No, we have no protection from the king. When we went back to our village, we saw that it was deserted. The Philistines had not laid claim to it. We hoped that the king would establish the towns and forts again to protect us from their incursions. But few settlers followed and the king apparently has given up on this part of the land. That leaves us open to attack from the Philistines. And they take the opportunity to pillage, to take the little they can get their hands on."

"We have to prepare ourselves here as well," Father said to Grandfather. His face had become increasingly anxious as he listened to the account of their guests.

"And now, where are you going now?" Father asked the man.

"To Jerusalem, although I don't know whether we will stay there. I have heard that the towns and villages in the highlands have not been destroyed. Maybe we will even go to the towns now established in the desert, along the shores of the Sea of Salt, or in the South."

"Stay here with us," Grandfather urged. "There are fields and a house for you here."

The man shook his head.

"We cannot. We will not be out of the reach of the Philistines here. No, I have to protect my family, have to get them out of harm's way."

"But this is our task, to settle the land, to make it bloom again. And the LORD will be with us. He will give us victory over the enemy," Grandfather urged.

"I believe the LORD will restore these lands to Judah once again. But what if I and my house perish while we wait? We may return once it is safe. For now we will go east."

No one spoke. Even Grandfather argued no longer.

"Thank you for your offer. We appreciate your hospitality," the man added quietly.

Leah and Rivkah gathered the drinking bowls together. It was already late. The guests stood. "May you rest in peace. May the LORD bless you," the man proclaimed.

"May the LORD guard you during the night. May he watch over your lying down and your rising," Grandfather responded.

Meshullam got up and handed the man a burning oil lamp. "To find your way."

Rivkah led them to the room where the bed had been prepared for them. Meshullam heard her enquire politely whether they required anything else. It seemed they were content. Meshullam climbed the ladder to the roof. He crawled under the light blanket beside Shimei. His sleeping brother hardly moved as he settled down at his side. He heard the girls and his parents come up a little later.

The sky was clear this night. He looked at the stars above, the lights dotted across the firmament, then turned on his side and closed his eyes. Sleep did not come immediately. And when it came, soldiers carrying swords and spears dominated his dreams. They demanded a lamb, nothing more, just a lamb. But the lamb was Uzi. Shimei did not want to give him up. No one could separate him from his lamb. He grabbed Uzi and ran down into the valley. The soldiers followed in pursuit. In horror,

Meshullam saw that they were gaining on him. Meshullam wanted to run to help Shimei. But his feet were as heavy as iron. He could hardly lift them. He saw that the soldiers were nearly upon Shimei. He tried to shout to warn him. But he had no voice. No sound would come from his mouth. With a jerk Meshullam woke up. He was wet with sweat. It was just a dream, he told himself, it was just a dream.

* * *

"Leah, where are you going in such a hurry?" Grandfather greeted her. He was sitting in his usual place outside the house.

"I need to talk to Mother and Father," she responded.

"You need to talk to Mother and Father?" he repeated loudly. "And so you will, no doubt, like a good daughter should. But be a good granddaughter and talk to your old grandfather first. Come, sit." Grandfather indicated a seat beside him.

"But . . ." Leah had not come to talk to Grandfather. She really wanted to talk to Mother and Father. When else would she get the opportunity to talk to them alone?

"Sit," Grandfather said again.

"I want to talk to Mother and Father."

"Talk to your grandfather first. Give your Mother and Father some time, eh? Come, sit," he urged her again.

What else could she do? Rivkah sat down next to him.

"What are the others doing?" Grandfather asked her.

"The same as every Shabbat. Tirzah and Shimei are playing with the other little children and Meshullam and Rivkah are sitting under the terebinth talking to Ahiel and the others."

"But you have come back here?"

"I need to talk to Mother and Father—alone."

"I will not ask you what you need to see them about. It must be important for you."

Leah just nodded her head. No, she wouldn't tell Grandfather, not yet.

He seemed to look into the distance, quietly observing the sky and the rows of hills stretching into the horizon, before he turned to her again. "How is life for you here in this village, Leah? Do you like it?"

"It's alright."

"You seem a lot happier now after the harvest than you were before it began."

"Really?"

"You know it yourself. You probably just didn't expect your old grandfather to notice. I'm not totally blind yet, you know."

"I know."

"I've also noticed that you and Rivkah are talking again."

"But we've always been friends."

"Always? Leah, don't think your grandfather is old and deaf. You didn't talk to each other for weeks, avoided each other whenever you could. But I'm glad that you've set aside whatever drove you apart. And your friendship has helped you heal, just as it has helped Rivkah."

Grandfather gently put his hand on her arm.

"Leah, you have been hurt. Be thankful for the healing. And be thankful for Rivkah's presence. At times you might have wished that she never had come. You were not always thankful for her presence here. Is it not so?"

"Yes," Leah admitted quietly.

"Remember that the LORD's ways are not our ways. At times they may seem strange and full of obstacles. But do not give up believing."

"So Grandfather, do you think the LORD brought Rivkah here?"

"I do, Leah. We humans may follow our own ways, but the LORD is still in control. And I believe that the LORD in his mercy has brought Rivkah here."

If Grandfather believed it, so would she. It only confirmed what Leah had come here to talk about. She looked at the door. She had already talked long enough with Grandfather.

"I see you are still keen to talk to your parents," he laughed. "Get up and talk to them. Just make sure they know you are there."

Leah jumped up.

"And Leah," Grandfather added, "it was good talking to you. Come any time."

Leah nodded and went into the house.

She did not have to look for her parents. They were sitting in the main room as if they were expecting her. Had they heard her talking to Grandfather? Father stroked his beard as he did so often. But Mother seemed somewhat flustered. Her dress didn't sit right, as if she had put it on in haste. Father looked sternly at Leah. Was this the right time to tell them? Leah wasn't sure anymore. But she couldn't go back now. They were clearly expecting her to talk, to say something.

"Leah, what is it?" Father asked. Was it that clear that she wanted to tell them something?

"I need to talk to you," she said.

"Then talk. Your mother and I are listening." Father smiled, but not at her. No, he was looking at Mother.

"It's about Meshullam and Rivkah."

"What about them?" Father turned towards Leah.

"Well, it's not right . . . if a young woman lives under the same roof as your son, especially since he is unmarried."

"What are you trying to say? Has anything happened? Have they behaved dishonorably?"

"No, no, they haven't. But people may think . . . "

"Let people think what they will. Rivkah is part of our family now. I will not send her away because some old women might gossip."

"That's not what I mean."

"Then what do you mean?"

"It's just that Rivkah . . . she is the perfect bride for Meshullam."

Father seemed surprised. "The perfect bride?"

"Actually, I have considered her as well, dear. Leah is right. She would make a good wife for our son," Mother said.

Father looked at her tenderly. "You have thought about it?"

"Yes," Mother smiled.

Leah hadn't expected that. Now she had an ally in Mother. It might be easier than she had feared.

"Do they . . . do they love each other, Leah?" Father asked.

"They don't admit it, not even to each other. But I'm sure they do. And they get on well together. Have you not seen them?"

"I have seen them. But, do you think they have talked about it themselves?"

"No, I don't think so. Maybe they're just too shy. But deep down there is love. They just don't know how to show their fondness for each other."

"Good," Father said, "I hope your observations are right."

"What do you think?" Mother asked him.

Father just raised his eyes and winked at her. Then he turned to Leah.

"Thank you for talking to us about it. We will consider what you have said. But don't say anything to anybody else. Leah, you can go now. Your mother and I need to talk alone."

Leah went outside. They certainly had not rejected the suggestion. But what would they do? It seemed Mother was quite taken with the idea. And Father looked as if he would listen to Mother, that today he couldn't refuse her anything. Maybe Leah had come at the right time.

* * *

"Rivkah, can you stay here for a moment," Ehud said as they were getting up from lunch.

"Now?" she asked.

"Yes," Merab said. Then she turned to Leah, "Leah go on ahead to the garden. Take Tirzah and Shimei with you. Shimei, you make sure Uzi doesn't eat anything in the garden."

"He won't," Shimei promised.

"Good, I'll be along soon, and if I see one leaf missing he'll know about it," Mother warned.

Rivkah stood as Leah took a basket in one hand and Tirzah's hand in the other; Shimei and Uzi trotted along behind them. Meshullam strapped some empty jars on the donkey and led it to the threshing floor while old Micah slowly walked to his favorite spot outside the house. Leah gave Rivkah a look that she was sure was meant to be encouraging. Did Leah know what this was about? Rivkah certainly didn't. She stood somewhat awkwardly in front of Merab and Ehud. It was clear they didn't just want her to help in some task; they wanted to talk with her. Had she done something wrong? Maybe they had some other work for her to do? What if they said she couldn't live here anymore? Rivkah was ready to go on to Jerusalem. She had always pushed her departure further out, but maybe now was the time.

"You can sit down again."

Ehud had never gotten up from lunch. Merab sat beside him, leaning against her husband, taking his hand in her hands and stroking it gently. Rivkah had not seen them together like this before. What was it? Puzzled she sat down opposite them.

"Rivkah, you have been with us now for several months," Ehud began.

"We have valued all you have done. You have helped us greatly," Merab continued.

"We have seen that you are a hardworking woman. You are skilled in housework and ready to learn new things. And yet you remain humble."

Why did Ehud praise her like that? Where was he going with this?

"You have been a blessing to us. In so many ways you have contributed to this household. You are nearly part of the family." Merab looked directly at Rivkah.

Was that it? Would they now say it could not continue like that? Rivkah leaned forward and with her right hand grabbed her dress, bunching the folds together. Would she have to leave?

But Ehud brought up something totally different, "I understand that you have no family left, no father or brother."

"Yes, they are all dead or captured," Rivkah agreed.

"That's why we are talking directly to you, for you have no one else who can speak on your behalf. Rivkah, we want you to be part of our family."

So she would not have to go! But what did he mean? Rivkah looked at Ehud questioningly. She noticed his wife nudging him. Why was this man—usually so confident—suddenly so nervous?

"I wanted to ask you whether you would agree to marry our son."

So, that was what it was all about?

"Meshullam?"

"Yes, Meshullam," Merab confirmed softly.

Rivkah's mind raced. She did like Meshullam. But becoming his wife? She hadn't really considered that. Of course, she had known of the possibility. After all, he was one of the few young men in the village. He was a good man, caring and diligent, but not really . . . exciting. Now his parents were looking at her expectantly. They wanted an answer.

"Will I live in this house?" Rivkah wasn't ready to say yes or no—not yet. She needed a moment or two.

"Sorry, I didn't tell you." Ehud suddenly sounded businesslike. His confidence returned. "We will build a house for you next to this one. You will be well cared for. And even though you do not have a father, I will provide a bride price. It will be your property forever. Your husband will not be able to touch it. I will give you twenty shekels of silver. Of course, we will provide you a wedding dress and new clothes. Your house will be furnished: bowls and jars, wool for bedding, and blankets will be yours."

Rivkah only half listened to the promises of silver and clothes. She knew it was a good offer. She couldn't deny that. And she would be able to remain here with the family. She would truly be part of the house of Micah the prophet. Wasn't that what she had wanted? But what about Jerusalem, her plans to find a new life in the city? All that she would have to give up.

Ehud cleared his throat.

How could she deny them their wish? They had been so good to her. And the offer showed that they did hold her in high regard. She should be honored. But Meshullam, he was hardly the man of her dreams. He was certainly no prince, just an ordinary young man. People wouldn't call him handsome, but not bad looking either. He had an open honest face. People seemed to trust him easily. He would be a good husband, she was sure of that.

She thought of the harvest time, when he had taught her songs, when he had made all the hard work feel like fun. He had looked after her, done everything to ease the burden on her. It had been a happy time.

"Yes," she whispered.

"What?" Merab enquired, eyes shining.

"Yes, I will marry him," Rivkah said louder.

"My daughter, my daughter!" Merab rushed forward and embraced Rivkah. Tears flowed from her eyes. Rivkah could feel the wet kisses on her cheek. She hadn't known it was that important to Merab. Had emotions, deeply hidden before, now welled up in hope and joy? Rivkah hugged Merab. "Mother." It was the first time she had addressed her by that name.

Merab stroked her hair. "My daughter, you have made me glad."

Rivkah extricated herself from Merab's embrace. She smiled at her.

"May the LORD bless you." Ehud didn't show any rush of emotion, but he seemed pleased at the arrangement, at having successfully concluded a deal.

"From the time of your betrothal until you enter the house of your husband you will live in the house of another family. It will all be arranged." Ehud sounded so practical.

Merab turned from Rivkah and embraced her husband. "Our son will marry a good woman," Rivkah heard her say. She wondered whether Merab would still say that if she knew all about Rivkah, her faults and doubts, her past and her ambitions. Rivkah wondered whether she would be able to live up to their expectations. What did they require of the wife of their son?

Ehud kissed his wife, then stood up. Rivkah stood likewise.

"Thank you, Rivkah", he said.

So that was it? She turned to go.

"We will talk more tonight."

What else was there to say?

Rivkah hurried to the door. She needed to be alone, needed to understand what had happened. Micah was outside the house, sitting where he usually sat.

"Shalom, Rivkah," he greeted her. She did not feel like talking to him now. She hardly acknowledged him and walked out of the yard. He must have known about it. Could he have said something to her earlier? Would it have made any difference?

Rivkah went past the houses of the village. She wasn't sure where she was heading. To the cistern? Down into the valley? Just away, some place where no one would look for her. She certainly wouldn't go past the garden. That's where the others were.

With her eyes to the ground, she didn't see him approaching—nor the donkey laden with grain—until he spoke to her.

"Rivkah, how did it go?" Meshullam's voice was so cheerful it grated. So he knew! Did he think she would be bursting with joy, running to embrace him? He was wrong then. Meshullam must have sensed something was not right. "Rivkah?" He sounded concerned.

Without looking at him she hurried on.

"What . . . what happened?" It seemed he didn't understand. She was sorry, but she just couldn't face him now. She would be his wife, yes, but somehow she felt betrayed by him. Had he just been so kind to her, laughed with her, taught her new skills, because he wanted her to be his wife? Had he seen the real Rivkah in her, or just a girl of marriageable age? What had been his motivation? And then he had gotten his parents to lean on her, had not even dared to ask her himself. It might be how things were done here, the proper way to ask for marriage, but it was hardly romantic or courageous. She hurried on, away from the village.

Rivkah sat down among thistles and the parched, summer grass. She mourned the loss of dreams and rejoiced in the fulfillment of others. She marveled at the mysterious path that had led her here and recalled the sorrow that seemed to constantly break into her life. She looked into the future with hope and trembled at the thought of the expectations placed on her. She was comforted by the trust of others but felt annoyed by their scheming. She was glad to have found a home but apprehensive about what it would hold for her. The sun was already setting by the time she made her way back to the village, back to the house of Micah.

* * *

Maybe one or two loads more to carry the rest of the grain from the threshing floor to the house. Meshullam checked that all the jars were securely tied on the donkey's back. "Let's go then!" He gave the donkey a slap on the hindquarters and led it along the path to the village. It came willingly today and so he reached the houses quickly.

Rivkah was coming towards him. Why wasn't she in the garden? That's right. Father and Mother had wanted to talk to her. He wondered what it had all been about. "Rivkah, how did it go?" he asked. She glanced at him with a confused, nearly angry, look. What was wrong?

"Rivkah?" Had Mother and Father complained about something? Whatever could that be? What could they have said?

Rivkah walked right past him, eyes downcast.

"What . . . what happened?" Something wasn't right. He looked after her. It appeared there was nothing he could do right now. She clearly didn't want to talk to him. Maybe it was just one of those strange moods girls sometimes seemed to have. They could get upset at the slightest thing.

Meshullam tugged the rope of the donkey. "Go!" At first the animal strained against the rope but then must have decided otherwise and followed willingly.

He didn't think he could ask Mother and Father about their conversation with Rivkah. But maybe they would at least give a hint of what it had all been about.

They wanted to talk to him immediately.

"Tie up the donkey, Meshullam. We need to talk to you," Father greeted him as he entered the door.

"The jars?" He couldn't just leave them on the donkey.

"Yes, we'll take the jars off first."

Father came over and carried some into the back room. Once the jars were all stowed safely away, Meshullam led the donkey to the stalls. He joined Mother and Father in the main room.

"Meshullam, you are a man now. You showed at the harvest that you are no longer a boy."

Meshullam sat down. What was Father getting at? Was this praise, or had he done something wrong?

"You know how to work the land, how to work together in the village. You know the rights and responsibilities of a man. I think you can take care of a family. It is time for you to marry."

Meshullam shifted uncomfortably. Of course he wanted to marry. Had he not listened to love songs pretending to be disinterested and yet wishing they were about him? Did he not sometimes look at a girl and wonder what it would be like to touch her and hold her? And, once he was married, he would be recognized as a man in the village. But what would be expected of him? His whole life would change. And he was not really good with girls. Did Father expect him to find a wife?

Mother continued, "Your father and I have chosen a wife for you, a good woman."

So they had chosen already. Who would it be?

"You will marry Rivkah," Father said.

Rivkah? Meshullam had never allowed himself to think of her in that way. After all, she lived with them. He had always told himself she was more like a sister. Now that he considered it, Rivkah was what he had always been looking for in a wife: she was a good Judahite, hardworking, humble yet confident; she was kind, observant, and appreciative of beauty and life. When he thought about it, he had probably never felt so happy around any other girl. She was really nice and was pretty enough. Even more important, he could not really think of any faults, none that mattered any way. Yes, she would be a good wife.

"What do you say?" Mother wanted to know his reaction.

"That's great." He smiled his approval.

But then Meshullam remembered how troubled Rivkah had seemed when he had met her. What about her? Did she want to marry him?

"Did you ask her?"

"Yes," Father replied.

"What did she say?"

"She said yes," Mother told him. She leaned forward and stroked Meshullam's arm. "Rivkah is a good woman."

"I know. Was she happy when you asked her?"

"She was emotional. I think she only just realized what it would mean for her."

So that's what it was! People called it being "emotional". That would describe Rivkah when he had met her. Maybe that's what women did. But he still didn't know whether she was happy, what she really thought about the plan. All he could see was hurt and confusion when he recalled Rivkah's "emotional" face, no happiness. Did she have other dreams and hopes? He was sure she didn't loath him, but marrying . . . ? Did she agree to it out of a sense of duty? What were her real feelings? What would their life together be like?

"From the time of your betrothal until your wedding Rivkah will not live in this house. She will live with another family, maybe the house of Joel. We will build a house next to this one. It will be your home."

"Good." Meshullam nodded. There would be time. Time to think about the new life, time to prepare for their new responsibilities, time to get to know her, time apart and time together.

* * *

The noise from the grindstone drifted from the floor below. That could only mean one thing—time to get up. Meshullam turned over lazily. Just a few more minutes' sleep, that's all he wanted. He was dead tired. Twisting and turning throughout the night, it was not until early morning that sleep finally and mercifully gave his troubled mind some rest. The news of the previous day had dominated his thoughts. He had tried to imagine the future, had puzzled about what would happen next. He had tried to think of all that Rivkah had said to him, all she had done. What did she think of him? What would life bring for them? He had found no satisfactory answers in the night, no rest. Shimei had kicked him once or twice, unhappy that his sleep was disturbed by his wakeful brother. Now the other side of the bed was empty. Shimei was already up. Meshullam sat up and rubbed his eyes. With a yawn he got out of bed.

Downstairs the family was already at breakfast.

"I was up before you," Shimei challenged him.

"Wow, well done."

Mother lifted her eyebrows at the sarcasm in Meshullam's voice.

"But I was," Shimei maintained.

"And you even looked after the animals, didn't you?" Mother encouraged him.

"Good Shimei," Father put in, then turned to Meshullam, "There's nothing urgent to do today. We've got all the grain in from the threshing floor. I looked at the sesame field. We'll start the harvest in a week. Today I'll do some work on the house. Can you get some wood, please? Take the donkey."

Leah passed Meshullam some bread.

"Should I take the ax?"

"Yes, get some well-sized pieces. I noticed a withered olive tree at the end of the upper grove. That would make some good wood."

"I know the one you mean."

Meshullam cut off a piece of cucumber and ate it with his bread. Rivkah didn't look at him. Eyes downcast she chewed on her bread and talked quietly to Tirzah about the sheep and goats in their flock. The two girls knew the animals, their characters, and each individual trait. Rivkah did the milking most days and Tirzah often took them to pasture. It was a familiar topic.

"Rivkah, do you want the cucumber?" Meshullam didn't know whether he should have asked the question. But Rivkah looked up and smiled at Meshullam, hesitantly at first, then her eyes sparkled as Meshullam returned the smile. "Yes please."

He leaned over to give her the cucumber. Their hands did not meet, but at the moment they both held it, their eyes locked, held each other more firmly than hands could. It was over in an instant. But it changed everything for Meshullam. He knew there was more to this than his parents' search for a wife, more than a plan to increase the numbers in this village and nurture a new generation. Rivkah was in this together with him. This was about Rivkah and him, their future. In that moment Meshullam saw Rivkah in a new light. It was as if a stab went right into his heart. He thought he had never met such a beautiful woman before, never seen a face so lovely. If he hadn't been sitting down his knees would have buckled under him. He became aware that his mouth was wide open. Don't be a fool now, he told himself. He reached for his cup filled with water. It was what he needed now.

Rivkah ate the cucumber with the dry bread she had nibbled on before. Meshullam guessed she was just as uncertain about what was happening as he was. But he knew nothing would be as before.

After breakfast, Meshullam saddled the donkey and tied the ax and ropes to its back. He saw Rivkah busy with the goats, but they didn't exchange any more words or looks that morning. With a last glance in her direction, Meshullam led the donkey out of the yard.

The sun sparkled in the dew that lay on the grass and hung on the trees. Like pearls covering a precious mantle, so the droplets covered the land. A thousand little suns spread across the ground, reflected the light from the sun above. Meshullam breathed in deeply, tasting the moisture-laden air. The beauty of the earth and the brilliance of the sky awakened an echo in his soul. It joined the hymns of thanks chirped by birds and repeated by hills and valleys, flowers and trees. At first the song rose within him silently, but as he made his way along the ridge it broke out and his voice proclaimed thanks to the creator of beauty and splendor, of joy and love.

"The heavens declare the glory of God;
the skies proclaim the work of his hands.
Day after day they pour forth speech;
night after night they display knowledge.
There is no speech or language
where their voice is not heard.
Their voice goes out into all the earth,
their words to the ends of the world.

"In the heavens he has pitched a tent for the sun,
which is like a bridegroom coming forth from his pavilion,
like a champion rejoicing to run his course.
It rises at one end of the heavens
and makes its circuit to the other;
nothing is hidden from its heat."

Today Meshullam would give all praise and honor to the LORD; today he would not hold back his thanks. How could he keep from singing on such a morning? How could he remain silent? His heart overflowed with joy, his eyes could not fathom the wonders of the earth. How often had he travelled this path, had walked these hills yet had not seen what he saw today? But today he saw the world with new eyes, for today he knew what beauty was, knew the answer to his longings. All his yearning dissolved into the desire to know, understand and love her. Did not the sparkling landscape display the same beauty that he first beheld when he saw Rivkah this morning? Did not every bush and tree, every flower and stone breathe her name? "Rivkah!"

Just as the LORD showed his goodness to all through this land, so, and more clearly, did he show his loving-kindness towards Meshullam through Rivkah. This he knew. She was the answer to his dreams, the one to whom he would give all his strength and love.

When Meshullam arrived at the withered olive tree he took the ax off the donkey and tied the animal to a nearby tree laden with fruit. But the withered tree without fruit he cut down.

* * *

The blazing fire inside the bread oven had subsided; the smoke dissipated, leaving red, glowing embers that heated the sides. That was the moment to put the bread in the oven. Rivkah sat next to it, the tray of leavened bread at her side. It had been rising for several hours now. Leah knelt opposite her, right in front of the oven. Beside her was a stone platform. Rivkah took one of the balls of dough and worked it into a flat shape. She placed it on the stone platform. Leah picked it up, flattened it some more and then in a single movement slapped the bread against the inner wall of the oven. She quickly drew her hand out of the baking heat. Rivkah had already taken the next ball of dough, turning and throwing it with her open hands to shape it into the flat loaf she then placed beside Leah. She brushed aside a strand of hair that fell across her face and peered into the oven. The first bread was just about ready. The smell of freshly baked bread wafted into her face. She drew in a deep breath.

Leah completed forming the flat bread, put it back down on the platform and then reached into the oven to get the baked bread. She easily loosened it from the wall. "Oops, I nearly dropped it."

"No, you didn't?"

"Just nearly," Leah assured her. Luckily she didn't. Otherwise the bread would have just been burnt in the embers. What a waste of good flour that would have been. Leah picked up the next bread and slapped it against the inner side of the oven.

"So, you will live with Rachel's family now?" she asked.

"Yes. Her father Joel has agreed that I can stay in his house until . . . you know . . . until spring."

"Until the wedding?" Leah smiled at Rivkah.

"Yes, until the wedding," Rivkah giggled.

"What do you think of Meshullam?" Leah lowered her voice.

Rivkah briefly stopped turning the next bread. "He's alright."

"Alright?! Come on, you like him."

"I do." Rivkah started slapping the dough again. "He's nice. I just didn't really think of marrying him."

"And now?"

"Now I'm somehow looking forward to it. But, I'm still not sure how he feels about it."

"He really likes you."

"I hope he does."

"You know he does. You can see it."

"Why didn't he tell me earlier then? Why did he leave it to your parents to ask me?"

Leah didn't reply. She took the baked bread out of the oven, and placed it on top of the other, then slapped the next one against the oven wall. Finally she looked up, rolled her eyes and just said, "Men!"

"I know. Sometimes they just don't know what to say." But Rivkah wasn't fully satisfied with that answer. Meshullam hadn't really spoken with her since his parents had asked her to marry him. In fact, he had seemed strangely shy around her since then. Maybe she was too. Had she tried talking to him? She probably should. Tradition would keep them apart from the time of their betrothal.

"Meshullam is a quiet one sometimes. He often doesn't talk about the things he cares about most. I've noticed that. I still remember when Father gave him a donkey of his own. Meshullam had never asked for it. But you should have seen his face when Father told him about the donkey. Meshullam was overjoyed. Of course he tried not to show too much emotion. But I tell you, no donkey in the whole village was as lovingly cared for as that old beast. Unfortunately, we couldn't keep it in Jerusalem." Leah stopped to exchange the baked for the unbaked bread in the oven again. "He had a favorite psalm, I remember. But he never wanted it sung. Still, I heard him singing it in the fields when he was looking after the sheep and he thought nobody was around. That's just how he is. I thought I'd better warn you."

"But sometimes he speaks very earnestly, as if he is talking about something really important to him."

"Oh, he can sound really concerned, but I'm not sure that he shares much of what he really cares about."

Rivkah nodded. She had often wondered whether Meshullam's words meant more than they appeared to on the surface. Maybe he had said something to her and she just hadn't picked it up. But then, how would she have reacted? What would she have said if he had told her that she meant more to him than any other girl he had met, that she was not just a refugee to him? She wasn't sure whether she would have been able to respond to his love then. Not only did she have other plans, the hurt was still raw. After Nadab had betrayed her, after he had rejected her, she did not know whether she could ever trust a man again. She was certainly more cautious. Nadab had left his mark: wounds that had not yet healed, feelings that had not yet passed. Meshullam would be different. He would not draw back from her, would not play games.

Maybe it was better that his parents had talked to her first. For now she knew. Now she saw Meshullam in a different light. Looking back, she could see some signs of his desire for her, small, apparently insignificant, signs. She had not noticed then. Now she cherished them. Now she would respond. She hoped he would be able to talk to her, to share what he really cared about, to trust her.

"Rivkah?"

"What?"

"That bread is more than flat," Leah laughed.

Rivkah looked at the dough in her hands. She had beaten it nearly wafer thin. She hadn't really noticed. "Oops, sorry."

"Well, less work for me. And it's the last one. All that bread should be enough for a few days, I would say."

"That depends on what else your mother has planned for our meals," Rivkah said.

"Maybe a lamb? Some meat would be nice."

* * *

It was not long before they had lamb for dinner. The betrothal of Meshullam and Rivkah was held within days. She—happy, but uncertain. He—shy, but radiating joy. They looked good together—not totally at ease, but very much captured by each other. Still, the happiest person was clearly Mother. She beamed at the pair, embraced them both throughout the evening and praised them repeatedly. Was it because her oldest son was now becoming a man and, once married, would take his place among the other men of the village? Was their marriage the fulfillment of her most ardent prayers?

Leah sat and watched the joyous occasion. She could be more than satisfied with what she had achieved, she thought. It may not have been only of her making, but she took the initiative at the right time. She had not been wrong in her observation; Rivkah and Meshullam were made for each other. Their paths joined here in this place. Maybe good had come out of the disaster that had befallen their land—at least some good. For how else would have Rivkah found her way here? Had the LORD brought something beautiful out of this destruction? His ways were marvelous indeed.

But what about herself? What plans did God have for her, Leah wondered. Where was the man that would one day be at her side? Of course, she thought she had found him, but it had turned out to be a false hope. Was it a hint of envy or a pang of loneliness that added the taste of sadness in the midst of this joy? As much as she was delighted for Meshullam and Rivkah, it was hard to see them so happy while she sat alone.

The betrothal was not an elaborate celebration: an exchange of promises, a recognition of their will to become husband and wife in the future, to have no one else. Meshullam and Rivkah gave those promises and Grandfather spoke a blessing over them. They enjoyed a festive meal and sang psalms of thanksgiving, but there was no dancing or feasting. That would be left for the wedding. As simple as this evening was, it was a day of great significance for Meshullam and Rivkah, for the house of Micah, and for the new, struggling village of Moresheth-Gath.

At the end of the night Rivkah left their house and went to live in the house of Joel. From there she would go to her husband's house on her wedding day. It would be hard not having her around. Leah was sure she would miss her friend. Rivkah had not gone far away. She would still see her often, she was sure. But for now Rivkah would live in another house, would work with another family.

Chapter 16

The evening breeze gently rustled in the green leaves that covered vines heavy with clusters of grapes. In the twilight, the dark of the grapes was no longer distinguishable from the jagged mass of leaves. After the heat of day, the evening cool felt refreshing. Rivkah even pulled a light blanket over her shoulders to ward off the hint of chill in the air. She sat outside the hut on the watch platform in the middle of the vineyard. It wasn't a sturdy hut, just built from the branches of the carob tree and the elder bush. But it was strong enough to last for this one month. It gave them shelter from the sun during the day, from the wind and dew at night. They were here to guard the grapes and ensure a plentiful harvest, to chase away birds from morning to afternoon and jackals in the evening. Leah, Rachel, Zeruiah, and Rivkah were all here, along with Shiphrah, the only married woman among them. Of course they had to watch the vineyards to make sure that the grapes ripened and were not stolen by bird or beast, but they still had time together, time to talk and sing, to tell stories and share their problems and hopes. They would dance, sometimes wildly, sometimes slowly—totally uninhibited, for no-one else would see them. It was absolutely prohibited for any man or boy to enter the vineyard during the ripening of the grapes when the women watched the fruit.

It was a time Rivkah would always remember. Next year she would be married, bearing the responsibilities for a household. This year she was still a girl, free to roam the vineyards, to sing and dream of the love she would receive. Of course, she looked forward to her wedding. Did not the many love songs she sang reflect that? But maybe this was a time to farewell the girl she was and welcome the woman she would be. Maybe it was the last, great exuberance of her childhood, a reliving of the carefree days of her younger years. It was the end of a passage from the city girl to a woman of the land. How her life had changed in little more than a year! Sorrow and sadness, serendipity and joy, they had all overwhelmed her life. But this evening she would be happy, she would remember the good things and think of the dreams she held.

Rachel sat down beside her. It was time. With a strong, penetrating voice, Rachel began to sing:

"Let him kiss me with the kisses of his mouth—
for your love is more delightful than wine.
Pleasing is the fragrance of your perfumes;
your name is like perfume poured out.
No wonder the maidens love you!
Take me away with you—let us hurry!
Let the king bring me into his chambers."

Voices from across the vineyards joined in the chorus, Rivkah among them.

"Daughters of Jerusalem, I charge you
by the gazelles and by the does of the field:
Do not arouse or awaken love until it so desires, lelele."

Now Rivkah continued the song. And as she sang she thought of Meshullam. Would he be strong for her, give her his protection and love? Would he be passionate and rejoice in her? Would he be tender and understanding, different from the gruff mass of men?

"Like an apple tree among the trees of the forest
is my lover among the young men.
I delight to sit in his shade,
and his fruit is sweet to my taste.
He has taken me to the banquet hall,
and his banner over me is love."

"Daughters of Jerusalem, I charge you
by the gazelles and by the does of the field:
Do not arouse or awaken love until it so desires, lelele."

Even Shiphrah joined in loudly. It may not have been appropriate for a married woman, but out here Shiphrah ignored such rules and enthusiastically sang sensuous love songs. She sang the next verse with ardor:

"Strengthen me with raisins,
refresh me with apples,
for I am faint with love.

His left arm is under my head,
and his right arm embraces me."

Rivkah could clearly make out Leah's voice as she joined the chorus from across the stone wall.
"Daughters of Jerusalem, I charge you
by the gazelles and by the does of the field:
Do not arouse or awaken love until it so desires, lelele."

It was Leah who sang the next verse, her voice at times shivering with emotion.
"My lover is mine and I am his;
He browses among the lilies.
Until the day breaks and shadows flee,
turn, my lover, and be like a gazelle
or like a young stag on the rugged hills."

"Daughters of Jerusalem, I charge you
by the gazelles and by the does of the field:
Do not arouse or awaken love until it so desires, lelele."

The song had hardly ended when Zeruiah started the next one, carried on the wind from the farthest corner of the vineyard:
"May you live, my friend, lelele.
May your brother live, lelele.
May your sister live, lelele,
and the children of your uncle, lelele
May the brothers of your mother live, lelele,
who gave your mother in marriage, lelele,
yarvedele, ledele lo.

"Oh my jailer, you jailer, lelele,
grant me escape from your prison, lelele,
you, with whom are silk and fine linen, lelele,
seducing with finest clothes, lelele,
yarvedele ledele lo."

She sang with expression, but the words did not speak to Rivkah of love, of that intimate feeling between a man and woman. Yes, they spoke of the fascination for the lover, but also of the burden of the bond of love, that helpless desperation of attraction. Somehow, it seemed a crude, hollow approximation compared to her own feelings.

Rivkah listened into the stillness after Zeruiah ended the song. And she heard a song; whether it welled up from her heart or was carried to her from afar by the night wind, she did not know. But it was a song of her dreams, a song of sensuous union, the moment no words could fully describe, that could only be sung about in ecstatic allegory:

"May the wine go straight to my lover,
flowing gently over lips and teeth.
I belong to my lover,
and his desire is for me.
Come, my lover, let us go to the countryside,
let us spend the night in the villages.
Let us go early to the vineyards
to see if the vines have budded,
if their blossoms have opened,
and if their pomegranates are in bloom—
there I will give you my love.
The mandrakes send out their fragrance,
and at our door is every delicacy, both new and old,
that I have stored up for you, my lover."

Leah joined in seamlessly, completing the song, as if she gave her blessing, uniting the lovers by a common bond:

"Eat, oh friends, and drink;
drink your fill, oh lovers."

The girls were silent, each left to their own thoughts. In the east the full moon rose from the horizon, casting the land, the rows of vines and figs into silver light. The girls watched the disc as it stood silently over the hills, commanding in its presence, and appearing round and large.

Rachel punched Rivkah, "Come on!" No, this night was not over yet. The moon would light their dances. Rivkah and Rachel hurried over to the other vineyard, clambered over the wall and met with the others, who, as if by an unspoken signal, had all gathered round Shiphrah.

Zeruiah hit the drums, Shiphrah played the flute. Rivkah, Leah and Rachel began to dance, slowly at first, then faster and more wildly, the moon casting elongated, moving shadows across the ground.

* * *

The tree groaned as if it had suddenly gained a voice to protest against the wounds inflicted on it, as if it lamented its demise. But it still stood. Meshullam lifted the ax again and struck another blow. The tree shuddered and started to lean.

"More! Strike it again!" Father urged.

Meshullam drove the iron blade of the ax into the wood again. The groaning grew louder and increased in intensity as the trunk rotated slightly.

"Stand back!" Father shouted.

With a roar the tree fell, branches cracking and splintering as it hit the ground. Then there was silence, although a few branches still snapped into place, giving the odd creak as the tree settled.

"Well done, son!" Father praised him. "That fell nicely." They walked over to the tree. Father looked it over. "It's nice and straight. It should be perfect."

It was a pine, well grown and yet not too thick. They would simply have to remove the branches and it would serve as a roof-beam. Good trees for house construction were not always easy to find, but they had found a few pines that were just right: strong and straight, and long enough to straddle from wall to wall. This one was the first large tree that Meshullam had cut down by himself. Father had just watched. And that's how it should be. After all, the beam was for Meshullam's house, the house they were building for his family, for Rivkah. Father and the other men worked on it when they could find the time, but Meshullam put everything he had into building that house. It was his future life, the cornerstone of his dreams. Once it was finished, he would lead Rivkah home as his wife.

"Good, let's get the branches off." Father jolted Meshullam out of his reverie. Meshullam hacked off the branches with the ax. Father cut the smaller ones with a knife or tore them off with his hands. The two of them worked over the tree like vultures picking over a cadaver, first removing the branches on the upper side. Meshullam pushed the comparison from his mind. It didn't really fit. After all, they were making something useful, were bringing order to the jumble of wood, needles and branches to get that important beam. When he cut some of the larger branches, sap flowed from the tree. It rubbed into his clothes, its strong scent enveloping him. That smell was one of the things he liked about working with wood, but not the stickiness of the sap. It glued his hands to the ax handle. Meshullam moved on to trim some of the branches from underneath the trunk so that they could roll it over.

It took some time to fully prepare the log. The tree had fallen so quickly under his blows and yet it had taken years to grow. Another tree would grow in its place. It was all part of the rhythm of the land, through which God gave them everything they needed. The house they were building would stand for many seasons to come. Perhaps he would build another one in the future, when his sons and daughters were ready to marry. The young saplings struggling on the forest floor would have grown by then. Maybe they would serve as beams for that house.

Meshullam cut down another tree that morning. They hitched the donkey to the two beams and led it up the hill and across the ridge to the building site of the new house.

* * *

The house was nearing completion. Already the roof-beams had been put in place. Soon this would be her home. Rivkah could not help but come here occasionally to see how things were progressing. Really, she should stay away from her future home. What would happen if she met Meshullam? Tradition required them to keep apart until the day of the wedding. Of course, it was not possible to totally avoid each other in a small village. They did encounter one another now and then, just briefly. Then they would smile at each other, would try to talk with their eyes, but they did not speak to each other, for that was not allowed. It was hard. There were so many questions she wanted to ask, so many things she wanted to talk about. She wanted to get to know him better before the wedding. Now she had to wait—wait until this house was finished. What would her life be like in here? She was looking forward to it, though with some trepidation.

Suddenly she heard footsteps behind her. Who was it?

"Rivkah." She knew that voice. It was Micah's. She turned around to greet him. "Shalom."

He nodded his acknowledgement. "Looking at your house, I see?"

"Yes," Rivkah said hesitantly.

"There's nothing wrong with that. It looks nice, does it not?"

"I think so."

"Have you had a look inside?"

"No, not really."

"Come on then! Meshullam isn't here at the moment. You won't meet him."

"But . . ."

"It's alright. I'll be there. Come!"

Rivkah wanted to see what her house was like from the inside. She needed no further persuasion. Micah motioned her through the door, then followed her. It was spacious inside. Actually, it seemed larger than her childhood home in Lachish. Maybe that was because this house was so empty, only a few tools and bricks lying in a corner. It wasn't a home yet, but she could envision it fully furnished. They would make it a home. There would be stalls for animals to one side behind the pillars. There in the main room they would have their meals. She would have to weave a carpet to cover the floor. That would be her task for winter. And then over there, they would put the bread oven and the kitchen bench. It would be close to the back room where they would store their jars of food. To the side, two rooms were partitioned off by mud brick walls. "Bedrooms," Rivkah concluded.

"I don't think they'll put a second storey on it, at least not this year," Micah commented.

"It's big enough," Rivkah assured him. She looked into the two rooms. Yes, they would be comfortable. "It's nice," Rivkah told Micah.

"You like it?"

"Umh, yes. There's so much we can do here. I will really be able to call this home."

"Yes, having a home, a place to rest, a place where you know you belong, that gives us comfort and helps us face the many challenges of life. But I think you know what it means to long for a home. You have roamed from place to place ever since your home was destroyed."

"I hope this house will never be destroyed."

"I, too, hope that war will never again touch this land."

"No more war? Is that possible?"

"It will happen. When, I do not know. I cannot tell you when he will come."

"Who will come?"

"The true heir of David, the one who has been of old, the one who will bring peace."

What was he saying? Rivkah looked at Micah, confused.

"You don't know about the promises? I haven't spoken about them much lately. In the face of the destruction wrought by the Assyrians on this land, they seemed unreal, unbelievable. And yet, it is exactly in times such as these that I should recall them. We need to be reminded that there will be a time when there will be no more war, a time when our land will not be plundered by the enemy."

Micah took a mud brick and put it against a wall. "I will tell you about God's promises and remember the words which I spoke so many years ago." He took another mud brick and placed it beside the first. "Rivkah, come sit."

And so Micah told her about the one who was to come. He told her here in the shell of her future house with sunlight streaming in from above through the unfinished roof.

"But you Bethlehem Ephratah,
though you are small among the clans of Judah,
out of you will come for me one who will be ruler over Israel,
whose origins are from of old,
from ancient times.

"Therefore Israel will be abandoned
until the time when she who is in labor gives birth
and the rest of his brothers return to join the Israelites.

"He will stand and shepherd his flock
in the strength of the LORD,
in the majesty of the name of the LORD his God.
And they will live securely
for then his greatness will reach to the ends of the earth.
And he will be their peace."

"But who is he? Is he a prince, the son of our king?"

"He will be an heir of David. But I do not think he will grow up in the palace of Jerusalem nor rule through officials and pompous ceremony. No, he may be from humble beginnings, but he will be from

God, sent by the LORD who rules heaven and earth and who raises the humble and lowers the proud. The LORD will be with him."

"When will it happen?"

"I do not know. Maybe it will be a long time until this ruler is born. But I hope Israel will not have to wait much longer. For I do not think there will be peace until he comes."

"No peace?"

"There are always times of calm between wars when nations gain new strength. But he will not simply ensure a time of quiet when weapons are sharpened for the next battle. He will bring lasting peace."

"But what if the Assyrians attack? What happens then?"

"When the Assyrian invades our land
and marches through our fortresses,
we will raise against him seven shepherds,
even eight leaders of men.
They will rule the land of Assyria with the sword,
the land of Nimrod with drawn sword.
He will deliver us from the Assyrian
when he invades our land
and marches into our borders."

"Did you tell the people that?"

"I did. And at the time I told them, it seemed even more unbelievable. The threat of Assyrian power appeared overwhelming, especially after we heard of the destruction the Assyrians had wrought upon Samaria. The people of Judah were afraid. And now we have witnessed the destructive force of the Assyrian army here in Judah. You have experienced their cruelty. The Assyrians ravaged the land. But they were not all victorious. Jerusalem did stand and so did much of the hill country. Maybe now we can see that even the mighty Assyrians can be turned back. Their withdrawal was sudden, pressed by the plague, by enemies from afar, and by the resistance of the cities they attacked. The might of the Assyrians is not absolute and brute force will not always win."

"But they destroyed Lachish."

"They did. And only when the heir of David comes will we live in peace."

"You do not think it is Hezekiah, the king?"

"Hezekiah is a king in the line of David, a courageous and wise king. But he is not the one. Though Jerusalem was able to withstand the Assyrian invasion, Hezekiah paid heavily for it. And he is far too involved in the dealings and schemes of Judah's leaders to administer justice among the people. No, the heir of David will come when we least expect it, and he will not be clothed in royal robes. Just as David, an insignificant shepherd boy from Bethlehem, rose to lead the people in the power of the LORD, so his heir will appear insignificant until his deeds will show him to be the anointed of the LORD."

"So he will come from Bethlehem?"

"Maybe. He will come from the remnant of this people, from among those whom the LORD protects through all the punishments and calamities which beset Israel. Maybe I did not even understand the words fully myself when I proclaimed them, but now I perceive more clearly, now I know what a remnant really is. For we are the remnant in this land. Listen!

'The remnant of Jacob will be
in the midst of many peoples
like dew from the LORD,
like showers on the grass,
which do not wait for man
or linger for mankind.
The remnant of Jacob will be among the nations,
in the midst of peoples,
like a lion among the beasts of the forest,
like a young lion among flocks of sheep,
which mauls and mangles as it goes,
and no one can rescue.'"

"But we are not like that. We have no power. We are helpless in the face of the Philistines."

"You are right, Rivkah. That is not us. And yet it is. We are here in this place, despite all attempts by our enemies to destroy us, enemies from within and from without. Like the dew on a field, we settle quietly on this land and the schemes of Assyria cannot prevent it. And though they may seek to destroy the LORD's people, we will rise again. For the LORD will not forsake us."

Micah must have seen the puzzled look on Rivkah's face.

"People count numbers, trust in the strength of armies, the size of their cavalry, the technology of their weapons. They fortify cities and strongholds, they train their young men for war. But it will not be so in the days of the LORD's anointed. For their strength will be in the LORD, not in military might. They will no longer trust in idols, will not bow before Asherah poles or seek comfort in the gods of Egypt. The will put their hope in the LORD alone."

Micah did not seem to see Rivkah clutching the figure of Isis under her dress. Was this an idol, a foreign god that had no place among the people of the LORD?

Micah continued, "The LORD will purify his people and cast out all that is wicked, all the things they misguidedly put their trust in.

'In that day,' declares the LORD,
'I will destroy your horses from among you
and demolish your chariots.
I will destroy the cities of your land
and tear down all your strongholds.
I will destroy your witchcraft
and you will no longer cast spells.
I will destroy your carved images
and your sacred stones from among you;
you will no longer bow down to the work of your hands.
I will uproot from among you your Asherah poles
and demolish your cities.
I will take vengeance in anger and wrath
upon the nations that have not obeyed me.'"

Rivkah shivered. Was this a threat or a promise of peace?

"Remember," Micah said, "remember that letting go of those false gods, those false securities, will bring us closer to God. Only then can we see his purpose for our life, can we become more like the people we were supposed to be."

"Even if we have to give up amulets that have protected us from our mother's arms?"

"Especially then. Rivkah don't keep holding onto old comforts if they are false and stand between you and the LORD. Draw close to God!"

Micah looked directly at her. Rivkah averted her eyes and instead let them wander around the room, the pillars and poles of the house.

Micah spoke again, "Sometimes I despair when I look at this people. Even though they have heard the word of God, they do not listen. They cling to their old habits. But I do not give up hope, for the LORD himself will take away their false gods and their God will dwell with them."

He stood up. "Now I have told you about God's promises, and in your future home too. Just believe that this is a house of promise, part of God's plan for you." He gestured towards the door. "Come, it was good to talk to you, good to be reminded of the hope I have spoken of in years past."

"Yes, I'd better get back."

But Rivkah did not return immediately to Joel's house. She first went down to the western side of the ridge where scrubby bushes covered the hillside. There she fumbled with the cord around the neck and finally untied it. The little figurine of Isis felt heavy in her hand. She resisted the temptation to trace the hieroglyphs on its back one last time. Closing her eyes she hurled the amulet into the bushes. She did not know where it fell. It was gone. She had done it. Even though she felt somehow happy, as if a heavy load had been taken from her, she also felt so unprotected—nearly naked without the figurine that had lain against her skin for so many years. Would this do? Could she now really be counted among the people of the LORD? What did it mean to put all her trust in the LORD, the God of Israel?

She ran back up the hill, only slowing down as the houses came into sight.

* * *

Bending low, Leah picked up the olives from the ground and threw them into the basket beside her. The oil in the hard fruit stained her hands. Yes, they would have a good pressing this year. Maybe it was because they had started the harvest somewhat later than in previous years. At least it seemed so much later in the year. The days were becoming shorter, the sun no longer burnt with summer heat at the height of the day, and the nights had become colder. Leah didn't think it had been this chilly during previous olive harvests. The cold wind seemed to blow faster between the trunks of the olive trees, penetrating her clothes and numbing her fingers. They had had to do so many other things before they were able to go into the olive groves: the sesame harvest, the gathering of dates and grapes. Some of the grapes had been dried but most were pressed and the new wine filled many jars. They picked apples and pomegranates, then collected firewood and made their houses ready for winter before they finally started the olive harvest.

Leah cleared all the olives under the tree and dragged the basket to the next one in the row. She paused briefly before she bent to pick up more olives. Farther up the row, Meshullam was climbing among the branches of a tree, stripping the olives from the branches, and beating the outer ends where he could not reach with a stick. He seemed to enjoy the work, climbing trees like a boy. Would that change once he was married? Of course he would still work with them next year. But it would be different. He would have his own house, his own family and a separate household. And Rivkah would be there. What would it be like to work with her then?

Maybe it was something to look forward to, having her brother and Rivkah as neighbors, working with them. Leah saw that she had got it right when she gave that little nudge to bring them together. Meshullam certainly seemed to have boundless energy when it came to building a house for Rivkah. The shell already stood. Now he was talking of making furniture and fitting out the building. He had already thought about the animals he would acquire. He didn't say much about Rivkah, but Leah didn't really expect him to. For Rivkah really mattered to him and he always found it hard to talk about those things that were close to his heart. But Leah saw the signs. Whenever Rivkah's name was mentioned, there was the sudden twitching of his foot or the quick breath that betrayed his emotions.

And Rivkah? During their time in the vineyards she had certainly been excited, had sung of love and the mention of Meshullam had made her blush. She had found joy, a new sense of purpose. Yes, Leah had got it right.

She was happy for them, glad that they were fond of each other. But sometimes she wished there would be someone for her, too. To be promised in marriage to a man who really cared, that's what she dreamt about. She did not long for Nadab anymore. She had learnt too much about him and his family, had had enough time to think about the events of spring. Maybe it was good to remain single, to let time heal her before she trusted a man again. Just sometimes she wished.

The basket of olives was full. Leah set it to the side. The men would collect it later. She walked to the end of the grove to get another basket. In one of the trees she could see two feet dangling. That must be Shimei!

"Hey Shimei! What are you doing up there?"

"Getting olives. Can't you see?" he shouted.

"I can see two feet dangling from the tree, but I cannot see any olives falling out of it."

The two feet disappeared among the leaves and a little later olives dropped to the ground.

"Here they are. Can't you see them?"

"Now I can. Do you always work that hard?"

"I have been working hard all day. I just had to sit down because my feet hurt."

Leah now stood directly under Shimei and looked up at him. He stopped brushing olives off the branches.

"That looks good, Shimei. Are you getting all the olives?"

"All the ones I can reach. Father will knock the others down with a stick later on, he said."

"I'll wait until he has done that before I come and gather the olives from your row. What do you think?"

"Fine with me," Shimei responded.

Suddenly something hit Leah's knees. "Ow!"

"Uzi!" she shouted at the same time as Shimei also called the lamb's name.

"Don't do that!" Shimei scolded him again. But Uzi tried to butt Leah again. She evaded his attack this time, grabbed his woolly back and turned him around before pushing him away. "Off with you!" She looked up at Shimei. "Your lamb is getting cheeky."

"I know. I tell him so many times not to do it. Sometimes he even butts me."

"Don't let him get away with it," she warned. "Back to your olives, Shimei!"

Leah walked to the wall and got the empty basket. On the way back Uzi followed her. He trotted behind her peacefully as if he would never even think of doing any mischief, the perfect example of an innocent lamb. But when she bent down to pick up more olives, he must have changed his mind. Out of the corner of her eye she caught a glimpse of him charging at her. Leah was able to get out the way. This time she kicked Uzi. "Go away!" He shrank off. But moments later she heard a bump and then a clatter as olives spilled all over the ground. He had charged the full basket!

"Uzi!" Leah screamed. "Now you have really done it." She ran over to the basket. "Look what you have done! Shimei, come here! Get here at once!"

Shimei was not the only one who came running. Meshullam and Mother responded quickly to her call as well. Shimei caught Uzi and held him still. Meshullam just shook his head and started to scoop up some of the spilled olives.

"Get Uzi out of here," Mother told Shimei.

"Take him to the other sheep," Meshullam added. "He has to learn he's a sheep, not a child that plays tricks on others."

"But they are so far away. I don't know where Tirzah took them," Shimei complained.

"You'll find them," Leah said.

"Leave him with the sheep in the morning then, Shimei. He's a menace! And you know what Father would have to say about that," Meshullam warned him.

Nearly crying, Shimei dragged the struggling lamb out of the olive grove.

"Come back here after you have left him with the other sheep," Mother called after him.

Then all three heaped olives back into the basket.

PART FOUR

Chapter 17

The first rain came before the olive harvest was complete. It was only a light rain, more a drizzle, but it spurred the harvesters on to greater urgency. For Rivkah that first day of rain was a day of remembering. Had only one year passed since she saw the rain come down, sitting in that cave with people who were strangers to her? How lonely had her life been then: her home destroyed, her family gone. She had been glad to find some place to lay her weary head, some place to keep out of the rain and cold. But she had no hope, no idea what the future would hold for her. She had learned a lot in that year, had met many teachers. She had learned to hope again, had searched for a place in this world, and had finally come here. She had loved and lost, had been disappointed, and surprised by joy. And now her future husband had built a house and was preparing it for her. How much had happened in one year!

Soon the rains became stronger, enough to moisten the soil. The men hitched the cows and oxen in front of the plow and worked the fields. The proceeds from the plentiful olive harvest had allowed the men to buy cattle in the highlands and the village's stock numbers had increased. Rain fell on the plowed fields and the men scattered the seed—barley and wheat. They planted lentils and beans. They went to the fields again and plowed the seed into the ground. In prayer they commended the plants to him who makes all things grow.

When the west wind drove swathes of rain across the land, the animals in their pens and the crackling fire in the hearth warmed the houses. Rivkah watched as the first lamb was born, helped to deliver healthy kids into the world as one of the goats gave birth. Here was new life right in the midst of the dark winter. On good days the sheep grazed near the village, on other days they were fed the chaff and straw of wheat and barley. Humans and animals alike preferred to stay inside on those wet days unless urgent work called them to the fields.

Rivkah spent many hours in front of the loom, weaving blankets and rugs for their new home. Meshullam's family supplied the wool. She enjoyed the weaving, not for the task itself, but because through it she worked for her future home. Just as Meshullam worked to put the finishing touches on the house, so she contributed her labor to make the building more than a house—a home, their home. At times it was late at night—after the house was already quiet—before she extinguished the oil lamp and crept under the blanket.

But the best time was when she went around to the women of the village to try on her wedding dress, or rather, different parts of it. None of the women would have missed the chance to prepare for the wedding. And so they all worked on different parts of the dress. One made the undergarment of fine linen, which fitted tightly against Rivkah's skin, another the short tunic. Then there was the flowing dress itself, falling from the shoulders down to her ankles, intricately decorated and matching Rivkah's figure. A belt, veil, and shoes with laces of finest wool completed the bridal dress. The family of Micah had not shied away from the expense of fine cloth and the women gave of their time freely.

Rivkah enjoyed the measurements and fittings. She liked to see the progress as the dress took form. When it was finished and she wore all the pieces together for the first time, she could not but marvel at its beauty. Was she really the woman that looked back at her from the bronze mirror? She seemed so grown up—a woman, no longer a girl. Together with Rachel she went to the spring to see her reflection in the pool. Fabulous! She had never seen a dress like it.

On a fine spring day, when the first flowers pushed through the ground and hesitantly started to bloom, Rivkah married Meshullam. The birds sang in the sunshine, the air was brilliant and fresh, yet with a promising hint of summer warmth. The joy of nature was reflected in the prayers, praise and hymns of the people that day. It was a feast to remember. Meat and fine bread were served in large portions. Sweetened cakes and dried figs, raisins and nuts filled plates and bowls. The wine flowed as never before in this new village.

Shimei strutted around proudly. He made it clear he was the bridegroom's brother and knew the bride well. Tirzah could not keep her eyes off Rivkah, gaping when she saw her in the wedding dress. Leah smiled at her, apparently satisfied with the success of the day. Merab hugged her son and her daughter-in-law. Ehud fulfilled the role of host perfectly. Micah gave the pair his blessing.

And Meshullam? His eyes held hers firmly. At times sparks of joy flashed in them, sometimes his glances were nearly shy. He said the words of vow and affirmation with conviction and yet at one point his quivering voice betrayed his emotions.

Despite the planning, despite the dreaming, Rivkah could not have imagined a wedding day like it. It all seemed so perfect, so right. This was her place, this was where she belonged. She felt at home here among these people, she felt loved by the man at her side. And she promised him her love.

The festivities lasted long into the night. Meshullam took Rivkah into their home. They were husband and wife.

* * *

Sunlight streamed through the small window, illuminating a rectangular patch on the opposite wall. As a dutiful wife Rivkah should have been up by now, should have started her daily chores. But she was still sleeping, blissfully unaware of the sunlight that ushered in a new day. Meshullam would have it no other way. No, he would treasure this moment forever, etch the sight into his memory. He sat there beside Rivkah on the floor, just watching her sleep, tracking her features with his eyes—the black hair, slightly unkempt in the morning, the slender nose, and the full cheeks that combined perfectly with her jaw. He marveled at the peaceful expression on her face, the eyes closed, the mouth slightly opened with the occasional smile playing around her lips. The slender neck showed the softness of her skin. The blanket just partly covered her upper body. Her chest rose with the regular rhythm of her breathing. This was Rivkah! This was his wife! Tenderly he reached out his hand and brushed back a stray strand of hair from her face. His hand hovered briefly above her head. When he touched his own cheek, he noticed her soft scent lingering. He wanted this moment to last. Was there anything so beautiful? He was sure he had never beheld a woman so lovely. He watched with amusement as wrinkles creased her forehead, giving her that quizzical look. He laughed softly. That was so Rivkah! She probably did not even realize she did it constantly, even in her sleep. What dreams was she dreaming? What thoughts came to her in her slumber? Was she dreaming of him? They shared so much. Sleep would not separate them.

Meshullam shifted onto his knees and quietly whispered, "I love you Rivkah." Thankfulness welled up within him and he could not but praise his God.

"Oh Lord, you have blessed your servant beyond measure
and let your grace shine upon me.
My cup flows over with love,
my heart sings with joy,
so that my lips proclaim your praise
and my spirit will give you thanks."

He closed his eyes briefly in contemplation, only to see the outline of Rivkah's face imprinted before his inner eye. No, he would not forget this moment. He gazed at her. Age would also work on her features. But Meshullam was sure she would never lose that lovely expression. And he would be there alongside her. They would grow old together. He did not know what the future would hold for them—happiness and grief, distance and closeness. He prayed their love would stand the test of time.

Meshullam did not know how long he knelt watching her. Somewhere from the adjacent room came the protesting bleating of a goat. It hardly entered his consciousness, but must have penetrated Rivkah's sleep. For now she stirred, kicking one leg and moving her head around. Had she opened her eyes? He couldn't tell. She sighed and seemed to return to sleep.

Meshullam stood up. She would wake soon. He started to walk to the door, but could not tear himself from her presence. He noticed how more light was flooding into the room as the sun rose in the sky. The light touched her body and Rivkah opened her eyes, blinking into the bright day. Meshullam moved back to her side, briefly shadowing the light. He knelt down beside her again, gently took her hand in his and brushed her hair with a kiss, "Good morning, my love."

* * *

The smell of the fennel hung in the still air. When Rivkah broke off its woody stem, its fragrant juice rubbed on her hands. She placed the fennel in her bundle of herbs. Spring added variety to their daily meals. The fresh growth gave them enough food to stretch their dwindling stores of wheat and barley. Rivkah was thankful for that, but why was she sent out to gather the greens? After all, she was now the wife of Meshullam, not some refugee seeking shelter, not just a daughter of the household. So often they treated her as they had done before the wedding: it was Rivkah who milked the goats and sheep of the house of Micah, Rivkah who went out to forage for herbs, Rivkah who helped to grind the flour and bake the bread, Rivkah who worked in the field and garden with Leah, Rivkah who sat among Ehud's children to celebrate Shabbat. Meshullam did not really remind them that she was his wife; he did not ask them to show her more respect. Sometimes even he treated her as if she was his sister, as if she was just another member of the household. It was not as she had imagined it. Couldn't he understand that she dreamed of more, that she wanted more control over her life and house?

In so many ways he tried to please her and showed his affection, but how special was she really to him? Couldn't he stand up to his family on her behalf? Would he dare to change things? She just wanted some more respect. She just wanted them to treat her like a woman.

Rivkah reminded herself of those things she did control, the things that just she and Meshullam had together. They had their own house, which was hers to arrange. They were building up their own flock of sheep and goats and the wool would be hers to spin and use. Maybe she should be grateful for that. Not all married women had as much. Tinshemet and her husband still lived in the same house as her brother-in-law.

The wind picked up. Rivkah hugged her mantle closer around her. She smelt the newly dyed wool, which was not yet worn out by months or years of constant use. Lifting her eyes to the sky she could see dark clouds gathering in the west. It looked ominous. Would it rain soon? The sun was blocked out, the black sky a threatening mass of dark clouds billowing high across the land. Then she saw the first bolt of lightning flash towards the earth and heard the distant rumble of thunder. Time to go home! Rivkah hurried across the fields, shaken by cold gusts of wind. She reached the path to the village. The lightning flashes seemed brighter, the thunder louder. The thunderstorm came directly towards her. The air was palpably laden with suspense. She listened for the sounds of the fields, but could hear neither the song of birds nor the drone of insects, not even the faraway bleating of a lamb. She climbed the path to the village, past trembling bushes and creaking trees.

And then it was upon her. Heavy raindrops pelted against her face, drenched her mantle within minutes and churned the ground. The rain was so intense that little streams flowed down the path. Rivkah struggled up the muddy slope, her clothes clinging to her body, restricting her movements. A bolt of lightning struck the earth close-by, shaking the ground and throwing her into the dirt. "LORD, help! Let me reach my home!" she shouted in terror. She got up again, stumbled over her dress and fell. She spit out the water and mud from her mouth and slowly pushed herself up. Fighting against the wind, eyes half-closed she pressed on. She should be close to the village now.

Suddenly she heard her name: "Rivkah!" She couldn't see anyone. Again: "Rivkah!" Somebody was calling her. She answered. A dark figure broke through the storm and ran towards her. It was Meshullam! He embraced her, though she was smeared with mud and soaked in rain. Taking the wet bundle of herbs in one hand and holding Rivkah's hand with the other, he led her back to the house. He opened the door and let her in, together with a gust of wind and rain. Hurling his weight against the door he pushed it shut. Inside the house it was quiet, the sheep and goats calmly moving quietly in the pens to the side. Rivkah stood in the room with dripping clothes. Meshullam threw the bundle of herbs to the floor. "Here we are," he laughed. His expression changed as he looked gently at Rivkah. "I didn't know where you were. I couldn't leave you in the storm alone."

"Thank you," she mumbled.

"I am so glad I found you," he added. He came closer, touched her wet mantle and said, "I think you need a change of clothes, something dry."

Rivkah smiled back at him, "So do you. Yours are pretty wet, too."

He looked up and down at his clothes. "I suppose you are right." He reached out and rubbed away some mud from her chin with his finger tip. "And afterwards we'll light a fire to keep us warm."

* * *

The plentiful rain had not only made the wheat and barley grow. The weeds had also sprouted and grown among the grain. There were thorns and thistles, flowers like campions and poppies, but especially that false wheat—darnel. If gathered with the wheat, its grains had to be separated after the harvest. Otherwise its seed would make those who ate it sick, both animals and humans. It was best removed before it grew tall.

Leah pulled out the darnel and poppies with her hands, putting the plants into little heaps among the wheat, to be thrown onto the path where the sun would dry them out. The thorns and thistles she hacked out with a hoe, making sure she got the whole plant out. Rivkah, Tirzah and Mother were out here, too, weeding the field with her. The men were plowing other fields, sowing the summer crops.

Rivkah still had difficulty distinguishing between wheat and darnel, at times plucking out wheat she was not meant to, sometimes leaving behind the darnel she was supposed to remove. Leah couldn't understand what was so difficult about it. It was true they looked very similar—she herself had to concentrate to get it right—but the leaves of the darnel were so much thinner than those of the wheat. You just had to know what to look for. Maybe she had done too much weeding in her life so that she recognized the weeds so readily. Sad, but true. She could have certainly done without so many hours in the field. Rivkah, on the other hand, had hardly done any weeding, and certainly not in the field. It was her first season and maybe for that she did quite well.

"How is this?" Rivkah called Leah over. Walking along the row that Rivkah had just worked on, Leah could find a few heads of darnel still left in the ground, but not many. She picked some out.

"It looks good," she told Rivkah, "you're getting them."

"You know, I have never really done this before. Maybe I'm too careful. I just don't want to pull out the wheat."

"No, if you're unsure it's better to leave it in the ground. Just try your best. The less darnel, the better of course. You're doing quite well, Rivkah."

Leah looked over the field and turned to Rivkah. "Still a lot to do."

"It does look like it," Rivkah sighed.

"Don't worry, we'll get through it in the end. It's never pleasant, but necessary. This year we won't have to sort so carefully through the grain after the harvest as we had to last year."

That didn't seem to comfort Rivkah. Harvest was still a long time away.

"I always think of something else when pulling out weeds to make the time go by," Leah suggested.

"So do I, until I pull out the wrong plant."

"Or a thistle stings me," Leah added. "That wakes you up."

She squatted down, pulling out a few weeds. "I'll work beside you for a while again. That way we can talk."

Rivkah agreed. "It makes it less of a chore."

Leah threw a few weeds on a heap. "I really like the rugs in your house. Did you make them yourself?"

"Yes, when I was living in the house of Joel. I was able to set up a loom and had time to weave."

"The colors are really nice."

"You think so?"

"Yes, sure."

"Tinshemet helped me to dye the wool. We were quite successful with the black and brown."

"How did you do that?"

"We used pomegranate peel."

"Is that why it's got that slightly red tinge?"

"Yes. Can you see it?"

"Just."

"Black seemed easier than any of the other colors. That's why we ended up with so much black wool."

"And how did you dye the wool red?"

"We used madder for that?"

"Madder?"

"You know, the little shrubs with the dark-red berries. The leaves sprout out from the stem like stars."

"Yes, I know it. Do you use the berries?"

"No, it's the roots you need. We were able to get some."

"That must have taken you some time."

"Yes, it wasn't easy. And the dye did not turn out as Tinshemet had hoped. But I like it."

"And the other colors?"

"We were also able to make some yellow dye. We used tamarisk for that, though it came out lighter than we expected. I would have liked more colors, but we didn't have the time."

"But your rugs and blankets look beautiful as they are."

"Yes, but sometimes another color would have fitted the pattern better."

"I like the patterns, especially the one with the flowers."

Leah had thought it particularly pretty when she had first seen it.

"That one! I worked hard to get that one right. But it turned out nicely, didn't it?"

"Nice? Beautiful! Where did you learn that?"

"I thought of it myself. I just imagined it might work."

"You thought of it yourself? That's amazing, Rivkah!"

"You know, it just felt right."

"Will you make more?"

"Maybe in winter when I have enough time. I do hope our sheep will have nice wool."

"I think Meshullam looked out for that trait when he selected them."

"I know he did. Their wool is really white. I think he knew it's important to me. It just makes it so much easier to get the colors right."

Leah had to admit that Rivkah seemed to know what she was talking about. And her weaving was without doubt better than her own. Not that Leah did not appreciate colorful clothes with intricate designs, she did. But maybe she just didn't have the patience to make elaborate fabrics. Maybe Rivkah had more experience weaving clothes, just as Leah had spent more time in the fields. They all had a gift. They all contributed differently. That was why it was so good to have Rivkah in the family.

* * *

Shabbat! A day to rest from labor, a day to relax limbs and soul, to let go of the cares and worries of the working week for just a few hours. Tomorrow would bring troubles of its own. Let them be! He would not get anxious over them now. Meshullam got up from the rug on the floor. Lunch had been a slow and leisurely affair. It had just been Rivkah and him, just the two of them in their own house. They would have a whole, lazy afternoon before they joined the others at the end of Shabbat to sing psalms and hymns.

Rivkah was clearing away the few dishes. Meshullam stepped outside the house into the brilliant sunlight. The seasons were changing and the sun, which at times had been obscured by clouds and had stood low in the early spring sky, now shone strongly. Grandfather sat outside in the courtyard, leaning against the wall of the house.

"Ah, Meshullam, what a nice day."

"It is getting quite warm."

"It does my old bones some good. Come, sit with me, Meshullam."

He hesitated.

"You do have time, don't you?"

"It is Shabbat, Grandfather."

Meshullam looked back to the house.

"Ah, you're looking for your wife. Tell her to come, too."

Just then Rivkah appeared in the door. "Meshullam . . . ?"

"Grandfather has asked us to sit with him."

"Oh yes, that would be nice."

And so they both sat down, Rivkah sitting between Meshullam and Grandfather.

"I see that married life suits you well."

Meshullam saw Rivkah smile as he himself nodded in agreement.

"You two are part of this family, the house of Micah, but you have also formed a new unit, a family apart from this one, a family of your own. And with that comes the task of determining your own way, determining how you will live as a family in this world."

"You mean choosing our way of life? Knowing what is really important to us?" Meshullam asked.

"Yes, that's it. Even though there is so much uncertainty in life, we have to walk our way with purpose, especially as a family."

Grandfather stroked his beard, gathering his thoughts, then looked directly at them.

"I have been thinking lately: about our responsibility before God as a nation, as a village community, as a household, as a family—such as you now are—and as an individual person. Whatever we do, our life has to be in tune with what God requires of us. For if there is discord in our family how can the village or the nation live in harmony? And if our nation is in strife does it not affect our families and ourselves?"

"I think so," Rivkah agreed. "Did you preach about this in the past? Did you tell the people how their own actions affect the life of Israel?"

"I don't think I said it as I would say it today. But the LORD gave me the words to speak. He filled my mouth with speech. They were the right words at the time. They continue to speak today. If you listen and take them to your heart you will know that God's words speak across time and place. For his loving-kindness endures forever."

Grandfather paused and closed his eyes for a moment before he continued, "I can still remember when God first gave me these words. It was in the days of Ahaz. Judah had again turned from the LORD and was following idols, as it had done so often through its history. The LORD called out to them, for he always continues reaching out to his people. I have repeated these words often through the years and I hope that some have listened."

Meshullam sat still as Grandfather intoned the speech, as he summoned the earth, the mountains and hills, the whole cosmos to witness the LORD's dispute and reconciliation with his people:

"Listen to what the LORD says:
'Stand up, plead your case before the mountains;
let the hills hear what you have to say.
Hear, oh mountains, the LORD's accusation;
listen, you everlasting foundations of the earth.
For the LORD has a case against his people;
he is lodging a charge against Israel.
My people, what have I done to you?
How have I burdened you?
Answer me.
I brought you up out of Egypt
and redeemed you from the land of slavery.
I sent Moses to lead you,
also Aaron and Miriam.
My people, remember what Balak king of Moab counseled
and what Balaam son of Beor answered.
Remember your journey from Shittim to Gilgal,
that you may know the righteous acts of the LORD.'"

"But in these words the LORD did not spell out his accusation, did not place his complaints about Israel before the hills and mountains, did he?" observed Meshullam.

"He invited the people to find fault with him," Rivkah added. "Of course, they could not."

"No, they could not. But he calls them to remember, he calls them back to him. When we come before the LORD we often expect accusation, condemnation, and judgment. But we forget who the LORD is. When the covenant is broken and our relationship is ruptured, he calls us back to himself. He pleads with his people to return to him once again, to return to the one true God. All the comforts his people seek from the other gods are false. People may think that the LORD no longer acts, that he is not powerful in the face of the gods of the nations. And so the LORD reminds them of their origins, of the mighty deeds when he brought them out from Egypt and freed them from slavery. The LORD reminds them of the family that he sent to lead them. Just so, the LORD will lead his people once again, even in the face of many foes. Like Balak, enemies may seek to curse his people, but Balaam had to bless them, for he could not do otherwise. The word of the LORD is true and a prophet cannot but speak it.

In trust the people crossed the river Jordan on their journey from Shittim to Gilgal. They entered this good land which the LORD gave them. If they only continue to trust him, the LORD will give good things to his people. That's what the LORD keeps reminding his people of, that's what I have been called to tell the people once again."

"Was the LORD not angry when his people turned away from him?" Meshullam wondered.

"Angry?" Grandfather reflected. "Yes. But more hurt than angered, deeply hurt. He cares for his people, loves his people passionately. He longs for them to repent, to come back to him."

"What does he expect of them, of us?" Rivkah asked.

"True repentance, a change of heart that is reflected in action. We know we have sinned and are not worthy to come into the LORD's presence. Therefore, we may seek to give our most valuable possessions, everything we hold dear to be reconciled to the LORD again.

'With what shall I come before the LORD
and bow down before the exalted God?
Shall I come before him with burnt offerings
with calves a year old?
Will the LORD be pleased with thousands of rams,
with ten thousand rivers of oil?
Shall I offer my firstborn for my transgression,
the fruit of my body for the sin of my soul?'"

"Offer the firstborn?" Meshullam looked at Grandfather in horror. "Who would do that?"

"There is no greater sacrifice. But the LORD does not require it of us. He does not seek our possessions. He seeks a change of heart, a change to our way of life.

'He has shown you, oh man, what is good.
And what does the LORD require of you?
To act justly and to love mercy
and to walk humbly with your God.'"

"Walk humbly with our God," Rivkah echoed. "Is that what you meant when you talked about our family's way of life?"

"It is. For this attitude has to start with you, Rivkah, and it has to guide the life of your family, Meshullam. We all have to take it to heart in this household, in our life together, so that it will also touch our village. Only in this way can Judah become what it was meant to be, can it enter into God's presence."

* * *

"To act justly and to love mercy
and to walk humbly with your God."

That's how her life should be, that's what the LORD required. Rivkah stopped milking for a moment and pressed her head against the side of the goat. What did it mean in her life? She did not sit in the gate in judgment over anyone, she was not in any position of control. And yet, justice was more than giving judgment. It was about treating others rightly: not looking at a person's status, nor eyeing the return we might get by favoring one over the other. It meant helping those in need, to ensure everyone got their share, to treat others with respect. That was hard enough.

The goat stomped her foot. "It's alright," Rivkah murmured and patted the animal's back. She put her hands on the teats again and sprayed more milk into the bowl.

At times it was so hard to see past her own self-interest, to understand others, to put herself in their shoes. What attitude should she have towards Merab, her mother-in-law? Merab was so concerned for the welfare of her family—including Meshullam—that she could not bear to see anyone idle? What would understanding her mean? Probably not silent acceptance. Perhaps Rivkah could somehow show her there was no need to worry.

What did it mean to act in mercy and loving-kindness? It was so much more than just understanding. It required real empathy with other people. It sought the best for them. It was not hard to wish the best for Meshullam. But what about people who had wronged her? Rivkah thought back to the time in the cave, to Naarah, to the many times that woman had falsely accused her. What did loving-kindness mean with her in mind? Forgiveness? Probably. Silent acceptance of the lies? Never. But Rivkah decided to forgive Naarah now, to hope that her life had turned out well, that life in Shechar treated her kindly.

Rivkah stripped the last drops of milk from the udder. "Well done!" she said, "that's plenty of milk today." She gave the goat a quick rub and moved on to the next one. "Let's see how much you can give today, eh?" Plenty it seemed. With the exuberant green growth, the goats were giving record quantities of milk.

Was this part of what Micah had meant by walking humbly with God? To do the job at hand, to take her place in the community of his people? Was this what she was meant to do? To milk goats, to look after the house, to help others? Was there not more? She was sure there was. And if God called her to new tasks she would follow that call. Still, for the moment she should be content with her life. Had she not been given so much? A place to call home, a secure future, a family, a husband. She was grateful for that, gave thanks to God.

The bowl was full and the goat still had more milk. Rivkah was glad she had brought the juglet along after all. She poured some of the milk into it, leaned it against the wall and went back to finishing the milking.

* * *

Meshullam pressed the plow hard into the ground. He urged the cows to move on. Justice and mercy! Justice and mercy! Meshullam knew that these were two attributes ascribed to the LORD. Still, they so often seemed in conflict. Did not the justice of the LORD so often demand condemnation? Yet in his mercy he held back; he even restored what was broken, and healed what was wounded. How often had not his people rebelled against the LORD? And yet, because of his mercy and loving-kindness the LORD did not destroy. No, he came to the aid of the tiny nation, cared for it and called it back to himself. How often did he, Meshullam, break the commandments of the LORD! And yet, he knew he was not doomed. For the LORD had mercy on him. Meshullam remembered the famous words from the old writings:

"The LORD, the LORD, the compassionate and gracious God, slow to anger, abounding in love and faithfulness, maintaining love to thousands and forgiving wickedness, rebellion and sin. Yet he does not leave the guilty unpunished."

This was the LORD! And now Grandfather said that he, Meshullam, should do likewise, that he should act justly and love mercy. But he was not God!

Meshullam noticed his plow hitting a stone and tilting around, coming off the line. He called the cows to a stop, placed the plow again and worked it into the soil as the cows moved ahead.

He was just a young farmer in a small village. How could he reflect something of God in his life? Maybe that's where the other part came in—to walk humbly with his God. By committing his way, his path in life, his daily tasks to God, he might become so immersed in God's ways that right actions would flow from his life.

Meshullam arrived at the end of the row. He gave the cows a quick break, then turned them around and started the next furrow.

But acting rightly was never easy. And Meshullam knew that justice and mercy towards others often required the very painful negation of self-interest. How could he treat others without fear or favor? How could he give them another chance when they not only wronged him, but also offended against the LORD's commandments? Maybe he had been too hard on others, had written them off too soon. Maybe he had been anything else but humble. He thought of Nadab. Not that it was Meshullam's fault, but had his remarks helped to alienate Nadab from the village and even from the LORD? Had he done wrong while he was trying to do right?

In the middle of the field he stopped the cows, leaned heavily on the plow, his head bent:

"LORD, I have wronged in so many ways.
Sometimes I do not know the way to go,
sometimes I do not know the deed to do,
sometimes I do not know the words to say.
Walk with me now and always.
Teach me to reach out humbly to others.
Grant me to understand my neighbor.
Give me a mind to determine what is true and just.
Make my heart strong in mercy and loving-kindness."

Meshullam lifted his face and looked towards heaven as he added, "Your love, oh LORD, endures forever. Do not abandon the works of your hands."

He shouted to urge the cows on again, "Cut the ground, cut the ground!" He had only done half the field and there were still many more chick-peas to sow.

Chapter 18

The heat of early summer had ripened the barley and wheat. They had already harvested most of the barley and soon would get onto the wheat. It was a good harvest. Now that they had been carefully plowed, sown and weeded, the fields were yielding plentiful crops. Unlike last year, the ears of grain stood closely together with few weeds interspersed among them. Men and women rejoiced over the bounty and worked diligently to bring in the crop. But the harvest was hard on Rivkah's body. This last week had been particularly painful. So often she felt sick and dizzy. It was hard to go to the fields early in the morning, hard to work alongside Meshullam gathering the sheaves. Sometimes even the walk home from the fields was a struggle when that sickness struck. Was it the burning sun that beat down on her mercilessly during the day? Was it all that bending down low to the ground?

This morning was worse than any other day. She couldn't even get up out of bed. Meshullam was up already, preparing to leave for the fields. "Rivkah, are you coming? Do you want something to eat?"

"Yes," Rivkah answered with a moan.

"I'll leave some bread and cheese out," he called.

Rivkah got up, swaying as she walked to the main room. Meshullam had the sickle in his belt and was about to go out the door as she sat down to eat a bite. Somehow the smell of the food was too much for her. Her stomach churned. She jumped up and ran to the door pushing her surprised husband out of the way. She was just able to reach the courtyard before she vomited. She stood bent over retching, tears coming to her eyes.

"What's wrong, Rivkah?" Meshullam asked with concern.

"Sorry," she sobbed. "I'm sorry."

He touched her awkwardly. "What's wrong, Rivkah?"

"I don't know. I just feel sick. I'll be fine soon. Don't worry, I'll come down to the field."

"Rivkah, you look pale. You're not well at all. I don't think working in the fields is the right thing for you just now. Wait, I'll get you a cup of water."

He was back in a moment. But she spewed out the water immediately, unable to hold it down. At least it washed out her mouth. As she quietened down, she was able to swallow a few sips.

"That's better," Meshullam encouraged. "Now, you should lie down for a while. You can come to the fields when you're better. I'll ask Tirzah to help me. I think she has gone with the others already." Meshullam led Rivkah back to the bed and helped her to lie down.

"I have to get on with the harvest," he said.

"I know," Rivkah said, weakly.

"Shalom, until later," Meshullam mouthed. Then he was gone.

Rivkah's head throbbed. She felt so weak. Whatever was wrong with her? Was the work too much for her? Was she not cut out for the life of a country woman? She did not want to let the others down. Anxious, she tossed and turned in the bed. She must have dozed for a bit for, suddenly, she heard someone call her name. "Rivkah!" It was Merab. Had she come to get her to the fields? Would she berate her for not doing her job? Rivkah sat up on her elbow.

"Rivkah, can I come in?"

"Come in!" Rivkah steeled herself for the accusations that Merab would fling at her. But when she peeked into the room, Merab seemed to be excited rather than cross. "Meshullam told me you did not feel well and that you had vomited."

"Yes," Rivkah said guardedly.

"Have you often felt sick recently?"

"Yes, most days in the past week or two. But not this bad."

"Really? That's good."

"Good?"

Merab paused, seemingly trying to find the right words. "Have you had . . . your regular flow of blood lately?"

Rivkah creased her forehead. What was that about? She tried to remember. "Maybe not. Why?"

Merab's eyes beamed with joy.

"Do you think you are with child?"

"With child?"

"Yes, all the signs are there: feeling sick, not having your regular period."

Rivkah couldn't remember her mother being so sick before the birth of her younger brothers or sister. But if Merab thought so . . . it could be! "Do you think so?"

"Of course I can't be sure, but it's likely. You had better rest, Rivkah. And don't try working too hard."

Merab clasped Rivkah's shoulder. "Wouldn't it be so nice?" she whispered. She closed her eyes. "A grandchild . . . ," Rivkah heard her murmur.

* * *

Mother was sure that Rivkah was pregnant. And she fussed over her accordingly. Rivkah was not allowed to do any heavy work, could appear late in the fields, and was served the best food. Mother told Meshullam repeatedly to take good care of Rivkah. And he did.

Father complained that it all went too far, that they needed workers for the harvest, and surely Rivkah could do her part. But Mother protected Rivkah and challenged him, "Do you want a healthy grandchild or not? Surely, a grandchild is more important than finishing the wheat harvest early. You don't want to be responsible for harming your first grandchild, do you?" Father didn't reply and quickly learned that he could not argue with his wife on this point.

Meshullam couldn't remember Mother being so careful herself when she was pregnant. She had worked right up to the birth of her children, as did most of the other women. But that hot summer of four years ago now came back to Meshullam's mind. Mother had worked in the field with them as she had done every harvest. However, there was one day when she had not come to the field. And after that day she was a different woman. Once or twice she started sobbing in the middle of a meal. He had even observed her weeping secretly at times. Every now and then her eyes were stained with tears and he knew she had been crying. It went on for several months. Mother continued to do her chores, seemed to work even harder than before. But Meshullam had noticed that she held every baby she could, and helped the young mothers in whatever way possible. Was that why she was now so concerned for Rivkah?

Due to Mother's excitement the realization also sank in for Meshullam. A child! Rivkah would have a child! He would be a father! He couldn't fully comprehend it, not yet. But it was only natural. That was what was expected in marriage. Now it had become reality. Somehow life took on a new dimension. Everything he did was no longer for himself, the family or Rivkah. No, it was also for this child. Soon the child would walk over these fields, would sleep in this house, would eat at this table. This child was part of him and yet different from him. He and Rivkah would care for this child and nurture it. It was the expression of their love for each other.

Meshullam prayed for the child, asked the LORD for a successful birth, a healthy childhood and a future of hope. And he gave thanks for the blessings the LORD had given them.

* * *

The news spread quickly through the village. Tinshemet was one of the first to congratulate Rivkah. Despite the demands of the harvest, she found time to see her one morning. Tinshemet carried her little daughter on her back, strapped in a colorful cloth. The little girl was only two months old. The baby seemed content on her mother's back, gazing dreamily at the world, looking only briefly at Rivkah.

But Tinshemet was not here to show her daughter.

"I have brought something for you."

Rivkah admired the small bundle of cloth that Tinshemet held out to her. It was woven from the finest wool and dyed an attractive light blue, two white bands around the edge. "Thank you, it's beautiful."

"Look inside," Tinshemet urged.

Rivkah could feel that the bundle contained something hard and heavy. She folded back the edges of the cloth and found a dark-red pottery figurine.

"A mother statue," she said surprised. The round, pillar-like body of the figurine featured ample breasts, held up by its arms. The head showed more detail than the stylized body—nose, eyes and mouth, and wavy hair.

"Yes, a prayer mother," Tinshemet echoed. "You will be a mother now. The prayer mother will aid you in your prayers for your children, the sons and daughters you are yet to raise. It will aid you at the time of birth and give you milk to feed them. It will focus your prayers on your family, the task that is set before you as a mother."

Rivkah turned the figurine as she looked at it. It wasn't the most exquisite statue she had seen. She had noticed them in many houses, the woman of the house bringing the prayers for her family before the prayer mother. And now Rivkah would be a mother as well. It was exciting! She would nurture a child through her body and her prayers. Her fingers enclosed the figurine as she felt its earthenware body.

Suddenly another figurine came into her mind—Isis! Her heart sank, grew ice-cold. She held the figurine away from her. "Isn't this one of the idols that Micah warns us about?"

"No Rivkah, it is not an idol," Tinshemet assured her. "This statue is not the image of a goddess. It is a prayer mother, a focus for your prayers to center your mind. Through it you can connect with the LORD's power of creation, and become conscious of the LORD who nurtures you and cares for your family with the love of a mother. It is your duty, your role, to pray for your family. The father of the family cannot do this, he cannot hold up the needs of the family like a mother can."

Rivkah had never thought that her role as wife and mother included intercession for her family. She had imagined the love she would give and receive, the respect she would be held in, the work she would be expected to do, the support she would receive. But only now did she begin to understand what being a wife and mother meant. Perhaps she did need a statue to teach her.

When Tinshemet had gone, Rivkah put the prayer mother up on the workbench at the back of the kitchen. There it stood, watching over the room, telling everyone that a mother cared for this house, and calling her to remember the family in prayer. Rivkah looked at the little statue for a long time. Finally words came: words asking for protection for the life growing inside her, pleading for an easy birth, for a healthy future for this child.

Rivkah knew Meshullam had noticed the prayer mother, but he didn't say anything and just accepted its presence. Maybe he knew that it was part of her becoming a mother, something he should not inquire into.

* * *

The fields yielded grain aplenty. Threshing followed the harvest. Winnowing followed the threshing. The summer crops—sesame and chick-peas—also grew successfully and filled many jars. Then it was time to guard the fruit of the vineyards. Again the older girls of the village lived in huts among the vines. Leah was there and Tirzah came for the first time. They sang, they danced, they told stories. But it was not like last year. Leah missed Rivkah. She had not realized how much Rivkah had been part of their group. Rivkah's love songs had seemed to well up from her heart, her dancing had looked so graceful, her stories had been so infused with hope. Her joy and her longing had touched all the girls. But this year Rivkah was not with them. This year Rivkah lived again in joyful anticipation, no longer as a bride-to-be, but as a wife expecting the birth of her first child. The signs were obvious now, the rounded belly clearly announcing the imminent birth.

Leah worked alongside Rivkah again at the olive harvest. Of course Rivkah could not work as hard this year, but she was there, bringing meals and drink, and somehow uplifting everyone by her very presence. The olive harvest was not as rich as last season but they would have enough oil.

As the first rains came, the flocks of sheep and goats no longer spent the nights in their outside pens but were held once more in the dry houses. This was the end for Uzi, unfortunately. Nobody could put up with his stubborn antics anymore. The butting, the willful destruction were just too much. Even Shimei grew tired of it. There were no loud protests when Father consigned him to the family's cooking pots. Even so, Leah found it hard to eat the meat. The image of the small, helpless lamb he once was, was still lodged in her mind. She could not forget how his jumps and wild chases through the house had made her smile.

Leah noticed the rounded bellies of the ewes and does more keenly this year. Was it because of her concern for Rivkah? Everywhere around her was the expectation of new life. The men went out to plow the fields and scatter the seeds as the rain soaked into the soil, moistening it for new growth.

And then, into the steady rhythms of life broke destruction and violence. The Philistines came on a fine day early in winter. It was only a small group of soldiers—six men—but the defenseless village was an easy target. Shimei saw them approaching the village. He ran home, warning the women and children. Mother sent him to tell the men in the fields. The news created confusion in the village. Some people ran into the fields, others stayed to watch over their homes. Leah tried to help Grandfather to flee, but the old man would not. He said he would face the intruders. What could he do against armed men? And then it was too late to leave. The Philistines were already here. Leah fled to the roof of their house and lay down flat on her belly. She peered over the edge. She heard them before she saw anything. They were smashing jars, overturning furniture, and shouting in one of the houses. Carrying their loot outside, they piled it high in a heap. They must have exhausted the treasures from that house, for now the men came to the compound of Micah. Grandfather sat still against the wall of the house, saying nothing. The soldiers stabbed a threatening spear in his direction, then ignored him. They entered Meshullam's house, one soldier guarding the entrance outside. Was Rivkah still in there? Leah wasn't sure. Meshullam seemed to think so. He came running from the field toward his house. Two of the Philistines were upon him immediately. He had to surrender himself. Leah clasped a hand over her mouth. Oh Meshullam, what have you done! Why did you put yourself in this danger?

The soldiers led Meshullam into his house. What could Leah do? Nothing but pray. With stuttering words Leah asked the LORD to protect her brother, "LORD, do not let Meshullam die, not my brother. Free him from the hands of our enemies who have attacked us. And Rivkah . . . let her live. Protect her, oh God. And the child, LORD, and the child. May the enemies take all that we have, but grant the lives of my family. LORD, LORD, protect them."

* * *

They were plundering his house and Meshullam was powerless to do anything. He had to stand and watch as they rummaged through their belongings, as they carried outside the rugs that Rivkah had woven, and raided the store room, taking the olive oil and the jars full of new wine. They would not find any valuable metals: the plow was in the fields, the sickles were in Father's house, and his knife was hidden in the belt under his mantle. One man stood beside Meshullam, holding a sword threateningly against his back. Another Philistine stood in front of Rivkah, her back against a wall. The tip of his sword played menacingly against her round belly. The man laughed raucously as he made a small jerking movement upwards.

"Later," his companion held him back.

Later? Did they think Meshullam could not understand them? It seemed they really did mean to harm Rivkah. But then Philistines were known for ripping open the pregnant women of their vanquished enemies. Beads of sweat formed on Meshullam's brow. Not Rivkah! Not her child! He had to do something. He could not just wait until they slaughtered his wife and child. But any move now would only bring the end sooner and more surely. Meshullam was certain the soldier would stab Rivkah if he made as much as a move to help her. They would both be dead—and the child.

The soldier gave Rivkah another poke then put the sword back into the sheath, leaving her leaning pale against the wall as he went into the store room to help his comrade with the plunder. This was Meshullam's chance! Now or never! In one quick movement he pulled out his iron knife, turned around and thrust it deep into his captor's chest. The man tried to strike Meshullam with his sword, but missed. Clattering, it fell to the ground as the man collapsed forward mortally wounded. Meshullam grabbed the sword. "Let's get out of here!" he shouted at Rivkah. She came to his side but the way out was blocked. One of the Philistines was coming back into the house for more plunder. He was surprised to see an armed Judahite coming towards him. Meshullam rammed the sword into his stomach and twisted it. The entrails spilled out of the man as he sank down, his eyes wide in shock. A gurgling sound escaped from this mouth.

But the fight was not over yet. His two companions outside the house had noticed the altercation and now ran towards the door brandishing their weapons. Would Meshullam be able to stand against so many?

"Meshullam!" Rivkah screamed. "Behind you! From the store room!"

Meshullam glanced behind him. The two soldiers in the store room had let go of their booty and come to join the fight. Meshullam certainly couldn't take on four men alone! He stepped back and slammed the door shut, pushing the bolt across. He spun around to face the soldiers emerging from the store room. Behind him he could hear the soldiers outside attacking the locked door. "Make sure the bolt is secure," he yelled at Rivkah. "And then hide."

He went to meet them. Swords clashed as they locked in combat. But Meshullam could not hold out against two trained soldiers. One of them cut a deep wound into his left side, the other struck Meshullam's right arm. His grip on the sword became weak. Suddenly something exploded in the face of one of the Philistines. The broken pot fell to the floor as urine dripped down his face. The man roared in rage. Wiping the filth from his eyes he must have spotted Rivkah behind Meshullam.

"Rivkah!" Meshullam shouted, "Get back! Hide!"

The man focused on her and jumped past Meshullam to pursue her. No! He would not get her! Meshullam turned and struck the soldier in the back. The man fell. Meshullam thought he got up again, but could not be sure. Out of the corner of his eye he saw the other Philistine attacking. Meshullam had just enough time to roll out of the way. He crashed into the bread oven, which was still warm. He was able to stand up again in just enough time to deflect the blow that was aimed for his stomach. But the power of the strike was not spent and the sword cut deeply into his thigh as it slashed downward. Meshullam struggled to keep erect. The Philistine's next blow flicked Meshullam's sword out of his hand. Meshullam sank to the ground. The little knife would not help him now. In desperation he thrust his hand into the bread oven, grabbed the hot ash and flung it into the attacker's face. It held his opponent back for a moment, but Meshullam could not turn the brief advantage into an attack. The man regained his composure, paused, and concentrated to deliver the final thrust.

Just then Meshullam heard the door shatter. Now it was all over! The Philistines had finally broken into the house. He could never have expected the wooden door to keep them out forever. But he would fight to the end. Meshullam stared at his opponent. What would he do next? Did Meshullam have any chance at all? In one quick move the man was over Meshullam, the sword coming down fast. Meshullam saw that he could not avoid the strike. He cried out.

In that instant the power seemed to go out of the strike. The man toppled backwards, his sword just grazing Meshullam's arm before it fell harmlessly to the floor. Then everything was quiet. Meshullam could hear his own loud breathing. He opened his eyes and looked into Father's grim face.

"Son, are you hurt?"

"I am alive." Meshullam got to his knees. "Rivkah, how is Rivkah?"

Father shrugged his shoulders, then turned. "I'll look for her."

Was she still alive? Had anything happened to her?

He heard Father's voice, "Rivkah." Then came her reply, "Father Ehud!" She was alive! Meshullam managed to get to his feet and stumbled towards their bedroom. That's where she was.

"Meshullam? Is he alive?" he heard Rivkah ask.

"I am here," he said as he entered the room. She seemed unharmed.

* * *

Rivkah flung the pot at the face of the Philistine. Her aim was perfect. It shattered around his head, the urine spreading over his face. Was it enough to help Meshullam? The humiliated man roared in rage. He wiped the filth from his eyes and fixed them on Rivkah. She suddenly felt exposed and unprotected. The Philistine totally disregarded Meshullam, intent now avenging this shame, bent on destroying this woman who had humiliated him. Meshullam must have noticed his intention. For now he called out her name, "Rivkah! Get back! Hide!"

She stepped back a few paces as the soldier pushed past Meshullam. But the man did not get far. With a cry he fell onto his knees. He leaned on his sword, trying to steady himself and turned around to face his attacker. But he did not have to fear another strike from the back. His companion was dealing to Meshullam.

The man now focused all his attention on Rivkah. He growled like a dog as he got back to his feet and charged Rivkah with new ferocity. She fled into the bedroom. In panic she searched for a weapon to defend herself, anything. All she could find were some loom-weights she had left in a bowl. The first one hit the surprised man in the chest as he came into the room. The second missed him and shattered against the wall. The third struck him in the mouth, causing blood to spurt from his lips. She also threw the bowl, which crashed harmlessly against his knee. But all these desperate attempts only held him back for a moment. The man was coming toward her.

Rivkah grabbed a blanket and threw it at him. It tangled round his body. The next blanket covered his head. As he tried to slash it with his sword, the weapon slipped from his grasp and rolled to the floor, wrapped up in the cloth. Rather than trying to recover it, the soldier decided to end things immediately and lunged at Rivkah, throwing his arms around her shoulders to drag her down. They both fell. Rivkah heard his head crash into the wall as they went down. The man came to rest on top of her. He was heavy, but made no further move, did not try to keep her down. Rivkah could smell the urine that dripped from his face and had soaked into his clothes. She felt as if she would suffocate. Gathering her strength she pushed the man off her. He slumped onto the ground beside her. Rivkah was too weak to get up.

She heard the house door being broken and the fighting in the main room. Meshullam must still be alive. She listened for his voice. But everything went quiet. Had they killed Meshullam? A man stepped into the bedroom. Rivkah was too exhausted for another fight, could not even get up.

"Rivkah."

She looked up at the strong figure, "Father Ehud!" Relief flooded over her, but only briefly. The dread returned, "Meshullam? Is he alive?"

Ehud jerked his head towards the main room, indicating that Meshullam was out there. But how was he?

Just then Meshullam came slowly through the door. "I'm here," he said and went down on his knees beside her.

"Meshullam," Rivkah breathed. He looked hurt. Blood came pouring from his arms, his side, his thigh. Bruises covered his body.

"Are you alright?" Meshullam asked.

Rivkah nodded.

"And the child?" He gently placed his hand on her belly.

"I think so." She took hold of his hand. He flinched in pain. "But you are hurt."

"It's nothing," he assured her. "You are still alive. That's all that counts. And the child too."

Ehud interrupted their reunion, "Is that man dead?" He pointed towards the Philistine still slumped beside Rivkah.

"I'm not sure," she responded.

"Better make sure then."

He slammed the iron plow tip into the man's chest. Blood spattered, sprinkling Meshullam and Rivkah. "That's done. We better take him outside and tidy this place up. You two need some looking after as well."

Other men from the village crowded into the house, surveying the bloody scene of the violent struggle. Ehud organized them to carry the dead outside and bring order back to the house. Merab insisted on cleansing and dressing Meshullam's wounds. She ordered him to come into their house. Leah stayed with Rivkah.

"Are you injured?"

"No, just exhausted. I feel so weak, Leah."

Leah gently dabbed away the Philistine's blood from Rivkah's face, her arms, her clothes.

"Thank you, Leah."

"I'm so glad you are alive, Rivkah—and the child. I prayed for you. I saw the men going into the house and how they captured Meshullam. I prayed so hard, but could do nothing else. When Meshullam shut that door in their faces, the men outside went berserk. They tried to break the door with their swords and spears. They were so focused on that they did not notice Father arrive. He had only his plow tip, but he made good use of that. Grandfather suddenly seemed to regain his old vigor and joined in the fight too. Then I dared to hope again, hope that the end had not yet come for you and Meshullam. So now, I give thanks to the LORD for your deliverance."

Rivkah nodded. "It could have turned out so differently. Thank you for your prayers."

"Here, drink this," Leah urged as she held some watered wine to Rivkah's lips.

Rivkah drank thirstily.

"You know, Rivkah. I have never really said it before, but I'll say it now: you mean so much to me."

"Leah . . ."

"Let me go on. The fear of losing you made me see it clearly. Rivkah, you are like a sister to me."

"Leah, you are dear to me, too. Thank you for all you have done."

Rivkah looked around the room. "This is a violent world. Destruction seems to constantly overwhelm us. And yet in this world, there are people who care, who love deeply. That's what I have found here. Even though evil also breaks into this place, it has not snuffed out the flame of love." Tears came to Rivkah's eyes. She felt cold, started to shiver.

"What is it?"

"I don't know. Leah, it was so awful. The men with their swords, the blood—all in our home."

Ehud came back into the room, "Right Rivkah, we better move you to the other house. We'll have to clean up this chaos."

Meshullam came hobbling after him. He insisted on helping Rivkah. The two men gently lifted her up. Supported by Meshullam and Leah, Rivkah slowly walked across to the other house.

"Thank the LORD!" Micah said as he saw her. She smiled at him, hoping it looked encouraging. Merab had prepared a bed for her and Meshullam. Tonight they would stay in the large house again, taking shelter there after their own home had been violated.

* * *

They buried the bodies of the Philistines in shallow graves the next day. They kept their weapons. They were too valuable to allow them to rust in the ground. The whole village pitched in to replace what was destroyed in the two houses that had been looted. The stains were all washed away, order restored. Rivkah and Meshullam moved back into their home. Life should have continued as before. But it did not. Leah sensed that something was troubling her brother and it was not just the imminent birth of his child. He was continuously tense and distracted. Could it be the wounds he sustained? But they were healing well and Meshullam soon returned to his work, plowing the fields and scattering the seed.

Once, in the field, Leah noticed him suddenly take off with quick steps muttering to himself before he stopped, looked around as if waking from a dream then continued his work. That was not the calm brother she knew. What was on his mind? Did the attack on his house still frighten him?

Leah decided to ask him as they were going home from the field one evening. Father had already taken the cows. Meshullam had strapped the plow on the back of the donkey and was leading the animal home. Leah walked beside him, the hoe she used to work the edges of the fields over her shoulder. "It's been a long day again," she observed.

"Yes, we struck some stony ground today."

"You seem to be coping really well, Meshullam, considering the injuries you received not long ago."

"They're healing quickly. They're hardly bothering me anymore."

"They don't?"

"These wounds heal quickly."

What bothered him then? "You're not scared that the Philistines will come again?"

"I don't know..."

"The ones that did come are dead and buried. No one will know where they met their death." She noticed the little twitch in Meshullam's face. The event must still trouble him.

"What is it?" she asked.

Meshullam stopped the donkey. "I killed them. I killed other men."

"Is that what troubles you?"

"Yes."

"But you killed them to defend yourself, to save Rivkah."

"I know. But Leah, I cannot forget the eyes of the man as I plunged the sword into him and he fell. The shock, the horror in his face was unbearable. And then his guts spilled out and his life ended. I ended his life. I killed another human being."

"But otherwise he would have killed you."

"Yes. Maybe I had to kill them. I hope the LORD forgives me for that sin." He gave the donkey a slap and they walked on again. "Leah, I don't know why men kill each other. Do they have no conscience? How can they bear to see another person die and know they are responsible? It is the whole business of war and violence that disgusts me, that makes me sick."

"Of course you're right. Sometimes, though, we have no choice but to fight."

Meshullam didn't reply.

"I am sure the LORD has forgiven you already. Did you talk to Grandfather?"

"No." Meshullam shook his head.

"Talk to him, Meshullam. Talk to him."

* * *

Rivkah felt the warm air of the fire rise pleasantly against her face. Her frozen cheeks, nose and forehead seemed to thaw in the heat. She stretched out her hands, warming them over the fire. It felt so good.

Micah also enjoyed the heat, leaning above the little fire in their living room.

"Thank you for sharing your fire with me," he said. He leaned back again as the flames caught another piece of wood and shot higher. "There's nothing like it on a cold winter's day."

"The wind outside just about froze my limbs right off. And when Meshullam comes back, he'll want a warm house."

Micah looked at Rivkah's large belly. "Not much longer now. The little one must be due soon."

"Yes. Merab reckons the child will come within a week or two. Not much longer."

"Are you excited?"

"Of course. I'm looking forward to this child. But I'm also scared. I hope the birth will be easy."

"I hope so." Micah's eyes darkened, then brimmed with concern. Was he remembering the birth of his youngest daughter, the day his wife died? But then he seemed to shake off the thought. "Meshullam is getting quite excited, too."

"Yes, he is looking forward to the child."

Rivkah paused, then asked Micah, "Did you talk to him?"

"About the killings?"

"Yes."

"I did. I'm glad he recognized the enormity of what he did in taking another man's life. It's better than killing without a conscience. But it is hard for him. In war even the victor loses, for he has blood on his hands. Sometimes the deed has to be done. Meshullam defended his home and family against a murderous band. He recognizes that. It would have been wrong to stand by and let you and the child be murdered. I think the LORD was with Meshullam that day and guided his hand. Sometimes the LORD, who alone has power over life and death, calls us even to take another life."

Micah stretched his hands towards the fire again. "I, like Meshullam, wish there would be no more war, that we could live securely, that nations would not live in fear anymore, that grievances were no longer settled by weapons, that land and possessions were no longer taken by force. And I believe that it will come to pass in the day when the LORD will rule over the whole earth from Jerusalem. Whenever I see violence and fear, I remember the promise."

"The promise?"

"Yes, the promise of the LORD."

Rivkah sensed that Micah remembered words he had spoken long ago, words he still treasured. "Did you preach about it in former days?"

"I did. Rivkah, listen to this vision, the promise of the LORD:
'In the last days,
the mountain of the LORD's temple will be established
as chief among the mountains;
it will be raised above the hills,
and people will stream to it.
The LORD will judge between many peoples
and will settle disputes for strong nations far and wide.
They will beat their swords into plowshares
and their spears into pruning hooks.
Nation will not take up sword against nation,
nor will they train for war anymore.
Every man will sit under his own vine
and under his own fig tree,
and no one will make them afraid,
for the LORD Almighty has spoken.
All the nations may walk
in the name of their gods,'
we will walk in the name of the LORD
our God forever and ever.'"

"Beautiful. But is it possible?"

"I know that in this world of wars, of cruelty and violent death, of fear and oppression, such peace is hard to imagine. But it is what we all yearn for. And it will come about in the last days when the LORD fulfills all he has promised, all he intends for this earth. When the LORD judges between nations, when people live according to his law, there will be no need for war. Men will no longer seek glory and riches through war. No, they will be content to farm the land and, in tranquility, enjoy the days of their life."

"But the Assyrians? Do they not consider a trained soldier the most admirable of men? How can they live without war?"

"Yes, a change of heart is necessary and the Assyrians, like so many others, will have to walk in new paths, paths they are not accustomed to. Everywhere, the way people live, their economies, will be radically altered. That's when they will beat swords into plowshares."

"You can kill with plowshares too," Rivkah interrupted.

"I know. But you cannot go to war with plowshares. Their main use is to till the soil."

"So everyone will work the land. They will sit under their own fig tree and under their own vine."

"Yes. They will rob and plunder no longer. They will not enrich themselves by taking from the poor farmer and by foreclosing loans. Instead every man will work the land. Rivkah, one fig tree and one vine is not much. Of course, they will have more fields, but for peace to really come we will need to be content with little, and not seek to amass land and riches. Then we will be able to live without fear and forsake war."

"But when will it happen?"

"When the LORD reigns from Jerusalem."

"Is that long away?"

"Yes, but by walking in the name of the LORD, we can bring about some of that peace here and now. Here in this community, this nation, we are still threatened by war, but if we trust in the LORD he will lead us along paths of peace. Even if the nations around us follow different gods, we do not dare let go of the LORD, his ways and his promises."

"I long for that peace," Rivkah mused. She put another piece of wood on the fire.

"So do I, so do I," Micah said.

* * *

Rivkah knew the time had come. Merab called together some of the older women of the village. They would assist at the birth. There was no midwife in the village, no midwife either among the people of Mareshah, who had just come back to settle the land. In a country so decimated by the Assyrian occupation, so sparsely populated, life had not yet returned to its usual ways. Rivkah wished Ayalah were here. She would have known how to help, would have known the herbs to ease Rivkah at this time. Rivkah was sure the women here had witnessed many births and knew what to do. After all, had they not delivered Tinshemet's healthy girl? But still . . .

Leah was there. Rivkah had asked her to stay with her.

The contractions seized her body, the pain took her breath away. She screamed in agony, sweated tears. The women around her encouraged her, but could they not see the pain, could they not feel what she was going through? Maybe Leah did. Her face was white and ashen. She held Rivkah's hand, tried to speak words of comfort. At times Rivkah smiled bravely, at times the pain became too much.

"Leah, Leah, what are you trying to tell me? I know you will not leave me. I know you will stay at my side. But I can understand your words no longer."

And then it was time. The women around her grew still. New life came into the world, but it was not an easy passage. Rivkah no longer knew whether she was in this body, no longer knew whether she was here or somewhere far away. And then a voice called her back, a baby crying, the voice of her child.

"A son! You have a son!" she heard them congratulate her. They placed him in her weak arms. Through the tears she saw the tiny face, contorted in angry outrage at the passage of birth. Her hands held his tiny arms, the struggling legs small but perfectly formed, the hands, curled in miniature fists. A son!

The women spread the good news throughout the village.

* * *

Meshullam's hand trembled. He looked at the flint knife he was holding. Why did it seem so hard now? He had looked forward to this day, when he would circumcise his firstborn son. There was no reason to be nervous, no reason to suddenly draw back. The knife was sharp, he knew. He had used it to cut the skin and flesh of animals. And he had confidently handled it then. But now that his son lay before him in Rivkah's arms, peacefully drooling and looking absentmindedly at the people surrounding him, now Meshullam was not sure whether he could go through with it. Could he really cut off the child's foreskin? What if he got it wrong?

Grandfather said another prayer, blessing the child, asking that God's grace may rest upon him and his family. The prayer finished. Now it was Meshullam's turn. All eyes were upon him. He had to do it! He stepped forward; quickly and without hesitation, he made the cut. The child screamed in pain and protest. The people around him erupted into shouts and exclamations, drowning out the boy's cries.

Meshullam looked more closely. Had he done it right? As far as he could tell, the cut had been perfect. He felt Grandfather's hand on his shoulder. "Well done." Meshullam breathed a quiet sigh of relief.

"What is his name?" Mother asked.

Meshullam smiled at Rivkah, gave her little nod. "Yohanan. His name is Yohanan," he declared. The LORD is gracious. He had experienced the LORD's grace in his own life and now his son's name proclaimed it.

"A good name," Grandfather commented.

"A fitting name," Mother said.

A name of hope, too.

"Yohanan . . . Yohanan." Shimei tried out his nephew's name. He touched the little boy, but his cries only got louder.

It took Rivkah a long time to settle Yohanan. The others had already begun the feast in honor of the child's birth and circumcision by the time she had got him to bed and was able to join them. Meshullam called her to his side and poured a cup of wine. This was a day for feasting. Mother and child had survived the birth and now another son of Israel had entered into the ancient covenant with the LORD.

Chapter 19

Yohanan stopped drinking. Rivkah looked down at him. He had fallen asleep against her breast. His face was so peaceful, so content. He had all he needed, all he wanted. She moved him and wiped the milk from his mouth. At the touch, his mouth responded sleepily, but he did not wake. Rivkah kissed him lightly on the forehead. She tucked the edge of her dress back over her shoulder and cuddled Yohanan close. He was so beautiful, really a little miracle. She took his tiny hands in her palms and marveled at them. So perfect. He made all the pain of birth worthwhile. The long months of pregnancy were insignificant when she looked at him, the short nights a small price to pay. What was all the hurt, all the loss she had experienced in her life compared to the happiness she now felt? She had come to the end of her wanderings, her search for a place in this world. Here with Yohanan, there was nowhere else she should be. All her questions, her doubts had passed. This was who she was meant to be—the mother of Yohanan, caring for this little boy. She had found her destiny.

Gently she traced her finger down his face, marveling at his soft, baby skin. "Yohanan," she mouthed. Her heart overflowed with thanks and she quietly gave voice to her prayer:

"LORD, thank you for Yohanan,
thank you for this son of mine.
You have given joy to my heart
and filled this house with laughing."
The words that at first came hesitantly now poured forth:
"I was wandering without aim,
I was lost, I did not know the way.
But you, LORD, found me
and brought me home.
You set my foot upon the right path
and made me walk in the ways of peace.
And now you have poured out your blessings upon me,
you have lifted me up high.

You have given me this child,
a son to care for and love.
He brings joy to his mother
and will make his father proud.
You, LORD, are gracious and good."

Rivkah had never prayed like this before. She had never felt so close to God before. She whispered the words again, "Thank you LORD, thank you for Yohanan."

God had given her so much, but this child in her arms was the greatest gift of all. Yohanan. The LORD was indeed gracious!

Softly she recited a psalm she had learned in the house of Micah, words that echoed her feelings:

"I will exalt you, my God the King;
I will praise your name forever and ever.
One generation will commend your works to another;
they will tell of your mighty acts.
They will celebrate your abundant goodness
and joyfully sing of your righteousness.
The LORD is gracious and compassionate,
slow to anger and rich in love.
The LORD is good to all;
he has compassion on all he has made.
The LORD is faithful to all his promises
and loving toward all he has made.
The eyes of all look to you
and you give them their food at the proper time.
The LORD is near to all who call on him,
to all who call on him in truth.
My mouth will speak in praise of the LORD."

*　*　*

Only a few high clouds drifted lazily across the brilliantly blue sky. The sun warmed the earth, encouraging crops to grow. A light breeze wafted through the village hardly moving the leaves on the trees. It was the perfect weather for shearing. The wool wouldn't be blown away and yet the breeze was enough to cool Meshullam's perspiring body. He pinned the sheep to the ground with his left knee as he stood over it. This old ewe wouldn't struggle. She had always been a quiet one. With her feet bound together, the animal couldn't kick or try to stand up; she lay silent and still before her shearer. Meshullam held the wool with his left hand, leading the knife in his right across the sheep's arched back. By keeping the skin stretched he could cut closely to the sheep's body without injuring it.

As the wool fell from the sheep, Leah gathered it up, sorting it immediately. She separated the dirty, short belly-wool and the stained wool from the luscious white fleece. It was good wool, Meshullam could see—pure, white, and strong. No thorns or thistles clung to it. Rivkah would be pleased. She could do so many things with it: dye it, or use the white in rugs or blankets. He looked up and smiled at her. She stood and watched, cradling their son in her arms. Yes, Yohanan would be well clothed. He guessed Rivkah was already thinking about the patterns and designs she would use the wool for, the clothes she would make for Yohanan. Not that she had been idle before his birth. No, she had woven cloths and blankets, had made tiny clothes for the child. But now that she saw Yohanan, he inspired her to ever-new creations. She had waited impatiently for shearing and had often asked Meshullam about the new wool. Now the day had arrived.

Lifting up the head of the sheep, Meshullam shore the last wool off its neck. "Shimei!" he called, and started to untie the cords around the sheep's feet. His younger brother had been sunning himself in the middle of the courtyard, watching the activity around him. Shimei jumped up and hurried over to Meshullam.

"Finished?" Shimei asked.

"She's done." Meshullam coaxed the sheep back up on her feet and handed her over to Shimei who dragged her over to the pen. He stretched his sore back and took a mouthful of water. "The wool is nice and clean this year," he told Rivkah.

"I saw that. It'll be quite easy to spin, I think. But the lambs look even better."

"Yes, their wool is really white."

"And so soft."

"It is. That new ram has passed on his best traits to his offspring."

Meshullam touched Yohanan's little nose. "That wool will make some nice new clothes for you, eh? Warm and soft they'll be, little boy." Yohanan gazed at him as if surprised by the sudden attention, then smiled broadly and chuckled.

"Meshullam! What sheep do you want?" Shimei called across the yard.

"I'll take a lamb! Wait, I'll be over," Meshullam shouted back.

At the sudden, loud voice Yohanan grimaced as if he was going to cry. "Ah, it's alright, Yohanan," Meshullam said quietly. It must have been enough, for Yohanan decided that there was nothing to be scared of after all.

Meshullam hurried over to the pen of bleating lambs. "That one there will do." He pointed to one and jumped over the bars to help Shimei catch it. Half-dragging, half-carrying it, he took it over to the shearing rug. He felt that this one would be a bit jumpy and would probably struggle. Ah well, there were always a few. But it did have nice wool.

Shimei sat on the lamb while Meshullam tied its legs together. "That's good. You can go."

But Shimei did not get a break.

"I've nearly finished this one here. Can you get the next one for me, Shimei!" Father called.

"No time to lie in the sun," Meshullam teased, but Shimei was already off to the pens. He was taking his responsibility seriously.

Father was shearing his flock, Mother and Tirzah were helping with the wool sorting. Father's flock was bigger than Meshullam's. Getting through them would take just about the whole day and Meshullam would help with the last few sheep. Then they would celebrate together. Mother and Rivkah had already prepared cakes and sweet yoghurt. It was another milestone in the year, not as significant as harvest time, not as joyous, not such hard work, but always a sign that spring had indeed arrived.

Shimei was ready with the next sheep by the time Father finished. Meshullam had to admit that his little brother was getting good at handling the sheep, not just the small lambs, but also the ewes. He had certainly grown this last year.

* * *

"Shh, Yohanan, don't cry, don't cry." Rivkah tried to soothe him and walked through the room rocking him gently. "What's the matter Yohanan? Whatever is the matter?"

He was so restless today, cried whenever she put him down and took a long time to settle. Most days he was a good child, happy and calm, but on some days it seemed as if something was bothering him. He clearly wasn't hungry. His little tummy was full and he was not interested in drinking any more. Rivkah gently slapped him on the back. His crying became more intermittent; he belched a few times and became quiet. Rivkah felt him snuggling contentedly against her. Was he asleep? She slowly lowered him to look in his eyes. No, they were still wide open, but she noticed the eyelids drooping occasionally. Rivkah carried him as she sang a lullaby:

"Hush little one, don't cry;
rest now and close your eyes.
You are my special child, dear to my heart.
Mother will watch over you.

"Sleep little one, don't fear;
Mother will dry your tears.
Nothing will harm you here, not in this house.
Angels will watch over you.

"Birds find their seed, sheep eat their grass, foxes their prey;
you, too, will eat; slumber in peace.

"Dream little one, I pray;
dream of the future days
when you'll be strong and brave, here in this land.
The LORD will watch over you."

The room was quiet after she finished the song. Yohanan breathed regularly and deeply. Rivkah sat down and saw he was asleep. She held him close, supporting his head, running her fingers through his short, fine hair. Would he wake again if she put him down? He seemed so peaceful. Rivkah laid him down in his cot. He did not stir, but slumbered peacefully. She covered him with a blanket she had made for him and made sure he was comfortable.

Rivkah gazed at him with love. This was her son! This was the baby she bore, the child who depended on her. She quietly sang the lullaby again, watching Yohanan's face. He was still so small, but she could see how he was growing, how he became bigger each week. Soon he would no longer be a little baby. She was sure he would be strong and would make his father and mother, his grandfather and grandmother proud.

Rivkah had not known how much hard work was involved in being a mother, how exhausting it could be. She had not thought that, at times, it would be so frustrating. But she also had never imagined the joy, the love she would feel for her child. And that surpassed all else. The satisfaction of her role, the knowledge that Yohanan depended on her, gave meaning to her life.

"Yohanan, sleep now. And I will be here for you when you wake. I will care for you. I will love you forever." Tenderly Rivkah brushed his face.

* * *

Lunchtime! Leah carried the sheaves to the edge of the field and placed them with the others to be carried to the threshing floor. She walked over to the shade tree and sat down out of the direct heat of the sun. Rivkah had brought lunch into the field: bread and cheese, hummus and gherkins, and nice cool water. Rivkah did not work the whole day in the fields this harvest. Part of the day she stayed back at home and did the housework. She baked bread, made cheese and, of course, looked after Yohanan. But she always came to bring lunch and eat with the others.

Leah watched Rivkah playing with her son. She held him up and blew against his tummy, moving her head back and forth. Yohanan giggled and kicked his little legs in glee. She lowered him down and made silly faces. "Who's a happy boy? Who's a big boy?" she asked. Yohanan reached for her face and grabbed some of her hair, pulling it towards his mouth. Rivkah bent her head forward, but then started to extricate her hair from his grasp. "Hmm, you like your mother's hair, eh?"

Leah laughed. Yohanan was such an adorable child. She was happy for Rivkah, glad that she could take pride in her son. Still, sometimes Leah wished she could have a child, too. Sometimes it was hard to be reminded that she was still single, with no husband, no child in sight.

She held out her arms. "I'll take him for you."

Rivkah handed Yohanan to her. He knew her, did not cry, as Leah bounced him on her knee. She waved his stumpy little arms as he gurgled excitedly. He must have looked funny, for Meshullam laughed loudly then grimaced at his son. Even Father couldn't help but smile. Mother, of course, wanted to hold her grandson and Leah had to hand Yohanan to her.

The lunch break was all too brief and the whole family returned to the field again. Even Rivkah helped with the harvest for a while once she had fed Yohanan who then slept peacefully in a swing suspended from the tree.

The sun was hot now, the air warm. Luckily, a breeze had picked, giving some respite. Leah worked alongside Rivkah, gathering the stalks that Meshullam cut. Even though it had been a dry spring, the harvest would be sufficient, enough to feed the whole family.

* * *

The harvest was over. The men were still threshing and winnowing the barley and wheat. Everyone knew they would not have the plentiful yield they had last year. But it was not altogether a bad year, the old people said. There had been years that had been much worse. Somehow this talk of good harvests and lean yields, of average years and bumper crops, was still somewhat unfamiliar to Rivkah. She listened, talked with Meshullam about soil moisture and plant growth, but she had nothing to compare it with, no knowledge from past years.

In Lachish her mother had occasionally complained about the price of grain, and at other times had been relieved at how affordable wheat was. But Rivkah had never known, or cared, what made the prices vary from year to year. Now she slowly learned to relate weather and harvest, understood the importance of the rain in its season, appreciated the work and the prayer that went into a good crop. She watched the sky in winter, waited anxiously until harvest time and then rejoiced as the grain was gathered.

And now there was someone else to think of. Now she had responsibility for this child. Now it was his future she was considering, his welfare she cared for. Though he did not know it yet, the success of the harvest would affect his life too. He just looked to her, his mother, and expected his needs to be met. He relied on her, but she could only provide what the harvest would give.

Rivkah watched Yohanan lying there on a rug, playing with a little wooden toy Meshullam had made for him. He was fascinated by it, took it into his mouth, sucked on it, chewed on it, then waved it excitedly in the air. "You're a wild one, you are," Rivkah laughed. It only seemed to encourage him. His arms moved even faster and he flung the toy away from him.

"Oops! Where has it gone, eh? Where has it gone, Yohanan?" When he noticed it was no longer there, he looked confused. Then his lower lip pouted and quivered slightly.

"Don't cry my darling, don't cry." But she had hardly finished her words when the first sobs developed into strident cries of protest. Rivkah sighed, put down the spindle she was using and reached over to get the toy. "Here it is, Yohanan. No need to cry, is there? Here you go."

Just as quickly as the storm had come upon his face, the sunlight now shone from his eyes. The crying ceased, replaced by a sparkling smile. Yohanan reached for the toy, grasped it with a happy yelp. After he had studied it with fascination, he put as much of it as he could fit into his mouth.

"Is that nice, is it?"

"Ehh . . . ," he drooled, then decided to bang it against his tummy.

"All good now." Rivkah tickled him. His smile grew even wider. She leaned over him, touched his nose with hers, took one of his hands in her hand. He grew totally still.

Suddenly she received a blow against her cheek as he decided it was time for action again and hit her in the face with the toy.

"Ouch, what are you doing?" It didn't really hurt.

He babbled excitedly as if he had something important to tell her.

"Ah, that's right. Interesting. I didn't know that, Yohanan," she acknowledged his string of unformed words.

He didn't stop his story when she picked up the spindle whorl again. She wound wool round her left arm and fed it to the right hand that was forming and twirling it. When she had wound a sufficient length she hooked the wool in the notch of the staff, rolled the whorl on her right thigh and lifted her left hand as the spindle whorl spun round. As the thread grew thinner, the spindle whorl nearly reached the floor. She lowered her hand and wound the thread on the distaff, the long part at the bottom of the spindle. She proceeded to form the next length. It would make good yarn, she knew. The wool here was so much better than anything she had worked with as a girl in Lachish. And it was so white.

"Our sheep have good wool, don't they?"

Yohanan totally agreed.

"I'll make you something nice."

He was pleased with that.

"What would you like? A new cloak?"

Yohanan didn't utter a sound.

"No? Maybe just a robe? Yes!"

It seemed he looked forward to it.

* * *

The evening wind wafted across the ridge, no longer in strong gusts as at noon. As the day started to fade into dusk, the west wind had become lighter and more constant—perfect conditions for winnowing. Meshullam had spent the afternoon on the threshing floor throwing the grain into the wind. The other men of the village stood nearby, each beside his own pile of grain.

Meshullam had his back to the setting sun as he worked on the pile of wheat. With his fork he lifted the threshed wheat high above the pile. The grain fell back onto the pile, the straw and chaff were carried farther to the east forming another mound. The lightest parts were scattered far and wide across the land. Wheat and chaff were separated by the wind, the one to make bread, the other for animal feed. It all had its uses.

Meshullam moved to the northern part of the pile and threw the wheat into the wind, working towards the centre. The men continued to work into the night, the moon giving them light.

Finally, Ahiel seemed to think they had worked long enough. He would spend the night here anyway. It would be his turn to guard the piles of grain tonight. He brought two jars of wine out of his bag. "Hey, do you want a drink?" he shouted to Boaz.

"I won't turn that offer down," came the reply.

"Meshullam, come, join us!"

Meshullam hesitated. It was late already. But what harm would one drink do? Just a quick one, he told himself.

"Sure," he answered. Father wasn't here to cast him a disapproving look. Meshullam might not have sat down with the others if he had. The men congregated around Ahiel, the cup passing from hand to hand as it made its rounds. Only Joel said he had to leave. "I can't stay. I guarded the threshing floor yesterday. My wife won't forgive me if I'm not home tonight."

"She should be glad not to have you around for another night," suggested Boaz, the wine already freeing him from any inhibition towards his elders.

"You can talk, young Boaz. Wait until you have a wife, then we'll talk again. Just because you can drink wine beside a heap of wheat, doesn't make you wise."

"Ouch." The others laughed as Boaz was put in his place.

"Get home safely, Joel! And don't stumble over anything," someone called as Joel disappeared into the moonlit night.

Ahiel lifted the cup. "A round for a good harvest."

"Not as good as last year," Meshullam mumbled.

A few of the other men nodded. "But still better than we feared in spring."

"Yes, not bad considering..."

"Enough to give you bread and some sweet cakes."

"But not enough to fatten a nice bull-calf."

"No, no luxuries like that this year."

"Your bones will creak as they did before. They won't be rich with fat and marrow."

"Not that they ever were."

"As long as we've got a good grape harvest I don't care for fattened calves or bulls or goats," Boaz joined the conversation again.

"Hear the wine talking."

But Ahiel had already filled the cup again. "To the grape harvest!"

The men drank enthusiastically and Ahiel had to refill the cup halfway through the round.

Meshullam remembered that he had wanted to go home soon. He got up.

"Where are you going?"

"I better get back home."

"Come, stay for another round!"

"No."

But he had to stay for the next toast: "To Meshullam and his young son." Ahiel poured a whole cup just for him. And Meshullam sat and drank it. He did think of Rivkah. She would be alright. She would care for Yohanan far better than he ever could. She would sing him to sleep, put him to bed. She was much better at it anyway. Meshullam did hold Yohanan at times, of course, but so often he did not know what to do with the screaming child, couldn't talk to him like Rivkah could. She was able to quieten Yohanan so much better, knew what he needed, understood him. She wouldn't miss her husband if he came home later tonight.

Meshullam sat in the circle when the cup came round again. The conversation had passed from matters of the village to those of national significance.

"King Hezekiah will expand Judah to the west again. Soon the Philistines will feel the force of our armies."

"The king does not have the money to equip an army."

"He soon will. Have they not found precious metals in the southern desert?"

"Yes, Judah will rise again." Meshullam was more confident of that tonight than he had been for many months. Any objections were quickly overcome and soon all the men on the threshing floor were united in foreseeing a glorious future for their nation. They drank to that future and no further discussion was needed. So it was natural that the conversation thinned and man after man lay down beside a pile of grain, or wherever he was sitting, and rested from his labors. When morning came, dew settled on the sleeping forms of men.

* * *

Rivkah carried Yohanan through the room, humming quietly. He was getting heavy, and screamed whenever she put him down. Right now he was finally sleeping placidly in her arms. She didn't dare to put him in his cot, not yet. Soon Meshullam would be back and she hoped he would hold Yohanan for a while, just to give her a break. She hadn't even been able to cook a good dinner tonight. Yohanan had been too clingy. Not that Meshullam would expect a big meal, not that late at night. Rivkah knew he would be late. With the bright moon and the constant west wind, the men would take the opportunity to winnow more wheat. She just hoped he wouldn't be too late.

Rivkah had already eaten, had done all the daily tasks she could with a little child in her arms. She was tired but she kept walking through the room. When she finally decided to put Yohanan to bed, he continued sleeping. Relieved, she tucked him in. But Meshullam had still not returned. Finally she went to bed. She left Meshullam's meal out in the kitchen. Would he still want it this late?

Tired though she was, she did not go to sleep immediately. She wanted to tell Meshullam about the day, wanted to ask him about the winnowing, wanted to talk. But he was not here. Would he come home tonight?

When Yohanan woke her early next morning Rivkah saw that the meal she had prepared for Meshullam had not been touched.

* * *

"Rivkah!" Micah called her.

"Good afternoon, Father Micah," she replied and walked over to where he was sitting in front of the house.

"How's our little boy, eh?"

Yohanan smiled at his great-grandfather.

"He's growing all the time," Rivkah said bouncing him on her hip, "and getting heavier."

"Yohanan, come to your old great-grandfather." Micah stretched out his arms towards Yohanan. Rivkah let him slide from her hips into the expectant hands. At first Yohanan looked at her as if he wanted to question how she dared to let go of him, but then happily settled into Micah's arms, all shyness quickly dissipating.

"Eh, young man, you're getting stronger each day. Soon you'll be running around and I won't be able to catch you."

Yohanan grabbed Micah's beard. He was always fascinated by it.

"Hey, be gentle," Rivkah admonished him.

"No harm done," Micah assured her, but grimaced nonetheless. "Don't you want to sit down for a while, too, Rivkah?"

"I'll have to take the dyed wool back to the house."

"Do that. And then come back. It's only a few steps after all."

Rivkah hesitated. She still had to prepare dinner, but resting for a few moments would be nice. It would not do any harm. "Alright, I'll be back shortly." She hurried into the house and put the basket of wool beside the loom.

"Pleased with the wool?" Micah greeted her as she sat down beside him.

"Yes, the dyeing has turned out quite well. We did the red wool first. Soon the pomegranates will be fully ripe and we can dye some wool brown and black. Tinshemet is really quite good at it and Rachel is learning too."

"You'll need to make some new clothes for this boy soon, the way he grows."

"I know," Rivkah sighed and pulled at Yohanan's clothes.

"But better that way. Better he's big and strong than a sick child. You can be grateful for that." Micah brushed Yohanan's hair. "Yohanan—the LORD is gracious. This child gives us all hope, points to the future full of promise, a land resettled. The LORD has not forgotten us. He is with us still."

"I am thankful for Yohanan, so thankful for the son the LORD has given me."

Micah looked at her. "You know, I believe only a mother's heart can come close to understanding the love the LORD has for his people. He cares for them passionately. He can never give up on his people."

"No matter what?"

"He loves them no matter what they do. He calls them back to himself when they have gone astray. He yearns for them."

"And what if they have done evil things?"

"The LORD cannot accept sin, cannot tolerate injustice. He will seek it out and punish it, exactly because he cares for his people. But he loves them still."

"But you have seen much injustice in Judah, haven't you?"

"I have. And I reminded them. I told them of the LORD's love, but also pointed out their sin."

Micah held Yohanan close as he remembered words spoken long ago:

"Listen! The LORD is calling to the city.
Hear, oh tribe and assembly of the city.
Shall I acquit a man with dishonest scales,
with a bag of false weights?
Her rich men are violent;
her people are liars
and their tongues speak deceitfully.
Therefore I have begun to destroy you,
to ruin you because of your sins."

"So the LORD is angry."

"The LORD cannot stand sin. Sin is not only an abomination, it is contrary to the very being of the LORD. You always have to remember the hurt sin causes. A poor man starves because he has been swindled. A young child dies because its mother cannot afford food. A family is driven from its land and is reduced to begging and eating the refuse from the street. The powerful break the lives of the poor, their actions fill the houses of their victims with tears. Sin may seem attractive to get rich quickly, to seize what they want, but others suffer, others hurt. The sinners don't realize that they not only destroy the lives of others, but their own as well.

"Adultery may seem exciting, but it breaks apart families, hurts others even if they never find out, and always hurts those who have become unfaithful.

"Lies destroy trust. And how can we live together, how can we live in community, without trust? If we deceive each other, we destroy each other; we entangle ourselves and many others in a web that will drag us to destruction and suffering.

"Many people do not care about others, do not care that their own heart grows cold to the hurt they are causing. And nobody hurts more than the LORD who hears the cries of the widows and orphans, who feels the tears of disappointment of the swindled, who takes up the silent calls of powerless anger."

"The LORD feels the hurt caused by our sin?"

"Yes. He weeps at the things we do to each other and his anger is kindled by the sins that destroy his people. And so I had to pronounce the LORD's judgment:

'You will eat but not be satisfied;
your stomach will be empty.
You will store up but save nothing,
because what you save I will give to the sword.
You will plant but not harvest;
you will press olives but not use the oil on yourselves,
you will crush grapes but not drink the wine.
You have observed the statutes of Omri
and all the practices of Ahab's house,
and you have followed all their traditions.
Therefore I will give you over to ruin
and your people to derision.'"

"A terrible judgment," Rivkah observed. She thought of the work that went into planting and harvesting the wheat and the olives. All that for nothing?

"Yes, we may think we are in control, that we have made our plans and ensured our future, but then the LORD's judgment comes over his people, as he can watch their sins no longer. I think the invasion of the Assyrians was just punishment for our wrongs. I hope the people have taken it to heart. Sometimes I despair because they seem to continue in their old ways and have not really changed. And so the LORD still calls, calls us back to him and away from sin."

Micah's voice seemed hoarse with emotion. He put Yohanan on his knee and bounced him absentmindedly up and down, hardly looking at him.

"Do you think that people still do not understand the effect of sin?"

"Taking a little advantage of others now and then may not seem drastic. The odd bribe or the occasional white lie appear to move us ahead and make things a little easier. A small indiscretion, a lack of care for our family, may make life more comfortable and pleasant for a short time. But it does not stop there. Sin continues to grow until it infects everything around us, from the royal court to the most intimate reaches of families. There is no justice any longer. Children are lost, have no regard for their parents. Marriages break apart. If there is no trust, life together becomes unbearable. If everyone only looks out only for themselves, sin takes hold over every aspect of life. It paralyzes. And the hurt, the hurt becomes overpowering. The LORD grieves at the sin, grieves at the pain of his people.

"I had to tell the people, had to hold the mirror to their face, so that they could see how sin and deception distorted the whole of society, the whole people, everything they held dear:

'What misery is mine!
The godly have been swept from the land;
not one upright man remains.
All men lie in wait to shed blood;
each hunts his brother with a net.
Both hands are skilled in doing evil;
the ruler demands gifts,
the judge accepts bribes.

'Do not trust a neighbor;
put no confidence in a friend.
Even with her who lies in your embrace
be careful of your words.
For a son dishonors his father,
a daughter rises up against her mother,
a daughter-in-law against her mother-in-law—
a man's enemies are the members of his own household.'"

Micah was quiet for a moment before he continued:
"But as for me, I watch in hope for the LORD,
I wait for God my Savior;
my God will hear me."

"In all this sin, we still need to turn to the LORD? Is that what you mean?"

"Yes."

"But are we not also affected by the sin of others?"

"We are, but we have to start with ourselves, turn to the LORD and leave sin behind. If the LORD's healing does not begin in us, where else can it begin?"

"What do we have to do then?"

"You know," Micah smiled.

Rivkah remembered. "Act justly, love mercy and walk humbly with my God."

"Though it may be hard, that's what we are called to do."

Yohanan was getting impatient. Nobody was paying him any attention. Irritated, he pulled Micah's beard again, then began to squeal. Rivkah took him from Micah and quietened him down, giving him a drink. "Yohanan, what's the matter? Are you hungry?"

He nuzzled contentedly against her. She gently stroked his cheek. How could anyone harm a little child? How could they totally disregard what effects their actions had on these little ones?

* * *

Despite the dry spring, the olive harvest was good this year. They had been able to bring sacks full of olives from the groves. Now they had to be crushed. Meshullam spread a few sacks of olives in the flat, rectangular basin cut into the rock. Father rolled a heavy, stone roller over the olives while Meshullam turned the crushed olives with a wooden pole and pushed the ones in the corners back into the middle of the basin. Soon it was a pulpy mass. Father and Meshullam pushed the crushed olives together and heaped them into the adjacent deeper, but smaller, basin. Meshullam checked the water that had been quietly heating over the fire nearby. It was hot enough, near boiling in fact. Together they poured it over the olives. Meshullam stirred the mixture. Soon the oil began to float on top. It was time to skim the oil off with a shallow bowl and pour it into the jars.

"I think we're getting some help," Father said. Meshullam looked up. Mother was coming towards them and behind her was Rivkah, holding Yohanan. Meshullam put the bowl down and walked towards them. "You've come just in time. We're skimming off the first oil"

"Does it look good?" Mother asked.

"It does, and tastes even better."

"I'll have to try it." Mother went to the basin to test this year's first oil.

But why didn't Rivkah come? She had stopped and stood several paces away from him. "Meshullam."

He looked at her. What was it?

She smiled and put Yohanan down. He clung to her dress standing on his little legs. "Watch him," she said. Then she gently nudged Yohanan away from her. "Where's Father, Yohanan? Where's Father?"

Yohanan babbled excitedly as he spotted Meshullam and pointed his little fingers at him.

"Go to Father, go to him," Rivkah urged.

And then Yohanan took a step away from her. He was shaky on his feet, but he did not fall. Another step towards Meshullam. He was walking! Yohanan was really walking!

Meshullam crouched down, held out his arms towards Yohanan. "Come here Yohanan. You can make it!" Another step. He nearly fell backwards, but regained his balance. "That's it. Another step. One foot at a time," Meshullam encouraged him. His steps now became faster, and for the remaining distance he nearly broke into a run. He would have fallen if Meshullam had not gathered him up in his arms. "Yohanan, you have done it! You can walk!" Meshullam held him up and whirled him around. Yohanan squealed in delight.

Rivkah beamed at Meshullam.

"He can walk, he can walk on his own," he said.

"He walked freely for the first time this morning. I thought you may want to see it. That's why I came out here."

"Thank you. He's learned so fast." Meshullam held Yohanan's little head close to him as his son snuggled against him. This was his son! And he had just witnessed his first major achievement. Yohanan could walk. The excitement as he walked towards his father's outstretched arms, the joy in his eyes, touched Meshullam's heart deeply. "Yohanan," Meshullam whispered.

He set his son down again. Yohanan tried to walk another few steps, but got ahead of himself. Meshullam was just able to catch him before he fell.

"A bit more practice needed, eh?" Even Father had come over to watch his grandson. "So, he can walk now. You'll have to watch him then. You can never be sure where he'll be off to." Father cast a warning look towards the fire and the basin full of the hot water and olive mixture. "And keep him away from the fire," he warned.

"I'll look after him," Rivkah assured him.

Meshullam let Yohanan go and watched in delight as he walked into Rivkah's arms. Meshullam turned and helped Father to spread the next load of olives in the crushing basin. But as he worked he could not help but look at Yohanan again and again.

Chapter 20

Yohanan coughed. It was a deep, throaty cough. Rivkah was worried. Something was clearly wrong with Yohanan. He cried a lot, just lay down in a corner somewhere and had no interest in any games. He did not follow her around, did not pull over pots and jars. Maybe she should have been glad that he did not cause any trouble, that she did not have to watch him constantly. But she was not. Oh, that he would be his lively self again. She wanted him to play, to wander through the house, to investigate the world, to be excited by what he found. Instead, he was so still, took no interest in anything.

And then there was his breathing. It had become so rapid, as if he was constantly out of breath. That strident sound worried her. What was blocking his throat, his lungs? Rivkah did what she could. She made him drink chamomile tea scented with marjoram. She lit a fire in the middle of the room to keep the house warm. But it did not help. He seemed to feel colder, chilly tremors shook his body. His breathing became even faster, more labored. He was deteriorating before her eyes, getting weaker as she watched and there seemed to be nothing she could do.

She just sat beside him and held his hand. What else could she do? She brushed his cheeks tenderly, talked to him gently. "Yohanan, all is well. Just be quiet now. Mother is here with you. Just rest. I know it hurts. But you will get better. And soon you will run through the house again, will play and be happy." Rivkah was trying to reassure herself as much as she was trying to quieten Yohanan.

Finally Yohanan slept, a fitful, restless sleep, interrupted by coughs. Twice he woke up screaming. Twice Rivkah was able to gently rock him back to sleep. He must be in so much pain and so exhausted. Rivkah felt for him, but she could not relieve him of his pain. She did not move from his side. She did no housework that afternoon.

* * *

Meshullam tied the donkey up outside Father's house. He took the plow off the animal's back and carried it into the house, one part after the other. Then he led the donkey to his own house. "Shalom!" he called, as he took it to the stable beside the main room. Rivkah did not reply. She must be busy somewhere. As he rubbed the donkey's sides he noticed how warm it was in here today. Rivkah must have felt cold and heated the house.

"That should do," he said and offered the donkey a handful of barley. He poured some more into the manger. "We did some good work today, eh?" He patted the donkey again. He was looking forward to dinner himself. Plowing made a man hungry. What would Rivkah have cooked today?

But when he stepped back into the main room, he could not detect the smell of a hearty dinner, just smoke from the fire. And there beside the fire was Rivkah, kneeling silently at Yohanan's side. She looked at Meshullam with desperate, fearful eyes, the worry clearly showing in her face.

"What . . . whatever has happened?" he asked. This wasn't a scene he expected after a hard day in the field.

"He's sick, Meshullam. Yohanan is very sick."

Meshullam crouched down beside them. He heard Yohanan's fast, labored breathing. He felt the hot forehead, saw the reddened cheeks. "But now he is sleeping." He tried to sound hopeful.

"He's still getting worse. Can't you see how restless his sleep is?"

Meshullam could hear Yohanan moaning, could see him rolling and twitching. This was no healing sleep. "Have you given him anything?"

"I gave him chamomile, but he will hardly drink."

"I'll get Mother. She might know what else we can do."

Rivkah sighed. "Yes, get her."

Mother initially seemed overwhelmed at the sight of Yohanan's condition. He was awake by now and stared at her with feverish eyes, crying weakly, stopping only to cough. She shook her head. "He is really sick. We have to lower the fever. Rosemary, that should help. And sage too. I don't know whether I've still got some. Rivkah, do you have any?"

Rivkah shook her head.

"You will also have to make him sweat by draping hot, wet cloths around him. That should drive the disease out of his body."

Mother sprang into action and heated water. She asked Tirzah to get some more cloths from the other house. Then she seemed to think of something else. "Have you eaten?" she asked Meshullam.

"No."

"And bring some of the dinner over," she called after Tirzah.

With Mother there, the disease no longer felt so threatening. She was, after all, doing her best to fight it. Meshullam put his hand on Rivkah's shoulder. "It'll be alright, you'll see. It will be alright." It seemed she didn't share his confidence.

Soon everything was ready: the cloths soaked in warm water, and Yohanan lying uncovered on a blanket. Quickly, Mother and Rivkah packed the cloths around him. At first he screamed, but then a coughing fit silenced him. He was too weak to fight the wet cloths. It did not take long and Meshullam could see beads of sweat on Yohanan's forehead. He was quiet now, even his breathing became quieter. Meshullam hoped it had worked.

They ate the dinner that Tirzah had brought them. Meshullam swallowed hungrily, but Rivkah hardly ate anything, not taking her eyes off her son.

Mother helped Rivkah dry Yohanan off. After Rivkah had laid him back on the mat beside the fire, Mother wished them a good night and promised to be back early in the morning.

"Rivkah, we'll have to go to bed now."

"I'll stay here beside Yohanan."

"Rivkah . . . " But he could understand her. How could she leave their sick child alone?

"I'll get our mats from the bedroom." He arranged the bedding on the floor of the main room, close to Yohanan. "Come now, you have to sleep. Don't be too anxious. He will get better." He saw the doubt in her eyes as he made the bold statement. She was right. It still wasn't over. Sickness was always serious.

"Rivkah, let's pray. The LORD can help. Let's commend Yohanan into his care." Together with his wife, Meshullam knelt at the side of their son.

"LORD, we cry to you,
cry to you for our son
who is ravaged by disease,
sick and smitten by fever.

We pray that you will heal him,
restore him to health once again.
Any guilt that we have brought upon us
do not bring it down upon him
do not punish this child for the sins of his parents.
Be gracious with us
and look upon us with compassion.
For you are our rock and our help,
the God in whom we trust."
"Amen," Rivkah affirmed the prayer.

Peace enfolded them. They had entrusted Yohanan into the LORD's hands. .

The night did not pass quietly. Yohanan woke several times and Rivkah looked after him. None of them got much sleep.

* * *

Yohanan did not get better. He lay on the bed coughing and wheezing. He spat out light-yellow mucus whenever he coughed which Rivkah caught in a bowl. His cheeks and forehead burned with fever; his whole body was hot and he shivered as if he was cold. Rivkah put blankets around him, and piled more wood on the fire which she kept going constantly. Yohanan was so weak he didn't even cry; he just lay there whimpering occasionally, breathing loudly as if he was fighting for breath. He was too weak to eat or drink, too weak to even accept her milk. Desperately Rivkah held him against her breast until she was able to drip a few drops of milk into this mouth. Even swallowing milk seemed to hurt. She cradled him close, kissing his hot little face.

"Yohanan, drink something! You have to get strong again. Mother's little boy, come, drink." Her words seemed to have some effect. He swallowed a few more drops. But the next mouthful ran out of the corner of his mouth, moistening her dress. She gently wiped his cheeks. Oh, Yohanan! What could she do?

Her gaze fell on the prayer mother, the little clay figurine that stood above the hearth. She focused upon it. Now, more than at any other time she interceded for her child, her only son. She prayed that God would nurture her family, have compassion on them. Could she expect any strength, any power from the prayer mother? The ample breasts of the statue seemed to mock her. She had plenty of milk, but her child would

Daughter of Lachish

not accept it; he was wasting away before her very eyes with plenty of food around him. "Oh LORD, oh Ashera of the LORD, save my son! Restore Yohanan to health! Please LORD, LORD . . . LORD! Save him. Oh, save him, I pray. Be gracious to him! Have mercy on him, on this child of your people! Please LORD . . . " Her prayer passed into an incomprehensible babble. After some time she became aware that she was sitting silently, numbed and staring beyond the prayer mother.

She clasped Yohanan more firmly again. What would she have to give for the life of her son? What did the LORD require? She thought of Micah's words. She had tried to apply them to her life, to walk humbly with God. But perhaps she had failed. It didn't seem enough. With the life of her son in the balance, she resolved to give more. And so she pledged to offer two lambs and two kids as a sacrifice if Yohanan recovered. "And," she murmured, "no wine or strong drink shall pass my lips from now until the Passover festival, this I vow."

Did the LORD hear her, here in this little house far away from any temple or sanctuary? Did her prayers ascend to the throne of God? Did the prayer mother channel them to the LORD? "Oh," she groaned and buried her face against Yohanan's weak little body.

That's how Merab found her. Merab was shocked at Yohanan's condition. But she would not give up. She considered more desperate remedies. When she was unable to give Yohanan some of the herbal drinks she had prepared, she suggested steaming the herbs so that Yohanan would inhale the scented steam. With Leah's help, Rivkah held Yohanan above hot stones as Merab poured herbal concoctions on them. He sputtered and even attempted to put up a fight, but then just suffered the procedure. His face became red and moist. His breathing became even faster and he seemed even more exhausted. Rivkah was glad when it was over. The pain Yohanan suffered was too hard to watch. And so they laid him down again. Rivkah wiped the sweat off his brow with a cloth.

Meshullam returned early from the field, even before lunch. He looked grim when he saw Yohanan. Merab described what they had done to try and help him. Meshullam listened to her quietly. When Merab left the house, Rivkah told him about her vows, her pledges of offerings. He looked at her sadly and started to pace across the room.

"Did I do right?" she asked.

He didn't answer. "There must be something else," he finally said. He stopped still. "I'm going."

"Going where?" Leah asked.

"To find a healer. I have heard there is one near Hebron. If I go now, I might make it to Hebron today. I'll travel fast and light." He took a measured look at Yohanan. "I don't think there's enough time left to go to Jerusalem to consult the priests at the Temple."

It was that serious then? But finding a healer may be their last chance. Rivkah nodded in agreement. "What do you need?"

"Stay with him," he replied. "I'll just take a bag with some bread. I won't need much."

Rivkah watched him as he rummaged in the kitchen and stuffed a few things in his bag. "Are you sure you will be alright? Don't you want to take a blanket?"

"Too heavy."

"Take this small one at least, so that you can lay your head on it."

He stuffed in into his bag.

"I'll be back tomorrow, I promise."

"God be with you," she called, looking after him as he left the house. She sighed and looked at Leah.

"He'll get help, you'll see," Leah assured her.

If it wasn't too late, Rivkah thought. She knew Meshullam realized his mission was a last desperate attempt. But they'd try anything. And all the time Yohanan grew weaker.

She sat with him all afternoon. Leah left to prepare dinner. As evening came, Yohanan finally lay quietly in her arms, breathing fast, but regularly. His little body finally got the sleep it needed.

"Sleep, Yohanan, and get well. Don't cry, Mother is here with you. Sleep now," she whispered. As she rocked him she quietly sang him a lullaby:

"Hush little one, don't cry;

rest now and close your eyes.

You are my special child, dear to my heart.

Mother will watch over you.

"Sleep little one, don't fear;

Mother will dry your tears.

Nothing will harm you here, not in this house . . ."

She didn't continue. Tears fell from her eyes onto his little face and stifled sobs rocked her. Yohanan!

* * *

"Forty shekels of silver! But I don't have that with me."

"Forty shekels now and forty shekels when I see the boy. Nothing less."

"I can pay! I can pay. Just come with me now," Meshullam pleaded. Why hadn't he brought more money? But forty shekels! How could he ever obtain such a sum? Maybe if he sold most of their olive oil, he would have enough, but then another forty. Impossible!

"I'll not go anywhere until you have given me the money," the healer insisted.

"But my son, my only son, he's dying."

"What is that to me? Children are dying every day. And if he is not worth this trifling amount to you, why do you bother me?"

Trifling amount! The cost was beyond his reach. Maybe the healer knew that and didn't trust Meshullam to come up with the money. He was, after all, just a poor farmer from the country, and from the frontier at that, where life and property were not exactly secure.

"Have mercy, my lord, and heal my son!" he tried again.

"No!" The man spun around to go back into his house.

"Can't you do anything at all for my son?" Meshullam shouted.

The healer turned around slowly and smiled at Meshullam. "I can give you something for your son." He grasped Meshullam round the shoulder. "Come!" The healer led him through the door into the house.

The room was large and high, but dark and unlit. A little light fell through the doorways leading to side chambers. Jars stood lined up against walls; shelves, stacked with bowls and juglets, were fastened to the walls above the jars; and in the middle of the room stood a bench with pounders, pestles and pots. From the ceiling hung bunches of herbs. The floor was bare and plain. No rugs covered it. Meshullam could see all this, now that his eyes had adjusted to the dim light. The house seemed cold and uninviting.

The healer walked with him across the room until they stood in front of a high shelf. He squeezed Meshullam's shoulder, then reached up and carefully took a juglet from the shelf with both hands.

"I can help you. Here I have a potion to heal the breathing of any child. It will heal the boy from the inside. It seldom fails." He gingerly and carefully brushed the little juglet, then gave it to Meshullam who took it in his sweating palms. It seemed to burn in his hands, an icy cold burn.

"This is what your boy needs. It is yours for only seven shekels."

Seven shekels for a potion? None of Mother's drinks had been effective. How would this help?

"Consider your son," the man urged.

Meshullam hadn't come here for a potion.

The healer sensed his hesitation. He reached for another juglet and held it before his face. "I have an even more precious elixir. It restores life to the weak, gives strength to the weary. It does have a higher price. I can give it to you for just fifteen shekels."

Meshullam looked at the juglet in the healer's hands. Intricate painted patterns made it look exotic and precious, but also made Meshullam uncomfortable. Since the juglet clearly wasn't from Judah, could he trust its contents? And fifteen shekels. He shook his head. "It is too much."

The healer placed the juglet back on the shelf. "Oh, if it is the price you are concerned about, I do have something else." He walked over to another shelf and moved several items before he returned with a small jar. "This is a balm. The jar costs only three shekels. If you spread it on the boy's throat and chest, it will give him heat, helping to heal him. I admit it is not as effective as the potion you hold in your hands, but maybe it is all you can afford."

Potions, elixirs, balms! And all for a price he could hardly afford. He had hoped the healer would be eager to help, would come with him to heal Yohanan. Maybe he had been wrong to come here.

"I will seek help from the priests in Jerusalem. Maybe they will come and heal my son." Meshullam thought they might have more compassion. And somehow it would be more reassuring to deal with official priests.

The healer took the juglet from Meshullam's hands. The smile on his face became rigid and cold. "As you wish. But I must tell you that the priests in Jerusalem are even less prepared to travel, especially to the frontier. And my charges are moderate in comparison to what they ask. I warn you, you will not get healing for free."

The man carefully put back the juglet. He led Meshullam to the door. "You know how I can help your son. Come back if you cannot find what you are looking for in Jerusalem."

Meshullam left the house quickly. He was glad to be in the open again. He hurried to the road. There was no need to go back to Hebron. He could follow the road directly to Jerusalem from here. He had to get there quickly. He half-ran, half-walked along the road that followed the ridge northwards.

Meshullam couldn't keep up the fast pace. Soon, he had to walk more slowly. Pictures of Yohanan flashed before his mind. He remembered his weak and decimated body, his inability to swallow food. He thought of the fever that ravaged him. And Meshullam realized that, even if he could convince a priest from Jerusalem to come to Moresheth-Gath, it would be too late for Yohanan. There was just not enough time. Going to Jerusalem would be a waste of time. And somehow he knew that the man was right: the priests would charge even more.

He walked on for a few more steps. He had promised Rivkah to be back today! He could not go on a fool's errand to Jerusalem.

Meshullam stopped. He had to go back to the healer. That was his only hope, the only way he could make something of this journey. He had ten shekels of silver with him, enough to buy the healer's potion. Determinedly he turned back.

The healer was not surprised to see him. "You have come back," he smiled. "How can I help you?"

Meshullam struggled to catch his breath. "That potion that heals breathing . . . I think I will buy it."

"Yes, it does wonders. I recommend it. I'll get it for you." The man motioned Meshullam to enter. "Come in."

Meshullam stood in the dark room by the door. He didn't want to go any farther.

Before the man reached for the juglet, he turned to ask Meshullam. "Seven shekels? Do you have seven shekels?"

"I do." Meshullam took the silver out of his bag.

"Put it on the table. I'll weigh it." The man placed the juglet on the table. He took a set of scales that hung from a shelf and placed the weight-stones into one of the pans. He put some of the silver into the other pan, taking a piece off and then placing another one on it before the scales balanced. "Yes, that is good. Thank you." He emptied the silver onto the table and swept it into a small pile. Carefully he gave Meshullam the juglet. "Guard it well. Be careful not to spill it. Give your son a sip each morning and evening and he will soon recover."

"Thank you."

Meshullam put the remaining silver back in his bag but held the juglet in his hands. He bid his farewell and hurried towards Hebron. He passed through the city's streets stopping only to drink water and buy some bread. It was already late in the afternoon. Why had he not taken the healer's advice immediately? His foolish idea of going to Jerusalem had delayed him many hours. It had already taken him until late morning to locate the healer in the first place. Meshullam knew he wouldn't be able to make it back home today. He would have to stay in the village along the way. These days, there was only one village along the road once he had left the highlands behind.

But Meshullam never left the highlands that day. He walked until darkness enclosed him. He had hoped the moon and stars would allow him to walk until late, but dark clouds hurried across the night sky. It was no use trying to continue on. He'd just stumble and break the juglet. So Meshullam lay down beside the road. He was glad for the blanket Rivkah had urged him to bring. Shivering, he drew his legs up against his body. He couldn't sleep. It was too cold, the ground too hard and the worries too great.

"LORD, I cannot make it home today. Watch over my son Yohanan. Keep him alive, heal him. At least, let me see him again, I pray. And be with Rivkah. Comfort her. Oh LORD, hear my prayer. Come and listen to me."

* * *

Micah knelt beside Yohanan's weak form. Rivkah hoped he would be able to do something, would somehow save her son. He was a prophet, after all. But Micah had not given her much hope. He was only a messenger, he had said. Still, he had agreed to pray over Yohanan. Rivkah observed him rocking back and forth, holding his hands over the boy.

"Oh LORD, God of Israel,
hear the prayers of your servant
and incline your ears to me when I call to you.
I beg you to preserve the life of this child of Judah
and to restore the body of this son of your people.

Do not take away the breath of life from Yohanan
and do not deprive a mother of her son.
Have mercy on us, oh LORD,
do not forsake us now.
I beseech you, oh God,
heal this child."

Micah continued swaying in silent prayer, an isolated groan escaping from his mouth at times. Suddenly he sat still and breathed in deeply. His chest heaved as he drew in long gasps of air. He leaned down over Yohanan, face touching face. He put his lips around the small mouth and started to blow gently. Yohanan spluttered and coughed, but did not even open his eyes. It sounded as if he was suffocating, as he noisily drew in his breath. Micah sat back in alarm. Rivkah quickly reached for Yohanan's hand. She did not want to interfere, for if Micah could not heal Yohanan, who could? But she was concerned. Micah's attempts to blow breath into Yohanan's mouth only seemed to make things worse. Yohanan was struggling for air, gasping noisily. Micah turned and looked at her sadly. "I did what I could. There's nothing else I can do."

Rivkah nodded. She gently brushed Yohanan's cheek. "It's alright," she whispered, whether to comfort Yohanan or Micah, she did not know.

Micah rose. Slowly he walked to the door. Shoulders slumped, steps shuffling, all strength seemed to have gone out of him. He put his hand on the door post. Leaning heavily on it, he turned and faced Rivkah. "You have to leave him to the LORD now, Rivkah. Commit your care to him. Give Yohanan into . . . " His voice broke.

So there was no hope! Even Micah had given up on her son. Rivkah heard the door close as Micah left the house. All alone! How could she face these dark hours alone? Hours without hope, hours filled with Yohanan's suffering, hours of letting go the one she loved most on this earth. Even Meshullam was not here with her. She had little confidence he would return in time. How could he? The distances were too great, the time too short. She did not even dare to put any hope in whatever help he may have been able to get. No, better to prepare for the worst. And so Rivkah had to watch over Yohanan alone, the light of his life dimly flickering and about to be extinguished at any moment.

A hand lightly, hesitatingly, touched her shoulder. She froze. Who was it? She felt scared and comforted at the same time.

"Rivkah . . . " She had forgotten that Leah was still here with her, standing silently in the background, never leaving her. Quietly, Rivkah reached for the hand on her shoulder. They touched lightly. One hand embraced the other. When the grip loosened, Leah let go and silently walked to Yohanan's side, sitting down opposite Rivkah.

"I'll stay here with you."

Leah did not give her any false words of hope, did not offer any desperate prayers, did not attempt any last cure. But she was here—she remained with her when all seemed lost, shared the sorrow. And her presence was like a spark in the darkness, like the lamp she lit when evening fell.

Rivkah and Leah sat and listened to Yohanan's labored breathing, watched feverish chills shudder through the tiny body. Twice Rivkah tried to give Yohanan something to drink. He drank only a little, most of it spilling onto the mat. Once he opened his eyes. In a moment of clarity he recognized Rivkah and smiled at her. He lifted his arms towards her. She heard his tiny voice once more. Had he really said "Mother"? Had he really called her name? But the arms fell limp against his body as she embraced him. The eyes closed once more and a violent cough shook his chest. He continued his loud breathing. But soon he was silent. The breathing had stopped. Rivkah did not want to acknowledge it. She glanced towards Leah, who did not dare to meet her eyes. But they both knew. Leah looked up and Rivkah could see the tears in her eyes. It was over! Their eyes told each other.

And Rivkah started to cry, quietly at first, but then in loud sobs as she cradled Yohanan's lifeless form. Leah took up the wailing. The cries went from house to house and the women of the village wept loudly. They all knew. Moresheth-Gath, the village that had been reborn, was in mourning.

* * *

As soon as he entered the village the next morning, Meshullam knew that he was too late. He heard the keening as he walked towards the house. He noticed the sorrowful eyes that followed his progress. His heart sank. Should he hurry home to see for himself? Or should he hold back, delay confirming his fears and avoid having to look into Rivkah's eyes? And so he trudged on, reluctantly and yet urgently.

Grandfather sat outside Father's house, his head bent low, his whole body sagging. It seemed he had aged years in these last days. Meshullam did not speak to him, did not want to disturb him. He went directly to the door of his own house.

"Meshullam!" Grandfather called quietly.

"Yes, Grandfather?" Meshullam could see Grandfather's eyes now, eyes full of anguish.

"He died yesterday."

"I'm too late then."

"There was nothing anyone could do."

"But . . . "

"You did what you could. We all did."

Meshullam said nothing, just sighed.

"As night fell, he slipped away. There was no way to hold him back. Leah was with Rivkah at the time. But go now, go! She needs you," Grandfather urged.

Meshullam entered the house of mourning, his house. Women sat around the tiny body of Yohanan laid out in the centre of the room. There were Mother and Leah, there Tinshemet and Shiphrah. Even Tirzah was here. Their wailing was subdued, intermittent. Too many tears must have already been wept this morning. But when Tinshemet noticed Meshullam, she broke into loud howls of mourning, and was joined by the others.

Meshullam made his way to Yohanan's side. His knees buckled. He sank to the ground. His son was dead! The realization of the loss hit him. He would not see Yohanan grow up, would not teach him to farm the land, to know the LORD, would not hear him speak his name. He placed the now useless juglet with the healer's potion beside the lifeless body. Tears welled up in his eyes. A lump formed in his throat and he swallowed hard.

He felt someone looking at him. Through moist eyes he saw Rivkah's face. She stared at him quietly, her expression empty. Meshullam got up and went to her. "I'm sorry. I'm so sorry," he said as he embraced her. "I did bring . . . " He decided not to tell her about the medicine. It was no use now. Why had he not been here with her yesterday? He had promised to be back. But he had failed her. "I went as fast as I could."

Rivkah just hugged him more tightly, nearly taking his breath away.

"Our son," she whispered.

"I know . . . Yohanan . . . he . . . " What could he say? He had no words, no explanation, no comfort.

Rivkah lowered her head to his chest and started to sob violently, her crying echoing within him.

* * *

They followed the body. The men carried it ahead, the women walked behind, lamenting the death of such a young child. The outpouring of grief was real. Leah was devastated. Yohanan, the joy of the family, the child of so much promise, was dead. She cried, she shouted in anguish, she tore her hair so that it fell before her eyes in a disheveled mass. She had never loved a child so much, had never felt the loss of another person so profoundly. It was not just losing Yohanan. It was also what it meant for Rivkah: her one and only son snatched away by disease! Leah had grown so close to her, had not only gained a sister-in-law, but a friend. She had rejoiced with her at the birth of her son, and had watched him grow. She had been there when Yohanan's short life had fluttered like a weak flame in the wind and finally been blown out. Leah knew it broke Rivkah's heart.

She looked at Rivkah now. Somehow she was strangely calm. Yes, Rivkah wailed with the others, but not uncontrollably, not wildly. Her voice seemed oddly serene in comparison to the shrill, raw cries of the other women. Her face seemed composed, not distorted with anguish. Yet her shaved head, and her dress of sackcloth—hastily stitched together—showed her mourning. The tears that stained her face displayed her grief.

The funeral train progressed along the valley. Leah knew the tomb where they would lay Yohanan's body to rest, the tomb of Micah's family. It was years ago since they had laid a member of the family here. Leah could still remember the day her little sister Abijah was buried. It had been in late summer. Abijah had succumbed to an infection that spread through her body after she had been injured. The wounds had not appeared serious. Leah could not remember Mother worrying about them. And yet Abijah had died. Leah had wept. She had wailed. It had been the first time she had joined the women in mourning. And after the grief, life had continued as before, or nearly so. But Leah did not know how things could return to normal now. Life would never be the same again, not for her and certainly never for Rivkah. Life would continue, she was sure, but the wound was deep.

They stopped in front of the grave. Father said a prayer, committed the body of Yohanan to the LORD, asked for peace and rest as he descended to Sheol to dwell there with his forefathers. Grandfather had already prayed over him at the house. He had not been able to make it to the tomb. Too old to walk the distance, too weak to climb back up the hill, he had stayed in the village.

The men walked down the steps into the tomb, maneuvering the bier through the small entrance. They laid Yohanan on a bench that had been occupied by so many dead before him. Their bones now lay in the pit at the foot of the bench, gathered to their fathers. The men filed out of the grave and stood around the entrance. Meshullam entered the tomb and placed oil lamps, a bowl of food and two blankets woven by Rivkah beside his son's body: tokens of his former life. Yohanan would not arrive in Sheol empty-handed. He would have light in the everlasting shades. Meshullam emerged from the grave ashen faced. Father must have sensed that he could ask no more of him and signaled two men to help him heave the stone back in front of the cave entrance.

Rivkah uttered a single piercing cry as the tomb was closed, the other women responding with loud wails.

Chapter 21

The house was so still. Rivkah would no longer hear her son crying as he woke from sleep, would not hear him babble as he played in his cot. His light footsteps would no longer sound through the house. Yet Rivkah still listened, expecting to hear him again. She imagined his tiny voice, his loud cries for his mother, his happy smile. But the sounds she thought she heard always turned out to be something else: the sheep stomping in the stall, pigeons cooing outside, the wind tearing past the house—never Yohanan, never her son. She would have to get over this, she knew. And so she worked. She spun, wove and sewed. And she cooked meals for Meshullam, elaborate meals. She did not give herself any rest, no time to think. But sometimes when Rivkah was alone at home, when she was working quietly, sorrow seized her heart uncontrollably. She would lie on the floor and weep, crying out her pain, her anger, her disappointment. Then she would quieten and return to her work.

Once, Meshullam came into the house when she was crying for Yohanan. She got up quickly, recovered herself and continued to cook. But he must have heard her. "What's the matter Rivkah? Has anything happened?"

"I'm just tired," she said. And it was true. She was tired. Ever since Yohanan had become sick, she had not been able to sleep soundly.

"But are you alright?" He must have heard her complaints.

Rivkah nodded. "I'm alright," she lied.

But she sensed that he knew. He wanted to say something. She could see him searching for words, "Rivkah . . ." He did not continue. After an awkward silence he walked towards the store room. "I just came to get some leather for Joel. I should be back soon." Then he sniffed the air. "Smells good," he said. "I'm looking forward to dinner."

Yes, she knew the food was good, but dinner was so quiet these days. Before Yohanan had been born they had talked and joked. Later, Yohanan was at the center of their family life. Now, there seemed to be nothing. They just lived, one day following the next, without purpose, without aim. They worked hard, they tried to please each other. She tried to be a dutiful housewife. Meshullam spared no effort to help her, to fulfill her wishes. Only, she had no wishes, for what she longed for was impossible. Yohanan could not come back. He was dead, his body rotting in the grave. Meshullam's efforts seemed in vain.

The one thing that bound them together was grief. Not that they talked about Yohanan, questioned his death or relived happy memories. It was too painful. Rivkah left that to those times of agony when she was lying alone on the floor in tears. "Why, oh why, why did he have to die? Why my little Yohanan? He was an innocent child, who had done no evil, the happiest child ever." It made no sense. Yohanan had given her life purpose and direction. It was for him that she worked, for him she planned and dreamed. Had not her many wanderings, the twists and turns of her life brought her to this task, to be the mother of this child?

"LORD, I cannot understand. I thought I saw your hand in my life, for I had found hope and joy. I was the mother of a precious child. But now the pain is deeper than I could ever have imagined. Oh, that I had never known happiness!"

Tears flowed down her face.

"Yohanan, Yohanan, I love you. I will always remember you. I shall never forget you. Oh Yohanan!" As her sobs became quieter, her thoughts turned to the things that needed to be done, the tasks she still had to do. And so Rivkah always returned to her work.

* * *

The plow parted the earth, cutting furrows into the land, loosening the soil. This was to be the last field of wheat Meshullam would sow this year. If the land held its promise it would be a good harvest. The fall rains had come in their season, the winter rains had penetrated deeply into the soil. If the spring rains did not stay away, the wheat would grow and the fields yield plenty. With a short call Meshullam slowed the two cows as he lifted the plow out of the last furrow. Tomorrow he would sow, scattering the seed across the field, but for today he had done enough work.

He would have to hurry. It was already getting late and darkness would soon cover the land. Not that it had been a bright day. The dull, cloud-laden sky had given it a somber mood. Meshullam fetched the donkey, which had been tied to a tree at the edge of the field. Where was Shimei? He had come here to help him get the plow and cows back home, but Meshullam had taken longer than expected. He must have gotten bored and disappeared somewhere. "Shimei!" Where was he? "Shimei!"

"Yes?" His brother finally appeared.

"Come, help me get the plow off."

Shimei slouched towards him slowly.

"Hurry, it's getting late!"

"Yes, I'm here."

These days it was hard to get much work out of Shimei. He just didn't take it seriously. They took the yoke off the cows and then disassembled the plow. Meshullam fastened it to the donkey, the long shaft trailing on the ground. "Right, that should do."

Shimei walked on ahead, leading the donkey, Meshullam came behind with the two cows. The two brothers didn't talk, each lost in their own thoughts on the way home. Home! Would Rivkah be better today? She never complained, never voiced her grief, but Meshullam knew that sorrow was eating away at her. He ached for her, but did not know what he could do. He tried to reach out to her, to comfort her, but it often seemed as if she drew back from him. At night she avoided his touch, shrank back when he tried to hold her. She seemed to have withdrawn into herself, hardly speaking to anyone. When she did, she was controlled, sometimes even cheerful. Most days she just claimed she was too busy and tired. She worked constantly. That was her consolation. Meshullam had organized some fine, dyed linen in the hope it would please her. She started weaving it immediately, but nothing changed. Meshullam sensed that the ache remained. What else could he do? He had tried talking to her, but at any mention of Yohanan's name she just shut off, she just did not respond. Oh Rivkah! Yohanan's death has hit you hard! At times worry for Rivkah overshadowed Meshullam's own grief for his son. He had loved Yohanan. Now he felt the loss, but it seemed he had also lost his wife when their son died.

"Does the donkey need a drink, too?" Shimei pulled Meshullam back to the work at hand.

"Yes, but I'll feed him inside. It's already too dark out here. Just take him into my house. Rivkah should be there." Meshullam took the cows into Father's house. He didn't stay there long. Of course, he had to talk with Mother, confirming that he had indeed finished the plowing and that, yes, the field looked good. Then he went to his own home, a light shining from the door welcoming him. As he stepped inside he was glad to feel the heat warming his bones. Rivkah must have lit a fire.

* * *

Black stripes and a red border contrasted with the brilliant white. Rivkah wove the cloth for the tunic out of the finest wool their lambs had given this year. She was sure it would be comfortable, would suit any little boy. The tunic should fetch a good price. It was woven in that tradition of Judahite quality even valued in Syria and distant Babylon. Rivkah could take pride in it. Maybe it would be worn by the son of an officer or a court official.

Carefully she threaded another row through the warp, making sure the weft was tightly woven, pushing it up with a comb. She stepped back and cast a critical eye across the cloth. No, she could find no fault. She was going to continue weaving when she thought she saw an untidy border. She rubbed her eyes. She looked at it again and tried to focus, but everything just swam before her eyes. She noticed the tears running down her cheeks. This tunic should have been for Yohanan, not for some unknown boy somewhere! She had dyed and spun the wool for him. For him she had dreamed up this design. She had imagined him wearing those clothes. Now it was all for nothing! He was gone. And she was making clothes for strangers. Why should she work for them? Why should cold money buy a garment woven with her mourning, her tears? Rivkah laughed bitterly. In anger she flew at the loom and started to undo the weaving row by row. But something suddenly held her fingers. She could continue the destruction no longer. Sobbing she turned away, walked across the room and just stared at the wall, quietening down. The anger, the grieving, the memory passed and numbness engulfed her again, that shell that did not let any feelings through. She breathed deeply, getting ready to go back to work and repair the damage.

And then her eyes fell on the prayer mother. Full breasts held up by folded arms. What a cruel reminder of her loss! Her son no longer needed her milk, no longer drank at her breast. All the prayers for her family had come to nothing. Now she had no prayers left, no children to care for and nurture. Angrily Rivkah grabbed the prayer mother and threw it across the room. It shattered against the wall and with it shattered her dreams of motherhood. The pieces lay scattered on the floor. How could she have believed that she could ever be a mother, that she could protect a son? They had all given her false confidence: Meshullam, Merab, Tinshemet and that prayer mother. Maybe she was just never meant to have children, never meant to be a mother.

Rivkah did not want Meshullam to see the smashed pottery pieces. She fetched a broom and swept them up, throwing them outside behind the wall enclosing the yard.

She went back inside meaning to continue the weaving. But she was too tired, so exhausted. She had worked from morning to night these last few weeks. She could do it no longer. She had no energy left. She was drained.

Rivkah crawled into bed in the middle of the day. She didn't know what Meshullam would say when he found her there. She didn't care. She just couldn't go on like this, just couldn't keep working. She had to rest. Not that she slept. She just dozed, closing her eyes and descending into a restless nothingness.

* * *

The night was clear, the sky cloudless. Myriads of stars stood in the firmament above, sparkled high above the earth. They looked beautiful, but cold. Rivkah remembered Meshullam saying that they weren't gods, that they had no life, that they did not determine the ways of humans. They were just lights in the sky, signs to mark seasons, days and years. Rivkah believed him. They looked lifeless, parts of an uncaring universe where humans—dwarfed by spaces infinite—wandered aimlessly, trying to eke a living out of the earth, trying to make sense of their existence. Was there any purpose to their lives? Or did they just flow in an incessant, unstoppable stream towards death? Did life just revolve in rhythmic circles without destiny, season repeating season, year recalling year? Were men and women struggling to make a mark on this world only to return from where they came from? From dust they came and to dust they would return.

Rivkah bent down, turning her eyes from the starry sky. She scooped up a handful of damp soil, rubbed it between her fingers, and let it crumble back to the ground. She shivered as she sat down, hugged her knees as she drew them up close. She looked up at the stars. They were unceasingly appearing in their due season. For what? In meaningless eternal motion? The LORD had put the lights in the sky, Meshullam said. But did the LORD who set times and paths for heavenly bodies care about the lives of mortals? She could see no direction in her life. The LORD seemed distant, further even than the stars shining above.

Rivkah curled up, leaned her head on her knees as the cold enveloped her. She did not know how long she sat there. Time seemed to be unending.

"Rivkah, Rivkah!" She knew that voice. How did he know to look for her here? Why had he come? Meshullam held a lamp above her. He was not angry, did not shout, just looked at her sadly. Did he understand? What meaning did he still see in life? Meshullam helped her frozen body up. Slowly he led her through the darkness, took her home.

* * *

"Can you smell it in the air?" Leah asked.

"The weather is getting warmer," laughed Rivkah.

"Soon the spring flowers will clothe the hillsides and cover them in many colors," Leah said.

"Yes, I look forward to that. The colors are so bold. It seems as if the hills have suddenly put on their festive robes."

"I always think that not even kings in their splendor are clothed as richly as the flowers of the field in spring. And when you see whole fields of them . . ."

"I know a small valley that was totally filled with flowers the last time I saw it. It can't be far from here. You see, I came across it just before I first met you," Rivkah explained.

"I remember that evening." Leah could still picture Rivkah: wearing worn clothes, exhausted, and thin. Not that she looked much better now, not in the last few weeks. Her hair was short; it still had not grown back after cutting it for the funeral. She still wore clothes of mourning made from uncomfortable sackcloth. Once, she had worn colorful dresses like the ones she still made, but no longer for herself. Now she sold all the clothes she made.

"Yes, I remember that evening," Leah said again. "It was spring and we had just moved into our house. It had been an exciting day. Just imagine the shock when I saw you standing on the path. It was totally unexpected. I think . . . yes, it was here." They had come to the bend in the path where Leah had first spotted Rivkah. It had been here.

"You were singing—until you saw me."

"Should I have continued singing, or what?"

"You should have. Something like 'welcome Rivkah,'" Rivkah warbled a few notes.

"Sounds very welcoming," Leah giggled.

Rivkah continued singing:

"Welcome to our village, dear.
get a jar and fill it there.
We need water, need it now.
Fill your jar, come go."

Rivkah made it sound so melodramatic.

"Hee-hee," laughed Leah. "Stop, you'll make me drop the jar."

"That's alright. You can carry mine back then," Rivkah quipped.

Leah wondered how Rivkah could still have any sense of humor after the tragedy. She knew she wasn't always like this, knew that often Rivkah had a heavy spirit. Today was the first time in weeks that Rivkah had gone with Leah again to get water. Most days she preferred to be alone, staying at home and working on the loom. She wanted to be left alone, wouldn't talk to anyone. And then there were days when it seemed that nothing was wrong, when she put on a brave face, even a happy face.

They filled the water jars at the spring. Just as Leah was putting the jar on her head, Rivkah somehow bumped her. Leah nearly dropped the jar. "Hey! You really want that jar shattered on the floor. Are you trying to get out of carrying yours home?"

"Sorry. I didn't look."

"It happens." Leah wasn't angry. "Speaking about broken jars, did you know there's a potter in Mareshah now?"

"Really?"

"Yes, Father went there. You know Mareshah has been rebuilt? Well, it seems they have a potter and a tanner, just like any other town. I imagine you will soon be able to buy jewelry as well," Leah said.

"People are coming back to this land."

"We should go there one day. Just to see what they've got."

Rivkah hesitated, "I don't know."

"Come on. You know you want to."

"I'll think about it."

Why were her answers so evasive? Didn't she want to go and see? It seemed Rivkah had little energy for anything but her weaving. Even the normal housework suffered, Leah knew. Sometimes Meshullam would sneak over to their house to get bread. His wife just didn't get round to baking. What else did she fail to do? She just wasn't the same active, conscientious Rivkah anymore.

They came to the bend in the path again.

"That's where I stopped singing." Leah tried to go back to the joke.

"Uh? Oh, yes." It seemed Rivkah had descended into a world of her own thoughts.

"Welcome Rivkah," Leah sang.

But Rivkah no longer saw any humor in it.

"I'm glad we met back then," Leah said. Maybe that would encourage Rivkah.

"Thank you."

"How much has happened since then!" Leah saw immediately that she had said the wrong thing. Rivkah suddenly wept, tears filling her eyes, silent sobs rising from her chest.

"What's wrong?" Leah asked. Of course she knew. The pain was still there and it came to the surface so quickly.

Rivkah turned away from Leah, not wanting her to see her crying. She controlled herself quickly, wiped away the tears. "I'm alright," she said. Rivkah smiled at Leah. "Silly me, crying like that. Don't worry, I'm alright."

* * *

Light shone through the small window. Rivkah stretched, yawned and looked up from the loom. It must be sunny outside. She decided to go out into the sun. Just a quick break. She would go back to work immediately afterwards. Stepping out into the bright morning light she blinked in the sunshine.

"Yes, the sun is nice."

Rivkah swung around to see Micah sitting in his favorite spot in front of the house.

"The warmth does these old bones good."

"Yes, it's nice."

"We haven't spoken for a while, Rivkah. Come, talk with old Micah."

"I can't. I don't have time. I have to work, have to weave."

"Rivkah, you do have time. The work can wait for a moment. Sometimes it's good to talk. Come, sit."

"But . . ."

"Rivkah, do an old man a favor."

It seemed there was nothing she could say, no way she could deny his request. Hesitantly she sat beside him. She hadn't talked to him since . . . since Yohanan, not really. Now that she sat beside him, memories came back to her, memories of the many lessons he had taught her. She couldn't recall any details, just remembered how he had made sense of the world for her, how he had helped her to see things differently. But nothing would ever make sense of Yohanan's death. And right now she didn't feel ready to talk about it.

"I know it's hard." Micah went straight to the heart of the matter. "I loved him. He was such a happy boy. And he was your son, Rivkah. I have seen many deaths in my long life, but. . ." Micah shook his head. "Yohanan's death was so painful. My spirit is deeply distressed."

Rivkah was silent. Why did he open the wound? The pain was so deep. Why did he make her hurt?

"I had so much hope. Hope for him, hope for you, hope for this village, hope for this land. Yohanan seemed the child of hope. You know Rivkah, when you first came, you made this old heart glad, a gladness that increased when you stayed, married Meshullam, gave birth to a son. I could not wish for a better wife for my grandson, and Yohanan was the great-grandson I longed for. Now this . . ."

"Maybe you were wrong. Maybe I should never have had a son."

"Rivkah!"

"Maybe I should have perished in Lachish, died like the rest of them."

"Never! The LORD led you here."

"But why has misfortune followed me wherever I have gone? I should have died in Lachish. The city was doomed, given over to destruction and I cannot escape from my destiny."

"I don't know why the LORD chose you and saved you, Rivkah. But he has a purpose for you. Through all the tragedy he has remained with you."

"But Lachish was destined for destruction, was it not?"

"Yes, it was," Micah conceded. "I warned the people." Micah paused. "I have already told you so much of what I said. I'll tell you these words as well:

'You who live in Lachish,

harness the team to the chariot.
You were the beginning of sin
to the Daughter of Zion,
for the transgressions of Israel were found in you.'"

"The beginning of sin?"

"Was Lachish not full of idolatry? Did the people not follow the gods of Egypt and Canaan?"

"Yes," Rivkah said quietly. Her own mother had prayed to Amun-Re, her father to Baal. And Isis had been her own goddess.

"And did the men not whore with the prostitutes, did they not lie with the goddess?"

Bath-Shua!

"And didn't the rich landholders of Lachish exploit the farmers from the villages?"

"But they owned the land."

"They hadn't always owned it. Once it was the heritage of the village. How did they get it?"

Rivkah shrugged her shoulders.

"Through opportunistic loans with exorbitant interest, through wheeling and dealing and shrewd action in the gate," Micah claimed. "Such were the sins of Lachish, a city where the commanders of the army were in league with the rich landholders to lead the people astray. And this idolatry spread to Jerusalem, where people turned away from the source of true life. Lachish sowed the seeds of its own destruction. And so it fell. The LORD gave it over to the enemy."

"I worshipped Isis. I should have gone with it."

"No Rivkah. Now is the time of redemption. The LORD is not angry forever. Now is the time to live in the land again. The LORD has rescued you from the ruins of a burning city. He is gracious to you and will guide you."

"Why does the LORD then bring all this suffering on us? Why does he torment me so?"

"It's hard. I don't have all the answers, but he may have a purpose."

"A purpose in suffering?"

Micah rubbed his forehead and sighed. "You once told me your father was a blacksmith?"

"Yes."

"Can you remember how he made the tools and weapons?"

"Of course."

"He would take a shapeless piece of iron, heating it in the hot fire until it glowed. And then he would beat it again and again, pound it into shape. The hammer blows would twist and stretch the iron. Then he would put it back into the fire and beat it with the hammer until it had the desired shape."

"Yes. And at the end he often cooled it in water."

"Maybe our life is a little like that. God continually works on us, gives us shape. The fire, the hammer, the water may hurt, but they form us into that person we are meant to be."

Rivkah thought back to the times she had watched her father. Yes, she felt she had as little control over her life now as that steel had had under her father's hands. But she felt she couldn't stand the blows any longer. "If we break, what then?"

"The LORD does not want to break you. Rivkah, have hope and trust."

She could see that, maybe, at times, loss in her life had given her a new direction, but she could see no sense in Yohanan's death. He should have lived. Or?

"Did Yohanan die because of me, to make me suffer?"

"No, Rivkah. That's not what I'm trying to say. I do not know the reason for Yohanan's death, but you have been changed by it. You will never be the same. Let God work on you through it. We do not choose what happens to us, but we can let God shape our life through whatever happens to us. We are more responsive to God's shaping when our spirit is broken, just as iron is more malleable when it's hot. So trust in God's love and let him shape you at this time."

"God's love? But Yohanan?"

"The LORD loves you, Rivkah, just as he loves Yohanan. Don't ever think Yohanan's life was without purpose. He is precious to God, so precious. And when he died, the LORD mourned with you."

"I will never forget Yohanan."

"Remember him, Rivkah! Remember the beautiful child he was. And be thankful. For you were given joy, a son to love. You loved much and therefore you suffer much. Do not withhold your love now, Rivkah. Nothing will bring Yohanan back, nothing will replace that hole in your life, but you are still needed."

Rivkah ached inside. She longed for Yohanan. But somehow the sadness shone with warm light. "I miss him so," she said and leaned against Micah's shoulder.

* * *

"Cut the ground, cut the ground." Meshullam urged the cows to haul the plow along the next furrow. Dutifully they pulled as Meshullam pressed the plow into the soil. Behind him Father dropped the sesame seeds into the furrow opened by the plow. It was the time for summer crops to be sown.

"We'll stop for lunch when we get to the other side of the field," Father decided.

That was fine with Meshullam. He needed a quick break and a drink. It seemed the cows could do with a rest as well.

"Come up, come up," Meshullam called at the end of the field, slowly lifting the plow out of the ground. He guided the cows from the field and directed them toward the carob tree near the dry stream.

"Where are you going?" Father called.

"To the carob tree, why?"

"With the cows?"

"Yes."

"Leave them here. It's not so hot that they need to stand in the shade. And they'll only attract the flies."

"But . . ."

"I don't want flies buzzing round my head."

Of course Father was right. But it grated Meshullam. Why did he still treat him like a little boy at times?

Meshullam dug the plow into the ground and called the pair to a stop. They stood. Heads down the cows sniffed at the grass and lazily swung their tails to chase away the flies. Meshullam and Father walked on to the carob tree. Father broke the bread after they sat down.

"Do you want the oil?" he asked.

"Hm," Meshullam mumbled. He took the juglet and poured some olive oil on his bread and ate it.

Meshullam felt something touch his arm. "What?"

"Leek?"

Wordlessly Meshullam took the vegetable. They didn't have leek all year, only in spring. It tasted quite nice for lunch, but he didn't like it for breakfast, he had to confess. Now he munched lazily on the stalk, and took bites from his piece of bread.

After he had given Meshullam the water flask, Father cleared his throat. He did it again. Did he want to say something? Meshullam looked at Father.

"It can't go on like this," Father started.

"What?"

"You have to sort out Rivkah."

"What's wrong?" Meshullam retorted defensively.

"She's going too far in her grief."

"She's getting there. And she's not troubling anybody."

"She's neglecting her duties. You've come over several times now to get bread. Sharing some bread with you is not a problem. We're willing to help. We're the same family. But you have to control your household. I don't know what else she doesn't do."

Meshullam didn't respond. What Rivkah and he did wasn't Father's business. Things were difficult enough without Father trying to set them right.

"I know it can be hard for a mother when her child dies. When your sister Abijah died, Mother was inconsolable for weeks. She came round eventually. But she never failed to do her duties. I insisted on that. Daily work keeps us steady when events disrupt our lives. It gives consistency to the ups and downs of our days."

"Rivkah weaves."

"I know she weaves. It seems it's all she does do since Yohanan died. She has to get back to normal life. She should bake bread, carry water, work in the garden, gather herbs. Will she weed the fields? Mother started in the fields yesterday and I don't think I saw Rivkah there."

"I'll talk to her."

"Do that."

"I don't think Mother even asked Rivkah."

"She shouldn't have to. Rivkah keeps to herself too much and doesn't talk to the others. That's what the problem is."

"Give her some time. And maybe it's not only Rivkah's fault."

"What are you suggesting?" Father lifted his eyebrows.

Meshullam turned away. He couldn't accuse anybody else. He knew it wouldn't be fair and Father would only get angry.

"I know your son's death isn't easy for you, Meshullam. But you have to stop making excuses for your wife."

Meshullam didn't look up from the ground.

"Do you think I didn't grieve over the death of my first grandson?" Father nearly shouted. "But life has to go on," he said more quietly. "We have to work the land, have to keep house and village in order."

Meshullam got up. "Yes." He would only incur Father's ire if he tried to contradict him. "I think we should get back to plowing the field now," Meshullam suggested.

"You think about what I have said."

"Yes," Meshullam mumbled.

Father didn't understand them, didn't understand Rivkah. But Meshullam could see that things would get difficult if they didn't go back to their old lives soon. But how could they leave behind what had happened to them? They couldn't just go on as if nothing had happened. Yohanan had been too important for them. Meshullam felt for Rivkah. How, oh how could he make her happy again? He'd be prepared to carry the grief for the rest of his life if only he could lighten hers.

Father took the plow in his hands, and led the cows to the field.

"Don't you want to give them some water first?" Meshullam asked.

"That'll take too long. We'll continue with the plowing. The cows should be alright."

If he said so! Meshullam didn't care. He would have led them to the water first. Ah well! Meshullam took the sack of sesame seeds and followed Father to the field.

* * *

She had vowed not to drink any wine until Passover. But Yohanan had died. So why should she still respect her vow, why should she do what she promised if God had not come through for her? A cup of wine or two might just help to dull the ache inside her, the loss that at times still seemed to tear her apart. But she knew she would have no peace. Her conscience would accuse her. Should she offend the LORD, add yet another sin? She couldn't do it. It wouldn't be long until Passover, anyway. Then she would be released from her vow.

Rivkah left the house and looked around the yard. No one was there. Not even Micah sat in his favorite place. Rivkah wanted to talk to someone, to take her mind off the sorrow that continually shivered through her even while weaving. But Leah and Merab had gone to weed the fields. Meshullam had asked her to go with them, but she had replied that she would be busy. Now she longed for their company, just as much as she had dreaded it this morning.

Rivkah went back inside. Maybe she should do something else for a while, something she could do outside. She could always do some spinning. She still had plenty of wool. But then she thought of the large quantities of milk the goats were giving at the moment. Maybe she should make some butter. It would be nice to have some in the long days of summer when the goats would give less milk. Two jars of milk had soured overnight. She would use that.

She poured the sour milk into the leather butter skin and hung it on the tripod she had carried outside. The tripod only consisted of three sticks bound together at the top. Rivkah sat beside it and pushed the skin backwards and forwards. Each time it swung towards her she stopped it with a thump, churning the milk inside the skin.

Swish, thump! Rivkah was caught up in the rhythm of the movement as the skin hit her hands again and again. At first it seemed to dull her mind, but then the thoughts returned. How often had she held Yohanan when she crossed this yard! He had laughed with her, clung to her, sometimes cried. He had been her joy and, at times, the reason for her exhaustion. But the times when he smiled were more vividly etched into her memory. Then her mind recalled the time of his illness. She had still had him then, but already she had begun to fear losing him, already suffering had begun to overshadow life. When he died, darkness broke into her life, and into the life of the entire house of Micah, and the village. At first she had not been able to get the picture of her suffering son out of her mind. But now the memories of days when he was full of life came back to her more often. The memories were sweet, but they broke her heart.

Rivkah rocked back and forwards with the movement of the butter skin. Swish, thump! Swish, thump! She wanted him so much, wanted to hold Yohanan again. But she would never see him again, never feel his little hands, never hear his delighted squeals. She would live with the pain forever. She stopped the butter skin and covered her face with her hands. Would sorrow be her constant companion? Would she never experience happiness again?

"LORD, I am worn out from groaning,

all night long I flood my bed with weeping
and drench my bedstead with tears.
For the joy of my eyes has been taken away
and I am in sorrow."

Rivkah started the butter skin once more. Swish, thump.

"Grant me comfort in my grief, my God
and heal the wound of my anguish.
Though my loss is deep
and my son is gone forever
grant me peace once more.
Let me remember him in gratitude."

Not that the prayer took away her pain, but it opened her eyes to the others dear to her. Meshullam, Leah, Micah, this village. She could never bear to lose them, too. Maybe now she started to appreciate the gift they were, all part of the LORD's people. Rivkah thought of Micah's words. 'You are still needed,' he had said.

"LORD, take this broken life of mine. Shape it, make it into something beautiful."

The butter was ready. Rivkah put her hands into the skin and took out the butter. She put it in a jar, adding salt to preserve it. She poured the buttermilk from the skin into a pitcher, skimming away the water. Yes, she would be able to make some nice meals and bake delicious cakes with the butter.

Chapter 22

Happy Passover! The greeting was repeated again and again as Leah hurried through the village with the water jar. There was still so much to do and prepare. And the afternoon was nearly over. Soon dusk would approach and everything had to be ready. For days now the women of Micah's household had worked to prepare for Passover. They had cleaned the house and searched for any scrap of leavened bread to remove it from the house. Tirzah had been so eager she even went and helped Rivkah to go through her entire house. They had cooked and baked for days, had prepared sauces and dips. And today had been so hectic. Many of the dishes could only be prepared on the day itself. They had gone into the fields to gather bitter herbs for the meal and had made salads. They had baked the unleavened bread this morning, had mixed the hummus dip. And they had burned any remaining traces of leavened bread, searched and cleaned the house one last time. Mother had gotten out the table cloth reserved for special feast days and they had all helped to decorate the house with green wreaths of spring. It looked amazing.

Leah saw Rachel ahead, rushing around on some errand.

"Not quite ready yet?" she called.

"Nearly there," Rachel puffed. "You know how it is."

"Yes, I know. We've got to hurry."

"Is it just your family at the Passover meal?"

"Yes, just us. Meshullam and Rivkah too, of course."

"Plenty of meat then."

"I don't think Father chose the biggest lamb, but we'll have plenty to eat, that's for sure." Leah paused. "Hey, I've got to keep going. See you tomorrow at the assembly!"

"Happy Passover!"

Leah hurried home. The table was already set. Mother and Tirzah were bringing the dishes from the kitchen.

"Ah, good! You're back, Leah. We'll use the fresh water for tonight."

"To drink and for hand washing?"

"Yes, for both."

Leah poured the water into the jugs and bowls and placed them by the table. Mother put more wood on the fire. This was where they would roast the Passover lamb. Father and Meshullam had already taken it outside to slaughter it. Still, Leah did have some time, enough to put on some nice clothes.

She had been uncertain which dress to wear. Really, she only had a choice of two, but that choice was difficult enough. She had thought about it for days and in the end had settled on the red dress. But now she looked at the two dresses again and made a last-minute decision to go with the light-blue one instead. Its border was not as nicely decorated, its design not as bold. Delicate and somewhat understated, maybe it would be more appropriate this year. And it was more comfortable. Leah put it on. She brushed her hair and oiled it lightly. She splashed on some perfume. That would have to do. She was already on her way downstairs when she remembered the bangles. She shouldn't forget them on a day like this. And so she went back and put them on her wrists and ankles.

Downstairs, Father and Meshullam were carrying the lamb inside and put it on a spit. The lamb's blood stood at the door in a big bowl. Everything was ready.

"Where's Rivkah!" Leah asked.

"She said she'd be here soon," Meshullam replied. "She just had to do something."

And Rivkah came. Leah looked at her, stared at her. Rivkah had put away her mourning dress of sackcloth. Instead she wore a dress of fine wool. And what a dress! Delicate curves of many tones formed patterns, swirled and shone, blended and contrasted, drew and yet eased the eye. The dress seemed molded to her body, fitting her perfectly. She must have bathed and oiled herself, for her skin looked smooth and clean. Her hair was not long yet, but it had grown and she had made the most of it. It was combed to the side, oiled and shining. Her earrings sparkled like dewdrops as she entered the house. And the subtle hint of eye shadow emphasized the features of her pretty face. Leah was not the only one to notice. She saw Meshullam's mouth drop open when he saw his wife. Rivkah just smiled at them and walked to her place at the table.

"Rivkah is here," Tirzah said, the first to find words.

"We will sprinkle the blood on the doorposts then," Micah said.

"Let no one go outside the door until morning," added Father.

As dusk turned to night and the pale light of the full moon flooded the land, Father sprinkled blood on the doorposts, purifying and cleansing those within the house.

The lamb on the spit was roasting above the fire, turning slowly. Mother poured the wine and gave a cup to each of them, though Tirzah's and Shimei's cups were not full. Grandfather recited the blessing:

"For the fruit of the vine, we praise you, LORD.

For your bounty we give you thanks.

Bless this wine and those gathered around this table."

They all sipped the wine, even Rivkah, Leah noticed. Rivkah's lips tightened as if surprised by its bitterness and a shadow seemed to cross her face. She had not drunk any wine for several months now. But the moment passed and she looked attentively at Grandfather as he continued his prayers. He gave thanks for the increase in the flocks during winter, for the lambs born during the cold months. He prayed for flocks and shepherds that would move farther away from the village in summer and spend more time in the hills. He sought the LORD's blessing over house and fields, over those sitting at the table, over the village and nation. And he asked for forgiveness:

"Make us clean, oh LORD

and acceptable in your sight.

Let your mercy shine on us

and bless us in our going in and our going out."

This was when he would normally close the prayer, Leah thought. But after a brief silence Grandfather continued:

"Into your hands we commit the sorrows of the past,

the loss of a precious son.

We remember . . . Yohanan

a child of hope and laughter.

LORD, dry our tears, grant us peace,

and let your face shine upon us."

Grandfather did not shrink away from the hard times they had been through. Leah glanced over to Rivkah. The hurt was still visible in her face, the mention of her son bringing up painful memories. But Leah could see no anger. Rather, the pain seemed to have softened her features. Eyes closed, Rivkah's face was upheld, as if she was seeking comfort from above. Grandfather concluded the prayer.

They all joined together in the first psalm:

"Praise the LORD.
Praise, oh servants of the LORD,
praise the name of the LORD."

After another psalm, they started the meal: first the leafy salad dipped in oil, then the unleavened bread dipped in fruit mince of raisins, dates, nuts, almonds, and wine. Finally Father carved the first pieces of the lamb and gave it to them. It was nice and tender. Only a few months old, Father and Meshullam had chosen it four days ago, and dedicated the young male lamb for this purpose.

Mother filled the cups with wine again. Now it was Shimei's turn as the youngest male in the house. He had been waiting for this moment.

"How is this night different from any other night? For on this night we eat only unleavened bread. On this night we eat only bitter herbs. On this night we eat only roasted meat."

Grandfather replied, "My father was a wandering Aramean, and he went down to Egypt . . ."

Leah let the familiar words wash over her. She had heard them so often, knew them by heart, but the story still gripped her. The LORD's mighty deeds when he brought Israel out of Egypt would forever be recounted. Generation told them to generation and found hope and meaning in them.

"He brought us to this land, a land flowing with milk and honey," Grandfather finished off. Especially now in spring, Leah thought, when goats and sheep were giving plenty and the hills were still clothed in luscious green. Then the land indeed flowed with milk and honey.

Shimei moved onto the next question. "What does this ceremony mean to you?"

Grandfather answered, "It is the Passover sacrifice of the LORD, who passed over the houses of the Israelites in Egypt and spared our homes when he struck down the Egyptians."

In silence they ate a few bites, then started the next psalm:
"When Israel came out of Egypt,
the house of Jacob from a people of foreign tongue . . ."

Leah thought of that night all that time ago, when families were huddled in their poor slave hovels, ready to leave on a long journey, a journey through sea and desert, through hard times and many trials. And yet, the children of Israel finally arrived in this land, a land in which the LORD provided so richly for them.

More psalms followed and Mother urged them to eat more meat, "Eat! It all has to go." Leah grew tired as she drank more wine and the night grew long. She was hardly able to keep her eyes open. Rivkah, in contrast, seemed alive, enjoying the night and joining loudly in the psalms. Meshullam sat beside her and played the flute.

"I will exalt you, oh LORD,
for you lifted me out of the depths.

"Sing to the LORD, you his people,
praise his holy name.
For his anger lasts only a moment
but his favor lasts a lifetime;
weeping may remain for a night,
but rejoicing comes in the morning."

* * *

The assembly was over. Slowly the families left the threshing floor and walked back to their houses. They had prayed for the harvest about to start, had dedicated the season, the village and themselves anew to the LORD. Soon they would no longer eat bread made from the flour of the previous harvest, but would grind new grain. Just so, they should leave behind the old things that held them back, and turn away from their sins. That had been Joel's message. They all agreed it had been a good message. But Rivkah had her doubts. She knew she could never leave the memory of Yohanan behind. It would be with her throughout her life. And it was no sin. Micah had told her that she should remember Yohanan. She knew that remembering was not everything, could not fill her entirely. She had to live. And maybe in that one aspect Joel had been right: she needed to look into the future, to trust God in this new season. The psalms they sang together, the assembly gathered in worship, the women, men, and children, they had given Rivkah hope that life would go on, that she still had a place here.

"Rivkah, you look amazing!" Rachel approached her. Rachel had waved in her direction earlier. They hadn't really had a chance to talk. "Did you make that dress?"

"You like it?"

"Like it? Of course I do! It's stunning." Rachel touched the dress. "So soft."

"Yes, I've used lamb's wool."

Tinshemet joined them. "Rivkah, it's just beautiful!"

They talked—about dresses and weaving, about flocks and shepherds, music and dancing, plans for the festival and the harvest. Maybe that's why Rivkah didn't notice where Meshullam had gone. She couldn't see him anywhere. He must have gone ahead with Micah.

"See you at the dances tonight!" Rachel and Tinshemet turned to go to their house.

Meshullam wasn't at home. Maybe Micah hadn't been able to walk that quickly today and she had missed them. His old bones just made it difficult for him sometimes. Rivkah poured herself a cup of water. She knelt in the kitchen to wash some lettuce. It would just be a light lunch today. After the celebration of the previous night and more to come in the evening, they wouldn't need much in the middle of the day.

"Rivkah." The voice was quiet, nearly hoarse. She turned around.

"Meshullam."

He stood in the doorway, somehow shy, somehow uncertain. "Rivkah," he said again.

She waited. What did he want to say?

"I've brought something for you." He took his hand from the doorpost and slowly walked towards her. She stood up and went to meet him. They met in the middle of the room. He held a small bundle in his hand. He gently folded back the cloth and held his hand out to her. "For you."

"A necklace!" Rivkah said in surprise.

"I didn't think you had one like this."

"No, I don't." Certainly not like this. Colorful carnelian beads polished to perfection delicately lined up in symmetry. "Beautiful!"

Meshullam smiled.

Rivkah took it gently in her hands and let it glide through her fingers. It was a masterpiece.

"Where did you get it?"

Meshullam just put a finger on his lips.

"Please!" she tilted her head and winked at him.

"I bought it in Mareshah," he conceded.

"It's exquisite!" Rivkah held it against her neck.

"Looks good." Meshullam gave his opinion.

She tried to tie the ends together.

"Should I help you?"

"Please."

Meshullam went and stood behind her. He fumbled with the cord. It took a while until he was able to tie a good knot, but Rivkah enjoyed his fingers moving against her skin, savored his attention.

"Comfortable?" he asked.

"Yes."

He lightly brushed her neck and let his hand rest on her shoulder. "Let me see." He slowly turned her around. He didn't say a word, but his eyes spoke volumes. Rivkah went to him, held him. She yielded to Meshullam's passionate kisses.

* * *

Rivkah went to Ehud's house with a rug. She had long wanted to make one for Merab. Now it was finally finished. It was not large at all, but Merab was still overjoyed and thankful. She would treasure it, she said.

"It's not really that special. I just made it for everyday use," Rivkah said.

"And I will use it every day, Rivkah. Now I have my own special rug."

Rivkah just about skipped the few steps to her own house.

"Happy?" She hadn't seen Micah sitting there. She stopped, feeling slightly embarrassed.

"Yes," she smiled.

"Good." He nodded his head, then pointed to the space beside him.

Ah, well! She didn't really have anything urgent to do this morning.

"You would make an old man happy."

Yes, she could sit with him for a while.

"How did you like the festival?"

Rivkah sat down, straightened her dress and was still for a moment before she answered, "The singing, the stories, the prayers, they all touched me. I have never celebrated a Passover like it. It was as if I heard everything with new ears, saw everything with new eyes. It was familiar to me, yet so different, so new. I marveled at the LORD's mighty deeds, his plans for his people. But I also knew that I did not yet fully understand. The questions came flooding back."

Rivkah paused.

Daughter of Lachish 353

"You felt everything more deeply this year?"

"Maybe that's what I'm trying to say. Loss and joy, wonder and pain, they felt so much deeper and mingled within me. I don't know whether it was the stories, the people, or the celebration."

"Great loss can bring us to feel more keenly the joys and sorrows of life. And somehow, the LORD can touch us more deeply, can infuse us with awe. I think the LORD is present in our celebration. For in it we draw close to him, confess again that we are his people and declare his mighty acts. We also acknowledge our dependence on him, who makes all things grow."

The two sat silent for a while.

"Rivkah, you seemed happy to celebrate with us. I think a few people noticed."

"I enjoyed it. I enjoyed the meals, the music, the dancing. And it seemed people were happy to see me, happy I was there with them celebrating. How could I not be happy?"

Rivkah studied her feet. "And yet, I don't know how I can dare to be happy. I remember Yohanan at every moment. Is it not an affront to his memory to be happy? Have I forgotten him so soon?"

"I don't think so. You will always remember him. He will always be a part of you. If you're happy, you are not forgetting him. You are seeing the joys of life again, the things in life that his death made you realize are so important."

"I still miss him so, even when I feel happy. Suddenly the pain wells up in me." Like now. Rivkah tried to suppress the sobs. Yohanan! How she had wanted him to share in all this celebration! What would it have been like if he were here with them? She wiped away the tear that had stolen into her eye.

"How can you feel so happy and so sad at the same time, Father Micah?"

"You can. I think it is hope that comes out of brokenness. Not a false hope that one day you will be lucky again, not a numbness that just accepts life as it comes. It is hope in the God who holds life and death in his hands, who has plans of good for us."

"Even for me?"

"Especially for you. Sometimes loss makes the future seem hopeless. But we cannot give up. Trust in the LORD!"

Micah's eyes shone, as if he was not only reminding her of that hope, but as if he had just rediscovered it himself and wanted to tell the whole people.

"When disaster has come upon his people, when they are broken, they have to learn to hope once again. They have to see a future, a future with their God.

'Shepherd your people with your staff,
the flock of your inheritance,
which lives by itself in a forest,
in fertile pasturelands.
Let them feed in Bashan and Gilead
as in days long ago.'

"We may seem lost, without direction, but the LORD will care for us again, will be with us. His mighty arm has not ceased, his love has not grown cold. And so he tells us:

'As in the days when you came out of Egypt,
I will show them my wonders.'"

"He will save his people."

"And we are part of that, Rivkah. He cannot turn away from his people."

"Even if they have sinned? Didn't you say that the LORD was offended by the sins of Lachish, the sins of Israel and Judah?"

"He is. But the LORD is gracious."

Rivkah drew in a sharp breath. The pain was still there. Yohanan—the LORD is gracious! Did Micah realize that he had mentioned his name again? She couldn't tell for he continued, "The LORD will have compassion." He lifted up his face as he said words of prayer, no longer trying to explain:

"Who is a God like you,
who pardons sin and forgives the transgression
of the remnant of his inheritance?
You do not stay angry forever
but delight to show mercy.
You will again have compassion on us;
you will tread our sins underfoot
and hurl all our iniquities into the depths of the sea.
You will be true to Jacob,

and show mercy to Abraham,
as you pledged on oath to our fathers
in days long ago."

* * *

The wind sent swaying ripples across the golden fields of ripened barley. The fields were ready for harvest. The stalks were heavy with grain, the ears full with the nourishing seeds enclosed by straggly yellow spikelets. Meshullam looked across the bountiful barley fields, saw that the slowly whitening fields of wheat beyond also promised a plentiful harvest while sesame and chick-peas were still growing in pale green. The people of Moresheth-Gath would not hunger this year. No, the fields promised a year of plenty.

He leaned down again, brought the sickle down swiftly and cut the stalks, gathering them into a bunch. Rivkah was following him, gathering the bunches into sheaves. She was working hard. Somehow it was like that summer all those years ago when he first got to know her, when the harvest was less plentiful, the fields full of weeds and the work of the harvesters so much harder. With how much hope had they set the sickle to the grain then, confident that Moresheth-Gath would grow again, that the LORD would bless them. And the LORD had blessed them. The land was fruitful again, yielding its crops, some years more, some years less, but always sufficient. Their flocks had increased, their cattle bred without fail.

The community had grown together, had weathered the challenges together, had learned to trust. But the village had not grown in size. No new families had joined them. Some asked in disappointment, why not? Was the LORD not with them? Would this land remain empty? A few children had been born over the years. Young and old had welcomed them, had rejoiced at the new life. And some had married. Only this spring, Boaz had led home a wife from the re-settled town of Mareshah. And of course, he had married Rivkah. But there was no child. Their son had died. And with him their hopes for the future had died, at least for Meshullam. For Rivkah, too, he knew. The hardship they endured no longer made any sense, the toil seemed in vain.

Meshullam straightened again, stretched and rested for a moment. He let his eyes wander across the land. He loved this land, oh God, he loved this land. The hopes he plowed into it, the desperation with which he worked it, the blessings he harvested, the toil he put into it. They all bound him to this land. It was the place of his life. He could not give up on it. This land was his future. It was the future of Moresheth-Gath, the future of Judah. And he would serve the LORD here in this place. Resolutely, Meshullam went back to work.

"Hey, you've suddenly picked up speed," Rivkah called behind him. "Do you want to harvest the whole field in one day?"

"That would be a plan."

"You might need a few more people to gather the sheaves behind you."

"Come on, you always knew we should set a new harvesting record."

"Maybe if we start at this speed right from the morning we could get there."

"Sure."

"If we really want to," Rivkah added.

"So maybe not today?"

"Maybe tomorrow . . . or the day after, or . . . "

"Fine with me. That was just practice then."

Meshullam looked up. Rivkah was still working at full speed. He loved her, loved her so much! They had shared so many good moments together, but it was the sorrow, the pain of loss that had made him realize how much she meant to him. It had been hard. In their mourning they sometimes felt so far apart. They had hardly talked at times. But they had realized they still had each other. And they had dared to love again. It had been as if dawn had broken anew, when Rivkah opened herself to him again, when she was ready to receive love and give love. It was not easy, he knew, for through it they had exposed themselves to further hurt, to new disappointment. What if something should happen to them? What if the tender shoots of their dreams were hacked down and collapsed around them? What then? But they had chosen to love again, to hope and trust. It would be amazing to see what plans the LORD had for them, what he would make out of their lives, lives marked by brokenness and loss.

"What?" Rivkah looked up at him. She must have understood. "Meshullam, harvest record or not, I'll be there with you."

The sheaf in one arm, she stood straight and followed his gaze as it swept over the land.

"I know," he said, "I know."

* * *

Even the distinctive silhouette of the hill on which the town of Mareshah stood was swallowed by the night. The dark hills stood silent. No light reached her from the town or the one or two tiny villages scattered among these ridges and valleys. Rivkah could not even see the light from her own village, Moresheth-Gath. Trees hid it from view. But the night sky sparkled. As darkness fell, star after star appeared in the heavens and soon clothed the firmament in glittering lights.

Rivkah leaned back and looked at the stars. Awesome, just awesome! All this God had made. The stars reflected his glory! Could anyone fathom his greatness? Could anyone understand his wonders? She felt small in the face of such splendor. "How great is the LORD!" And yet she knew he cared for her, loved her. She felt the gentle night wind in her hair and it was as if a loving hand was caressing her, comforting her. She felt the embracing love of the LORD, the compassion of her God. The LORD took her up in the hollow of his hand, held and protected her. She could hear the whisper in the wind: "I am with you Rivkah. I will be with you forever."

All her joy, all her sorrow were taken up in that moment of knowing the closeness of the LORD. Rivkah stood up, lifted her hands to heaven in adoration and gave praise to the LORD. Arms outstretched, she worshipped the God whose faithfulness she had come to know, who had been with her through hard times and good and whom she trusted to lead her in the future.

Bibliography

Aharoni, Yohanan. *Investigations at Lachish: The Sanctuary and the Residency.* Tel Aviv: Tel Aviv University, 1975.

———. *The Archaeology of the Land of Israel.* London: SCM Press, 1982.

Albright, William Foxwell. *Yahweh and the gods of Canaan: A Historical Analysis of Two Contrasting Faiths.* London: Athlone Press, 1968.

Andersen, Francis L., and David Noel Freedman. *Micah.* New York: Doubleday, 2000.

Aubin, Henry T. *The Rescue of Jerusalem.* New York: Soho Press, 2002.

Baker, Margaret. "Hezekiah's Boil." *Journal for the Study of the Old Testament* 95 (2001) 31–42.

Batal, Malek. *Wild Edible Plants: Promoting Dietary Diversity in Poor Communities in Lebanon.* Beirut: International Development Research Centre, American University of Beirut. No pages. Online: http://www.wildedibleplants.org.

Ben Zvi, Ehud. "Micah 1.2-16: Observations and Possible Implications." *Journal for the Study of the Old Testament* 77 (1998) 103–120.

Berquist, Jon L. *Controlling Corporeality: The Body and the Household in Ancient Israel.* New Brunswick: Rutgers University Press, 2002.

Blakely, Jeffrey A., and James W. Hardin. "Southwestern Judah in the Late Eighth Century B.C.E." *Bulletin of the American Schools of Oriental Research* 326 (May 2002) 11–64.

Bliss, Frederick Jones, and R.A.S. Macalister. *Excavations in Palestine during 1898-1900.* London: Palestine Exploration Fund, 1902.

Borowski, Oded. *Daily Life in Biblical Times.* Atlanta, Georgia: Society of Biblical Literature, 2003.

Brueggemann, Walter. *The Land: Place as Gift, Promise, and Challenge in Biblical Faith.* Philadelphia: Fortress Press, 1977.

———. *Worship in Ancient Israel.* Nashville: Abingdon, 2005.

Bunimovitz, Shlomo, and Zvi Lederman. "The Final Destruction of Beth Shemesh and the Pax Assyriaca in the Judean Shephelah." *Tel Aviv* 30, 1 (2003) 3–26.

Carey, Brian Todd. *Warfare in the Ancient World.* Barnsley, South Yorkshire: Pen & Sword Military, 2005.

Chiera, Edward. *Lists of Personal Names from the Temple School of Nippur.* Philadelphia: The University of Philadelphia University Museum, 1916.

Clements, R.E., ed. *The World of Ancient Israel: Sociological, Anthropological and Political Perspectives; Essays by Members of the Society for Old Testament Study.* Cambridge: Cambridge University Press, 1989.

Cogan, Mordechai. *Imperialism and religion: Assyria, Judah, and Israel in the eighth and seventh centuries BCE.* Missoula, Montana: Society of Biblical Literature, 1971.

Contenau, G. *Everyday Life in Babylon and Assyria.* London: Arnold, 1954

Cook, Stephen L. *The Social Roots of Biblical Yahwism*. Atlanta: Society of Biblical Literature, 2004.

Cross, Frank Moore Jr. "The cave inscription from Khirbet Beit Lei." in *Near Eastern Archaeology in the Twentieth Century. Essays in Honor of Nelson Glueck*. ed. J.A. Sanders. New York: Doubleday, 1970: 299–306.

Cuff, Yvonne Hutchinson. *Ceramic Technology for Potters and Sculptors*. London: A&C Black, 1996.

Dagan, Yehuda. *Archaeological Survey of Israel: Map of Amazya. Volumes I and II*. Jerusalem: Israel Antiquities Authority, 2006.

———. *Archaeological Survey of Israel: Map of Lakhish*. Jerusalem: Israel Antiquities Authority, 1992.

Dalman, Gustaf. *Arbeit und Sitte in Palästina, Band I: Jahreslauf und Tageslauf, 1. Hälfte: Herbst und Winter*. Gütersloh: C. Bertelsmann, 1928.

———. *Arbeit und Sitte in Palästina, Band I: Jahreslauf und Tageslauf, 2. Hälfte: Sommer und Frühling*. Gütersloh: C. Bertelsmann, 1928.

———. *Arbeit und Sitte in Palästina, Band II: Der Ackerbau*. Gütersloh: C. Bertelsmann, 1932.

———. *Arbeit und Sitte in Palästina, Band III: Von der Ernte zum Mehl: Ernten, Dreschen, Worfeln, Sieben, Verwahren, Mahlen*. Gütersloh: C. Bertelsmann, 1933.

———. *Arbeit und Sitte in Palästina, Band IV: Brot, Öl und Wein*. Gütersloh: C. Bertelsmann, 1935.

———. *Arbeit und Sitte in Palästina, Band V: Webstoff, Spinnen, Weben, Kleidung*. Gütersloh: C. Bertelsmann, 1937.

———. *Arbeit und Sitte in Palästina, Band VI: Zeltleben, Vieh- und Milchwirtschaft, Jagd, Fischfang*. Gütersloh: C. Bertelsmann, 1939.

———. *Arbeit und Sitte in Palästina, Band VII: Das Haus, Hühnerzucht, Taubenzucht, Bienenzucht*. Gütersloh: C. Bertelsmann, 1942.

Dar, Shimon, Aren M. Maeir, and Ze'ev Safrai, eds. *The Rural Landscape of Ancient Israel*. Oxford: BAR International Series, 2003.

David, A. Rosalie. *The Ancient Egyptians: Religious Beliefs and Practices*. London: Routledge & Kegan Paul, 1982.

Davies, Philip R. *Memories of Ancient Israel: An Introduction to Biblical History—Ancient and Modern*. Louisville: Westminster John Knox Press, 2008.

Davies, Philip R., and Volkmar Fritz, eds. *The Origins of the Ancient Israelite States*. Sheffield: Sheffield Academic Pres, 1996.

Dorsey, David A. *The Roads and Highways of Ancient Israel*. Baltimore: The John Hopkins University Press, 1991.

Faraone, Christopher A., and Laura K. McClure, eds. *Prostitutes and Courtesans in the Ancient World*. Madison, Wisconsin: University of Wisconsin Press, 2006.

Faust, Avraham. "A Note on Hezekiah's Tunnel and the Siloam Inscription." *Journal for the Study of the Old Testament* 90 (2000) 3–11.

———. *Israel's Ethnogenesis: Settlement, Interaction, Expansion and Resistance*. London: Equinox, 2006.

———. «Settlement and Demography in Seventh Century Judah and the Extent and Intensity of Sennacherib's Campaign.» *Palestine Exploration Quarterly* 140 (2008) 168–194.

Fritz, Volkmar. *The City in Ancient Israel*. Sheffield: Sheffield Academic Press, 1995.

Gallagher, William R. *Sennacherib's Campaign to Judah*. Leiden: Brill, 1999.

Gibson, Shimon. "The Tell ej-Judeideh (Tel Goded) excavations: A Re-appraisal Based on Archival Records in the Palestine Exploration Fund." *Tel Aviv* 21,2 (1994) 194–234.

Görg, Manfred. "Persönliche Frömmigkeit in Israel und Ägypten." in *Fontes atque Pontes: eine Festausgabe für Helmut Brunner.* edited by Manfred Görg, 243–253. Wiesbaden: Otto Harrasowitz, 1983.

Grabbe, Lester L., ed. *Like a Bird in a Cage: The Invasion of Sennacherib in 701 BCE.* London: Sheffield Academic Press, 2003.

Guenther, Allen. "A Typology of Israelite Marriage: Kinship, Socio-Economic, and Religious Factors." *Journal for the Study of the Old Testament* 29.4 (2005) 387–407.

Hackett, General Sir John, ed. *Warfare in the Ancient World.* London: Sidgwick & Jackson, 1989.

Herzog, Chaim, and Mordechai Gichon. *Battles of the Bible.* London: Weidenfeld and Nicholson, 1978.

Hopkins, David C. *The Highlands of Canaan: Agricultural Life in the Early Iron Age.* Sheffield: Almond Press, 1985.

Jacobs, Mignon R. "Bridging the Times: Trends in Micah Studies since 1985." *Currents in Biblical Research* 4 [2006] 293–329.

Kern, Paul Bentley. *Ancient Siege Warfare.* Bloomington: Indiana University Press, 1999.

King, Philip J., and Lawrence E. Stager. *Life in Biblical Israel.* Louisville, KY: Westminster John Knox Press, 2001.

Kitchen, Kenneth A. "Egypt, the Levant and Assyria in 701 BC." in *Fontes atque Pontes: eine Festausgabe für Helmut Brunner.* ed. Manfred Görg. Wiesbaden: Otto Harrasowitz, 1983: 243–253.

———. *On the Reliability of the Old Testament.* Grand Rapids, Michigan: W.B. Eerdmans, 2003.

Macalister, R.A.S. *A Century of Excavation in Palestine.* London: The Religious Tract Society, 1925.

McNutt, Paula. *Reconstructing the Society of Ancient Israel.* Louisville, KY: Westminster John Knox Press, 1999.

Margalit, Baruch. "The Meaning and Significance of Asherah." *Vetus Testamentum* XL, 3 (1990) 264–297.

Mayer, Walter. *Politik und Kriegskunst der Assyrer.* Münster: Ugarit Verlag, 1995.

Mayfield, Sue. *Living with Bereavement.* Oxford: Lion Hudson, 2008.

Meyers, Carol L. *Discovering Eve: Ancient Israelite Women in Context.* New York: Oxford University Press, 1988.

Miller, Patrik D. *Israelite Religion and Biblical Theology.* Sheffield: Sheffield Academic Press, 2000.

Miller, Patrik D., ed. *The Religion of Ancient Israel.* London: SPCK, 2000.

Olmo Lete, Gregorio del. *Canaanite Religion According to the Liturgical Texts of Ugarit.* Winona Lake, Indiana: Eisenbrauns, 2004.

Parker, Simon B. "Graves, Caves and Refugees: An Essay in Microhistory." *Journal for the Study of the Old Testament* 27.3 (2003) 259–288.

Perdue, Leo G., ed. *Families in Ancient Israel.* Louisville, KY: Westminster John Knox Press, 1997.

Pinches, Theophilus G. *The Religion of Babylon and Assyria.* London, 1906.

Prosic, Tamara. *The Development and Symbolism of Passover until 70 CE*. London: T&T Clark International, 2004.
Richard, Suzanne. *Near Eastern Archeology: A Reader*. Winona Lakes, Indiana: Eisenbrauns, 2003.
Saggs, H.W.F. *The Might that was Assyria*. London: Sidgwick & Jackson, 1984.
Santillana, Fernando B. *Miqueas: Profeta para Latino America*. Bethesda: International Scholars Publication, 1998.
Shaw, Charles S. *The Speeches of Micah: A Rhetorical-Historical Analysis*. Sheffield: Sheffield Academic Press, 1993.
Sendrey, Alfred. *Music in Ancient Israel*. New York: Philosophical Library, 1969.
Sittser, Jerry. *A Grace Disguised: How the Soul Grows through Loss*. Grand Rapids, Michigan: Zondervan, 2004.
Spieckermann, Hermann. *Juda unter Assur in der Sargonidenzeit*. Gottingen: Vandenhoeck & Ruprecht, 1982.
Stern, Ephraim, ed. *The New Encyclopedia of Archaeological Excavations in the Holy Land*. Jerusalem: The Israel Exploration Society, 1993.
Sweeney, Marvin A. "Micah's Debate with Isaiah." *Journal for the Study of the Old Testament* 93 (2001) 111–124.
Tallqvist, Knut L. *Assyrian Personal Names*. Helsingfors: Societas Scientiarum Fennica, 1914.
Tetley, Christine M. *The Reconstructed Chronology of the Divided Kingdom*. Winona Lake, Indiana: Eisenbrauns, 2005.
Tufnell, Olga. *Lachish III (Tell ed Duweir) The Iron Age*. London: Oxford University Press, 1953.
———. *Lachish IV (Tell ed Duweir) The Bronze Age*. London: Oxford University Press, 1958.
Twigg, Graham. *The Black Death: A Biological Appraisal*. New York: Schocken Books, 1985.
Tylecote, R.F. *A History of Metallurgy*. London: The Metals Society, 1976.
Ussishkin, David. *The Conquest of Lachish by Sennacherib*. Tel Aviv: Tel Aviv University, 1982.
Vargon, Shmuel. "Gedud: A Place-name in the Shephelah of Judah." *Vetus Testamentum* 42 (1992) 557–564.
World Health Organization. *Pneumonia (August 2009)*. No pages. Online: http://www.who.int/mediacentre/factsheets/fs331/en/.
Yadin, Yigael. *The Art of Warfare in Biblical Lands in the Light of Archaeological Discovery*. London: Weidenfeld & Nicholson, 1963.

Scripture Index

Exodus	
34:6–7	107 (AT), 276

Numbers	
13:17–20	38 (AT)
13:27–28	38 (AT)
13:30	39 (AT)

Deuteronomy	
26:5a	349
26:9	349

Job	
37:2–5	69 (AT)

Psalms	
6:6	344 (AT)
19:1–6	240
30:1,4–5	350
31:9,14,15,17–19,24	104
56:4	150
57:1–3	93
65:1–2,9–10	150
113:1	349
114:1	349
145:1,4,8,9,13,14,18,21	298

Song of Songs	
1:2–4	246
2:3	146, 246
2:5–6	246
2:7	246, 247
2:16–17	247
5:1b	248
7:9–13	248

Isaiah	
37:30–31	127

Micah	
1:13	338
2:1–3,5	221
2:6–11	222
3:1–2	209
3:5–7b	209
3:8	210
3:9–12	208
4:1,3–5	293
4:6–8	210
4:10	128 (AT)
4:11–13a	211
5:2–5a	252
5:5b–6	253
5:7–8	254
5:10–15	255
6:1–5	273
6:6–7	274
6:8	274, 275
6:9	309 (AT)
6:11–13	309
6:14–16	310
7:1–3a	311
7:5–6	312
7:7	312
7:14–15	354
7:18–20	354

www.ingramcontent.com/pod-product-compliance
Lightning Source LLC
Chambersburg PA
CBHW061423300426
44114CB00014B/1506